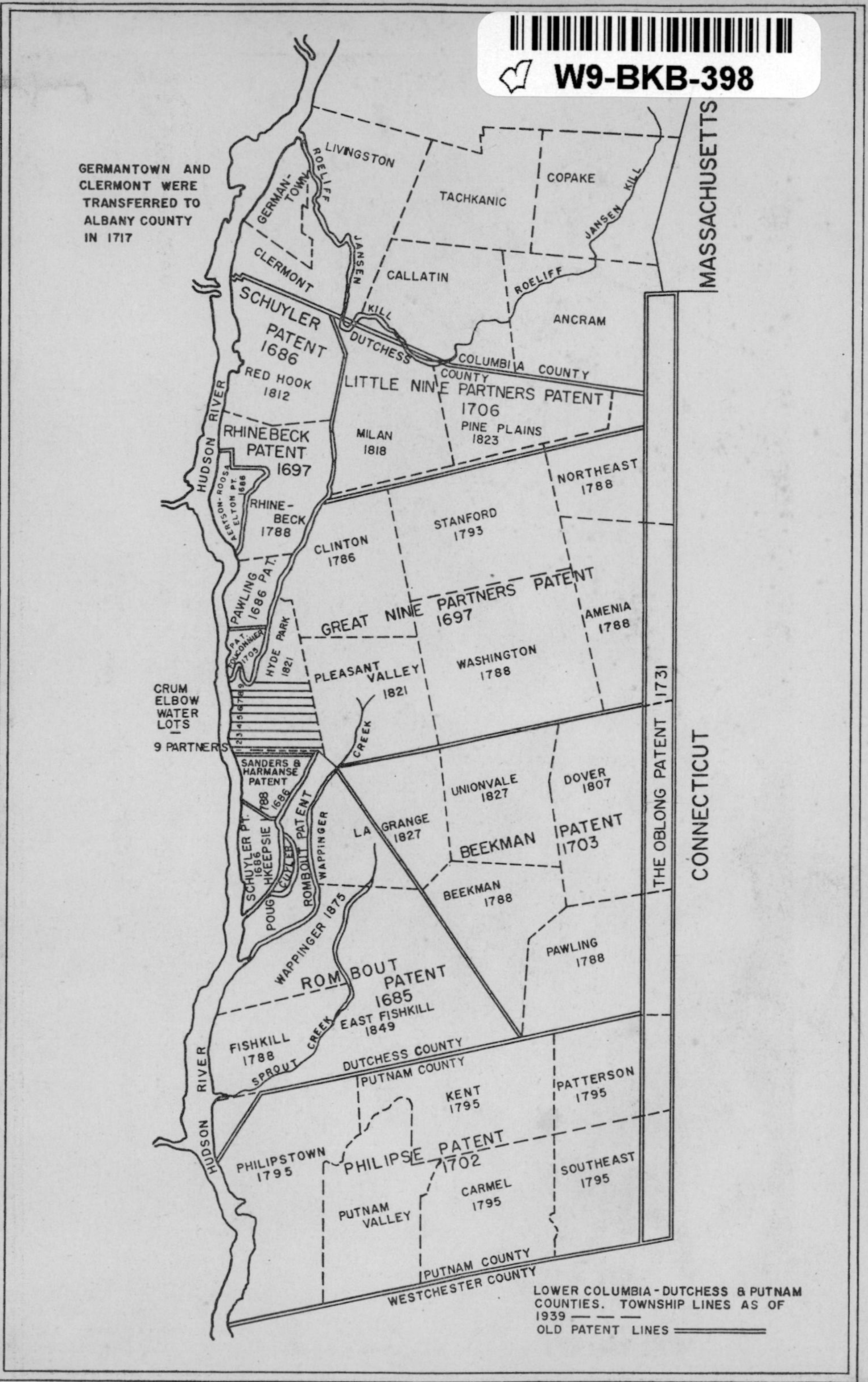
GERMANTOWN AND CLERMONT WERE TRANSFERRED TO ALBANY COUNTY IN 1717
LIVINGSTON
ROELIFF
GERMAN-TOWN
CLERMONT
TACHKANIC
COPAKE
JANSEN KILL
MASSACHUSETTS
JANSEN KILL
CALLATIN
ROELIFF
ANCRAM
SCHUYLER PATENT 1686
DUTCHESS COUNTY
COLUMBIA COUNTY
RED HOOK 1812
LITTLE NINE PARTNERS PATENT 1706
PINE PLAINS 1823
MILAN 1818
HUDSON RIVER
RHINEBECK PATENT 1697
AERTSON-ROOSELTON PT. 1686
RHINE-BECK 1788
NORTHEAST 1788
STANFORD 1793
CLINTON 1786
PAWLING 1686 PAT.
GREAT NINE PARTNERS PATENT 1697
AMENIA 1788
PAT. FAUCONNIER 1703
HYDE PARK 1821
PLEASANT VALLEY 1821
WASHINGTON 1788
CRUM ELBOW WATER LOTS
9 PARTNERS
1 2 3 4 5 6 7 8 9
CREEK
1731
THE OBLONG PATENT
CONNECTICUT
SANDERS & HARMANSE PATENT 1686
UNIONVALE 1827
DOVER 1807
SCHUYLER PT. 1686
POUGHKEEPSIE 1788
CUYLER
ROMBOUT PATENT
WAPPINGER
LA GRANGE 1827
BEEKMAN PATENT 1703
BEEKMAN 1788
WAPPINGER 1875
PAWLING 1788
ROMBOUT PATENT 1685
EAST FISHKILL 1849
FISHKILL 1788
SPROUT CREEK
DUTCHESS COUNTY
PUTNAM COUNTY
KENT 1795
PATTERSON 1795
HUDSON RIVER
PHILIPSTOWN 1795
PHILIPSE PATENT 1702
SOUTHEAST 1795
CARMEL 1795
PUTNAM VALLEY
PUTNAM COUNTY
WESTCHESTER COUNTY
LOWER COLUMBIA - DUTCHESS & PUTNAM COUNTIES. TOWNSHIP LINES AS OF 1939 — — —
OLD PATENT LINES

Old Dutchess Forever!

# Old Dutchess Forever!

## THE STORY OF AN AMERICAN COUNTY

by

Henry Noble MacCracken

HASTINGS HOUSE

Publishers New York 22, N.Y.

PUBLISHED BY HASTINGS HOUSE
NEW YORK 22, N. Y.

First Printing

LIBRARY OF CONGRESS
CATALOG CARD NUMBER: 56-12863

MANUFACTURED IN THE UNITED STATES OF AMERICA
BY HADDON CRAFTSMEN, INC., SCRANTON, PENNA.

To M.D.M.

*The love of anything is the offspring of knowledge, the love being more fervent in proportion as the knowledge is more certain. And this certainty is born of a complete knowledge of all the parts which, when combined, compose the totality of the things which ought to be loved.*

Leonardo da Vinci,
Anat., III, 241.

# Contents

# I. FORERUNNERS

## 1. The Tawny People

FOR A HUNDRED years the Dutchess ploughboy at the turn of his furrow would stoop to pick out a small three-cornered piece of hard stone that seemed different from the rounded gravel of the field. He would observe its sharpened point and its chipped edges, or perhaps its barbed stem. He would slip it in his pocket, to ask the folks about it, and push on.

He would learn from his father that his find was a spear-point, or an arrowhead. On the lookout for others like it, he would find more: an axe, scraper, grinder, knives of a crescent shape, stones with little holes in them, perhaps needles of bone. At the springside, where he took his nooning, he might spy in the eroded bank fragments of pottery, and could guess that Indians had taken their rest at the same spring, or camped overnight in their hunting season.

Perhaps, like a boy I know, he wandered afield in idle hours. From one such boy, a score of years ago, I once bought two thousand points, all of them found on a single river meadow.

"De oude wylt zyn vly." The old Indian's marsh. "Speck zyn kill." Spot's brook, or Spackenkill, we call it now. "Wappens Kill." The Wappingers' creek. "Waban," east. Indians of the East Shore. So run the names on the old maps. Indian bounds seem always to have run by water. At a rough guess, two hundred sites by water have been spotted, forty of them in Putnam County alone. Most of the larger sites lie along the Hudson shore.

Jack Hennessey, respected night watchman at Vassar College, picked up many points while on his campus rounds, where the gardener had dug to set bushes, or a contractor was setting his forms. On his own place he found a carved pipe-bowl of catlinite, a stone of the west, suggesting a traffic of distances.

Henry Taylor, another member of the college staff, made a handsome store in visits at Sopus Point, the Danskammer, Clinton Point, and the ridges of the Wappingers. Without digging a foot, he tracked hundreds of the best specimens. The college borrowed and exhibited them for years. Of earlier collectors Henry Booth is remembered.

In 1939 and 1940 Vassar College projected two brief surveys under the direction of Dr. Mary Butler Lewis. The workers were students from college and high school, with a few older amateurs. Thirty-eight sites were laid out and tested in the summer weeks. Constant in these were Woodland pottery of simple type, semi-lunar knives, scarcity of pottery pipes, great varieties of chipped stone in sequences consistently found.

The most interesting dig, at Crugers Island, where additional finds have been made by the society that followed Dr. Butler's work, comprised two levels, one with no pottery, but with broken bits of shell, the other later, and linked with Coastal types of New England.

There will be other digs than Dr. Mary Butler's, but none, I guess, will ever be gayer. I used to watch her ragamuffin crew, starting off in their rickety old truck, and would calculate my potential share in the resultant catastrophe. Her hard-driven scientists slept in barns and sweated out hot days in swamps and quarry slides, rock shelters and shore jungles. Folks derided them, but they sang

Yes, we're buggy archeologists, but we don't give a hoot,
It's buggy archeologists that bring home all the loot.

One cache, apparently a pre-historic workshop of some humble grinder and chipper of points, was so near the highway on Bear Mountain that many got their first glimpse of the gay science of archeology, and the New York newspapers made them popular.

A Mid-Hudson chapter of the New York branch of the Eastern States archeologists has since been organized with the help of the Director of the State Museum at Albany, Dr. William H. Ritchie. Almon Beneway, who is a railroad engineer by profession, and had followed the arrowpoint trail for many years, was one of the older members. "A hobby has no end," he told me. "It does something to you." It has lured him to the mesas of the far west, Louisiana bayous and Colorado cliffs. James H. Shafer is another member who has done an outstanding dig below Fishkill on a river "hook", near Polipel Island.

He found four levels, the two lower with occupations. An oyster-midden of some depth indicated a much more brackish river than is known at present. At the lower levels of his dig types suggestive of the earliest Indian culture, called Lamoka, were found, with the Laurentian overlapping. Transitional and early woodland types were found above them.

Dr. Ritchie is now completing his survey of the state, and perfecting his map of Indian pre-historic and historic cultures. The State Museum with its publications tells of cultures far surpassing in quality the meager finds and undeveloped arts of the Hudson region. We are fairly sure, at least, that the Valley has been occupied for some thousands of years by Indians, the Woodland and Laurentian strains being the longest-lived. The Laurentian claims priority in time, but the two strains run together in the later period. Coastal affiliations indicate that Dutchess was maritime even in its earliest human life.

Of Dutchess Indians in the days of New Netherland there is no history. Of the Wappinger Indians, whose council-fire was in Fishkill Hook and their ceremonial dance-place on the Danskammer, little was known beyond the fact that they were the head of a loose confederacy of nine tribes whose lands lay east of the river all the way to Manhattan. Their warriors were reported as far afield as the Connecticut, White Plains, and the Esopus. They were said to have robbed a barge of hundreds of beaver-skins on their way to New Amsterdam, "a nation with whom we had never the least trouble before." This was in

1644. Their good offices were sometimes sought in mediation, and once a Dutch sloop wintered in Wappingers Cove.

The Dutch writers were singularly incurious about their Indian neighbors. Their accounts either varied so widely as to be almost useless as history, or were slavishly copied from each other. They were tall and strong, and loved to be used as runners and messengers, always faithful in this. Their daughters were modest and fair, and Indian hospitality to guests resulted in many children of mixed parentage. Indian culture melted away like snow in the sun, so that by the time of white men's concern with Dutchess, 1683, their major arts were gone.

Of variety in Dutch description, the question of Indian color may be used for illustration. De La Rasieres, the earliest writer, 1628, thought the Indians "of an orange color, like the Brazilians." Hudson had called them swarthy. A friend of Governor Kieft called them "of an ordinary stature, strong and broad-shouldered; olive color, light and nimble on foot, subtle of mind, of few words which they previously well consider, hypocritical, treacherous, vindictive, brave and obstinate in self-defense, in time of need right resolute to all." This was written after Kieft's war upon the Indians, when the white men far outdid the savages in the ill qualities. Van Der Donck of Yonkers called the Indians "yellow, as yellow as the people who sometimes pass through the Netherlands and are called gypsies." The Iroquois called themselves brown, as the Dutch reported. Verrazano the Italian thought them lighter than his countrymen.

One color they never thought of: red. The term "redskin" is not quoted from English or American sources before 1790. It seems to be a product of the romantic era. And there we may leave them until they appear in our history.

## 2. The Perils of New Netherland. 1609

THE "DUTCHESS'S COUNTIE" was a tiny fragment, and a wholly neglected one, in the story of New Netherland. During the entire period it remained in the domain of two Indian tribes: the Wappingers occupied the south and west, and the Mahikans the north and east. The land bore no other names on any map. Doubtless the Dutch fished its shores, while the Indians and an occasional white trapper entered its upland for furs. But in the half-century there is no record of Dutch residence, or even of Dutch travel through its trails.

Yet though its history falls wholly within the era of the English province and of the State that replaced it, the Dutchess remained in its early days a Dutch land, and its own adventures are so deeply rooted in the history that heralded it, that its own color and feel cannot be caught at all without some sense of the flavor of Dutch origins.

Three periods mark early European concern with Hudson's River: from Cabot to Hudson, 1497-1609; from Block to Stuyvesant, 1613-1648; and Stuyvesant's term, 1648-1664. The English took over without bloodshed, and with the goodwill of its inhabitants almost entire. The event was an administering rather than an occupation or a conquest. British officers ran the province with a merely token garrison, as the bloodless reoccupation by the Netherlands in 1774 amply proved. With almost no fresh migration from England, and with New Englanders soon forming the bulk of the people, the governors' yoke was easy. They found that the policy paid well.

A stronger English tone was sounded in 1683, when the

twelve original counties were formed and an English charter projected. The date of the birth of Dutchess is therefore our starting point, and the terminus of the Netherland era.

The search by Spain and Portugal for new routes to the Indies in the southern hemisphere were soon followed by the northern Atlantic powers. The first voyages were guided by foreign pilots. John Cabot and his son Sebastian, pilots from Venice, claimed the whole coast from Labrador to Florida for England. Giovanni da Verrazano of Florence explored New England for Francis I of France. He even entered New York's Upper Bay, calling it "a very beautiful lake with a circuit of about three leagues". Estevan Gomez of Portugal had carried Spanish colors when he visited Carolina, Cape Cod, and the Penobscot. Thus when the newly organized East Indies Company of the Netherlands employed an English captain, already experienced in Arctic waters off Europe, to find a Northeast Passage, it was carrying on an admirable precedent. Like the predecessors, too, its later voyages were all led by its own nationals. When another English captain defended his alleged right to trade at Albany by citing Hudson's English citizenship, he had no case, and he knew it. But as one Dutch writer remarked, "No Englishman ever stopped for law". Might ruled then as now.

Hudson's fame as the discoverer of a River, a Strait, a Bay, and a great Territory has quite suppressed his own unhappy temper. On the New England coast he had landed among poor Indians and "took our spoiles of them, as they would have done of us", a brusque foreword to the Indians' story of New England. News of it must have traveled fast along the Coast, for when Hudson kidnapped two Indians in New York Bay his own men paid for it, and all the Indians below the Highlands were hostile, both then and for long after. Indians had very good memories.

The Dutch themselves did not approve the continuance of international courtesy in pilotage, when Peter Minuit, who had been the first real director of the little colony in Manhattan, later undertook to lead some Swedish colonists to the shore of the Delaware, at Newcastle and Swedesboro. That was coming too close home.

What accidents determine history! Hudson's mutinous crew, half Dutch, half English, forced him in 1609 to turn back from Nova Zembla and seek fresh fish off Newfoundland Banks. Meeting no more encouragement in seeking a Northwest Passage, he bethought him of the great bay of which his friend Captain John Smith had written. This looked promising as a way to China. He sailed thither, found Delaware Bay too shallow for his ship, and turned north to give his own name to the "Great River of the Mountains".

Whether Hudson planned to desert his employers on his return is unlikely. But as an Englishman in Dutch employ he was certainly ill-advised to touch at Dartmouth after so famous a discovery. His jealous countrymen detained him, and sent him in a later voyage to his fate on the frozen shore of Hudson's Bay. Only his report of the Great River reached the Netherlands at the time. But their hardy skippers at once sailed west, and within fourteen years had mapped the whole coast from Cape May to Cape Cod, established friendly relations with the Indians, and built up a small but flourishing trade in furs.

In 1613 the Dutch captains Christiansen and Block erected Fort Nassau on Castle Island near the site of Albany. When Adriaen Block lost his ship there by fire, he built his own ship, the Onrust (Restless) and sailed it through Hell Gate to the Sound. His careful mapping of the shores established the Dutch claim to the Fresh (Connecticut) River.

But the Hollanders were not precipitate. Their deliberate planning was characteristic of the business acumen that had brought wealth and stability to their great cities. It was 1624 before Cornelis May brought thirty families to Fort Orange (Nassau) and to another small fort on the Delaware. Next year came the three ships carrying cattle and sheep, and more families shepherded by Director Verhulst and a passenger, Peter Minuit, who soon succeeded him. Minuit wisely concentrated the tiny settlements in Manhattan, which he purchased from the Indian tribe for 60 guilders. Legend has come to laugh at the bargain, but it ranks high among later deals by comparison, and it initiated the honest Dutch custom of peaceable purchase and legal occupancy, things which other Americans soon forgot to remember.

Three hundred settlers in twenty-four years is no great title to fame. Yet Peter Minuit was a good enough director. He was of Walloon or French stock, a native of Cleves, and a competent manager. He built up the fort and the village of New Amsterdam, exported half a million guilders worth of furs, and constructed a great ship of 600 tons, the "New Netherland." Nothing could have better advertised the ambition and the skill of his people, or the resources of his colony.

But a director cannot lift himself very high by his own bootstraps, and Minuit left or was removed in 1632, though he stayed till his successor was appointed. This was an office clerk, Van Twiller (1633-1638). He probably owed his appointment to his uncle Kiliaen Van Rensselaer, a director who had taken a real stake in the Company as the patroon of Renssalaerswyck in 1629. Van Twiller's term was not unsuccessful, though the credit cannot be traced to him. At least he did nothing to prevent the adoption of improved rules in 1635, which brought increase of settlers on better terms. The colony grew more rapidly, and with a better leader might have become strong enough to insure permanency. But though the West India directors adopted good rules for the company, they were poor judges of men. Their next choice, Willem Kieft, was their worst. In five years he brought New Netherland to the verge of ruin. There had been a few Indian outbreaks, in every case the result of white aggression. Kieft decided to wipe out the Wappinger nations in the vicinity of New Amsterdam. Taking a leaf from the New England book, he carried out two massacres in 1642. In one case, that at Pavonia (Hoboken), he became the bloody murderer of the innocent Indians who sought his protection. He was so incompetent that he occasioned a real reform in the one-man government of the company's colony. The "Twelve Men", the first deliberative assembly of the colony, were called by him in order that he might have their support in calling for war expenses against the Indians.

The "Twelve Men", however, demurred to the director's project and accepted it only on restrictions, and after all efforts at conciliation were exhausted. Kieft promptly dissolved them, but when his measures had brought desolation he found himself driven to the same extremity. The "Eight Men" were then summoned, and joined effectively in the work of reconstruction. Five years later, when Stuyvesant became governor, the "Nine Men" were selected from an elected list of eighteen, representing merchants, burghers, and farmers. The "Eight Men" brought about Kieft's dismissal in 1647, and the "Nine Men" secured new privileges for New Amsterdam and local government elsewhere.

There was in New Netherland at this time a Dutch planter, David de Vries. His "notes", supplemented by other records, give a vivid picture of the little colony. He traded with Virginia and Connecticut, visiting both; voyaged up Hudson's River to Ft. Orange, and finally pitched upon Staten Island, where the patroon began to plant his colony. He also owned land on the Jersey shore.

De Vries knew and trusted the Indians, and was trusted by them. But when Kieft's Massacres in 1643 precipitated a universal butchery he left the colony and returned to Holland. Col. Peter Stuyvesant replaced Kieft in 1648, and ruled firmly and tyrannically till the surrender of New Netherland in 1664. He was honest and honorable, but built for valiant and obstinate defense. He could not lead a forward movement.

Nevertheless the colony prospered. From 2500 it increased to near 8000, if the population of English settlers in western Long Island, and the settlers in the Jersey be added. Immigration steadily increased, new villages sprang up in Long Island and the Esopus flats, and Ft. Orange became Beverwyck.

Trade also increased. Dutch sloops ran the coastwise traffic for New England in great measure, and traded in the West Indies, where Stuyvesant had begun his career as governor.

But the testy colonel was harsh, a martinet in discipline.

He persecuted Quakers and Jews until he was reprimanded by the Company. He sent captive Indians to the West Indies as slaves, following the Spanish custom he had witnessed. Thus he started an Esopus war of his own, which nearly ended that little hamlet.

Meantime the English war-clouds which had been threatening all the while burst at last in 1664, and his rule ended in surrender and futility. But Stuyvesant, alone among the governors, stayed in his American land and died in peace. He had stopped Connecticut and Sweden from settling the Delaware, thus preserving the Jerseys as an adjunct to Manhattan's Bay. He had kept the Indian frontier easy, had stood off Massachusetts to the very end, more by good luck but partly also by his brave stand in conferences. In 1653 and 1654 these colonies had almost come to war against him, but Cromwell's peace with the Netherlands in 1655 had ended their hopes. In 1664 they were ready to strike again, when the Duke of York, subtly encouraging their plans, determined to forestall them by gaining a colony for himself, from which as a beachhead he could launch his power against all the colonies when the time came.

There runs throughout the story of New Netherland, so briefly sketched here, a note of strain and nervous tension. Our records tell little of the daily life of the colonist and of his family. We read the endless complaints of the governors and their critics, sent over to the company for adjustment. The Indian wars take up a tragic part of the story, obscuring the fact that the Dutch domines taught the Indians, and lived with them on friendly terms, anticipating John Eliot's New England service.

Numerous Dutch agents learned the Indian languages, traversed their tribal territories, and settled treaties of great future importance. The English fell heirs to this happy outcome, and upon it built their successful campaigns against the French.

We learn by reading between the lines how content the Dutch were at first with their River and its estuaries, so like their dear canals at home. In sheer exuberance they dug a canal across Manhattan, at Canal Street. They sought islands to live upon, at Manhattan, Canarsie, Ft. Orange, and Esopus. They fished to their hearts' content in the great stream, naming the river opposite Southern Dutchess Fisher's Reach. As experts who had long fed England with their herring, they soon followed the Indians in netting the shad and herring of the North River. The Dutch word for shad is "elf"; it means also eleven. "Elf, twaalf, dirtien", they cried (shad, striped bass, drumfish), and they hauled them in. The name Magdalene for Madalin Island is said to be another name for herring. Podlapel or Polipel at the southern end of this opulent county is the Potladle that dishes out the wonderful fish-pot.

The unpoetic Netherlanders went on to name the two frowning sentinels of the High Lands (so written in early documents) for a rick of hay (Hoyberg) and a mound of butter (Boterberg). Slipsteen Island looked to them like a grindstone. But they did not perpetrate the classical Esopus for the Sopas Indian tribe.

Their enthusiasm began to fade at the prospect of woods and hills. They were no axemen, even if Governor Dongan praised them for their skill in garden, orchard, and farm. At first they waited until the forest had been burned over by Indians or stubbed by slaves or hired Irishmen. Their province remained a mere ribbon along the river and its tributaries. Vlaaktje (flats, plains) were their favorite soil.

At any rate, we hear of no starvation, or of being fed by charitable Indians, as at Jamestown and Plymouth.

They brought over their favorite seeds and animals. On one voyage three vessels named the "Horse", "Cow", and "Sheep" entered the harbor. De Vries tells how at Fort Good Hope, at Hartford, the Dutch commander entertained a company of fifty English folks, including Hartford's mayor, feasting them on the ripe cherries from the trees about the fort. This was less than twenty years after the little fort had been built.

But though they knew all these things, they were in early years the servants of a furtrading company. The colony was an afterthought. Throughout its history trade came first; but that which endured was the little company of less than five thousand Dutch men, who had brought into their own culture an equal number of outlanders. Their contribution to American life has been in relation to their priority and their situation, and out of all proportion to their numbers in the United States census. In this contribution the citizens of Dutchess played their part.

Among their perils not the least was the rivalry of Canada and the French traders. Throughout the years Jesuit priests made heroic journeys to the Iroquois, hoping to win them to Christ and to the French. French commanders were less successful, the battles of Champlain and other captains engendering a bitter hostility on the part of the Five Nations, who fiercely resented the invasion of Iroquois territory by Algonkians from Canada. No sooner did the priests convert an Indian nation than Senecas and Mohawks set upon them. The great Indian wars in which the Huron, Neutral, and Erie nations perished were the result. The Dutch, meanwhile, applied to the Iroquois for help in making peace with their Esopus-Wappinger Indians, a system followed in the eighteenth century by Conrad Weiser and his American successors. All the English had to do was to follow this policy and win a continent.

With another group who might have proved a real peril the Dutch were far more successful. These were the refugees. There were first of all the French Huguenots and Walloons, of the Reformed religion, who were readily absorbed into Dutch culture. The Belgians have been very active in claiming credit for most of the settlers of New Netherland; a Belgian tapestry depicts Minuit and his compatriots in the act of holding title. Certainly many came from the land now called Belgium.

Francois Rombouts (also correctly spelt Ro(u)mbout), was from Hainault in Flanders. There were many other refugees, however; the Scots and Irish, whose early settlement in New York were larger than usually stated. Long Island in the first grant was a patent of William Alexander, Earl of Stirling, and the Alexander family were later very prominent in New York. James Alexander, whose son claimed the earldom, was active in several Dutchess patents. Leonard Lewis, the first Dutchess judge and sheriff, was of Scots-Irish descent.

Then there were French Protestants from Canada, as well as French Catholics. Scandinavians of all the north, occasional Spaniards and Portuguese—but above all English refugees from New England, who could not endure what the Dutch called "the intolerable tyranny" of New England. These settled towns on Long Island, and soon were found elsewhere, as in Westchester. They included Quakers, Baptists, and the rest of the dissidence of dissent.

All these were given mere tolerance. Many of them, like Baxter and Underhill on Long Island and Samuel Munroe in Dutchess, became active radicals, plotting against the government. Most of them became good citizens, adding energy and originality to the more deliberate Dutch substance.

Dutch relations with the English citizens and governments of New England were their chief peril; well-grounded fears lent color to their profound distrust. "In short, according to the claims of the English, it belongs to them, and there is nothing left for the subjects of their High Mightinesses. One must have this far, and another that far, but they all agree never to fall short." This proved to be no prejudice but the literal truth.

It is more than likely that the English in New Amsterdam in 1664 were active in persuading the Dutch to submit to the Duke's fleet, pointing out that their fate would be far better as subjects of a Catholic Duke who was known to favor tolerance, than in the hands of the Puritans. Doubtless many of them, as refugees, feared for their own skins. It is certain that the Dutch leaders, whose petition forced tough old Peter Stuyvesant to surrender, had long been dealing with the English colonies. They regarded the Duke's intervention as a godsend, and served him loyally in every office. There is no record, so far as I know, of any serious disaffection on the part of the Dutch population.

Such disaffection as there appeared came from Long Island, where there were three sets of towns of English settlers. At the eastern end were towns which had for many years been under Connecticut rule, and were now in 1664 transferred to New York law. Then there were towns east of Oyster Bay, transferred to Connecticut through piracy and force majeure between 1660 and 1664. Finally there were towns west of Oyster Bay that had lived contentedly enough under Stuyvesant, and though settled chiefly by refugees from New England, were yet English in political sentiment. These now made common cause for the grant to New York of a government like those of New England, and a general assembly with a governor and council. For twenty years they agitated until it was granted by the Duke of York.

From many of these towns settlers came to Dutchess County, looking for its richer soil. Most of them settled in central Dutchess, and became the leaders of its levellers and rebels, and its Revolutionary officers. The family leaders transmitted to their children a love of liberty that could not be extinguished.

Early governors worked for harmony with the Dutch population, hoping to keep them from migration, and to secure their loyalty. Since the Duke's government was proprietary, and the Duke ruled as absolute master, the Dutch, more used to such rule than the English, might be played off against them in the contest for power. The governors visited Albany and secured the frontier by treaties. Lovelace renamed Esopus Kingston, and aided its growth. While Nicolls had begun his conciliatory policy by the enactment of the Duke's Laws, he administered them with discretion. The Laws themselves, modeled on those of New England, were not too unfair.

Liberty of religion and freedom of conscience, recognition of the Dutch language, laws, and customs, as far and as long as possible, and the adjustment of offices to Dutch custom where necessary, made for perhaps the smoothest transition of a conquered province to free status again, in recorded history.

But neither the assiduous attention of his governors nor the fears of his opponents could prevent the Duke from giving away the "propriety" of the whole of New Jersey to his friends Carteret and Berkeley. All early governors protested the act in vain. True, the Duke reserved to himself the charge of the New Jersey government, but experience might have told him that government followed lordship. James Stuart was only thirty years old when he received his province, and must have been under some special obligation to his friends in the Navy. Whatever it was, the City of New York achieved control of its harbor only through interstate cooperative authority. But the chief concern of New York's early governors was James Stuart's need of ready money. He could not pay his debts for the expedition, nor make good his payment on the purchase of Long Island's patent from the Earl of Stirling. Neither could he reward his soldiers who had won his province for his Highness. If commerce and trade came first with the Netherlands, taxes and customs came first with New York. The citizens were not pleased. They raised the cry of taxation without consent, and sedition raised its head, more frequently after the Dutch interlude in 1674. The Duke managed to stave it off till Andros' term expired in 1681. He was dismissed for too great fidelity to his master, in claiming the administration of New Jersey. A New York jury, with an independence that soon became a habit of such bodies, declared for the freedom of New Jersey from the Duke, and the too eager Andros paid for it.

It was clear from the insistent demand for self-government, for the right of consent to be taxed, and for the limitation of the Duke's power in the Jerseys, that some concessions must be made. The new governor, Colonel Thomas Dongan, came there armed with instructions to reform the whole constitution.

A constituent assembly was summoned in 1683, which in two sessions passed upon more than forty laws, and in a third session two years later passed six more, all of which met the approval of the Duke. In its range and extent it was the most liberal session of any colonial legislature.

The most far-reaching of its acts, the Charter of Libertyes and Privileges, involved an almost complete surrender of proprietary sanction. The power of the commonwealth was stated to reside in the governor and council, and in "the people met in general assembly", a phrase twice repeated, and taken to mean something more than similar phrases elsewhere. No tax law was to be valid except by the consent of all three bodies.

Governor Dongan and the Duke gave their consent to all these laws, and the governor at first enforced them. But something happened between the cup and the lip.

The death of Charles II in 1685 made the Duke a monarch, and released him for his plan to erect all the North American colonies into a single royal province. As a first step he created the Dominion of New England, wiping out the charters of the Yankee provinces; to them he added New York and New Jersey a few months later. Thus he felt the new charter was superseded, and revoked it.

It had been operative in the province, however, and the people continued to believe in it and act upon it. They were never to give up their right to control their own taxation, nor the annual appropriation for the salaries of the governor and his staff. Every assembly, every jury, and a great body of lawyers were trained in the hundred years struggle for this liberty, which would end only with its final attainment in the Revolution.

Another, and for our story the most vital change, was the division of the province into twelve counties on the English model. For this marks not only the birth of our county, but its purchase and settlement. For twenty years of English rule, not a single pioneer had entered upon it.

Governor Dongan and his master the Duke were realistic. Westchester and Suffolk were already full of New Englanders who had already proven themselves refractory subjects. They gave them no excuse for further dissatisfaction by a change of name. But they meant to assert their lordship of this royal propriety by affixing royal titles to the rest. King's, Queen's, Duke's, Duchess's; York, Albany, Ulster (the Duke's English, Scottish, and Irish titles); Orange (title of his sister and his daughter, both named Mary); Cornwall and Richmond (both royal titles). No province was ever more firmly nailed down. Cornwall in Maine has been lost, and Duke's (the Vineyard, etc.) is now of Massachusetts.

Thus to east and west, the Duke's province blocked the further encroachment of Puritan New England. Massachusetts was never to swallow Maine, or Connecticut to appropriate the Jerseys or Pennsylvania, though history knows they tried hard enough. New York remained, as Emanuel Downing called it, "ill news for New England".

We are left with "the Dutchess's Countie". James' first wife, Anne, daughter of Edward Hyde, earl of Clarendon, had died (1671), and James in 1673 had remarried, choosing this time a princess of his own religion, Mary of Modena. To her title, then, he gave the last wholly unsettled tract, our county. Of its original boundaries only one, the river, persists. The Highlands are gone, and Roeliff of Jansen's lovely Kill no longer marks our northern bound. The Connecticut line shifted uneasily in the long squabble until 1880.

The man who carried out the Duke's will in the creation of the Twelve Counties ruled for seven years (1681-1688). He left a record unsurpassed in the annals of the forty-three terms of governorship officially listed by our state for the colonial period of one hundred and sixty years (1623-1783). Thomas Dongan might even come on top of the poll in a colonial Hall of Fame. He deserves a better statue than "Elmer Poughkeepsie", as the irreverent New York reporters dubbed his effigy when enroute to the summer White House at Hyde Park. That "Rogers statuette" in St. Mary's Park gives no hint of the vigorous, aggressive officer whose energy made his influence felt everywhere within and without his own territories. One of the best letter-writers of colonial times, he brought to terms the intriguing French and the encroaching Yankees. When the good but acquisitive William Penn tried to cut off New York's western lands, Dongan went straight to Albany and won from the Iroquois renewed pledges of fealty and recognition that the upper Susquehanna lay in New York. Thus Dongan is the savior of the Empire State.

# 3. The Dutchess Came Late. 1683

ON ONE FACT, and one only, our contentious Netherlanders were all at first agreed—the beauty of their River and the land it watered. How often have their praises been quoted! "As pleasant a land as one can tread upon". "As fine a river as can be found". "Very high mountains", "very good people", "very old men". The country "seems to lack nothing to do needful for the subsistence of man." "Well adapted for our people to inhabit, on account of the similarity of the climate and the weather to one's own." "The land is the finest for cultivation that I ever in my life set foot upon, and it also abounds in trees of every description." "The land is very pleasant and high, and bold to fall withal." "As pleasant with grass and goodly trees as ever they had seen, and very sweet smells came from them" . . . "good ground for corn and other garden herbs, goodly oaks and walnut trees and Chestnut trees, yew trees and trees of sweet odor, in great abundance, and great store of slate for houses, and other good stones."

So run the tales of Captain Hudson and his supercargo, Robert Juet, and the earliest reports of the voyage.

When it came to a closer inspection of the whole river, some were not so rosy. The Dutch had strict criteria of good land, and they did not find it everywhere. Too often it was rocky, stony, hilly, woody, boggy, barren.

The Labadist missionary, Jasper Danckaerts, was not so flattering in 1680. On his return to Manhattan from Ft. Orange, he and his companion, "as we were crossing the street, the lord governor (Sir Edmund Andros) passing by met us. We went to him, and he asked us what we thought of the lands around Albany. We answered, they were very good, but limited, being flat here and there, and that the woodland in particular was not worth much. 'But', he said, 'you have not been to Wappings Kill.' We replied that we had not. 'That is,' he rejoiced, 'a beautiful place about three-quarters of an hour inland, on a fine creek which you can navigate with yachts and it lies just through the Highlands directly opposite the Dans Kamer,' and with that he left us."

The Labadists, however, were not impressed, and soon left for Maryland, perhaps because the religious climate seemed at the time more wholesome.

One deterrent was in the very nature of rivers. By a law named for an American, Ferrel's Law, the right bank of rivers in the northern hemisphere tends to be higher, and the right channel deeper. Dutchess holds true to this law. The shoals and islands lie on its shore, and the sloops and yachts, having a fair and almost straight course along Fisher's Reach and the Long Reach, made haste on their way to safer anchorage under the western hills.

The flats about Wiltwyck (Kingston) and the Rondout Creek were more attractive, with their good slate and stone that Hudson had reported; but it was over forty years before the Netherlanders ventured so far, in 1652, (led by an Englishman, Thomas Chambers). The little neighborhood grew, soon hiving out into Nieudorp (Hurley) and New Paltz, and was ready in another generation to people northern Dutchess.

But Westchester and the land to the north gave an uncertain title, and no man knew his boundaries. The Indians were reported fierce, the Nochpeem of the Highlands being especially dangerous. The boisterous kintakoye on the Danskammer could not have added any attraction to the region for the lone settler. De Vries records, April 27, 1640: "Towards evening came by the *Dance Chamber,* where there was a party of Indians who were very riotous, seeking only mischief, so that we were on our guard." As far as Katskill de Vries found the whole river "up to this point stony and mountainous, unfit for habitations." Only two years later the Wappinger Indians were raiding the barges of beaver as they sailed downstream, sometimes taking prisoners and killing others in the struggle. Though they acted only in retaliation for Kieft's massacres, their reputation cast a deeper shadow than the Blue Hills on the eastern shore.

There were Dutchmen who preferred that it should be so. Of such was Francois Rombouts, Mayor of New York, who closely and jealously questioned our Labadist, Danckaerts, before he set out for Ft. Orange. The little episode is unique in the annals, and may be inserted here, since Rombouts, whom we know as Rombout, was the first patentee of Dutchess a few years later.

The Mayor first explained that the Labadists were asked to come because they had failed to register, as was required in Europe.

Danckaerts replied that they knew of no such strange law. Rombout knew better. "You know it is the custom in Europe." "It is only so required upon the frontiers." "We are no frontier," said Rombout "but a capitol, and it must and shall be so in the future."

Danckaerts then gave his occupation as a wine-racker—not a very frank reply. His companion was a theologian; both were of Friesland in the Netherlands.

But why did they come? What was their purpose and intentions?

"To look at the country."

"How to look at the country? Some come to look at the cities, others at fortifications; some to learn the mode of government and policy, others the manner of regulating the militia; others again to learn the climate and times and seasons, and you run and travel through the country without giving any notion why."

They said they were interested in the soil, and "might go around mornings and evenings".

Then Rombout came to the point. Were they to be looked upon as citizens or foreigners?

"Well, then, you are forbidden to carry on trade, particularly with the inhabitants."

It is not unlikely that Rombout, who from 1667 had been the partner in the fur trade with Gulian Verplanck, knew of Andros' interest in securing a settlement at the Wappingers, and wished in some way to forestall him. He had been Schepen under the Dutch and seven times Alderman under England. He had been lieutenant under Beekman against the Swedes on the Delaware. Thus he was in a good way to know the governor's mind.

What was in his own mind was indicated when he took out his patent. From that time till his death in 1691, he showed no interest in selling or leasing his land, much less in any division. It should remain a happy hunting-ground for his friends the Wappingers. His daughter and heiress Catharyna was of a different mind.

Except for the Duke's need of money, and the people's distaste for the remedy, the province enjoyed quiet. Colonel Nicolls, the Duke's first governor, was succeeded four years later by Francis Lovelace. In 1674 came a Dutch interim under Capt. Anthony Colve. Governor Andros ruled after the peace and the resumption of English rule in 1675. Anthony Brockhols acted for Andros during several months' absence. All but he were military men. The Duke's Laws were conciliatory, and the transition to English custom was deliberate. After all, the Dutch knew something of administration. It was easy for schouten to become sheriffs, and for schepen to become aldermen.

The Duke of York all these years was fighting the Battle of Britain. He had but little time to waste upon his purchase. He would have had no leniency for New Haven, which had sheltered the regicides Goffe and Whalley. Nor was Connecticut in higher favor, which had sped its soldiers overseas to join the Ironsides. The total loss of Long Island by Connecticut was a foregone conclusion, and that part of New York forever was snatched from their grasp. But the Puritans had powerful friends at court, and their nonconformity could be played off against the Anglican power, in the interest of his own Catholicism. For the time James went no further, and settled for a boundary line with the Yankees that became the beginning of the tangled tale of the Oblong.

So little did the Yorkers prize their Dutchess, that a Boston parson was the first to describe its back country. In 1694 the Reverend Benjamin Wadsworth set timorously forth upon a mission to Albany, in attendance on the commissioners who were to conclude a treaty with chiefs of the Iroquois at Albany. With Connecticut's first Colonel Allen and sixty-five dragoons to guard them, they made twenty-five miles a day through the Berkshire woods.

At a place called Ousetonnuck "formerly inhabited by Indians" they "came upon a very curious river".

Along the river they spied "parcels of pleasant, fertile, intervale land". But the next day they plunged into "a hideous, howling wilderness", but pushed on till they found Kinderhook, and another "curious" river and very rich land.

The houses of Albany were "generally low; but very few of them have a built upright chamber; the corner rooms are built very high, the houses are generally covered with tile, and many of the houses themselves built with brick". "Rensler's Island" had a very curious farm.

"The Maquase, Oneydes, Onnondages, Caouges, and Sennekes came twenty-five of them, two by two, singing songs of joy and peace. They also sang of peace before they began the treaty."

On the homeward way from "Clavrick" to "Turconnick" they crossed "a very stately farm of Mr. Leviston's". They used the wagon way, but passed bad swamps, bad bridges, a bad hill. The land "seems to be good; 'tis clothed with a young growth of wood, especially white-oak." (Perhaps it had been fired for clearing, or for hunting, as was the Indian custom).

At last they found the Dutchess somewhere below Ancram, named for the Livingston's Scottish home. "On our left a hideous high mountain; it had but little wood. It seemed to be a continued rock." Passing by "a long pond" ('Indian Pond'?) they came to Ten Mile River, which was not deep, but had "a very strong bottom".

"Before we came to this river, we met with a boggy meadow, where several horses were mired. Before we went half a mile farther, we met with a little green hill which, though narrow, was as boggy as the other. After we were over the river, we went over a very high, long tedious hill. Ten Mile River runs into Weyantennuch River by the side of which we rode, I believe, six or seven mile (Bull's Bridge to Milford?) and then passed the same a little after sundown." They reached Woodbury at night, seventy miles by the Rev. Mr. Wadsworth's bones, but probably fifty, a good day's ride in any saddle.

Wadsworth hit off "the dead way" as "very woody, rocky, mountainous, swampy; extreme bad riding." These were the four deterrents that had kept the Dutch from the same venture for eighty years. No one could put it more "curiously". But what would we not give for a little less thought of his own discomfort, and a little closer inspection of our woods!

The bogs and swamps, common in all beaver country, were really most promising signs of fertility. They are indicated in our earliest maps clearly enough. Some of them persist along the Sprout Kill.

# 4. The "T" in Dutchess

AFTER THE SECOND noggin of applejack, it is not safe to introduce the subject of our chapter—one would be lucky to escape a duel. Even without assistance tempers rise when the fatal "T" is mentioned, and the greater the ignorance the greater the heat. It would probably be the part of wisdom to leave the squabble where it is, and it is not with the hope of putting the question to rest that the following remarks are addressed to future contestants at any degree of conviviality. Facts are of no importance on such questions; it is a matter of honor. Indeed, those who for generations past have vociferated in defense of their "T" will turn over in their graves to learn that they were right without knowing it, while those who are convinced that no Dutchman ever learned to spell English will continue to jeer.

The trouble is that from the historical point of view both are probably right. There must have been among the early settlers a notion that Dutchess was somehow a compliment to the Dutch. The spelling "duytsar" occurs in early documents, and the Dutch of Dutchess would have been more than human if they had failed to associate the name of their favorite county with their honorable ancestors.

"Michael Hallenbeck, lately dwelling on some land in Dispute between this Government (Mass.) and that of New York, was some time past imprisoned in Dutchy's County Gaol." Thus the official minutes of the House of Massachusetts Bay, in 1753.

There is myth as well as history behind this point of view. Every old resident has been told that a hundred years ago some reformers of the liberal enlightenment persuaded the State of New York to take the "T" out of Dutchess, and that the enraged Dutch farmers changed their party, put the "T" back in Dutchess by the law of use and possession, and have ever since voted the true Republican ticket. But it is true that people, some people, believed that Dutchess somehow was the feminine or plural of Dutch, that the "T" was taken out by some most respected authorities, and put back again by unanimous consent, without benefit of the slightest knowledge of the grammatical truth.

Of these there are two major points to be made. The first fact is, that from Elizabeth's death to Victoria's birth, Dutchess was the correct and customary way to spell duchess, in the English of London and everywhere else. Shakespeare in King Lear so spelled it.

Samuel Johnson in his Dictionary defined DUTCHESS as "the lady of a duke", and DUTCHY as "the domain of a duke". And so it remained until the beginning of the nineteenth century, when for a time both spellings were "permitted", until in a few years the present spelling was accepted.

The second point is, that from the moment Dutchess, so spelled, became the legal appellation of this county, it became subject to the law of names, which is, that most names yield unwillingly to fashions in spelling, and prefer to retain the original spelling long after the pronunciation of the word has shifted. There are innumerable examples. Fetherstonehaugh is still spelled though pronounced Fanshaw. Clerke, Clarke, and Clark are all variants of the common "Clark". Smythe is a proper name from the universal Smith, Whyte for White. Peirce is still retained by a great family, though others go on to Pierce, pronounced "purse" still.

Thus, once given the appellation Dutchess, the county was privileged to preserve the *name* in the spelling then current, whatever might be the history of the common noun "duchess" in years to come. Only pedantry could insist upon the change, hallowed as the "T" has been in records for two hundred and seventy years.

Moreover, it is a law or practise of patents, that a peculiar spelling has a marketable value as a trademark or individual sign. Thus we have Tydol, from Tidewater Oil; Jetheet, for a company in heat engineering. Dutchess in its seventeenth century spelling is not merely quaint; it has a value in public relations that is beyond computation in good will.

In historical grammar, the "T" has a curious history. It was probably cooked up in William Caxton's printshop at Westminster. There the custom had arisen, in the confusion resulting from new importations of French words with the spelling ch, to double the "c", making cch, whenever the word took the harder "tsh" sound instead of the "sh" sound of French. Thus we have in the language doublets like the early crotchet and the later crochet. The "c" of the time was very like the "T", and as the fonts gave out of "Cs", a "T" was substituted. This is, at least, a theory—the spelling is certain.

On this theory the English town of Lichfield kept its spelling, although the fashionable Earl of Litchfield and his highborn spouse the Countess, a natural daughter of Charles II, came to live at No. 10 Downing Street in 1682, the exact year of the first application for land in Dutchess. The house had been built by Sir George Downing, the natural enemy of the Dutch. The Connecticut village and county of Litchfield preserve the seventeenth century spelling, just as Dutchess does; but Lichfield Cathedral is still the gem of all small cathedrals of the world. Meanwhile the Countess of Litchfield's home is the capitol of the British Empire, and no one gives a thought to the two spellings.

A distinguished Frenchman also went astray on the word. Mr. F. E. Milbert, the French landscapist, published his "Itinéraire Pittoresque" in 1815 on his return from America. He found the brookfalls along the Hudson exquisitely wild, and painted them. One of them, the lower brook on Mrs. Montgomery's place, he painted and reproduced in the volume. The falls, still in Livingston hands at Mrs. Tracy Dows', deserved his praise. Unfortunately the romantic artist left to an assistant the filling in of figures and animals; a gentlemanly hunter clad in a correct cutaway and wearing a beautiful fob, watches his dog pursue a hyena down the ravine. Somehow he does not carry conviction.

But Milbert's book was a great success. A Vassar professor learned that the German poet Goethe subscribed for the book at the circulating library in Weimar, and from it derived some of the real enthusiasm he soon displayed for the new land.

Milbert was delighted, too; and determined to like everything, even the inn at Hudson where the guests before supper plunged their heads into a common trough at their ablutions. From them, or some other, he learned and set down in a footnote the pleasing fact that the County of Dutchess is so named for "les dutches".

In an article in the New York Evening Post, the American poet-editor William Cullen Bryant opined, perhaps from his cottage at Williamstown, on the spelling of Dutchess: "a curious error has crept in—it being usually spelled with a "T", possibly from confusion with the early Dutch settlers along the Hudson. A similar mistake is made in the spelling of Litchfield, a town and county in Connecticut, whereas the English Lichfield, whence the name comes, is never so spelled."

The schoolmaster, with his almost complete ignorance of language, is evidently abroad. Every statement of Bryant is quite erroneous. But Bryant's authority, or his own fanciful myth-making, induced the Dutchess historian Benson J. Lossing to urge the elimination of the "T". His own name, if he wished to be true to its original spelling, should have been Laassen, for the good Benson was a lineal descendant of Pieter the Brewer, who was the famous Squatter that lived on Clinton's Point. Our first County historians followed him, with confusion, until Hasbrouck's "County of Dutchess" set us right again.

# 5. The Duchess of York. 1673

"A FAIR FLOWER, brought from Italy, planted in England, brought back, planted again, grubbed up and sent to wither and die at St. Germains." This is a brief epitome of the sixty years of Mary of Modena, the tribute of a compassionate well-wisher of her time. "Queen of Tears", a modern pen labels her. Both are most unjust, for although she could dissolve in weeping on all appropriate occasions, and fainted before her husband's bier, she was also a woman of great personal courage and resolution, and long endured the torture of a growth at the breast with the patience of a saint. Indeed, had she not tried so hard to obtain beatification for her somewhat less than saintly husband, she might herself have been a candidate for the name. "She was tender in her nature as any of her sex" wrote one, "not an ambiguous, but a real saint". The sentiment was often echoed in her day.

Maria d'Este of Modena traced her lineage back through five generations, ennobled by marriages of women of Savoy, Parma, and Medici families, to the first duke of Ferrara and Modena. As the Popes had appropriated the family estates, the dukedom had become a mere seignory, the especial care of the pope, and a pawn on the diplomatic chessboard of Louis XIV of France.

Looking for a second wife to replace the good Anne Hyde, James Stuart at first rejected the Italian princess. True "she was tall, admirably shaped, (somewhat thin, to the taste of the age), hair as black as jet, and so her eyebrows and eyes; but the last full of light and sweetness, with power to kill and to save." This was the unqualified encomium of the noble scout who had faithfully performed his master's instructions to look him up a satisfactory mate among the princesses for sale. A widower of a full year's respectability, with two daughters but no legitimate son, James knew a male heir would clinch his claim to the throne. He was an unblushing libertine himself, but he had strict notions about his bride.

She must be beautiful, young, a good Catholic, and so related as to be politically helpful. No Cinderellas. A list of eleven had been submitted, and reduced to five. Mary stood at the head of this list, but was at first crossed off because although the King of France sponsored her, her mother had designed her for the veil. The others were then duly inspected, but rejected for reasons of weight, age, brains, or beauty. King Louis became impatient, (was he not supporting the Stuart regime with mistresses and subsidies?). The Pope intervened with a personal letter to the young devotee, urging that her duty lay in England. To these behests she bowed, received a dowry from her sponsors, and at fourteen years was wedded by proxy (a Protestant one). The Pope was irritated. He was working out a treaty of religious autonomy for his young envoy; and he refused sanction.

But an English priest was found in the emergency, whose patriotism outweighed other loyalties; and after a most leisurely two-month's honeymoon without a bridegroom, including a sail down the little Loire in a decorated canalboat, and a stay at Fontainebleau in most uncomfortable quarters, she met her impetuous spouse of forty at Dover in September, 1673, just ten years before she sponsored her county in far-off New York.

She had many crosses to bear. James had good qualities, but not much room in which to play. He was a good sailor, a brave captain, an active and ambitious man. But his devotion to Catholicism, and the temptations of a licentious court, had almost reduced him to the level of a debauchee no better than the rest of the Restoration. His two bastard sons, the Dukes of Berwick and of Albemarle, later gave very good accounts of themselves, showing a not unworthy unbringing. Berwick had a brilliant career as a French marshal. But during these years James Stuart did not change his ways merely because he had married a beautiful woman. He kept his mistresses, and forced one of them, the Duchess of Dorchester (Mrs. Sedley, actress) into his wife's presence.

Nor was it comfortable for Maria to know that her cousin Hortense Mancini was one of the King's most unscrupulous mistresses. But these were petty annoyances, compared with persecution of Catholics in England. Popish plots were the witch-hunt of the day, (though real ones, too, were numerous in England) and Titus Oates may fairly be credited with driving James Stuart and his Duchess into exile for four years, one in Holland, three in Scotland. In the latter land James proved a stern administrator. It is perhaps a matter for congratulation that in all this intrigue James had little thought of his province.

Mary was not without some responsibility for the national feeling about the Catholic danger, for her own chaplain begged money for Père La Chaise to "give the greatest blow to the Protestant religion". But the storm was out of all proportion to the provocation, and though Charles II bowed before it, he at last rode it out. James at one time was threatened with the loss of his command as Lord High Admiral unless he gave up his religion. But Charles lived long enough to give time for the Duke to return to the capital, and to strengthen his claims. James was crowned in 1685, (the year of the first land-grant in Dutchess) and Mary, too, was crowned as his consort. Her influence was at once felt, and respected. "She had the Italian turn of thought, that consists, as I take it, in jealousy, penetration, and thought." The poet of her coronation ventured to hint it:

> "Your matchless beauty gives our fancy wing;
> Your judgment makes us careful how we sing."

Her majesty had done her best for her King in another field, the family. For twenty years she was almost constantly pregnant, with many griefs. Five of her eight children who came to birth died before her own death, one of them a much-desired boy, being kissed to death by a little sister convalescing from small-pox.

It was, however, the birth of her second and surviving son (James Stuart "the Old Pretender"), that did his family more unwitting harm than all the outcries of the Rev. Titus Oates. For now it was certain that Mary's son, brought up a crusading Catholic, would end the Protestant succession for good or ill. The news dismayed the colonists. James went doggedly ahead, dismissed Dongan because he could not put across a Catholic governor of the new Dominion of New England, and sent Andros after the colonial charters of the Puritan commonwealths. The rebellion that followed fortunately synchronized with the "Glorious Revolution" at home, or it would have gone hard with the independent Bostonians who threw Andros in jail.

Paradoxically, in that age of universal intolerance, it was James' act giving Catholics and Dissenters political standing which upset the English applecart. The "Glorious Revolution" is a good deal of a myth, because its "Bill of Rights" had been long proclaimed in common law, advocated in political philosophy, and accepted as the working basis for a united people, though not, of course, intended to apply to enemies of the state. On the other hand, Catholics and Dissenters in England suffered even greater hardships than before, being rated third-class citizens.

Queen Mary, she of Modena, had good ground for her bold challenge: "I leave the whole world to judge if hatred of religion has not been the cause of the treason and revolt of our subjects; if we have not lost our own kingdom for having sought to further Christ's." Certainly, with New York's Anglican governors like Cornbury, Cosby, and Clinton, the suppression of freedom of religion, of the press, of Nonconformists and Catholics, bore out the charge, and became one of the fruitful sources of our own Revolution.

Whether completely sincere or not, the terms of governors

appointed by the Duke of York were looked back upon by members of the Presbyterian and Reformed faiths as eras of comparative good-will and good government.

The Duke's toleration, however, was a good idea, but a bad thing. The timing was unpropitious. The two daughters of James Stuart, who were to succeed to his throne, had no compunction in joining the popular cry that baby James was no son of the King, and no pity when their father was driven into his exile. Princess Anne, until that moment, had been her stepmother's companion.

Mary outlived them both, through thirty years of exile and intrigue, a pensioner of the King of France, selling her jewels and her robes to help her cause and feed her ladies. She obtained a Cardinal's hat for her uncle, and did her loyal best for her dissolute brother the Duke of Modena. She persuaded her indulgent host to recognize her son as Prince of Wales, and later as King of England. From the wars he financed, and the Stuart battles in Ireland and Scotland, came untold misery for these kingdoms. Mary of Modena has some personal responsibility for all the tragedy and suffering in the emigration of the Scots, Ulster Irish, and Catholic Irish to America. They had at first sought refuge in France, but when twenty thousand had arrived Mary closed this way to others, forcing the poor people into the hands of unscrupulous English shipowners for the long terrible American voyage.

During his exile Mary's prayers restored her husband to repentance and extreme piety. She herself was found in a hairshirt on her death-bed. Yet in her youth she had been witty and gay in moments of happiness, the very life of her circle. She rode to hounds in the fearless English fashion, and frequently took a ten-mile gallop over the downs. She loved music and art, and brought Italian painters and singers to England. A lineal descendant of Lucrezia Borgia, she loved intrigue for its own sake. Her letters in great numbers have been preserved and used by students and historians. They are well composed.

If she made mistakes, they are those of her time and her

circle. Religious wars were still in the air, their fallout still poisoning the kingdoms. It is said that when Duke James was proposed to her as her spouse, she had not only heard nothing of him, but knew nothing of England. She cannot be blamed for not fully understanding the complex ways of English people, or for placing a world religion above their national interests, or for caring nothing that her title graced a little county on the Hudson shore. What she had and was, she put to fullest use. She was a brave and ill-fated, and forgotten, princess. Nonetheless she has established a place quite similar to her sisters on equally losing battlefields of diplomacy, Margaret of Anjou and Constance of Brittany, who found England no less suspicious of a foreign princess.

# II. THE PLANTING

## 6. A Right Tight Title

THE MODERN SOCIETY—if by modern we mean the period since the industrial revolution—modern society thinks more highly of personal than of real property. Farmers, in Dutchess today, make up only one-tenth of our population. Land has residential rather than farm value. We keep our property in fluid assets, like stocks, and land is easier to sell if it carries a high mortgage. Government encourages us in these superstitions.

Yet with all this we cherish the myths of bygone squabbles, and though we think nothing of buying land on 80% mortgage, and paying interest on the mortgage, we are greatly prejudiced against landlords and rent, even though so many of us live in rented apartments. Rents were controlled until recently long after all other price-controls were lifted. Land produce, as crops, is supported by high parities on the other hand. It is all very confusing.

There was a time when prejudice and practice were not so confused. Land was property; indeed, so much of property was in the form of land, that the word property, about 1700, came to mean "a property", a holding of land. One spoke of one's "property" in the Wappingers. So all-inclusive was the idea of property as good, that John Locke asserted the aim of government to be the protection of property. He then quickly added, that every man had a "property" in himself, and that his self-property was the basis of all equity. So highly was property esteemed that property and propriety meant the same thing, and proper conduct meant the conduct that belonged to one's self, which was called property or propriety, indifferently.

Moreover, office was property, in the common opinion; no body objected to a man's making what he could out of it, so he did it with proper respect for the existing order. Also, by a certain common error in logic, since land was property, and office was property, office and land were synonymous. Land was the main business of government in the colonies. Land stretched out limitless, inexhaustible in fertility, awaiting its proprietor. Colonies were called proprietaries, when the propriety lay no longer in the king alone, but in a lord or a company.

A good man meant a landed man. Men voted who were good men, or as the landed George Washington called them, the wise and good. The "best" society was the landed one. Land conferred prestige. In the colonies, for the most part, great landlords were also merchants, and skippers. The landlords of Dutchess owned docks and sloops, and traded in wheat at New York. But none of all this brought social prestige—land was king. In later times, of course, cotton, coal, wheat, and tobacco, made kings in turn, but all of them were own children of the land. Not for a century was the country to speak of "steel kings".

We are limited here to an outline of forms and methods in normal and successful times. Nothing that happened in New York fell outside the experience of other colonies. Its governors sometimes complained that landlords' greed for land must be held responsible for New York's failure in population. Quite apart from the debatable question whether rapid increase is necessarily preferable to slow and steady growth, it has been shown that the real failure must be laid at the governors' door. What was Bellomont doing to allure settlers, while John Winthrop of Connecticut was touring Scotland? What was Admiral Clinton doing to encourage Moravian settlement, when Penn had completed his saturation of Germany with his migration literature? These also were the real culprits: Fletcher and Cornbury with their extravagant patents; the surveyors-general like Graham who did not survey; the collectors of rents who failed to collect; the secretaries who did not keep record. It was a failure of government, not of land tenure. Under the pressure of immigration the system of land tenure could have been further improved. The story of land in Dutchess, however, is a success story, not a failure, so far as the county officials were honest men, the landowners considerate, and the tenants and yeomen industrious. Within fifty years from the breaking of the land-jam nine-tenths of its land was in cultivation, with enormous crops and great herds of cattle. This good fortune came to pass under a system of leasehold and freehold inherited from Dutch and English practice, although slightly modified by American experience.

Theoretically in early English law the title to land derived from the king. In the United States, the lawyers of 1776 in Dutchess just scratched out "George the Third, by the grace of God, King" etc., and wrote instead "The People of the State of New York, by the grace of God free and independent". Such writs can still be found in the County Clerk's files. The king of England in his desire to be independent of his barons and his parliament naturally put all the charges he could invent upon his land. The death of an owner, the minority of a ward, the sale of land or transfer of tenancy, and especially the fines for days and failure to meet payments formed the natural occasions for the imposition of these charges. As the centuries went by they increased to the breaking-point, when partial remedies were found. With the growing class of yeomen, and the great increase of wealth all through England, there were fewer defaulters, while Parliament, at the price of sovereignty, was willing to bear the main charges. Thus by 1700 there was little left of feudalism in land tenure, and the term "feudal", so vague as to be meaningless, may well be dropped from the historians' glossary.

What was left was a combination of Dutch and English usage. New Netherland had an enlightened code. First of all, the Indian title was recognized, and the land purchased from the Indians. We may smile at Rombout's royals; how much did Plymouth pay? Second, the recording of all purchases was required, agreements and mortgages were registered in New Amsterdam, and the secretary's office became an office of land records. Third, the surveyor general became an important official, often rising to the rank of Lt. Governor. To his labors must be attributed the peaceful settlement of intercolonial boundary disputes, which otherwise would have resulted in armed conflict. Fourth, the approval of the director (governor) and his council was required to validate all sales. Fifth, planters were promised full ownership after ten years' occupancy from 1638. Sixth, small landholders as well as large were encouraged after the second Charter of Liberties in 1639. Seventh, as towns developed they obtained municipal charters. By 1664 there were 17 municipalities in New Netherland.

There was grumbling, and occasional refusal to pay, but whenever government was good the system worked well. Much has been made of the patroonwicks, copied from similar institutions in Holland; but only one existed for any length of time. Rensselaerswyck would doubtless have been better managed, had it been one-tenth the size. At least no New Englanders claimed its shores.

With English occupancy came in the quitrents, the quarter-sales, and the pre-emptions. Sales were made as we have seen in Dutchess, not to settlers in good faith, but to men of office, merchants in the fur trade, speculators and land-pirates looking for a fast shilling at the expense of the careless land buyer —and for these the governors alone must be held culpable. Back of the governors, of course, the English colonial authorities who appointed the governors must stand trial; also our governors were rather better than the general run of Englishmen. They were, in New York at least, brave soldiers who had loyally served their king. If they were inefficient in office, so were their superiors at home.

The system of land tenure exported to America was the most liberal of the many forms in England. In earlier colonial days grants of land were made to correspond with the practice in the Bishopric of Durham in northern England. Here the king had more authority, and the tenant labored under more charges both of service and rent, than in later times. In New York, as in other colonies at the end of the seventeenth century, land throughout the province was sold "as of the Kings Manor of East Greenwich in Kent." This meant that it was held in "free and common socage". Socage, from the Anglo-Saxon word *soc,* plough, meant that service was commuted to a very limited amount of days' work, in addition to the common rent of land, in general held at two shillings sixpence for each hundred acres, certainly not a high rent even then, when New York shillings were worth only half the sterling. In a word, the tenant did not have to fight for his landlord, nor to deal directly with the king's agent. He did not have to labor in his lord's fields. At most he had to work a full day each year on the roads or other improvement. Very often, the quitrent was taken in kind, and sometimes in trifles, as "three peppercorns" in the Brett deeds. As an example of the Dutchess, a Beekman deed may stand.

Col. Beekman reserved to himself all the minerals and water use, and all land needed for their exploitation, though he agreed to reduce the rent by the amount involved. The lease ran to George Elsworth, his sons George and Charles, "for the term of the longest liver". For the 205 acres leased, the tenant paid a yearly rent of "one Cupple of Live Fatt Hens" on Lady Day (March 25); one day's work, yearly, with a wagon, sled, or plow, and an able man to drive with horses or oxen, "to perform as in such case is reasonable" within twelve miles, or in failure, twelve shillings, after four years an additional rent of twenty bushels of good sweet merchantable winter wheat computed at ten bushels for one hundred acres, on the 21st of May. The landlord in explicit terms was given the right to distrain, to enter the premises and take property to equal the unpaid rent. The tenant must also give preemption or prior right of purchase of all his produce to the landlord, and a similar preemption of the lease. The tenant could not in any circumstance sell his lease without his landlord's consent. Finally, the tenant was forbidden to put any obstruction in a water course for a dam or any other purpose.

Our gorge rises as we read. But this form of lease was merely the standard of the times. The lease here copied was from a printed form, evidence prima facie of its general acceptability.

Sometimes a leasehold might be used as introductory to a sale in fee simple. In 1730 Andrew Teller sold a large farm to Matthew DuBois, the son of Lewis DuBois. The two deeds are worth comparison. The original of the earliest deed is now in the possession of Vassar College, to whose land in part the deed refers. Both are copied in the register in the office of the County Clerk. In the first deed "bargain, sale, and lease" were executed for one year, at the rate of one peppercorn. In the second, made one day later (28 March 1730), the property of 1337 acres was conveyed to have and to hold forever, for the sum of four hundred pounds. Only mines and minerals were reserved. The one year lease was executed in order to give the purchaser use and possession, though not dwelling on the land, and thus making him eligible to make a fee purchase later, being "seized" of the property. The cumbrous method of the day followed English law like the Wappinger Kill, in all its twists and turns. The same method was adopted by the Philipse heirs before their division of the great inheritance, in order to dispose of the restrictions of entail left upon the property by the previous owners.

Land records of freehold sales were more common than of leaseholds; for this reason no accurate estimate is possible of their comparative frequency. In Rombout and the Lower Nine Partners, Poughkeepsie and Schuyler's Patents sales were more frequent than leaseholds. In Beekman's Patents Henry Beekman seems to have been more liberal of sales than his two sisters. The steady diminution of his tax assessments seems to bear this out. Not all partners in the county groups had the same policy.

About the time that the Duke of Chandos was dreaming of establishing a manor in the Oblong of Dutchess, the governor of Massachusetts, Jonathan Belcher, wrote to him describing the sort of land tenure obtaining at the time in Massachusetts.

"A farm of 200 acres, with only a small house and barn (no living stock or utensils) and such a house and barn may cost about £30 st' and I would make a lease of 14 years. The tenant to be oblig'd in the term thorroly to subdue and bring to English grass (fit for the scythe) 40 acres of land, without ever breaking the sod . . . the landlord must find the grass seed for the land as it's wanted. For corn land we allow the tenant to break up what may be necessary in such places as the landlord directs, etc."

This was in Massachusetts, where, as in Connecticut, there were no quitrents or preemptions, but where at the end of fourteen years the land with its improvements reverted to the landlord, or in the case of freehold, to rent upon higher terms.

When after 1760 Governor Benning Wentworth of New Hampshire parceled out the "Grants" that became Vermont, he sold the townships, 6 miles square, to companies of families which were to be permitted to hold two fairs a year, and a market one or two days a week. A village of 68 one-acre lots must be laid out in the center of the tract. Each grantee must pay one ear of corn on December 25, and one shilling of Proclamation money for each 100 acres. The governor got 500 acres in each township for himself, one share for the Church of England, one for the glebe, one for the minister, and one for the school. Others were reserved for the the governor's personal friends.

Thus a New England grant, at the end of the colonial period, carried a religious charge, and many other emoluments quite unknown in Dutchess. Many well-to-do farmers in Dutchess speculated in these grants, but only a handful ever migrated. They thought twice before they traded King Log for King Stork.

But in general the large number of families that stayed on the land, and the frequent occurrence of their names in the county today, is the best evidence that conditions in the generality of Dutchess leases were fair and good. As times went on, and farmers prospered, conditions improved. Though some resented the terms, they would bear them as long as the good top-soil bore its increase.

A minor classic in this story is "A Guide in the Wilderness" written by Judge William Cooper, the father of James Fenimore Cooper. Set forth in an excellent style, much more concise than that of his famous but diffuse progeny, his book outlines the ideal method of land tenure. He believed in good surveys, quick and absolute sales in fee simple, loans of money and supplies to get started. What he failed to add was that in his case the chief profit came from his monopoly of stores and transport. Judge Cooper in his later years tried to bully his customers into his political party, with disastrous results. He wrote, too, of a time following the Revolution. But he was certainly successful in the "plantation" of some 40,000 settlers on 750,000 acres, in central New York.

# 7. East into the Woods

WITHIN A PERIOD of twelve years, from 1685 to 1697, the granting of thirteen lawful patents had secured to their purchasers every foot of shore line in old Dutchess. A few thousand acres were chiseled out of Pawling's Purchase, the Upper Nine Partners closed up the vacant lots between Livingston Manor and the Lower Nine, and a few gores were picked out here and there. But to most intents the job was done by the turn of the century, though sales did not mean settlers. Less than forty families were on the land.

The initiative in this purchase we must credit to three governors, Andros, Dongan, and Fletcher, all of them soldiers, all of them plagued by the incessant attacks upon the frontier of New York by its aggressive neighbors on east and west. Throughout their terms the preservation of provincial boundaries was their preoccupation. There hung the Dutchess like a ripe peach, ready for the plucking by Connecticut and Massachusetts. The governors were not lawyers, and they knew that military action against other English governments would not be sanctioned. But they knew at least that possession was nine points of the law, and that the charters of New England colonies entitled them to land otherwise unoccupied as far as the South Seas. To forestall them, therefore, occupation was the watchword of their own policy.

The basis of this assertion lies in their correspondence. Outward evidence appears in the effort of Andros in 1680 to interest Danckaerts' Labadists in the settlement on Wappings Kill, and Rombout's application in 1682. But the real proof is the success of Dongan in his five years of work, completely lining the Hudson with private bastions of property. From Rensselaerswyck to New York, practically the whole eastern shore was occupied. Colonel Fletcher inherited the policy, and though he was careless and intemperate in his actions, he did at least continue Dongan's work.

Too much has been made of the obvious fact that the ownership of land brought great profits, and that governors subsisted in part on the incidental fees of the patents. These were, indeed, abuses, and they required correction. But they were abuses of administration, and the governors were soldiers, ruling a conquered province for their Stuart Duke or King. Defense came first. With Dongan it was almost an obsession. His attempt to get a patent for Staten Island, in which he failed, was surely prompted by the danger that the proprietors of Jersey would occupy it, and thus control the harbor mouth.

The urgency of occupation necessarily brought trouble. The province was land-poor. Bankruptcy stared the English government in the face. The English garrison in New York was nearly starved. The wealthy among the Dutch did not trust the Stuarts. What wonder, then, that the governors indiscreetly parceled out wild lands like oriental kings among their own men? Their king at home afforded them every sanction by his own personal life and the favors he distributed at court. In the other colonies, also, one could find ample precedent.

The legal forms of purchase, the amounts of land secured by individuals and groups, and indeed all the steps leading up to each transaction, ran similar to those of other counties and provinces. Although many parts of New England were settled in a much more popular way by congregations headed by a pastor, with freeholds drawn by lot, and a village government set up in the parish, there were also vast areas purchased by speculators for their own profit as a purely commercial venture, and the colonists had to fight them almost as vigorously as they did the Indians. Harris' patents of 80,000 acres in early Rhode Island equalled Rombout's in Dutchess. It is necessary to say this, for New England sometimes stresses the "democracy" of New England settlement, while glossing the speculative feature. Even after the equitable division on the basis of church membership, a shrewd speculator often managed to get the land pretty much into his own hands; in new lands such as the Green Mountains and the Berkshires, the church system was supplanted by a company or an individual.

The governors found their purchasers for the shore from three groups: the great landed proprietors of Albany, Schuyler and Livingston; the government servants who had served as interpreters, scouts, and Indian agents; and the merchants of New York with interest upland. Kipsbergen, a small grant in Rhinebeck, went to three Ulster farmers, and the larger patents included lesser employees and favorites of the governors. But in the main the personnel of the first men of Dutchess was as good as the province afforded. Their influence upon the county lasted so long, that they deserve a more particular notice hereafter.

Colonial conditions determined the fate of many Utopian provisions that issued from England and were valiantly affirmed by the governor. The necessity of occupancy, and the lack of demand for land, and most of all the aristocratic land customs of England made mincemeat of the regulation that no purchaser should have more than a thousand acres. The deed from the Indians was often lacking when, as in upper Dutchess, the Indians had ceased to occupy. The survey cost too much to make, even if surveyors enough had been ready to make them, and no Dutchess patentee offered one. The description, based on Indian names of bounds and areas, was vague and inaccurate in most instances. Only the patent itself, duly approved by the authority, remained to attest the validity of the patent. Thanks to a good Dutch custom, the patent was recorded in books of land grants, which still remain in the possession of the Secretary of State at Albany. From them our titles descend, through the "Liber" series in the office of the Clerk of Dutchess County.

1. The Rombout or Fishkill Patent. Patentees: Francois Rombouts and Gulian Verplanck, merchants; later, Stephanus

Van Cortlandt. License, February 2, 1682; Indian deed August 8, 1683; and Crown patent October 17, 1685.

As our first valid patent the description for the patent deserves repetition:—

"All that Tract or Parcel of Land Scituate, Lying and being on the East Side of Hudson's River, at the North Side of the High Lands, Beginning from the South side of a Creeke called the fresh Kill, and by the Indians Matteawan, and from thence Northward along said Hudson's River five hundred Rodd bejond the Great Wapins Kill, called by the Indians Mawenawasigh, being the Northerly Bounds, and from thence into the woods fouer Hours goeing, always keeping five hundred Rodd Distant from North Side of said Wapinges Creeke, however it runns, as alsoe from the said fresh Kill or Creeke called Matteawan, along the said fresh creeke into the woods at the foot of the said High Hills, including all the Reed or Low Lands at the South Side of said Creeke, with an Easterly Line, fouer Houers going into the woods, and from thence to the end of the fouer Houers goeing or Line Drawne att the North side of the five hund Rodd Bejoyond the Greate Wappinger Creeke or Kill called Mawenawasigh" . . . etc.

This easterly line into the woods four hours going could scarcely satisfy the modern surveyor. Three definite lines saved it; the two streams and the mountains. But it took a judicial decision to determine that four hours going meant sixteen English miles. The mountains proved a vain thing for safety, and a competitor shaved off a southern slice. The Wappingers Kill changed its course, apparently, below Manchester, and cost a miller his mill. But in due time surveys made deeds hold water as well as land, and the Rombout titles are good ones.

2. The second patent derived from Albany October 24, 1686; Robert Sanders, Indian interpreter, and Myndert Harmense Van Den Bogaerdt, merchant, son of the surgeon of Fort Orange whose narrative of the Oneidas has been widely used: the Minnisinck Patent, also known by their own names. Their description was no doubt clear to them, though vague

enough to give trouble later on. It has, however, the simple flavor of the woods:

"A certaine Tract or Parcelle of Land, called Minisinck; lying on the East Side of Hudson's River, to the North of the Land of Severyn, alias called the Baker; with the Arable and wood Land, Marshes, with the Creeke called Wynachkee;

With Trees, Stones, and further Range or out Drift for cattle;

And the fall of Waters called Pondanickrien;

And another Marsh, Lying to the North of the Fall of Waters, called Wareskeecken".

As Severyn the Baker never established his claim, the deed obviously leaves something to be desired. Nevertheless, most of Poughkeepsie traces its title to this deed, north of the Fallkill and west of the Rombout Patent in the Wappingers Creek. Severyn afterwards gave up his baking and went to Ulster, where he married the fair widow Bruyn whose nose is the source of "Gertrude's Nose" at Mohonk Mountain. Severyn then inherited a family of fond stepchildren, who named their own children after him. He seems to have passed his time pleasantly killing wolves in the Catskills, for Ulster accounts record payments to him at twelve shillings each.

It was natural for an Indian interpreter to base his deed on three Indian areas, quite clear enough to him. Wareskeecken, however, meant merely "the end of the boundary," and if it referred to the boundary of this patent, would be wholly unsatisfactory. More probable is the fact that this area was near the boundary between the range of the Mahikans in the north, and the Wappingers in the south, a widely known line in the Indian world in which Sanders passed his life. In 1730 Daniel Nimham, an Indian, described this in his own way, as "about the Middle of Beekman's Patent". Now Beekman had two patents, and Wareskeeken lay adjacent to the north end of his southern patent.

3. To the south of the Minisinck Patent Colonel Peter Schuyler of Albany located his Patent, issued June 2, 1688.

"At a certaine Place called the Long Reach; Bounded on the North and East by a certaine Creeke that Runns into Hudson's

River on the North Side of a Certaine House now in the Possession and Occupacion of Pieter, the Brewer; the said Creeke being called by the Indians where it runs into the River Thanackonek, and where it Runns further up into the woods, Pietawickquasseick. Bounded on the North by the lands of Robert Sanders and Myndert Harmense and on the west by Hudson's River Aforesaid."

The two Indian terms mean "place of nut trees" and "high lands at the end of the bog". The Casper Kill, named for Jan Casper Hallenbeck, brother-in-law of Pieter the Brewer, runs through boggy meadows to a point where in other generations boys gathered chestnuts.

4. On the same day that Colonel Schuyler obtained his Poughkeepsie Patent he also obtained his patent to Red Hook. It ran from the shore adjacent to Magdalene Island at the mouth of the Sawkill, to a meadow Tauquashquieck, then to a lake Metambesen; thence northerly to a line due east from Sawyer's Creek (Saugerties), thence west to the Hudson, and south along the shore to the Sawkill mouth. Much of this Schuyler soon sold to Harman Gansevoort. His descendant Peter J. Schuyler lived at Rhinebeck, owning much land by inheritance and purchase.

5. A small strip between Schuyler's patent and the Casperkill was taken up in 1697 by Johannes Cuyler of Albany. It had been purchased in 1687 from the Indian Kaghqueront, but was left unfilled for ten years. Perhaps the gore was found when Schuyler made his purchase of the Indians and got his fellow-townsman to apply, to prevent others.

6. On the same day, June 2, 1688, that Governor Dongan granted his Patents to Colonel Schuyler, he also approved the Patent of Kipsbergen, to Gerrit Aertsen, Arie Roosa, and Jan Elting. On July 28 Hendrick Kip obtained an adjoining Patent. The Patent ran to only 1200 acres. Henry Kip became the sole owner, but the other families settled in Dutchess. Interest in Kipsbergen, however, goes back to 1686, when application for the license was made. It thus coincided in time with the

Poughkeepsie Patent, as well as with the great grant to Robert Livingston which included northern Dutchess County, above Red Hook.

7. The deed to Henry Kip's grant is interesting as containing the names of two famous Indians, who are remembered in Calicoon and Ankony Farms today. It seems odd that Sopus Indians should sell lands in Dutchess, but since at the time Ulster officers held charge in the younger county, the Indians might have claimed a similar priority. "We, the underwritten Ankony, one of the Esopus Indians, and Anamaton and Calycoon, two of the Esopus Sachems, do acknowledge to have received of Henry Kip, of Kingston, full satisfaction for a parcel of land lying over the Redout against the Redoubt Kill (Rondout) on the north side of Arie Roosa on the river, which is received by me Ankony, Anamaton, and Calycoon in full satisfaction for the above said lands, in witness whereof [we] have hereunto set our marks this 28" day of July, 1686. Testis Henry Pawling."

8. Colonel Pawling, prominent Ulster official, received a license from Governor Dongan about this time. The formal Patent known as Pawling's Purchase, or the Pawling-Staats Patent, was issued May 11, 1696, (confirmed May 1, 1698) to his widow Nieltje and her six children. The Purchase included the land between Crum Elbow Creek and the Hudson, but unfortunately the deed was described as containing four thousand acres only.

9. Seven years later a sharp-eyed official, probably Peter Fauconnier, discovered the discrepancy, and as he was the trusted secretary of Lord Cornbury the governor, he obtained the remaining acreage in this area, with a company headed by his attorney, Jacob Regnier, and three petty officials, Benjamin Ashe, Barne Cosins, and John Persons. Persons later testified, when Fauconnier was on trial for such things, that he had not acted in good faith, but was a mere front to secure the Patent. Fauconnier's Patent is one of the strangest on record, claiming the whole of Pawling's Purchase,

"except only such land, parcel thereof, to which Wyntie, John, Albert, Anne, Henry, and Mary Pawling, children lawfully begotten between Henry Pawling deceased and Nieltje his wife are duly entitled to".

10. Thus in three years, 1685-88, Governor Dongan could feel that he had saved Hudson's River by his patenting the eastern shore from Rensselaer to the High Lands. Only one piece remained, the Rhinebeck Patent of Henry Beekman, April 22, 1697, which may indeed, like Pawling's, have been originally planned by Dongan. He described it as "a place called by the Indians Maninquious, over against the Klyne Sopus Effly, being the north bounds of Pawling's Purchase", to "a stone creek (Stony Kill) over against the Kallcoon Hoek, which is the southerly bounds of Colonel Peter Schuyler, from thence so far east, as to reach a certain pond called by the Indians "Waraughkeemeek" and thence southerly parallel to the river, to meet a line from the place of beginning running easterly into the woods, this being the northern bounds of Pawling's Purchase".

11. At the same time Beekman obtained his vast Back Lots Patent, including four Dutchess towns, Dover, Pawling, Union Vale and Beekman, and the east part of La Grange. This he "improved" in a new patent from Cornbury, June 25, 1703. He coolly added Kipsbergen to his north Patent, but did not try to evict the real patentees, contenting himself with purchasing from them.

Lord Bellomont, who sounded off for rectitude whenever he could (though he had half the shares in Captain Kidd), wrote of these Patents "One Henry Beekman, a Lieut. Coll. in the militia, has a vast tract of land as large as the Midling County of England, for which he gave Fletcher a hundred dollars, about twenty five pounds in English, and I am told he values his purchase at £5000."

12. Colonel Fletcher was even more reckless in his grant in 1697 to Nine Partners: Col. Caleb Heathcote, Major Augustin Graham, James Emott, Lieut. Col. Henry Filkin, David Jamison, Hendrick ten Eyck, John Aertson, William Creed, and

Jarvis Marshall. This included Clinton, Pleasant Valley, Stanford, Washington, and Amenia; Hyde Park beyond Crum Elbow Creek, and the southern part of Northeast.

This grant, one of the two largest in the history of Dutchess, and in many ways the most influential in its effects, deserves reprinting. It picked up the only river lots Dongan had overlooked. "A Tract of Vacant Land Situate, Lying, and Being on Hudson's River in Dutchess County. Bounded in the west by the said Hudson River Between the Creek called Fish Creek (Crum Elbow) at the marked trees of Pawling (Including the Said Creek) and the Land of Myndert Harmense & Company then Bounded Southerly by the Land of the said Myndert Harmense and company as far as their bounds goes westerly by the Land of the said Harmense and until a southerly line runs so far south until it comes to the south side of a certain Meadow wherein there is a White Oak Tree markt with the letters H.T. then southerly by An east and west line to the Division Line between the province of New York and the Colony of Connecticut, and so Easterly to the Division Line and Northerly by the aforesaid Fish Creek as far as it goes and from the head of said Creeke by a parallel line to the south bounds east and west reaching the aforesaid Division Line."

This covered the eastern part of Hyde Park, the greater part of Clinton and Stanford, all of Pleasant Valley, Washington, and Amenia and the south part of Northeast, except for the Oblong portions then in Connecticut. The famous White Oak Tree at Rochdale was the point of departure for Rombout, Beekman, Poughkeepsie, and Nine Partners Patents. Governor Dongan had sold Dutchess to the Dutch. Fletcher had divided his grants between Pawling and Beekman, of Dutch extraction, and the English members of his council. Lord Bellomont persuaded the English Lords of Trade to forbid him to make further grants until abuses were corrected.

Lord Cornbury, who succeeded him in 1704, took up where Fletcher had left off. The Hyde Park group, all friends of his, cleared the way for another group of officials to capture the remaining lots.

13. These included Roger Mompesson, Rip Van Dam, Sampson Broughton, James Graham, Peter Fauconnier, Richard Sackett, Thomas Wenham, Robert Lurting, and George Clarke. Men commonly speak of their Patent as "Little Nine Partners", referring to the size of the grant as compared with its predecessor. School-children, however, quite literally think of them as smaller men, and, as the terms Upper and Lower better describe the geographical relation, they are here used. Certainly the Upper Nine Partners group was far more distinguished than the Lower.

Their Patent, issued April 10, 1706, comprised the land bounded on the south by the putative patent of Richard Sackett, "lately purchased" to "Wimposing, thence by the Mountains Easterly to the Colony Line of Connecticut and thence northerly by the said Colony Line and Wiantenuck River to the south bounds of Lands purchased by John Spragg & Company. At Owissetanuck thence westerly by the said purchase as it runs to the Manor of Livingston and by the south bounds thereof to the lands purchased and patented to Coll. Peter Schuyler over against Megdelons Island and so by the said purchase and patent. To the patent of Coll. Beekman for Land Lying over against Esopus Fly and thence by the said Land to the said southeast corner and thence to the place where it began."

14. On October 26, 1687, Jan Roelof Sybrandt and Lambert Dorlandt obtained a strip along the Hudson shore in the High Land, all the way from Anthony's Nose to Polipel Island, "east into the woods to a marked tree." No east bound was described. The governor gave no patent, no doubt awaiting further survey. Whatever propriety the buyers had obtained by the Indian purchase was transferred to Adolph Philipse on June 16, 1697; he next day obtained his patent from Governor Fletcher. His deed ran north to the great Fishkill, and thus overlapped the Rombout Patent, bringing later litigation. Easterly it ran along the line of the Rombout Patent, and also Beekman's (as was claimed). A second deed confirming the first, and this time running to Connecticut, bore the date

1702, and some Indian signers. This deed was not recorded.

This great estate of about two hundred thousand acres remained undivided until after 1750, although squatters and some tenants occupied farms as early as 1730. Chief Nimham of the Wappingers challenged the validity of this ownership after 1762. Timothy Shaw testified at the Nimham trial in 1767 that 24 families were settled in the patent before 1742, and 300 before 1756. In the taxlist of old Dutchess, 1728, none of the taxpayers in South Ward were located in the Highlands. The first survey, apparently, was that of John Alsop.

The best example of the incomplete patents was that of Arnout Cornelise Viele, (pronounced as in French, Vielé, and often so written) the noted Indian agent. Among the Indians his reputation for honesty and fair dealing was very high, and even the critical Bellomont chose him as official interpreter. Bellomont's engineer, W. Roman, who rebuilt the fort at Albany, wrote the governor that Viele was "a good and faithful interpreter, who lives in the Bay on Long Island". An account of Viele's journey to the Long House still exists.

This excellent public servant was rewarded by his Indian friends Calkoen, the Esopus sachem, Waspacheek *alias* Spek, who must have been of consequence in the Wappings Kill area, and Pillippuwas of the Wappingers. Their gift of land on June 15, 1680, included the whole Town of Poughkeepsie as far north as the Rust Plaets spring in the Rural Cemetery, an area of twenty thousand acres odd. The deed was attested by the Sakemaker of the Highlands, Unamnamapake. Viele received permission from Governor Andros to accept the gift, "in consideration of his long and faithful service to the Government as Indian interpreter. But unfortunately Viele had not recorded the deed, and five years later the Rombout and Schuyler Patents preempted the same land. Viele in 1704 appealed to Governor Cornbury for redress, and was granted the land; but even the governor could not overrule the rights of Property, and Viele lost. Some compromise may have ensued, for Viele's nephew Peter married Harmense's daughter and settled in Fairview.

Against this honest effort the petition of the landgrabbing Leigh Atwood, an appointee of the Earl of Bellomont, stands out starkly. His barefaced attempt to jump the whole northern end of the Rombout land is referred to in a later deed as having been granted, but this is very doubtful. Dr. Samuel Staats and Derick Vanderburgh granted a part of their riverfront and a passage through their land to the land "to the eastward granted to the said Leigh Atwood and Co. behind us." Their generosity was well meant, perhaps, but the Rombout proprietors defended their claims well.

This same Leigh Atwood, though a member of the Governor's Council, led the raid on the Westchester grant of Caleb Heathcote, and succeeded in bullying the great landlord into admitting him and his group as partners. Not all the piracy of the period happened at sea.

For good or ill, the governors had given the land away, with quitrent to the royal authority which the Monday morning critics swore might have been twice as much. What excuse they found for not collecting what little had been specified, they never told. The better governors by good humor and skill got some of it, though there were always arrears in the impecunious treasury.

A somewhat different view of the enterprise came from Robert Hunter, the most competent governor of eighteenth-century New York, in 1710. "The Proprietary governments, which were modelled according to the humours of their respective proprietors, consist of the governor and representatives, the council being a mere cypher, having no share of the legislatures, by which means the governors, being dependent upon the good will of the people for their daily bread, have been obliged to make such concessions, and passed them into laws, that if these governments be purchased and continued upon the foot they now stand, her Majesty pays for much trouble and no dominion. This is the plan of the government, however, they all aim at, and make no scruple to own it."

But Hunter came too late to do anything about the Dutchess Patents, and he confirmed Robert Livingston in his manor, allowing him to take his lands below the Roelof Jansen Kill out of the County in 1717. The governor set up the first county government in 1714, thus early helping the settlers to manage their own affairs. Next after the Irish Dongan we should honor the Scot, Hunter. He brought over the Palatines and set them up in East Camp, providing the first substantial group of landsmen in the county.

On their part the patentees might count their profits on paper, for their speculation was very definitely "risk capital". They knew nothing of the land's fertility, for the steep rocky shores and dense woods gave no promise of what lay behind. If they ventured up the streams, they found bogs. The Indians added an element of uncertainty. Trade in fur might beckon a few, and experts in Indian affairs might know more than the rest, but only where patentees or their widows and children led the way, did early settlement increase.

There remained the great river. It gave easy and immediate access. It bore the sloops that carried government officials on their endless errands. It promised law and order, and had separated the infant county from conflicts that ravaged the other shore. Though it exposed the western flank to attack, it could bring aid with equal speed to meet an invader. Neither the French nor their Indian allies ever ventured so far.

Unoccupied for a century, and barely opened after another half-century, Dutchess County in thirty years thereafter, to the amazement of observers, bounded to the top of the list in wealth and population. Her growth seemed miraculous only because the factors that operated lay concealed behind its woods.

On the Lower Nine Partners Patent the tax records afford conclusive evidence. Seventeen out of fifty-six names on the first tax list for Nine Partners Precinct had paid taxes in the area either on land or poll for years before the partition of the lots. How many of the rest had been squatters is uncertain. Twenty-two were newcomers to the tax list, and may have just entered the precinct. The remaining seventeen had paid taxes under the ward system (which lasted until 1737) between 1735 and 1737. There is no reason to believe that conditions were different on the Beekman lots, or elsewhere. New York records seem to lack any reference to shiploads of disappointed settlers going on to other provinces. Dutchess had her full share of the Scotch-Irish migration. Evidently, except for the relatively small quota of more enterprising pioneers, the land already opened sufficed to meet the demand. Although Americans coined the word "squatter" about 1800, they understood its meaning a century before. Out of every group of settlers a few determined men refused to be discouraged when they found company land unavailable because of delay in its partition. Where there's a will there's a way; and they simply moved in upon the woods. When partition came, they either bargained for the property, or moved on.

# 8. The Propriety

*Propriety: a private estate. Obs. exc. in American history: individuality. Now rare.*

OXFORD DICTIONARY.

THE HISTORICAL geography of old Dutchess grew out of personal association and human needs. Since the entrants had found a way east into the woods from the creek-mouths, the landseekers bounded their purchases by the kills or their watersheds.

The three partners Rombouts, Verplanck, and Van Cortlandt, all dealers in furs, secured the watersheds of the Wappingers, the Sprout, and the Fishkill, nearest New York, most likely to yield the beaver and otter which would be trapped by a fairly numerous and quite friendly Indian tribe. The Albany group, equally well-informed but a little late on the scene, chose upper landings and town sites with good land along their mill-streams. Ulster men, active farmers and responsible leaders, took land opposite the Ulster shore from Kingston south. The speculators, in three companies of partners, carved out the remainder. Only the latest among them failed to secure at least a foothold on the Hudson Shore, the county's only highway.

Thus in the first definition of the county, geographical nearness and personal interests determined the boundaries of the Patents. For over thirty years this remained the whole story. On June 24, 1719 sales of land at Poughkeepsie, Rhinebeck and Beacon warranted a division of responsibility, and three wards were created: North Ward, north of Crum Elbow Creek; Middle Ward, north of Wappingers; and South Ward, from the Wappingers south as far as Westchester. The three groups of settlers thus defined grew into almost autonomous societies. The affiliations of the North fell chiefly with Albany and the manor lords of the upper river. The Middle Ward identified itself with Ulster. The South Ward developed two major connections, New York with Long Island, and New England. The human interests thus created led to the loss of the county's northern patent, Livingston; while a century later New England ties led to the loss of Putnam County, with its New England name.

When wards were first mapped, only 183 families, in 1722, had ventured east into the woods. Twenty-five years later the total population had grown to 3418. Division had been made of the lots on the Rombout, Beekman Back Lots, and Lower Nine Partners, while small but thriving neighborhoods had developed at the three villages near the shore. Settlers were beginning to take up land in the Oblong running all along the back country.

On December 16, 1737, the colonial Legislature authorized a division into seven Precincts, following patent boundaries in every case but one, in which one partner's interests were so diverse as to warrant a different deal. Rynbeck included Schuyler North, Pawling-Staats, Beekman-Rhinebeck, and Kipsbergen. Northeast included Upper Nine Partners. Crum Elbow included the congenial Hyde Park and Lower Nine Partners. Poughkeepsie took over the lots of Rombout west of Wappingers, surrounding Poughkeepsie, and the other town patents: Sanders and Harmense, Schuyler, and Cuyler. Beekman Precinct followed Beekman Back Lots Patent in its entirety. Rumbout included the Rombout Patent, except for the lots beyond Wappingers already mentioned; and Adolph Philipse got his separate South Precinct for his patent.

The old patentees' boundaries remain in Poughkeepsie, Schuyler, Beekman, the two Partners tracts, Rombout except for its apex, and Beekman beyond and below La Grange. Though subdivided within themselves by town lines, the patentees might still claim five-sixths of all the Dutchess's bound, a notable achievement in this land of incessant change. They builded better than they knew.

Old Dutchess proved no attraction to the patentees so far as concerned their personal residence. Only Richard Sackett of the New Haven family of that ilk, after giving up ale-brewing in New York, boldly entered the Dutchess wilderness shortly after the turn of the century, and took up a putative patent at Dover (which may, for all I know, have been christened by him). He bought land of the Lower Nine, helped Governor Hunter with his Palatines, and afterwards beguiled some of them into the Upper Nine, of which he was a Partner. His sons became active citizens in later years.

But nearly all the patentees held their lands so long that they became a heritage, and so induced the children to join their fortunes with the Dutchess. The gift to the children goes far to atone for their own neglect of their purchases, and almost excuses the existence of the patents themselves. For many of these children became the leaders of county and provincial life, and even today, in the ninth generation, can be found everywhere in the county, good and useful citizens.

Two of them, Sheriff Henry Beekman, Jr. and Catharyna Rombout Brett, were our first citizens. William Beekman, whose given and family names adorn two streets of old Manhattan, was a fellow-townsman of Francois Rombouts. He left Hasselt in Flanders about the same time, and became equally well-known in New Amsterdam. Governor Stuyvesant's son married his eldest daughter Maria, and his son Gerardus, in his capacity as senior councilman, once acted the governor's part for a few weeks. Johannis, his youngest, founded the Kingston branch of Beekman. Cornelia married Isaac Van Vlack, of a family long known in Dutchess.

The father's link with up-river sprang from his appointment as commissary at Esopus in 1664, and as overseer in 1669. He served in the following year on the commission to set out new towns in Ulster, and served also as sheriff, but returned to New York when he was replaced after 1670.

Judge Hendrick Beekman, his son, must have followed his

father dutifully, for Governor Dongan appointed him a justice for Ulster in 1684. The good burghers of Wiltwyck, not yet subservient, protested his appointment in a petition, and requested the right to elect their own officers. The governor arrested all seventy signers, and only forgave them after they had pleaded guilty and humbled themselves.

It was not the first occasion of this sort. In 1667 the burghers had risen against Captain Daniel Brodhead of the English garrison at Kingston, who was carrying things with the high hand. Among the rioters—or patriots—was Albert Heymans, who was exiled for life, but soon returned, taking the name of Roosa. His son Arie, whose mother was Wyntje Ariens, became an associate of Judge Beekman in the purchase of land at Rhinebeck, and sold land at Kipsbergen to him.

Arie Roosa had been one of the seventy who withstood Dongan in 1684. Hendrick Kip, Jan Elting, and Jacob Aertsen Van-Wagenen, all good Rhinebeck names, were also among those arrested, as was Severyn Tenhout, our baker of Poughkeepsie.

None of them seem to have held any grudge against Judge Henry Beekman, when he obtained his patents in 1697 and enlarged them in 1703, even to the extent of absorbing their own Kipsbergen patent. The judge never pushed his claim, and bought some land from them later on.

In 1713 to 1715, Judge Beekman attracted the interest of the Palatines. Thirty families settled on his land, and the name Rhinebeck is said to derive from their wish to compliment him (Beeck, as then spelled) upon his kindness to the Rhinelanders. No direct proof exists, but probably the earliest use of the name occurs in their deeds. Beekman had also purchased much of the Schuyler patent, where many Palatines also settled. His son with a share of the Upper Nine Patents, and his neighbor Henry Pawling were equally fortunate in leaseholds where the indwellers were Palatines.

The judge represented Ulster in the first elective assembly directly under the king, in 1691, and was reelected in 1709, 1710, and 1715. A portrait reproduced by the Dutchess Historical Society shows a singularly handsome and agreeable man, dressed and bewigged in the best London fashion, giving a picture of him as an old man, living quietly at Rhinebeck with his wife, the daughter of Stephanus Van Cortlandt, perhaps the first citizen of New York in those days.

"Figure to yourself my old (grand) parent, very deaf and almost deprived of sight, sitting in his great chair, filling his pipe and calling for Miss Janet to read the newspaper. His constant word was "omit nothing, child", begin with the high and low water mark, the price of flour and wheat etc., not an advertisement left. This was my daily task, at first not pleasant; but I loved my parent, and was satisfied to add to his enjoyments. I began sometimes, almost choked by the vapor of the blessed pipe, and rose with half a voice."

Henry must have been the first man to assert his enjoyment in listening to commercials.

Thirteen letters of Col. Beekman to his agent and nephew Henry Livingston, Sr., clerk of Dutchess, have been preserved and published. They exhibit a man "diligent in his business", patient, tolerant, and unworried in the affairs of his great estate, and in his offices as sheriff of New York for six years, colonel in Dutchess militia, and member of the legislature (1716-1758).

As an assemblyman he resisted the Attorney General in his attempts to proceed without due process of law. "If they stand out I shall not fail to stand by them." He resisted land jumpers, too, and aided others in doing so. His realism is refreshing: "Money only hath sense", is his version of "Money talks".

His granddaughter's account of his interest in current events is borne out by the letters, for he frequently adds scraps of news to the details of land deals. He planned his feast for the others on election day. "Beef, Porck, and Backin, most all should be Buylt (boiled?) a day or 2 before ye Election brought to the Saverall Houses of ours, as Buys, Van de Bogart or Mrs. Ten Brock . . . 6 Barrels of Cider . . . the Cyder Should also be Distrebuted Before ye Day. I know not hoe shall Manage. Filkin & I am Tyered. Sum others I think should bear a hand."

He tells his "Loving Couzn" to let his suits drop against poor farmers, and shows no disposition to proceed against others in trouble. An examination of the County Clerk's records bears this out, for Beekman's name is absent from the long lists of suits against tenants.

Something of the flavor of justice in a midcentury Court of Dutchess lingers round this letter:

New York 2 March 1753.

Loving Couzn,

I Send yu by Jong Isaac Kup the newspaper You know we have to Defd Vs. Hofman suets of Great Consequences. The Jurrours are the Decisory: I find the Jurrours twin Hofn. & Benthuyse where those voted for him in the Last Election. Should the Sherif by him already be secured, as he is artful & understands Doabbing, I would venture the Sub, But how to come at Such Knowledge is a M - iry & could I be certain the Chief Sherif was Determined to penul. Them himself, would be for a struck Jury; give me your openjo soon, as our Lawyers requirer of me to Deside that Mater, as they may proceed by our aprobation.

Remain yr afectioneed unkle to Commaind
Henry Beekman

Old Beekman had died in 1737, leaving his estate equally divided between his two daughters and his son, known in his day as Colonel Beekman. The Rhinebeck Patent had already a goodly number of tenants, but the great Back Lots had not been surveyed. Doubtless there were squatters on so large a tract. The plan of its distribution in 1737 shows two tiers of lots, separated by two large irregular plots, one at the source of the Fishkill, and the other at the point of its effluence into the Rombout Patent. Roughly, these comprise the beautiful Clove valley. The tier lots extended three miles east and west, and a mile from north to south. There were twenty-four lots, two of them belonging jointly to the two sisters, the rest drawn by lot. In all, the Beekman purchases in the County might rise to 150,000 acres.

The two sisters were Catherine Beekman Pawling, widow of Albert Pawling, who gave her name to our town, and Cornelia Beekman Livingston, wife of Gilbert Livingston, a son of Robert of the Manor.

All this genealogy sets our hero in his time. In our day his birth and his landed wealth will count two strikes against him with some readers. But he called himself "a plain country squire", and he commended himself to his countians by his plain and unpretentious life. Young Alexander Hamilton of Edinburgh, the physician, met Beekman in a Poughkeepsie tavern in 1744, and thought him "at first possessed of the wisdom of the ages, but when he spoke, he knew no more than other men."

It is pleasant to record that Henry Beekman, Jr. undertook at his own expense to defend the Viele purchase against the aggression of the Nine Partners. The letter, published by the Historical Society, was found in a rat's nest in an old Poughkeepsie house. It is invaluable for the light it sheds on the whole land problem. The style suggests translation from the Dutch.

New York, December 29, 1743

Messrs Frans La Roy, Peter Parmentier, Pieter Vielen and Magiel Pelts:

Your letter sent by Mr. Turk has come to hand, together with the 4 inclosures, as well as the original Indian deed and patent of Robert Saunders and Mindert Harmense; also the deed from Col. Peter Schuyler and some other writings, including a copy of the patent to Johannes Cuyler, an Indian deed and a mortgage to Arinhout Viele, each of which papers I shall carefully keep. Your request to me for assistance I can not well refuse, being obliged thereto by long friendship as well as by our duty to assist our fellow man in good conscience as far as is right and equitable. For that reason I only wish that I had more experience and ability, since the business is so confused that it takes a better head than mine to disentangle the matter and bring it to clearness. However, I shall undertake it and spare no pains, as I do not doubt that justice will be done; in the hope that my services will redound to the benefit of the four of you.

First, it will take me some days to make a map of the whole of it, with explanations, according to the contents of the papers, in order to make the lawyer understand on what he is to ground his opinion. I mean Mr. Alexander. As soon as I receive this opinion I shall send it to you. Mr. Murray was spoken to by the 9 partners, but was still unengaged, so that I have asked him for his services in your behalf. He is an able man, by whose advice I am to confer first with Alexander and thereafter with him. He seems to have good hopes on account of your Indian deed, as no number of acres is mentioned therein, and the patent is based thereon, if only the bounds or limits thereof can be proved by the Indians and impartial men, whom you must meanwhile try to find. He also feels confident that your long and peaceable possession will count.

It will be best for you to say little about it to strangers, for fear that they may make evil use thereof to your disadvantage, but to be of good courage and to look your adversary confidently in the eye, for the old saying is, Who dares is sure to gain. I received by Turk seven pounds of your money, of which I shall keep account and which I shall spend to your service and satisfaction.

I not only hope but also trust that in my next letter I shall be able to give you greater satisfaction and courage that you will be released from the hands of your troublesome neighbors, for I shall put it up to them to prove that you are in possession of their land, without which they can recover nothing from you, and I suspect that they will not find it easy to do so. I lack information whether the Nine partners, at the division of their lands, measured off any land included in your Indian purchase and divided it among themselves. Also, from what place on the River they began to perambulate and whether the survey of Jarton's mill, up the River, is to be sent over.

I shall leave no stone unturned to show forth your right. I have unraveled other tangled threads and have no doubt but that I shall get the better of this ball also. You may rest assured that there will be no lack of willingness on my part. I expect to show my master-piece in this matter, as I believe that justice is on your side and I shall expect no other reward for this than your friendship, which will be enough for me.

I could write much more but fear that you would tire of reading it. Furthermore, I wish you and all my friends and acquaintances a happy New Year and remain (with good courage)

Your friend to command,
(signed) Henry Beekman.

Addressed:

To Messrs Capt. Frans La Roy, Peter Viele, Peter Parmentier and Mighil Peltz
at Poghkeepsie

Catheryna Brett made a name for herself unique in county and perhaps in all colonial history. She well deserves to be remembered as the "First Lady of Dutchess". Born in 1688, three years after her father had obtained his patent, and dying in 1764 two years before the repeal of the Stamp Act, she embraced the whole colonial existence of her heritage. No man in that whole period left a deeper impression upon its history. When in 1907 the first reunion of her descendants took place in Fishkill, more than a hundred and fifty met together to call her blessed. The county rejoiced with them.

Historians have made it the fashion to call her "Madam Brett", but she never used the word herself, and but one early document called her Madam. Another paper called her Mistress. It is the better title, for her life was one of mastery, mastery of the wilderness as of all other adverse conditions. Tradition, of course, plays up her arrival at church in a carriage-and-four, with coachman and footman; but it also admits that she could be seen any weekday, galloping astride her good horse on her round of visits to the farms.

The historical records tell rather of the competent woman of business, unafraid to borrow on credit, to sue or be sued, to withstand her opponents or stand by her friends; a woman generous and fair-minded, and of heroic fibre.

Catheryna Rombout's father, Francois Rombouts, merchant, alderman, mayor of New York, died in 1691, when she was barely four years old. He left her his house on De Heeren Street (Broadway) and his land, "the Wappins". To the fair widow, Helena nee Teller, who had been his third wife, as he was her third husband, he left 4000 guilders and the residue of his ample estate.

As guardians of the child Catheryna he appointed William Teller, her grandfather, expert at Albany with Indians and their trade; Peter de la Noy, leader in New York commerce; Dr. Samuel Staats of Albany, who had brought over the latest medicine from Holland, and who had beautiful daughters of his own; and Paulus Richards, wine merchant, and owner of a vineyard monopoly on Long Island.

Oddly, or perhaps naturally, enough, Mrs. Brett in later life exhibited traits that corresponded very closely with the above named skills. She proved expert in her understanding of Indians. She traded keenly and successfully. She loved to give her friends medical prescriptions. Her friends, who bought her lands, came almost exclusively from Long Island.

Formal education she never had, or very little. In the little Dutch town, slowly becoming an English colonial capital, the writing of good English must surely have been at a premium. But neither her guardians nor her English husband, Roger Brett, though he wrote Gentleman after his name and had served in her Majesty's Navy, ever succeeded in getting her to spell a single English sentence, hardly a single word, correctly. Her mis-spelling, indeed, almost amounted to genius.

Her mother, relict of Cornelius Bogardus, son of Domine Everardus Bogardus, and, later, relict of Jan Hendricksen Van

Baal, had a son Cornelius Bogardus, and a son and five daughters Van Baal. To Cornelius she left just five pounds, with the tart observation that she had "before that time paid considerable sums of money for his use". To Catharyna Rombout she left nine pence without a single word.

All the rest of the estate she left to Henry Van Baal, Maria (Mrs. Isaac) de Peyster; Margaret (Mrs. Nicholas) Evertson; Helena (Mrs. Gualthemus) Du Bois; and Rachel (Mrs. Petrus) Bayard; together with provision for their care of one-sixth for the youngest daughter Hannah.

This was in 1707. Catheryna in her sixteenth year had departed from the Dutch tradition by marrying her gay young lieutenant, Roger Brett, of Somerset in England, apparently of excellent background, for he had come from England with Edward Hyde, Lord Cornbury, first cousin of Queen Anne. The Bretts could boast that a certain Captain Brett in Elizabeth's time had battled the Barbary pirates. Cornbury kept Brett in high favor, for in 1709, in forwarding Brett's mail to him, he added: "On Sunday morning My Daughter sailed out of the hook with a fair wind; she gave her service to Mrs. Brett and yourself. I entreat you to give My respects to Mrs. Brett and believe that I am Sir, Your most humble servant, Cornbury."

How Catheryna could have read such elegant epistles, peeking over her husband's shoulder, and never have learned to spell a single word herself, passes all comprehension.

Speculation has not been idle about Mrs. Rombouts' legacy of nine pence. Catheryna said nothing about it, and if we may judge from the record, all her sisters remained her friends. De Peyster, Evertsen, and DuBois families bought her land; Bayard did business in Dutchess, and her son Francis named his second daughter Hannah.

Roger did not take it so well. His friend Cornbury had obliged him by appointing him to the lucrative post of executor of Mrs. Rombouts' will—scarcely decorously, for he was the youngest daughter's husband; and the will, soon discovered, had made other provision. Roger tried to fight in the courts by delaying the execution, but in vain, and he and his wife found themselves with a big house and no money.

Moreover, Lord Cornbury, himself in heavy debt, had stepped out of the governor's house into jail, to be bailed out later, and to become the Earl of Clarendon, if you please, but then in England. No hope in that quarter. Cornbury's friends were distinctly unwelcome in the new state of things. So, perhaps in despair, perhaps as one loyal descendant claims, because "the love of the forest and the hardihood of the pioneer settler" was "inborn in (her) veins", Catheryna found herself and her little family at "the Fishkills", after five years of gaiety in the governor's set. Henry Beekman's wife Gertrude van Cortlandt, we recall, had precisely the same experience, for she danced at these very balls, and became a country squire's wife.

In 1708 Roger and Catheryna Brett raised £240 on their New York house by selling a mortage to James Emott, (whose descendants came to Dutchess), and in 1709, 1711, and 1729, three additional mortgages were placed on Catheryna's property at the Fishkills. Between 1708 and 1713, five farms were sold to farmers at Fishkill. With the money they were able to build a mill and a miller's house, where they lived from 1713 to 1716, while their own house was a-building further upstream. The contract for the latter called for payment in land, of 100 acres to the carpenter Robert Dengee. When that time came, they added a bonus of ten acres; and it is clear they earned his good will, for he later was called in to witness one of their deeds of land.

Meanwhile Catheryna had given birth to three sons, Francis and Robert, who survived her, and Rivery, who died at eighteen. Rivery got his name from the fact that Catheryna had borne him while on her sloop in one of her New York trips. The same sloop that gave her a son took away her young husband, for at some time between the autumn of 1716 and the winter of 1718 he had drowned while sailing into the Kill, being knocked overboard by the sloop's boom. Not a very seamanlike death for a naval officer, it appears. It would have made a catastrophe for a young woman of ordinary spirit. Catheryna rose to the challenge.

For years her husband and she had left unpaid the interest on a large mortgage, held by George Clarke of Upper Nine Partners, Secretary of the Province and a relative and close friend of Lord Cornbury. He now secured himself by association with the widow "in equity" in the sale of two or more large farms. One of the deeds, in 1733, rehearsed the whole story, affirming non-payment for twenty years. The sale was in fee simple, with "right tight title and interest". Seven hundred and four pounds were paid for nine hundred and fifty-nine acres by Cornelius Van Wyck, whose daughter Margaret promptly was married to Francis Rombout Brett, and whose grandson Isaac Van Wyck married Sarah Brett, daughter of Mistress Brett's son Robert. One of the Van Wyck homesteads became the scene of J. F. Cooper's "Spy".

After a couple of sales more Mistress Brett shook free of George Clarke's clutches. She had reason to be concerned, for Clarke and his friend Leonard Lewis in 1712 had obtained an Indian deed from the well-wishing Wappings to Poughkeepsie land that fell within her patent. When in 1721 she obtained a license to survey this land her surveyors were obstructed and threatened, and some drunken Indians even entered Catheryna's house at Fishkill threatening to kill her. She escaped, however, perhaps through a warning from friendly Indians, and Doctor Colden finished his survey. His line, the famous parallel line (parallel 500 rods west of Wappingers Creek) still prevails in today's deeds.

Once free of Clarke, Mistress Brett sold her land without anyone's supervision. A letter of hers, which may appear here as well as anywhere, illustrates her knowledge of the intricate land practice, though it also gives delightful evidence of "creative" spelling and medieval medicine of the eighteenth century. Incidentally, it shows that Henry Livingston, county clerk for so many years, was her agent as well as her very good friend.

Readers will enjoy deciphering this letter, printed exactly as written. It is hoped they will not be too "pusseld" at first, for it is completely explicit and business-like.

To Mr Hennery Levenston at His hous at pocipsing
May the 13.1749
Sir

afther my Kind Respacks tou your selfs en T yours this Comes tou Retorn you thancks for your Favers tou your spous Sr en I had a Litel descors about her desorder sie has bin affectid weht wyle sie had that Dimnis on her syht en accorden tou wat axpirens I haff had I thack it that the esstirrix is the prinsibel cors thes drops ar vary goud tou supres the vapers my Dater has Resifd grat Rilyffe by thacken of them I houp to mersy the will be blest tou her the are to bie thacken 25 drops en the morning as sone as sie Ryses on 2 or 3 sponfulls of water for som days en alsoo at nyht when sie gous tou Bad I advysd Mrs. levenston tou Drinck way tou Coul her Blod en tou Bring her tou a nateral Body witcts I houp sie has had bennifit by becaus when sie begins tou thack this Drops sie soud not bie vary Costiff or Bond but being pretie naterell not Lous neither but pretie naterell en then thacken the Drops duly mornings en Evenings the well ciep her soo after a Wicks thacken of them sie mack yuse half wyn tou thack them en the are passentter tou thack en I wold not haff her bie afrad of a drop or tou moor for after 2 or 3 thyms taken them sie may thack forthie the wont hert for en case of a Collick wan may thack sextie. Sr Mr Everitt was hier this morning hie is tou geff mie sex fatt fols for quit en I Resarf half thie myns en hie is tou geff mie a morrigide on the Land for the tou other pamants wan half I must Resife now en the other half of the hole is tou bie en four pamants wan half of that half the naxt may en the other half the nax may Follerng en for the securitie of the same I thack a Morrigeed en a Bond en Sr Mr Everit en I ar agrid that hie is tou haff but 11-hondrid ackers I am tou Ciep the Remander out of the Remander is Laid out 59 acars By Johannes Swartwout en for moses DeGraff 19 ackers more en for Mr Tappen 100 ackers en for Mr Piter De Bous en Arie Van Vliet about 20 ackers it Lys yust By Arrie Van Vlits possessyon mr De Bous was Ron this out before en the Remander sr witcts I haff Resarfd I am tou thack en proporsine as I haff sold tou hiem goud en Bad as I haff sold to hiem as it sall bie agriyd en wan pies if it can suet for I would haff it weht tember on for I haff thacken som plans alridy I Donbeliff Mr Evrit en I sant Dessagrie

en Sr I mack Bold tou remynd you wans more tou Gard mie en that pynt that I only sell 11 hondrid ackers wehten Mr Coldens Lyne that en kays that the Land accorden tou the patant sold bie fond broder thn that must bie my Ryet still en his is tou giff the quit en preporsin of the patant en sex fatt fols tou mie my son will Sr Explan my crall tou you otherways you wold bie pusseld I Remane Sr weht du Respact tou your selfs en spous Sr your

vary ombell
Sarvant
Catharynn Brett

Sr you will bie plisd tou Lett know

And now her sales began in earnest, and the activity began in Fishkill, which may in great part be attributed to the energy of this indomitable woman. By 1760 Rombout Precinct was assessed three times as high as Poughkeepsie. She brought to the county the families whose sons were its officers in the Revolution: Swartwout, DuBois, Teller, Brinckerhoff, Van Wyck and Schenck, de Peyster, Storms, Rosekrans, and Van Voorhis, Adrianse, Southard, Montross, and Mesier, Buys, Hussey, Van Vliet, Peele, Wiltse, and Wambone—not all of these first on her land, but all purchasers.

Her most interesting achievement was Frankfort Storehouse on Aug. 6, 1743, an adventure in cooperative enterprise. Her name heads the list of a company which bought 12 acres from her son Francis, including a landing on the river. This lay north of Dennings Point between two large marked rocks on the shore. Each partner took one share or a fraction. (Two bought two shares each). All but four signed as "yeomen"; two were merchants, one a blacksmith, one a widow.

| | |
|---|---|
| Catheryna Brett | John Carman |
| Cornelius Van Wyck | Joshua Carman |
| James Duncan (Merchant) (2) | Thomas Storm |
| John Brinckerhoff | Jacobus Brinckerhoff (1/2) |
| Theodorus Van Wyck (2) | Laurens Losee (1/2) |
| Theodorus Van Wyck, Jr. | Isaac Brinckerhoff (1/2) |
| Abraham Bloom | Henry Du Bois (1/2) |
| Cornelius Wiltse | George Adrianse (1/2) |
| Benjamin Hawsbrook | John Van Vlackera 1/2 |
| Abraham Van Wyck | Abraham Adrianse 1/2 |
| George Brinckerhoff | Isaac Adrianse 1/2 |
| | total 20 shares |
| | 22 partners. |

The organization was of the familiar Hanseatic pattern. Each stockholder was entitled to one vote, decision was by majority vote. Mrs. Brett held no interest beyond one share, but her sloop carried much of the produce to the New York markets. Each share-holder had a room in the storehouse to which he brought his produce. Prices were agreed upon.

The account book is possessed by a descendant of Mistress Brett. The company ran till 1840, though closed for duration in Revolutionary times.

The Storehouse was a powerful argument for a highroad, which became one of the most traveled routes out of New England. The Verplanck storehouse borrowed from it, and the Farmers Landing at the Wappingers, produced another good road for the farmers on Verplanck leases, in the middle Rombout.

Equally interesting were the terms in the sales conducted by Mistress Brett. Unlike Beekman, she called for only a one-half interest in mines and minerals, though she often retained water-rights. But many of her deeds grant the purchaser the privilege of "grass and timber" on her "common land"—any of her as yet unsold and unsettled property. Sometimes she retained an equal right in her purchaser's land. The great majority of her sales were in fee simple. The leases were invariably "forever", with no limitation of lives. The rent of one peppercorn was often stated to be purely for the purpose of taking advantage of the English Statute of Uses—a device by which the "cestui que use"—the actual farmer—got an absolute possession.

By 1760 Mistress Brett was assessed on only £20 by the tax committee of the supervisors. Henry Beekman had over twenty times as much in the same year, and many in Poughkeepsie and Rombout paid higher taxes on their acreage. Catheryna Brett had single-handed disposed of some 30,000 acres of land, and lived among her customers, honored and deferred to.

A word of her kindness. She did not limit this to medical dispensation. Pieter Lassen the Brewer, though his patent was not valid, was left in possession of valuable land in Wappingers Creek. The Wappinger Indians were allowed to remain on land which they had sold Rombout and Company, and remained on good terms until the end of her life. These same Indians were fighting with the patriots in the Revolution. A letter from Mistress Brett, quoted elsewhere refers to her pledge not to disturb them. She gave this, she avers, in appreciation of a valuable service done to her.

Her will, drawn March 14, 1763, shows the same use of conventional form and personal vigor.

"In the name of God, Amen. I Catheryna Brett of Fishkill in Dutchess County and in the Province of New York, Widow, being aged and infirm in body but of sound and disposing mind, memory, and understanding,—Thanks be given to Almighty God for the same"—etc. Her body was to be decently interred at the discretion of her executors (it lies beneath the pulpit of the church she endowed and attended, the Reformed Church in Fishkill).

Francis Brett was given the share in Frankfort Storehouse, 100 pounds in money, a Negro woman Molly by name, five farms, and one half the estate. The children of Robert Brett, deceased, the second son, received the remainder. To them she left the Negro woman Coban, "and if sold she is to have the liberty of choosing her new master". The same was true of Molly.

One month after her will was made, her daughter Hannah married Henry Schenck. The homestead descended to our own times in the female line, as befitted a friend of the Indians. But her best known descendant, Francis Bret Harte, who bore her father's name as his own given name, and her husband's family as his second one, was never a resident of Dutchess. His people lived on the western Hudson shore, at Albany and elsewhere.

Of the thousands of suits over land in Dutchess recorded in the County Clerk's Ancient Documents, only two can be recalled as related to Mistress Brett. One of these gave as evidence an I O U of Jacob Musiar, in Dutch so quaint as to deserve preserving.

Febrary de 23, 1721/22

Jek onder geschreven beken schuldigh tee we en aen Ms Catharina Brett Wedue en Dutches Countye twe en darttigh Schepel goudye wenter Severbarre taerrue voor huer Van de Bouwerij dare ick op woon op peequeick en beloufe et haer tee Brengen of an har order Waenneer it sael waen myen Voorey-ghit werden dat getuyghick mett myn hant

Jacob Musiar

Cornelius Bogard

Colonel Peter Schuyler and his Scots brother-in-law Robert Livingston might stand for parallel lives in some future work of biography. Having married his Dutch wife and taken his position as Commissioner for Indian affairs in the province, Livingston joined and often led the local popular party. Though he amassed great lands in the mad race that infected everyone at the time, he so far slew envy as to be chosen speaker of the Assembly. Though in close association with all the governors of his time, he earned the hatred only of those whose disfavor did him credit: Fletcher, and Cornbury. Dongan, Bellomont, and Hunter were his friends, and generous ones. Whether he cheated the Palatines or anyone else must await a new study of the man. Most of the evidence comes from men sorely tried.

No such problem as that of the Palatines troubled Peter Schuyler, the beloved friend of the Indians. "Quedor" spoke their language and seems really to have thought them human. His journey with Livingston to Onondaga brought about an alliance with the Iroquois, of great importance. He led an expedition against their enemies.

But in Dutchess his interest evidently was to help out Dongan's policy of "occupying". Within two years he had sold out to Albany friends like Sanders, Knickerbocker, and Van Benthuysen.

Another Albany man, Dr. Samuel Staats, the friend of Francois Rombouts, who was connected with Livingston through his marriage with a Hawarden, purchased Henry Pawling's Patent, and thus bequeathed his name to Staatsburg. A successful physician and a liberal in politics, he was a supporter of Leisler and the country party. His partner in Pawling's Purchase, Dirck Van De Burgh, soon moved to the Poughkeepsie area and left a numerous line of county leaders. Staats was a friend of Arnout Viele, from whom, perhaps, he first learned the value of Dutchess land.

Of Viele, Sanders, and Myndert Harmense Van Den Bogaerdt, enough has been said in their Indian relations. All of them had children in Dutchess, Viele being the only one surviving in direct line and in numbers. But they must not be passed over without a tribute of appreciation for the inestimable privilege the county enjoyed of starting as a friend of Indians, honored by their marks of gratitude and maintaining, with two grave exceptions, a history of the friendliest relations.

Dr. Staats' fame in his day was not diminished by his six beautiful daughters, the belles of their day, who married into the Gouverneur, Coeymans, Van Cortlandt, Schuyler, White, and Morris families. Thus one grandson signed the Declaration, another was governor of New Jersey, another chief justice, another married an earl's daughter, another edited the text of the United States Constitution.

The story is told, I know not of what branch of the Coeymans, that Nicholas Van Rensselaer once came courting, and while the elder daughter kept him waiting while she prinked, the younger daughter entertained him so successfully that on her arrival she found her suitor betrothed to the cadette. A likely story, and probably to be found also in the Arabian Nights. But the Dutch lasses were capable of it, to judge from their sons.

The land of Pawling's Purchase was among the last to be divided (1751). Thus the Staats family have less personal connection than most others, but the name is not unknown in the county today. A small part of the Patent not owned by Staats or Van de Burgh came to Major John Pawling and Petrus de Witt, grandchildren of the original grantees.

The distinction of being the first white settler in Dutchess must probably go to some Unknown Squatter. On the earliest map "the French man" is listed at Fishkill. "Peche de Wall" is also a candidate; he may have been the Frenchman. Catherine Emigh, child of Palatine settlers, was the first child born in the county, so far as we know.

The most likely story is that of a settler somewhere between Pleasant Valley and Poughkeepsie, written by one Paul Upton. The letter, according to Pelletreau, was formerly in the possession of T. Van Wyck Brinckerhoff. It bears the marks of truth.

"In the year 1823, I saw Isaac Upton, a coaster from New Port, Who informed me that about 1760 he came up the North River to Poughkeepsie, and in company with another person went to Mabbitt's store in Washington on business. That on their return they took a circuitous route from Pleasant Valley and passed the house of a German settler by the name of Hoffman who was 118 years old. He supposed himself to be the first settler in Dutchess County. When young he deserted from a Dutch ship of war in New York, squatted where he then lived, built him a shanty and lived a number of years a solitary life without being able to find a white woman for a wife. Afterward he found a German family at Rhinebeck, married and lived where he then was to an advanced age. I was informed that he died two years afterward at the age of 120."

Hoffman may have been a Swede, captured at Swedesboro, and deserting from the ship of Van Couwenhoven, stationed at Wappingers during the Esopus wars in 1662.

The Company Patents, Rombout, the Nine Partners, and Hyde Park, resembled the personal patents, Pawling's Purchase and Beekman, in the problem of dispersal. Only the determination of young Mrs. Brett to live upon her estate was able to overcome the inertia that pervaded group ownership.

Hyde Park was divided in 1730. The Lower Nine, under the drive of David Jamison, the Attorney General of the province, initiated a division in 1723; but failed. In the winter of 1730 the act was finally passed, and in 1734 the partition followed. The Upper Nine act was passed in 1734, but the division was not made till 1744. Charles Clinton had surveyed all these.

Judge Henry Beekman had sold many lots in his river Patent (Rhinebeck) by 1720, but his Back Lots remained unsold at his death in 1737, when they were divided among Mrs. Albert Pawling, Mrs. Gilbert Livingston, and Henry Beekman, Jr., their brother. Henry received two large lots beyond the equal division, by his father's will.

Pawling Purchase, in the ownership of Dr. Samuel Staats, was distributed to his heirs in 1751. A small portion of the Pawling property had in the meantime been bought back by two Pawling heirs, Major John Pawling and Petrus De Witt, whose wife was a Pawling. It was the ancestral pull that led James Kirke Paulding of the same family to purchase Placentia further down the river as his home. The Paulding who captured Major André was also of this Dutchess stock.

Thus four-fifths of the land of Dutchess was not opened for settlement until after 1730, seventy years after the English conquest, and a hundred years after the first Dutch governor arrived. Historians invariably treat this as if something criminal was done; and certainly more than one governor lamented the fact. But from the point of view of fur-traders, of capitalist investors with land for sale elsewhere, and indeed from a broader view, the reservation of Dutchess fertility until the Revolution was no disaster, but a blessing in disguise. If New York's growth in colonial days seemed slow, the young state leaped ahead all too quickly in the following decades. The slow and steady growth of Dutchess from 1730 to 1790 perhaps suited the Dutch pioneers best, and gave time for the flowering of their culture.

But the latest actual division was that of Hyde Park. Although partitioned in 1730 by the patentees, Dr. John Bard put the patent together again. The famous physician had married Suzanne Valleau, granddaughter of the originator of the patent, Peter Fauconnier. The two young Huguenots made their home at the Patent, after long negotiations with John Morin Scott, the attorney for the estate. Sales and transfers by Dr. John Bard and his son Dr. Samuel Bard continued at intervals from 1768 to 1816. As with Pawling's Purchase, river estates resulted.

The Brett family allied itself through many marriages with famous families of the Dutch colony. Catharyna Brett was the daughter of Helena Teller, thus the granddaughter of William Teller of Schenectady who once affirmed that he had personally attended every Indian conference and treaty-fire at Albany for sixty years. The Tellers both in Fishkill and Hyde Park added greatly to the Dutch incomers. Through the marriage of Mrs. Brett's granddaughter Alice Schenck with her cousin Isaac de Peyster Teller, and their residence in the Brett house at Fishkill, the house changed its name to Teller in 1790, and is now known as the Teller homestead. It belongs to the Daughters of the American Revolution.

Mrs. Brett's halfsisters married men whose families became intimately connected with Dutchess. The Brett sons, too, made Dutchess marriages, Francis wedding Catharine Van Wyck, and Robert, Catheryna Du Bois.

Of the Lower Nine Partners Hendryck Ten Eyck, "Mariner";

Caleb Heathcote, Mayor of New York and Lord of the Manor of Scarsdale in Westchester; James Emott, attorney of high standing but called by Bellomont "Fletcher's lackey"; John Aertson of Ulster; and Jarvis Marshall, doorkeeper of the governor's executive council, sold their lots after the first survey in 1699. The four remaining partners, through their children, made an outstanding contribution to county life. Three sons and a daughter of Henry Filkin, Excise Collector and militia officer on Long Island, resided in Dutchess. Henry, the son, became High Sheriff; Isaac, the first supervisor of Crum Elbow; Francis, author of the "Country Store" accounts, judge of Common Pleas and General Sessions. The daughter Antje married Francis Hageman, and owned a river landing.

James Graham, Surveyor-General of New York, left his share to his son Augustine. His sister Isabella married Lewis Morris. Their daughter married James Graham II, a first cousin. Thus a Col. Morris Graham commanded a Dutchess Revolutionary regiment. The Jersey Morrises thus united Staatsburg and Nine Partners.

William Creed's son Augustine was an owner in 1740. A daughter Elizabeth married Dr. Theodorus Van Wyck of the Fishkills. A granddaughter was Mrs. James Kent; a grandson, U.S. Senator Theodorus Bailey.

Best known of all the Nine Partners was David Jameson, attorney of the purchase and its manager. As a boy in Scotland, he had been a member of one of the stricter Scottish sects, the "Sweet Singers". For this he was deported and bound out in New York to pay for his passage. His proficiency in Latin becoming known, he was bought and set up as a tutor. He became a clerk of the Council, and was admitted to the bar. Later he was Chief Justice, then Attorney-General of New York. In 1707 with Jacob Regnier of the Hyde Park syndicate as colleague, he successfully defended Rev. Francis Makemie. The acquittal of the famous founder of American Presbyterianism settled the position of New York on the question of freedom of worship. Jameson in his closing appeal said: "As this is the first time in this province's history that this question has been raised, so I hope it will be the last." So it would have been, but for Shekomeko.

Bellomont accused Jameson of stirring up riots and of drinking a toast "to those who stay honest in the worst of times". This lover of liberty had a daughter, Mrs. John Johnston, who built Lithgow, and a grandson, Judge Johnston of Bellefield, who married Susanna Bard, and lived at "Bellefield", on one of the Partners' Water Lots.

Of the Upper Nine Partners the most important was "the little man that wasn't there". George Clarke, Secretary of the Province, a close relative of the Earl of Cornbury, the Governor, had his own reason for preferring to be a silent partner, with his name omitted from the petition for the patent. He later purchased a ninth share, and his name appears in the distributed lots. Clarke was later Lt. Governor, actively connected also with the Oblong controversy. He made a fortune of a halfmillion pounds out of his office and retired to knighthood and the sanctity of a cathedral tomb at English Chester.

Next to Clarke came Rip van Dam, a liberal Dutch leader, friend of Leisler, President of the Council in 1731. He fought Governor Cosby's aggression upon the colony's rights, was active in composing the Coetus controversy of the Reformed Church, and in general made common cause with Alexander and Smith in the "country party". His granddaughter was Mrs. Robert Livingston (third Lord of the Manor).

Augustine Graham, Roger Mompesson and Peter Fauconnier we have known in other patents. Fauconnier sold out to James Alexander, of whom something will appear in the Oblong story. Mompesson sold out to Henry Beekman, Jr. Thomas Wenham, a worthy merchant and a Trinity Church man, was of the "wise and wealthy". Robert Lurting incurred the ire of Bellomont and may have been a friend of privateers, smugglers, and pirates, the fashionable law-breakers of the day. Sampson Broughton was a Speaker of the Assembly of New York, of whom we hear little otherwise. Captain Richard Sackett we shall know better before we are done.

# 9. Neighborhoods

WHAT'S IN A PLACE-NAME? Not just its literal sense, but its reference; the color and temper of the folks that gave it currency. A list in a county gazetteer will sound humdrum enough to the reader who spells it out, but the stories packed within could while away a long winter night.

Poughkeepsie, for instance. Not the "safe harbor" invented by historians, but the real story, as the Van Kleecks and Van den Bogaerdts, Vanderburghs and Laassens found it, and as Helen Wilkinson Reynolds, our own researcher, brought it to light from the old deeds and patents.

The name takes us in a moment back to the first contacts of Netherlander and Indian. The Algonkians were a bundle of contradictions to the Hollanders, for their morality did not jibe with European standards. Kind to children and cruel to enemies, lustful in behavior but loyal in marriage, great in endurance but weak in liquor, the Tawny People in one respect measured up to one highest mark of civilized conduct: the delivery of messages and goods. The earliest narratives note with pleasure the fidelity of the Indian runners and their willingness to fulfill errands.

Johan de Laet, a careful historian, after pointing out that "a wise and sober" Dutch rule could do much for the tawny people, adds: "They are, besides, very serviceable, and allow themselves to be employed in many things for a small compensation; even to performing a long day's journey, in which they discover greater fidelity than could be expected of such a people."

Isaac de Rasieres in 1628 wrote in the earliest eyewitness description of New Netherland:

"When we wish to send letters overland, they (the natives) take their way across the bay, and have the letters carried forward by others, unless one amongst them happen to be on friendly terms, who might venture to go there." No Indian custom is more fully substantiated in the old records. Commerce and communication between the Great Lakes and the whole Northeast flourished, and the runners made it possible.

The "Mohawk trails" in Massachusetts and Connecticut were of this kind, and the Hudson highways followed the old river paths. Beside one of these a small kill sprang in an open woodland where the cattail weeds waved in the wind above the rockpool. Crossing the path the killetje rippled down a little glade, and fell into the Hudson. This was Pakakcincg as it is called in the earliest record, or Pooghkepesingh, as Massany, the generous Indian giver, corrected the name of the stream that still splashes through the Rural Cemetery on its river bound course.

In 1700 a local deed speaks of it as a "Creek known and called by the name of the rust plaets or by the Indians Apopeesing". As "Rust plaets spring" in 1798 Henry Livingston, Jr. the surveyor marked it in his fine map.

Here, then, if we follow Miss Reynolds' surmise, lay a station along the Indian runners' path to the Manhattans, a "rest place", where mats woven from the reeds (upuhki) hung upon bent saplings to form a lodge-covering, or serve as mattress on the damp ground. Doubtless from a tree branch above the water-place (ipis - ing) dangled a haunch of venison to refresh the weary messenger. Count von Zinzendorf found such at a similar rest-place on his way to the Iroquois a half century later.

The spring may have been chosen because it flowed near the boundary of Mahikan and Wappinger confederacies; or it may have neatly divided the run, from the Hudson Ford at Albany to the island at the end of the Wappinger rule, into two days of seventy miles apiece, an average trot; or it may have appealed simply as a cool and never failing water in a pleasant spot, inviting rest.

Wareskeeken, the name of the northwest corner of the Minnesingh or Poughkeepsie patent, means "the end of the boundary." This may refer to the Mahican-Wappinger boundary, since it was apparently known by this name before the white man bought it. At any rate, the tribal boundary fell near this spot, according to tradition, and was confirmed by the late testimony of Nimham, a chief's son, as "near the middle of Beekman patent". This probably refers to upper Lagrange. Wareskeeken marks now the boundary of Hyde Park-Poughkeepsie. As we have noted, its extension, the Great Nine Partners line, was attested by both Mahikan and Wappinger sachems.

As the river sloops outsped the runners, the rust plaets lost its use, but the goodnatured Netherlanders retained the Indian word for their neighborhood, long as it was and subject since to delightful variety of spellings. Miss Reynolds lists some thirty, not one of which contains the "u" of today, a late eighteenth-century encumbrance.

The Dutch were no more original in their name for the second neighborhood. The "fresh kill, called by the Indians Matewan" (creeks join), soon changed to Viskill, or "the fish kills." Here the Hudson changed from brackish to pure water, and here in consequence was the best of fishing, as Hudson had found. Indians feasted on oysters below Polypel Island, and held their chief kintakoys on Danskammer opposite and upstream. Here, no doubt for the same reason, was the capital of the Wappinger river-tribes. No wonder, then, that Fishkill grew faster than Poughkeepsie, even without the superior competence of the Widow Brett. The great shadnets still hang to dry on Dennings Point. Below rise the bold sentinels of the High Lands, Boterberg (Storm King) and Hoyberg (Breakneck). Nathaniel P. Willis was too elegant to endure Butter as the name of his mountain; and here for once a fashionable name survived. "Breakneck" celebrates a runaway bull which climbed the mountain and leaped to its death when pursued. Sometimes it was spelled like Welsh Brecknock. Cold Spring, below it, celebrates a local water course, like Poughkeepsie.

The third neighborhood, Rhinebeck, again pays tribute to the appeal that water makes to those that dwell beside it. Spelled Rynbeeck in early deeds, it somehow compliments its first settlers the Palatines, from the Flemish Palatinate and other provinces, and comforted them for their unwilling exile. They had just escaped from the miseries of East Camp, and needed a friendly word. Henry Beeckman, Sr., is credited with its invention. It is not necessary to accept the "beck" of the second syllable as a reminder that Beeckman owned the land. There is a Rheinbach in the Eifel; but "beck", brook, may well refer to the two brooks, Beekman and Landsman's Kill, that meet at the village. It might seem farfetched to lug in a definition of beck from the Oxford Dictionary:

*Beck, a gesture expressive of salutation or respect.*

But certainly that was what Henry Beekman intended. He was shrewd but unpretentious, a "country farmer" as he called himself. He beckoned to very good purpose, for many of the county's best leaders came from Rhinebeck in later years.

Thus our three original neighborhoods in their names suggested shelter, food, and welcome. Not a bad beginning. For half a century Rust Plaets, Fishkill, and Rynbeck remained the only neighborhoods of any size. All else was countyside, little neighborhoods not exceeding a dozen houses, up to the times when Dutchess with twenty-five thousand people embraced the Revolution.

Of all its early place-names, only Dover is reminiscent. It is attributed to Jackson Wing by the county guide, but Richard Sackett is more likely, for the name occurs in 1735. Like its original it served as port of entry. Through its Webatuck gap streamed in the New Englanders to take up Dutchess.

We have preserved a score of Indian names. Their translations, none fully authentic, have engaged historians from Egbert Benson to Helen Reynolds. Only the better proved can be given here. There are Wassaic; Wiccopee, "nut trees";

Wappingers; Poughquag, "flaggy meadow"; Matteawan; Taconic; Poconnuck, "barerock"; Stissing, "big rock"; Shekomeko, "big lodge"; Sepasco; Sharparoon; Shenandoah; Winnikee, "good land"; Woronock, "hollow land"; Spackenkill, "Speck zyn kill," named for the friendly Waspacheek; Massany, equally generous, who gave Viele his land at Poughkeepsie in 1780, is forgotten.

Matapan and Minisinck are local names for a waterfall in Wappingers Kill, and for the ridge that borders the stream near Pleasant Valley. Minkinsing, corrupted to Mackenzie, names an inlet near the shore by I B M. Mawenawasigh, chosen name of the Poughkeepsie chapter of the Daughters of the American Revolution, has been shown to refer either to the land between the lower Wappingers and the Hudson, or the Great Wappinger Kill itself.

Finally, Webatuck (Indian "narrow pass" or "pleasant") is the name of our loveliest stream, a wayward escape to the Housatonic, after a scamper down the Harlem Valley, and flirtations with Ten Mile and Swamp Rivers. The name applies also to the neighborhood and to its pass through the Taconic ridge.

Like their friends the Indians, the Dutch kept close to water. The islands on the river shore bear Dutch names. Magdelijn means any shad or herring. Polipel or Bannerman's Island is commonly attributed a corruption of Podlapel, Dutch potladle. Slipsteen is a grindstone. Kaale Rugh (Kale Rock) is Bareback. Klein Sopus is of course Little Sopus. Some half-baked schoolmaster, remembering his Aesop, changed the Indian tribal name to Esopus, and the Encyclopaedia Britannica loyally printed it Aesopus, putting ignorant Americans right on classical spelling. The Dutch looked at the Blue Hills, as the English called them, but they saw only the brooks, and the mountains are named for the brooks, Wildcats Kills (Catskills) or Tomcats Kill (Kaaterskill).

Dutch brooks, most of them, still bear Dutch names. Beginning with the Fishkill, we have the Sprout (stream), the Clove (Du. Kloof, cleft) and the Casper (named by Pieter Lassen the Brewer for his brotherinlaw, Jan Casper Hallenbeck of Saugerties). The Fonteyn Kill (Spring Brook) is a little Dutch sister to Casper. Crum Elbow (De Cromme Elleboge, crooked elbow) comes next above Poughkeepsie's Fallkill. At Staatsburg (named for Dr. Samuel Staats), there is the Enderkill, and at Rhinebeck the Fallsburg, Landsman, Rhinebeck and Sawkill, with Roeloff Jansen Kill to close the list of Hudson streams. In the county there are few Dutch names. Verbank is Dutch, and so are Pawling and Beekman, who held patents and left their names in villages and towns, not by intention, so far as we know. Neighborhoods sprang up on the Rombout patent bearing the names of Brinckerhoff, Swartwout, and Hageman: they have survived, though the Post Office added a —"ville" just to be sure they referred to locality.

Otherwise the Dutch neighborhoods went unnamed. Only Henry Filkin the sheriff is said by tradition to have sought a name, and to have offered a barrel of rum to the farmers in Nine Partners, if they would name their crossroads for him. They agreed, and the old maps carried the "Filkin town Road" for many years. It is now the Dutchess Turnpike, Route 44, and Filkintown became Mabbettsville as soon as Samuel Mabbett's store and tavern became more popular.

Scots settlers were nostalgic. David Jamison, one of the Nine Partners, bought land which became Lithgow. His grandson named Annandale. Netherwood is Scottish, and Barrytown, and McIntyre. Love of Lafayette may have prompted the inn's name at the little neighborhood, which took the inn's name later. La Grange was the name of the Marquis' estate, but it seems farfetched to derive our town's name from it. Was there not a La Grange family among our Huguenot farmers?

And so we come to the English names, by far the most numerous group. In New England the settlers had entered upon the land in parishes, giving each church member a share in the allotment. A neutral name, usually that of some town in England, was chosen, all the way from Boston to Rutland. Not so in Dutchess. The incomers were no longer thought of as church members, but as persons individual. They bought separate farms, or became tenants in leasehold. If two roads come to cross next their farm, the family name was given to the corners. So it was if a mill or bridge was built, or a landing, pier, or wharf; or a store or inn, or if by some chance a neighborhood grew up among the children.

Bull's Head and Bear Market must have been inns. There was a Bull's Head Inn at Arlington, that nearly succeeded in giving its name to Vassar College land. Gayhead, a Martha's Vineyard name, drifted back to East Fishkill, for the New Englanders of Dutchess were not nostalgic.

The classical itch never struck our toponymy, although Robert Harpur, who is credited with giving New York State its classical placenames, was a Dutchess resident during the Revolution and a member of its Committee to Detect Conspiracies. It was not till years later that he went to Albany as Secretary of the State, and began his naming of Cato, Cicero, Hannibal, Scipio, and the rest. Upon him be peace! But we free Dutchers have celebrated our own folks.

Of "Corners" we have Jackson, Spencer, Pulver, Beeman, Clinton, Myers, and Leroy (Pleasant Plains). There are Chapel Corners, Union Corners, and Shenandoah Corners, too, for good measure. Of "Dales" we have Wing and Thorn. Of "Hollows" we have Clinton and Washington, and Fishkill too. Of "Mills" there are Hull, Hart, Moore, but Red Oaks Mill, a late-comer has distanced them. Millbrook residents have forgotten Hart's Mill and Hart's Corners.

Larger units, such as "Furnaces" (Dover, Fishkill) were beyond individual claims. So, too, were "Ridges" (Pleasant, Chestnut) and "Plains" (Pine, Freedom, Fishkill, Dover). But we still admire the straight road across the "Astor flats", where fast trotters once raced to the annoyance of the farmer's teams.

Ponds were private property. There were Black, Whalley, Hamersly, Ellis, Tyrrell, Upton, Hunn, Wallace, Thompson, Miller, and Rudd. There are three Mud Ponds, two Long and two Round, and one Oblong. Sepasco, Silver, and Indian Ponds are larger than any but Whalley, and are no longer personal in name. Silver was too prosaic, and became Sylvan (no improvement).

Along the river Denning, Clinton, Greer, Mulford, Lewis, Vanderburg, Knickerbocker, Clifton, Astor, and Cruger placed their names on points or landings, though many a good name like De Cantillon and Johnston has passed on.

Among the towns we still speak of Baxtertown as a Beacon neighborhood, where it is said still dwell some who claim descent from our brave Wappingers. Channingtown was formerly on the north side of Wappingers Kill, now incorporated in the Falls. Hortontown lies in the Shenandoah and Barrytown at the north end of the county.

The "villes" far outnumber them. The Post Office is suspected of perpetrating most of them. But there were a good many folks like the LeRoys and Montforts to whom ville would have had a welcome sound. In the south precinct were Reynolds, Storm, Beekman, and Johns. In the center and the east were Harts, Mabbets, Leeds, Perry, Stanford, Campbell, and Grove. In the west and north are Shook, Ogden, Lafayette, Milan, Schultz, La Grange, and Hughson.

Of the "burgs" we had only Arthur and Wurtemburg, the latter Palatine, the former attributed to a summer in a local grocery store passed by Chester A. Arthur. This one seems impossible to anyone who has seen a portrait of our Arthur. Old Attlebury is a lost neighborhood up Clinton way.

This suggests Oswego, a ghost village of the Quakers on the Beekman road, just beyond Moores Mills. Beyond Stormville lies Grape Hollow, recently unearthed in the hillside by a purchaser unsuspecting. There is, too, the City and the Square, ambitious projects of the northeast, now names only. Smithfield is such another.

Barnegat on the river shore, a burning pit for lime, and Wolvergat, a wolves' den on Hornyback Ridge, are of Dutch origins though not in any sense neighborhoods. But Hornyback or Hornbeck (by confusion with the Dutch proper name) is really a farmers' corruption of the Dutch Haanebergh, or

Cock Hill, the ridge east of Poughkeepsie where cocks first crew to greet the sun. Vassar students called it Sunrise for the same reason. Today it has attained the dignity of neighborhood.

A group of names represent industry. Mechanic was a lower part of Millbrook. Glenham, part of Beacon, is so called from Glen's Mills. Irondale and Hammertown, Dover and Fishkill and Clove Furnaces tell of the old mines nearby. Rochdale and Manchester on the Wappingers Kill speak of the early nineteenth century and the arrival of many English textile operators, leaving England's hard times for new looms in Dutchess.

A few families have left names unattached, some of them from industry, as with the Brockway brick yards. Miller, a contractor on the Harlem River Railroad, was popular enough to leave his name in Millerton, while the railroad gave its corporate name to the whole beautiful valley. It may have been due to this naming the Harlem Valley that Chard Smith was led, in his "Housatonic" in the American River series, to describe the Dutchess Croton, which rises near Sharparoon, as flowing into the Harlem. Some Croton water does cross the Harlem on the High Bridge viaduct, but conventionally the Croton ends at Croton-on-Hudson. Only the Webatuck of all our streams, escaped the Hudson watershed.

Other unattached names scatter through the county: Adriance, Brush, Billings, Husted, Lamoree, Lent and a host more, fugitive place names scarce lasting beyond the disappearance of the family.

Neighborhoods were named over and over. Scarcely a village has its original name. Rhinebeck was at Pinks Corners in its beginning. Beacon was Fishkill-on-Hudson, and Fishkill Landing before that. Chelsea was first Low Point, as New Hamburg was High Point. Low Point became the classical Carthage, but gave up the high name when the Chelsea Company made it a condition of its coming that the Point should take the company's name. This was done, and the company then backed out.

Dutchess has its share of odd names. There is Cotton Doll Road, attributed to two maiden ladies, who were doll's dressmakers. There is the Shunpike, by-passing the old toll pike from Amenia to Hart's Corners. There is Separate, and of course the Oblong, unintelligible without the story. There is the usual New England "Sodom Corners", like a gargoyle under the choir stall. Dog Tail Corners, too, Purgatory Hill, "halfway to nowhere", Eel Pot Corners. Hardscrabble (Red Hook), all the odd ones are to be found, vestiges of grim Yankee humor. The Dutch never thought names were funny, unless Spuyten Duyvil is humorously meant.

Roads follow the general rules of individualism, as do village streets. Beacon thus honors Brett, Rombout, Verplanck, and Poughkeepsie Livingston, Delafield, Roosevelt, and Pershing. Most of the hills have personal names: Delavergne, Horton, Honess, Preston, though also Molasses and Maple Syrup, and other oddities.

The "Places" on the Hudson were not neighborhoods, and so belong elsewhere. But one of them, Hyde Park, has become a town of ten thousand, and may well close this Homeric catalogue. Dr. John Bard, who had married Suzanne Valleau, and thus inherited more shares in the Regnier-Fauconnier Patent, bought up the remaining shares and became sole proprietor. He named the part in which he had built his home "Hyde Park". In his time, certainly, the name never included the whole patent. Dr. Bard would have resented the extension of his choice to the inn and to the neighborhood that began to gather round it. There is not the slightest evidence for the tradition that the name was given because Peter Fauconnier had been the secretary of Lord Cornbury's council during the unhappy term of that worst of governors. Dr. Bard, like his son and grandson loved flowers and plants, and desired to emulate the gardens of Hyde Park in London. He was, besides, a good loyalist, and lived quietly at home in Dutchess unmolested.

He would scarcely have cared to honor the family name (by which Cornbury was never honored in America), of a worthless scalawag whose careless hand involved Fauconnier in more than one doubtful deal.

There were other Hyde Parks, on Long Island and in Jersey, with no thought of Cornbury. Hyde Park can stand on its own good name as a parklike estate; the Vanderbilt National Monument of today, with its magnificent trees, a glorious lawn, and unsurpassed vista of the great river and its shores, is the graceful gesture of a fine old Tory to the city of his admiration, like Kew Gardens on Long Island today.

With all its variety, all its individualism, and all its indifference to the impermanence of its naming, the Dutch tradition still had room for a sense of neighborhood. We shall find it among both gentlemen and yeomen, Whig and Tory, Democrat and Republican.

Nothing could be more neighborly than an article on Titusville in our historical society's series, or the pamphlets on Quaker Hill, or the booklets on Old Pine Plains, Rhinebeck, Amenia, or Mrs. Crary's "Household of a Colonial Dame" at Mrs. Brett's in Beacon. It was not for nothing that our forecomers chose the word to describe their little villages, which were never so small that men and women could not be neighborly. There were disagreements, but no feuds. Men stood by their neighbors. The modern county is the heir of the spirit of neighborhood.

# III. THE WATERING

## 10. The Dutch in Dutchess

IS IT POSSIBLE, after two hundred years, with all the power of opposed components, to capture the slightest part of the quintessence we might call Dutch? I do not know. Only I remember forty years ago, when my wife and I left Northampton in Massachusetts for an old Dutch town, we felt the difference at once.

Dixon Ryan Fox, in his "Yankee and Yorker", has pointed out many of the differences. He noted with satisfaction how some of the harsher features in the Puritan attitude were softened and humanized under Dutch influence. Joseph Henry, a century ago, said something on the other side. "The Dutch are hard to be moved, but when they do start their momentum is not, as other men's, in proportion to the velocity, but to the square of the velocity. So when the Dutchman goes three times as fast he has nine times the force of another man. The Dutchman has an immense potential energy, but it takes a small spark of Yankee enterprise to start it off."

The first ingredient that struck our attention in Dutchess was its integrity. Not exactly in the moral sense, but in a general way. Dutchess seemed to us to be complete in itself, though not complacently so. It was all of a piece; a rural and urban setting without a trace of provincialism; in touch through its river and its roads with a great world, but not envious of it. Industrious without fanfare, slow to decide but coming through at a pinch, competent, steady and sane, the community had found itself, and was aware of its own identity.

How much of all this was attributable to its Dutch begetters, I could not say. We had not seen it in New England, where I had lived a dozen years, or in the metropolis from which we had first come. There seemed something original here. We set out to find it.

The Dutch had never been wholly Dutch, it seemed, but Fleming and Walloon and French. Beeckman and Brett were Flemings from Limbourg Province in the Low Countries. Robert Sanders was a Netherlandered Scotsman. So was Livingston, so was Leonard Lewis, who though a son of a Belfast man, could hardly write in English, yet was the first Justice in the county. So was Dr. Bartholomew Noxon, and many other good citizens. If we add all the High Dutchers, as Beekman called the Palatines, we have a diversity in the very first decade of the county's growth.

What led to this Dutch acculturation of such a varied group? I believe it was the very lack of any design or purpose of putting it across. The Dutch let things take their course, and that led, as naturally as water flows, into a Dutch pattern, because it seemed to those in a deliberative mood to be desirable.

The New Paltz French-speaking church soon changed to Dutch, and the Hasbroucks, Deyos, Lefevres, and Crispells that came to Dutchess with the DuBois and the rest were all of the Dutch group. Some of them like DeGraaf had been LeComtes.

Of the Livingstons very little but the name was left of the Scots descent; all the wives had been Schuylers, Beekmans, Staats, and the rest. Lewis Morris looks English enough, but he was a Marius of old Dutch stock.

The effect of all this was, that whatever the source of the incomers might be, they were a compact Dutch community speaking Dutch except when at law or paying taxes. Not until after 1750 was there much abatement in the use of Dutch, and the children at school spoke Dutch until their teacher threatened to "keep them in" from the playground. My old friend Houghtaling of Kingston told me that he spoke Dutch as a boy, about 1850. Here and there in remote spots it may still be found. At the Revolution it was still a living dialect. In 1788, according to G. A. Van der Kemp, Mrs. George Clinton, Mrs. Peter Tappan, and Mrs. Alexander Hamilton spoke Dutch with him. The Reverend John Livingston of Poughkeepsie had been trained at Utrecht in Holland, and the Verplancks in Amsterdam.

How the Dutch in Dutchess impressed men may be judged by the loan words that still come down the wind. "Dutch" added to a dish immediately whets the appetite. Some of them are good-natured jibes, but none bears the stamp of malice. "Don't that beat the Dutch"? needs no comment. "A Dutchman's breeches" for a patch of blue sky hurts no feelings. When a "Dutch uncle" talks to you, you know it's for your good. A "Dutch treat" smacks of equality as well as thrift. When a man gets "in Dutch", he seems out of favor, but not unjustly so. Judgment is exercised. "Dutch housecleaning" speaks thoroughness, "Dutch courage" is partaken by most that go into battle. A "Dutch auction" is one in which the auctioneer sets a high figure and lowers it until he gets a bid.

Innumerable tools and household effects bear the Dutch attributive. A whole house could be furnished with it. Vassar College still boasts a Dutch oven, though electric ones have superseded it. Evidently in household arts the Dutch were no whit behind their neighbors. No Dutchman ever starved.

A Dutch door, barn, roof, chimney were all distinctive. Farmers called the daisy "the Dutch curse", meaning to imply that a Dutchman expected every blade of grass to do its duty. Dutch clover was better. The bed in the alcove, the clock on the wall, the cheese on the shelf, the chop in the grill, and the pipe awaiting its master, all carried the Dutch trade-mark. The Dutchman's pipe and breeches might, of course, double as names for flowers, of which the Dutch were inordinately fond. Finally, he could top off with a Dutch sauce to a Dutch supper, as the cold buffet used to be called.

They liked the idea of a separate summer kitchen for cool comfort on hot days. Indeed a Dutch housewife had things her way, or she knew the reason why. When her market-stall was "cleaned Dutch," there was nothing but the stool to sell.

When the "skipper" came ashore from a "yacht", "sloop", or "schooner", he was Dutch all the way. From Dutch larboards on boats in the Hudson "coves", came the modern centerboard, according to Wm. E. Verplanck of Fishkill.

And the big barn with its open door in the mow under the gable, and the Frisian cattle, and all the rest. Dongan wrote home that "The Dutch are great improvers of land". At their own pace, neither hurried nor lazy, they stubbed the woods and plowed their fields, and made Dutchess a granary. According to Wertenbaker, the Flemings brought over the stone house with its gambrel and its roof with overhang or flying gutter. The great barns, too, have a Flemish air. The Dutch introduced the court with separate buildings inclosing a yard, unlike the extended Yankee farm-house of wood. Nowhere in Dutchess, so far as known, did men make loghouses except when the Germans were dumped into East Camp with nothing but axes to live by, or when the Continentals made their village.

Mud huts never desecrated Dutchess. Swedes liked log-cabins, too, and built good ones; and perhaps the Swede Cornelius Wiltsie lived in one when he first came to Frankfort Storehouse. The Hoffmans, too, were Swedes, and the Jansens Norwegians. Dutchers did not need to go to school in Delaware in order to make a logcabin. But they preferred stone, cool in summer, warm in winter. Miss Reynolds and her colleague in their books about Dutch homes have proved what an artistic job they made of it.

They took life in the same sensible way. Differing groups often used the same church, one in the morning, one in the afternoon or on alternate Sundays. The Dutch Reformed Church is the only church that ever split and reunited, so far as our reading goes. When Livingston split off a long slice of Northern Dutchess, the county made no complaint. When

Putnam left in 1812, the opposition was not on a linguistic but a political basis.

Anecdotes often give the color and feel of a culture. A Dutchess justice was rebuked for his unvarying custom of giving his verdict in favor of the plaintiff. "Do you suppose any man would be foolish enough to bring suit against another, if he did not think he had good ground for complaint?" The rebuker stood rebuked. The justice soon had a clear docket.

Another justice never decided a case unless his wife sat on the bench with him to give the benefit of her intuition.

When the Palatines opened their German Lutheran Church in Rhinebeck Hendrick Hermanse was delighted with the sermon and its sublime style. He was abashed in learning it was not Dutch he had heard, but good high German, of which he understood as much as some do of any sermon.

Over in Ulster, the mother county, a farmer came back from a meeting in English.

"How it did went?" asked a friend, proud of his new English.

"So it did went," was the reply, with a subbinder wallop to accompany it. Everybody understands a fist.

"I pronounce you one beef," said a J.P. to the newly married couple. Another Ulster Dutchman took his daughter to the Albany county line, turned her face towards Albany, and gave her a sound thrashing. "That way lies Albany."

He then turned her around and gave her a second thrashing. "That way lies Kingston."

The girl when a woman, so testified in a boundary dispute. Her memory was still clear. The custom, of very ancient origin, is also told in Reymont's Polish novel "The Peasants".

Indeed, the Dutch farmers of the Hudson were very simple people in those early years. More than half of the early jurymen had to make their mark in a verdict. But they were skilled in their craft, and the freed woodland produced wonderful crops at first. This alone would explain why life was so peaceful along the quiet river.

But there was more. The Dutch were rational, not emotional. They did not believe in witches. A dozen were hanged in Connecticut, but none in New Amsterdam. I was told they could not get through the wooden bridges on the Housatonic, "couldn't manage the broomstick".

There were no guilt-panics over fancied Negro insurrections. When the frightful massacre of 1742 struck New York, the governor issued a proclamation forbidding Negroes to gather on the street in groups of more than two. A group in Poughkeepsie were arrested on this charge, but the law took its proper course.

The Dutch named their children after personalities of the New Testament, while the New English named their children after those of the Old Testament. Matthias, Lucas, Marcus, and Johannis were favorites in Dutchess. To these must be added the Patriarchs, Abraham, Isaac and Jacob. But the Puritans ran the whole list of Judges and Chronicles: Jabez, Jedidiah, Samson and the rest, though most of them did not last beyond the second generation. Elijah, however was embalmed among the family of Tompkins, and so continues. But Cornelius, Philip, Peter, Thomas, Jacobus, Theodorus, Theophilus, Elias, and of course Martinus, Francis, Augustinus, and other saints were frequent in Dutch households. Along with these, and just as popular, went the names of their princely families: Adolphus, Frederick, Wilhelmus, Hendrick.

The Dutch possessed the trait of obstinacy in superlative degree. Franklin Roosevelt could be stubbornness incarnate.

A British officer wrote: "I can do nothing with this Dutch population. I can neither buy them with money nor subdue them with force." Such a spirit emboldened them to stand up for their liberties.

Free from ecclesiastical domination like that of New England, bound by no town vote allotting land, with each man fighting for his own hand, the Dutch made their way into the woods, now as squatters, now armed with a lease or a deed in fee simple. They lived in neighborhoods, or along the country lanes, extending for miles. George S. Van Vliet, our wonderful story teller, tells of the Traver neighborhood in Clinton where every farm for five miles down the road was farmed by a scion of old Sebastian Traver of the Palatines.

Individualists as the Dutch were, and not much concerned with political matters, the men of Dutchess were not, as is often asserted, mere rubber-stamps of their "aristocratic dictators". Shortly after Henry Beekman's withdrawal from serving at the assembly, the farmers easily defeated the two Livingston candidates for the seats. Later, after the Revolution, Dutchess again defeated the Federalists, electing George Clinton's men, and opposing ratification of the new Constitution in 1788. It is too often forgotten that the Dutch in Dutchess were the sons of a Dutch Republic that had been struggling for freedom during more than a century, citizens of the most advanced state of Europe, and by no means ignorant of the arts of self-government.

Professor Charles Andrews, for example, surmises that the Charter of Libertyes and Privileges must have come from the pen of Matthias Nicolls, the English Speaker of the New York Assembly which had adopted it. He argues that Dutch assemblymen could not have drawn up so forward-looking a document, as if they could not, after twenty years under the English, have heard of Magna Charta. When so sympathetic a writer as Andrews takes this view, the attitude of other writers can be guessed. The Hollanders, like Americans of our time, criticized their government and themselves fiercely, and were far better able to handle their affairs than most of the officials of the Stuart regime.

The Ulster citizens, from whom the Dutchess derived her government, had already petitioned for self-government in local affairs, when Dongan arrested them, as has been reported. In writing home of the New York public, he said rather scornfully, "of all sorts of opinions there are some, and for the most part of none at all". He could not have been thinking of the Kingston burghers.

In 1710 the New York assembly asserted its rights in the clearest possible way, without any help from Mathias Nicolls. Their quarrel was then with the appointive governor's council which liked to think of itself as an English House of Lords. The assembly affirmed:

"... the share the council have (if any) in the legislature does not flow from any title they have from the nature of that board, which is only to advise (the governor); or from their being another distinct state, or rank of People in the Constitution, which they are not, being all commons; but only from the mere pleasure of the prince signified in the commission. On the contrary, the inherent right the Assmbly have, to dispose of the money of the freemen of this Colony, does not proceed from any Commission, letters patent or other grant from the Crown; but from the free choice and election of the people, who ought not to be divested of their property, (nor justly can be) without their consent. Any former condescensions, or other assemblies, will not prescribe to the present Council's privilege to make any of these amendments, and therefore they have it not." They added that the opinions of her Majesty and her ministers could not conclude them.

This was passed sixty years before the Declaration of Independence. Dutchess County at the time was represented by Ulster in the Assembly, because of its small numbers, but it had sent two of its own men none the less, to act as observers though they had not a vote. The Assembly never surrendered this position. The Governors who accepted these terms had no trouble; those who did not had nothing but trouble.

The Dutch Livingstons may be taken as typical of the Dutchess temperament. Patriotic and conservative, they supported the Federalist party at first, changing to Clinton in later years. One of them, Peter R. Livingston, led a radical reform that greatly widened the suffrage though at the cost of the Conservative group. The family included such liberals as Elizabeth Cady Stanton and her daughter Harriet Stanton Blatch. The abolitionist radical Gerrit Smith was one of them, who largely financed John Brown's raid. So, too, is Eleanor Roosevelt of today, in her own mother's line of descent.

Martin Van Buren and Edward Livingston deserve much of the credit for electing Andrew Jackson and, as his Secretaries of State, for helping him in his struggles with the Olympians of finance and privilege. Van Buren came from Columbia (there were Van Burens in Dutchess, too), while Edward Livingston was of Rhinebeck. Incidentally, the Democratic party of today owes much to these men. But these are to be more fully told in due course. Here it suffices to say that of intelligent leadership the Dutch of Dutch lineage have given out of all proportion to their numbers.

# 11. The High Dutchers

BY 1710 the war of the Spanish Succession had drifted off the European scene. It had enriched His Grace the Duke of Chandos and impoverished the people of the Lower Palatinate, on either side of the middle course of the Rhine. These remote and irrelevant facts are to meet in Dutchess during the following quarter-century, as a result of which the poor Palatines shall live happily on the rich Beekman land, and the wicked Duke shall be thwarted in his villainous scheme of grab for the neighboring country-side.

For the present we must follow the poor pilgrims. As you slow up at the traffic light where Route 9 crosses Route 9-G, you will see ahead of you, on a little hill, an old graveyard. To the right a dusty lane diverges. This is Pilgrims Progress, leading from Emighville to the crossroads by the church successively known as Kingsbury, Kirch Hoeck, Rhynbeck, Monterey, and Pink's Corners. Here stood the first church and school in Dutchess (1719) and here our first Palatines are buried.

For nearly a century the Rhenish Palatinate suffered war and its horsemen. The conflict of religions in the first half-century was followed by Louis XIV's devastation, a wanton series of ravages that forever discrown him of his title of "Grand Monarque". The latest outrage had been in 1707, when the French raided at will through the whole area, plundering beyond the call of duty. The next year an unprecedented freeze set in to complete the disaster by killing all the vines.

Taxes scarcely made things worse, for they were already worst.

Religious intolerance may have spurred on the French raids, but Catholics suffered as well as Protestants, and of the refugees who came to London practically one-third were of that faith. Some of them had set out purely to better themselves, like Ulrich Simmendinger, who wrote of his adventures in 1717, after his return from New York. The High German Company of Thuringia by 1705 was working for an expedition to Carolina, with the aid of its governor. The Reverend Joshua Kocherthal wrote a pamphlet for them, and on the strength of it visited England to promote a new venture of his own. The company he brought with him, fifty-five in all, were sent by Queen Anne to Orange County, where they settled Newburgh, naming it after their Palatine Prince, whose title came from a little town of that name in Bavaria.

William Penn had long preceded them. As soon as he obtained his charter he began to advertise and to send agents to promote his province. His deep concern for religious freedom favored his enterprise and was welcomed in England, where the Protestant succession and the early advent of a German king were topics in the day's politics. In 1709 a naturalization law for German Protestants was adopted by Parliament. Its restrictions in religious affiliation kept out some sectaries, but the provisions for the naturalization of children, the right to hold land and do business, outweighed these defects. In bidding for German colonists, Britain was following a pattern already familiar. Her empire was expanding. The peace of Utrecht that was to follow three years later was to give her Newfoundland, Nova Scotia, and Hudson's Bay, among other prizes. There would be room for all.

Thirteen thousand five hundred Palatines had arrived in England by 1709. Of these 3500 Catholics were not acceptable, under the new law, and were returned. The remainder were fed at public expense, costing fourpence a day apiece. The landowners were very uncomfortable about it, and resented their lodging as an intrusion. Mob violence followed. In the fall 2000 were settled, or at least distributed, in Ireland, where a German element is still found, in the neighborhood between Limerick and Killarney.

A small planting of Palatines and Swiss developed at New Bern in North Carolina, but the greater part of London's guests were still the wards of government which racked its collective brain—or the lack of it—with every conceivable scheme for colonization. Apparently no effort was made to ascertain the need of migrants from any of the stronger colonies. But some earlier suggestions from New England must have lain dormant and revived in their memory, for they suddenly thought of "Hudson's River on the Frontier of New York". Let the Germans fight it out with the French and Indians, where we have not done so well of late. Bellomont had reported great losses in populations at Albany among both whites and Indians.

At the suggestion of Governor Hunter, the Palatines were placed under contract like indentured servants, to work out their time in making tar and other stores for the Crown. A convoy was finally assembled, and 3300 poor souls embarked in December 1709, remaining on shipboard until April, unable to sail for lack of orders. Naturally many died of "Palatine fever". The ships arrived in June of 1710, except for one ship wrecked on Long Island. Their cargo increased New York's population by one half. Governor Hunter and Pastor Kocherthal came with them.

Instead of assuming that the large landholders would compete for such promising workers, the governor was so bound by his own idea of profit in tar that he restricted the settlement to land held by the Crown. Of this there was but little left, where pitch pine could be found. That was on the Hudson "frontier" at West Camp above Saugerties. On the opposite shore the governor purchased 6000 acres from Robert Livingston. Since every effort has been made to blacken his share in this deal, it is but fair to state that Livingston did not make the offer to sell, nor suggest the site, which was determined solely by the recommendation of William Bridger, Surveyor of Woods in the Colonies. The price, £266 English, or 22¢ an acre, seems not unreasonable.

After months of waiting over 2000 Palatines were shipped up river and divided into camps near the river shores. They made log cabins as they best could, with their inadequate tools. The governor followed every step with the greatest interest. He was overtaken by plans for an invasion of Canada in 1711. With characteristic opportunism he recruited soldiers from the hungry Palatines to the number of 300, thus setting an example of employing German mercenaries against their foes in America.

Dr. Knittle, who has made the most thorough study of the records, inclines to the view that the colonial authorities did their best with the impossible assignment. England of that day was opposed to governmental control of such enterprises; Governor Hunter did not get a penny of salary from the contrary legislature, and the English treasury did not meet his bills for the project. Everything was contracted out with no sense of human relations. Imagine forbidding German housewives to bake their own bread! None of the Palatines knew anything about the reduction of tar from pitch pine, although for a year the project had been planned. Time was wasted for the lack of training and the rendering of the tar, ordinarily at least a two-year task, was postponed fatally for the impatient British. Even the cure of souls for which provision had been made, went wrong. The historian regretfully records that Kocherthal and Haeger, the two ministers, were soon at odds. The former, who had made the voyage with them, cared for the Lutherans, the latter worked for the Anglican missionary society, which at the time was charged with political as well as religious motives.

They forgot that the Palatines had minds of their own. Secret plans were made to leave the camps, to claim lands in the Schoharie promised them, and to break the contract. The plotters just missed capturing the governor in their "jail break". He revenged himself in ample ways.

While the Palatines received food at the London rate of

four-pence a day in sterling, the governor charged against this sum the entire overhead as well. Responsibility for the food rested with George Clarke, our friend of the Upper Nine Partners, with a thumb in every sack. He was not only Secretary, but Treasurer of the Province, and Commissary of Stores. His assistant deputy, Jean Cast, certified the food at East Camp as satisfactory, but complaints arose. Cast thought Livingston given to cupidity, and perhaps he was. But he had nothing to do with the meat contract about which the worst complaints were made. It must also be recorded that Livingston had other duties at this time, and that Cast was jealous of his opposite number in the West Camp.

The same jealousy developed between the director of the tar enterprise and William Bridger, the English Inspector of Woods in the colonies, who finally refused to instruct the Palatines at all. In this emergency Richard Sackett of Dover was employed by Hunter to take his place. The Dutchess farmer claimed to have learned tar-making down east, presumably in Maine, since he was of New Haven family. But his chief activity in earlier days appears to have been brewing ale.

Sackett barked 100,000 trees, built a bridge across Roelof Jansen's Kill, and filled 200 barrels with tar, which is one barrel for 500 trees, not a profitable average. Whether he used the best methods has never been decided. The trees may not have been the pitch pine, as our Dr. Poucher suggested, following Cobb's view in his book.

Our good friend and countian, Dr. L. Wilson Poucher, had spent his boyhood on a farm in Columbia County near West Camp, and recalls the pitch pine knots which he found and used as torches for night fishing in the kills. He was positive that any good method would have got plenty of tar from the pitch pines, great trunks of which still lay halfburied in the humus of the woods in his day. The dry and barren soil preserved them.

But the fiasco may also, and perhaps with more likelihood, be attributed to the utter distaste of the Palatines for the job. They hated it, and everything connected with it. They had left Germany and good farms to better their condition. They had no intention of learning to make pitch pine, and the easiest way to stage a slowdown being to assume ignorance, they played dumb. Governor Hunter seems to have run the gamut of feeling about the venture, from confidence in its success to utter despair.

The termination of the Palatine tar project did not arise from failure or delay in the first two experimental years. No engineers in his senses would abandon any project merely because one or two false starts had gone wrong. He would say that if Sweden could make tar, Britons could make it. The real failure came in London, when Queen Anne dismissed the Duchess of Marlborough, turned out the Whigs, and put straight Tories back in office. These immediately sought and won a general election, and proceeded to reverse every project the Whigs had sanctioned, the Palatine tar among them.

The Tories left Governor Hunter holding the bag, with the government indebted to him, personally, by more than twenty thousand pounds. To ensure its success, this uncanny Scot had pledged his own estate to keep the tar hot. The provincial assembly made a deal with him on a broadened naturalization, and paid up five years' back salary; but the debts owed in England were left unpaid, it seems.

Hunter was not a good loser, as it turned out. The Palatines, three hundred of whom had marched off to share in an ill-fated raid in Canada, were now left stranded at the Camps in 1712, with neither pay nor food. They scattered to seek a better fortune, as those left in New York City had done. Some went to New Jersey, and so it came about that Christina Rockefeller of Ancram married her cousin William at Germantown; their great-grandson, John D. Rockefeller, was born at Richfield Springs. A Rockefeller of Red Hook recently spent a year in France, tracing the family name back to Roque-feuille in southern France. The Flegelaers on the other hand, moved down to Fishkill Plains, and all the Flaglers descend from them. Some went to New York, where young John Peter Zenger, a bound-out orphan of the Palatines, was learning his trade as a printer, and in twenty years stood trial for freedom of the press.

But forty families set out from Dutchess for the Schoharie of their dreams. Hunter pursued them with most unsporting vindictiveness. The Indians had welcomed them and "given" them their lands. The governor forbade the acceptance, but other Palatines joined them, till nearly 600 of the 1500 on the Hudson were there. Then Hunter invoked the law. He granted a patent to Nicholas Bayard and six others, one of them Robert Livingston of Clermont. By the end of Hunter's term the two parties were at loggerheads. Burnet, Hunter's successor, offered them reasonable terms, but at least a hundred families went off to Pennsylvania, while the remainder settled on German Flats, near Herkimer.

Among the Pennsylvania families that of John Conrad Weiser stands out. The father was a natural leader, who struggled courageously for his people during the whole miserable and heroic affair. The son, Conrad Weiser, who lived as a boy in East Camp, became the most famous Pennsylvanian of his day, as the greatest Indian interpreter and envoy extraordinary in our history. By his influence more than any other man's the course of Indian power ran with increasing strength on the British side, until Conrad's place was taken by Sir William Johnson, and France's day was over.

In his old age John Conrad Weiser went back to Dutchess to spend his last days among his old friends near Shekomeko. It was there that his son found him and brought him back to the son's home in Tulpehocken, where the sturdy old Palatine leader sank to rest.

About 1716, Col. Henry Beekman, Jr., who had inherited his share of his father's patent, invited the families left at East Camp to live upon his land. They accepted, and by 1737, Beekman's land was partitioned among the two sisters Cornelia Beekman Livingston (Mrs. Gilbert), and Catherine Beekman Rutsen Pawling (Mrs. Albert), and Henry Beekman Jr., and deeds could be given. Until that time leaseholds evidently prevailed. Beekman gave a church lot to the Lutherans, and thus arose the tradition of 1719 as the year of organization of the Stone Church that became Kirchhoek. Beekman called it Rynbeck in his deeds and certainly our oldest records use this name, though the name "Beekmansland" in one early list probably refers to it.

A pastor's son, John A. Quitman, was born in the parsonage, and lived to distinguish himself at Monterey, in the war with Mexico. On his return the village at the crossroads was named in his honor, Monterey. Later, in true Dutchess fashion, the neighborhood reverted to the storekeeper, and became Pinks Corners. Today, they know it as Old Rhinebeck, or—what you will.

The Palatines did not stop at Rhinebeck. By 1719, 52 of the 94 names of families in the North Ward were Palatines. Soon the Rau and other families followed Richard Sackett back over his Upper Nine Patent, to Pine Plains, originally an exclusively German village, whose church lot was given them by the Partner, James Alexander. They kept on into North East, and down to Amenia, Dover, and Pawling. Along the Hudson they took up most of Staatsburg. Below Rhinebeck they crossed the hills. Wuertemburg Church is named for the home province of some, the Weisers among them. Schultzville bears the name of a family that ran the upper ferry at Kingston. They followed the Wappingers to Poughkeepsie and beyond. When I came to Vassar College, the college farmer was Albert Flagler, and his assistant Frank Dietrich, both Palatine names.

An interesting article of Miss Reynolds shows orthographic changes from Treber to Traver, from Kuehn to Coon, Froelich to Fraleigh, Mauser to Mosher, Schreiber to Schryver (often pronounced as in Dutch Skryver).

The Palatine Germans were noted for large families. Of the perhaps 200 families that made their home in Dutchess, either from the original transfer or by later return like John Conrad Weiser, there are thousands today in every walk of life. Houses near us have been erected by the contractor Raymond Feller. The Comptroller's secretary at Vassar was Mrs. (Cookingham) Downer (Kuckenheim). The Palatines were farmers, but they were also skilled in many other occupations. It has been easy for them to hold their own in every field. One of their descendants, the late Harry Harkness Flagler of Millbrook, was not only a great benefactor of music through the New York Philharmonic orchestra, but of the Millbrook School and many other enterprises. He loved Dutchess history, and owned many original records of old Dutchess.

Thus by the light of a pitch pine torch, Henry Beekman fished for the Palatines and caught them, and Nicholas Emigh and his family strolled up Pilgrim's Progress to the High Dutchers' Stone Church at Monterey.

Like the first settlers in New Netherland, the Palatines brought people of half a dozen different states of Germany, French from both northern and southern regions, Swiss and Alsatian families. The Palatinate furnished only a fraction of the group; but they furnished a good pronounceable name and one with which the English were familiar. The name has stuck at Palatine Bridge and in the Hotel Palatine at Newburgh. Why has Dutchess forgotten it?

Legend and speculation have busied themselves about Old Rhinebeck and New Rhinebeck. Col. Henry Beekman, it is alleged, used his influence with the province to divert the King's Highway into the village on the flats, and away from Pinks Corners. As he owned both sites, sufficient motive is lacking. If anyone should have the credit, William Traphagen seems a likely candidate. He built Beekman's Mill on the creek named for the miller Casper Landsman. Buying a good part of the Vlaaktje, he built himself a tavern, and like most taverners of the day soon won to prominence. Round his tavern the Dutch settlers gathered at first, and Henry Beekman in 1730 granted forty acres for a Dutch church. The two neighborhoods thrived, the Germans depending on the Eighmie mill, and the Dutch on Landsman's lower down. But when the great expansion started about 1800, and new Englanders came down the Sepasco trail on their westward trip, a turnpike was pushed through with tollgates to the Kipsbergen ferry. For a time the resentful farmers used the Shunpike to

Shultz's ferry at the landing on Rutsen's place, connecting with the old Kingston dock. But Rondout and the pike had the better road and the longer ferry, the tolls were removed, the Palatines fraternized with the Low Dutchers, and Old Rhinebeck became a ghost neighborhood, its church removing to Red Hook, its tavern gone. Janet Montgomery, to whom her mother Margaret Beekman Livingston had bequeathed the land comprising Rhinebeck, bequeathed one part to her brother Edward, and the rest to the Rhinebeck Improvement Company, with five shareholders. This led to better planning and more rapid sales. Rutsen and Suckley were Dutch, Schryver a Palatine, Platt and Cunningham New English, a good amalgam for future growth.

One likes to think that the good planning of Pine Plains, Red Hook, and Rhinebeck villages is due to the sense of order and discipline in German life. Streets at right angles instead of rambling cow-paths, well-built centers instead of one long street, famous inns still thriving on the old sites, seem to speak of old German villages along the Rhine and its affluents. A little Gemüthlichkeit still lingers in our northern outposts. Long may it survive! Peace to the "poor Palatines".

One of the wise acts passed in Governor Dongan's time had been naturalization of aliens and confirmation of land titles with which they may have been associated. The arrival of the Palatines brought the question up once more. The English Whigs had passed a generous act for their naturalization, but the New Tory government repealed it before their arrival in New York. The assembly and Governor Hunter disputed the matter for five years, until the governor in dire financial need because the assembly had withheld his salary, agreed to the new law in 1715. Under it Palatines could, and many did become citizens of New York, and all land titles derived through alien sources were validated.

Among the many craftsmen the Palatines numbered carpenters and wood workers, weavers and tailors, shoemakers and saddlers, masons and bricklayers, bakers and butchers, brewers and millers, miners, potters, and glaziers; there were also hunters and locksmiths, who made the German rifle. This weapon, so magnificently exhibited at Ticonderoga Museum, saved more than one day for American arms. The English had no rifle at this date. It equipped Morgan's Pennsylvanians, Jackson's Tennesseeans, and all our backwoodsmen with an accurate and enduring arm. It was worth a whole corps to us, and when we talk about Hessians in the Revolution we should remember the Palatines, and the Palatine General Nicholas Herkimer and his men from German Flats. We owe them the word "rifle" itself, I suppose, as it must be the same as the American-coined "riffle", meaning a groove in a river, like the grooves in a gunbarrel, creating eddies.

# 12. The Riverway Broadens

BETWEEN 1714 and 1790 Dutchess County increased a hundredfold, from four hundred to forty thousand. For some reason this figure is quite unsatisfactory to some historians, who follow the incompetent governors in blaming the slow increase of the province—they never quote Dutchess as exceptional—upon the land grants.

It has been shown that the large land grants were no deterrent in the case of Beekman and Brett. In the former the proprietor took advantage of the plight of the Palatines to secure tenants who stayed in his leaseholds. In the latter a capable woman through her family connections started the sale with both leasehold and freehold. It will be shown in a following chapter that when publicity attended the settlement of the eastern boundary, settlers poured in from New England. No system of leasing deterred them for a minute, nor is there any record of complaint. In both Beekman and Brett grants, the father's death brought an early division of the patent, but squatters already were occupying in some numbers.

On the other hand there were many other possible causes of slow immigration. An alien province, recently conquered, did not offer such inducements as other provinces with no language or culture problems.

Titles were uncertain because derived from aliens as yet unnaturalized.

Land was insecure except along the river because of hostile provinces on the east, and unreliable Indians on the west.

A succession of military governors, some of them notoriously unfit, did not create confidence. Unpaid soldiery in garrison, and unpaid governor in office, did not make for good will.

The provincial assembly was more concerned in defending its own liberties than in extending the province.

The fur trade, though fast diminishing, was still a rival to agriculture. Indians still dwelt on both shores of the Hudson, and made their living by it.

The French frontier was one of continuous danger not only during the frequent wars, but in the intervals as well. Unlike the New England frontier, attack was easy by the rivers and lakes. Defense was weak.

New York, which depended on trade, was restricted by the Navigation Act. It had only four thousand inhabitants in 1710. It was a poor market town for the back country.

Some of this, perhaps all, could have passed by word of mouth to the head springs of European migration, in Germany, Scotland, and Ireland. It was not an inviting picture. But Dr. Knittle has hit the nail, I think, in arguing that William Penn's extensive and persistent advertising was the weight that turned the scale. The Scots and Germans went to Pennsylvania because they had heard good things about it. They knew, because Penn had been among them, that he was a good pious man, who desired justice, and would treat them fairly.

We can therefore take the heat off the system of land tenure. It worked well enough in good hands, and badly enough in evil hands to bring violence and opposition as a warning. It died of obsolescence rather than by act of legislatures. Mrs. Ogden Mills had great difficulty in getting the last of her tenants to surrender their precious heirlooms of ancient perpetual leases, just a few years ago. Vermonters still pay rents to Ira Allen's heirs, and quitrents to the Church of England. Old customs die hard, but they do fade away.

If our incompetent Governors had persuaded the assembly to demand the immediate division of the grants into company shares, and their advertisement in Europe for sale, the province might have had more purchasers. Even then they would have faced keen competition.

So far as this county is concerned, the increase was deemed extraordinary in its day, and its prosperity and productivity became bywords. From the seventh county it grew to be the first, if we measure the present Dutchess and the present Albany.

At the early enumerations of families, nine-tenths at least were from the Low Countries and their immediate neighbors on the Rhine. The earliest groups to risk intrusion upon this fairly homogeneous center were the Irish and Scots, and their blend called in America Scotch-Irish. Newcomers today call themselves Ulster Irish, though others call them Ulster Scots. The term Scotch-Irish does not please a Scotsman who never uses "Scotch". Protestant Irish would perhaps be more accurate, for there were many Protestants in Ireland in the Pale, George Clinton himself among them, and Dr. Thomas Young of Amenia.

Here we will call them Irish and Scots. Their religious differences never prevented their making common cause in the eighteenth century, either on the old sod, or in the provincial wildernesses.

The county's oldest documents show such good Scots names as Livingston, Noxon, Lewis, Graham, Campbell, Christie, Hamilton (spelled Hambleton), Ross, Munro, McDougald, Scott, McDonald, and McGregor, among many others. The Irish include Kelly, Murphy, Cassidy, Cullinan, O'Brien, McCoy, McCabe, McManus, McDermott, McQuinn, McGarrah, McCord, McClave, O'Carlan, Kilpatrick, McCarthy, and many more. And since not all the Scots and Irish got into trouble with the law, we must assume many times this number at work in the county, most of them in the humbler occupations; far more than the "few" "scattered" "one or two" mentioned by our own analysts who did not have access to these records. The same evidence appears in the rolls of Dutchess regiments in the wars. There never was a time when the Dutchess people might not have derived from any of at least ten national stocks: Dutch, Flemish, French, German, English, Irish, Scot, Norwegian, Swedish, Welsh.

Many good folk of Dutchess, some of them of Irish or Scots extraction, will tell an inquirer that the Irish came to the country with the railroads, and the Scotch with the gardens on the estates. The official state history makes no mention of Scotch-Irish in the volume dealing with the eighteenth century, and no reference to the Irish. Our own historical society has thus far been silent on both branches of the Gael, and these observations must therefore be somewhat particular.

The patentees included names like Graham and Jamison. The Grahams claim descent with very good reason from no less than the great Marquis of Montrose. James Alexander of Little Nine was in the direct line of the Earl of Stirling. The Livingstons had similiar good claim to descent from the Earls of Linlithgow. Sanders is also a good Scottish name. Of all these, descendants lived in Dutchess.

Of the early settlers Leonard Lewis, the first judge, and Bartholomew Noxon were leaders. But the greatest number came upriver during the 'forties and 'fifties, when the Scotch-Irish move was on. That is the name they go by in Pennsylvania and the Middle West. In New York City they call themselves Ulster Irish, and in New England they are mostly Irish. It makes no matter.

Among the very earliest of the old documents occur the names of Manus O'Carlan, Patrick Murphy, and Bridget Force. A steady stream of Celts follows, giving color to the sober Dutch and German catalogue. Few of these names appear among the taxpayers or freeholders. They were laborers, of the lowest classification in the social stairs. They were constantly in debt, some of these people coming up before the justices again and again. The farmer and storekeeper Samuel Munroe easily carries off premier honors for prospering in continuous indebtedness. He failed at one time to pay a bill for some twenty quintals (500 lbs.) of codfish, a most extraordinary purchase for an upstater, with all the other fish in the River. Sam Munroe became chief aide and abettor of William Prendergast, an Irishman whose trial caused a great stir.

Munroe was arrested with him, but escaped, and later returned to the county.

We owe to one Peter Creely a pathetic vignette of Dutchess life, recorded in an old document.

Whereas by an Advertisement Printed at Philadelphia in a Gazette sometime in February anno 1737-8 that one Peter Creely an Irishman then lately went away from Salem County in West New Jersey describing the person apparrell etc. who was then suspected to have been murthered or made way with by one John King and whereas one Peter Creely with almost the same description as in said advertisement given sometime in July 1738 dyed his naturall death and was buryed in this place as appears by the following deposition,

James Willson Esq High Sheriff of the County of Dutchess being duely sworn on the Holy Evangelists of Almighty God deposeth that sometime toward the latter end of July in the year 1738 he this Deponent was sent for to the house of Mrs Samuell Mathews in Poghkeepsie Precinct and there saw a man lying sick who told this deponent that his name was Peter Creely and that he was an Irish man and was born in the parish of Cregen in the County of Armagh in Irland and that he came a servant to Salem County in West New Jersey and that he had served his time there and further the said Peter Creely told this deponent that after he left Salem which he said was some time in February then last year he had lent a mare bridle and saddle to a taylor who was supposed to have gone to Albany and that he the said Peter Creely was on his way thither in pursuit of the said taylor when at said Mathews his house there taken sick and this deponent saith that he the said Peter Creely at said Mathews house about the latter end of July dyed his naturall death. and that he this deponent saw him buryed in a Christianlike manner at the burying place of major Bunschoten in Poghkeepsie Precinct aforesaid and further this deponent saith that he the said Peter Creely was of a midle stature and had blackish lank hair did not speak plain English but on a brouge and was a laborer and about the age of 25 years and the apparrell that he the said Creely wore or had with him were as followeth viz: a blue drugget turned coat and jackett lined with blewish duroy course trouzers a striped homespun jirken jackett much worn an old pair of leather britches ill shaped two ozenbriggs shirts one garlicks shirt much worn a beaver hatt half worn.

James Wilson

Sworn the 21 day of October 1741 in open court

Margriitt Mathews wife of Samuel Mathews Poughkeepsie Precinct in Dutchess County being duly sworne on the Holy Evangelist of Almighty God deposeth that on Thursday the 15 day of July in the year 1738 one Peter Creely an Irishman came to her house and the same day complained that he was not well in health by reason that he had over heated himself the day before with hard labouring at Justice Van Wyck in said county and his illness increased til the Thursday following when and where he the said Peter Creely died his naturall death at her house and on Fryday being the 23 day of July 1738 he the said Peter Creely was buryed in a Christianlike manner in the buryall place of Major Bunschoten in Pogh-keepsie Precinct aforesaid. Between which said space of time this deponent had several conferences with the said Peter Creely relating to himself and his own affairs and that the said Peter Creely told this deponent that he was born in the Parish of Cregen in the county of Armagh in Ireland and that he came over from thence a servant to Salem and that he there served his time and sometimes before he died he was several times speaking of one Michaell More living at Salem who seemed to be a particular friend and acquaintance of him by his expres-sion and also he said that one John Mooty at Salem had bought a horse of him sometime before he the said Peter Creely left Salem and that said John Mooty was to give him fifty yards of linnen for said horse and that he Peter Creely had promised this deponent that Linnen for her care and trouble towards him and that said Creely told this deponent that he had lent a mare sadle and bridle to a taylor whom he supposed to have gone to Albany and said Creely was in his way thither and in pursuit of said Taylor when he came to her house and taken sick and died as aforesaid. (Remainder personal description and apparel identical with above)

Margaritta Mathews
her mark

sworn in open court the 21 day of October 1741

Samuel Mathews his mark

(in the matter of substance)

Justices F. Filkin, L. V. Kleek, W. Scott, J. Montross, W. V. Plank, J. Kip, C. V. Wyck, J. Germond, J. Krego

Beside Peter—rest his soul!—we may place a woman's picture, kind-hearted Mary Brisbane "who has been for many years supported by the town, aged about one hundred years."

"I find in your journal of this day an account of the death of Mrs. Brisban, an inmate of the poorhouse of this town, and that her age was 100 years. Sixty years ago I knew Mary and her husband, James Brisban perfectly well. He has been deceased several years; he was the youngest son of a Protestant clergyman in the north of Ireland and married Mary soon after his arrival in this country. They were a happy pair—too happy ever to be able to decipher the word Discordance. Always poor but ever honest. Charitably disposed, their hands were ever open and they never bestowed a mite without wishing it a pound. I think Mary Brisban was at least 108 years old. Fare thee well kind-hearted Mary! Green grow the tufts which cover thy humble grave and sweet the lovely violet which blooms over thy venerable form."

May 31, Poughkeepsie Journal 1810, letter to Mr. Potter the editor dated May 24, and signed: "A friend to merit however obscure."

Leonard Lewis, already mentioned, was the son of an Irish father and a Dutch mother. His writing indicates that Dutch was his mother-tongue. Of his children, two married Van Kleecks and, one a Kip, and one a Fitsoor (Fitchett to us). Dr. Noxon left a street, a highway, and a neighborhood named in his honor.

There were trouble-makers among the group, of course; we should deny their Celtishness were it otherwise. One of them, Hugh Ross, got into trouble with John Kane, who brought a suit for slander of a most original kind.

Hugh Ross
On a Plea of Slander 1770 at Poghkeepsie
John Kane brought suit against Hugh Ross; Crannell and Livingston, att'ys. Slander. The words complained of were: "the said Hugh declared "You have taken a false oath and I can prove it. Such fellows as you are known in my country by wearing a straw in their shoe." And the said John in fact saith that in the Kingdom of Ireland where the said Hugh was born these words to witt "Such Fellows as you are known by wearing a straw in their shoe," are well known and understood and do import a charge that such person of whom the same words are spoken is a Knight of the Post, who is one who for hire or reward will falsly swear anything to be true.
damage £200.

Some may think that it is futile to think of the Scots apart from the English, and they have a point. But the Scots in the provinces were thorns in English flesh. Some of them were old Covenanters, or even Stuart men of a later day. Governor Andrew Hamilton of New Jersey was removed by the Lords of Trade, who ruled America, because the right of a Scot to hold office in the colonies was doubtful, owning to the phrasing of the Navigation Acts of 1696. Such events only whetted the Scots' dirk. We shall read of many Scots who became Sons of Liberty. A typical one may well stand here for the rest. John Morin Scott, who held extensive lands in Dutchess, was perhaps the chief among the Sons. Like the others, he could boast a gentleman's status, however, for his great grandfather was Sir John Scott. Our John's mother was a Huguenot. Graduating from Yale in 1746, studying law with Judge William Smith, he soon rose to leadership at the bar. His most celebrated victory was along liberal lines: that no appeal in questions of fact lay from a provincial superior court to the governor-in-council. Thus he clipped one of the strongest pinions in the government wing. He fought for Whig Presbyterians, wrote vigorously in controversies; we may leave the recital of his war activities to another time. As trustee for the Widow of John Bard, he had much to do in Dutchess, and lived long in Fishkill during the Revolution.

Perhaps Dutchess' most famous Irishman was Samuel Neilson, one of the leaders of the Irish rebellion of 1798. The editor of the newspaper Northern Star, still a leader of Belfast, he was an organizer of the United Irishmen. With Henry Joy McCracken he raised Ireland's flag, but was arrested, and got away to America by a lucky chance, and came to Poughkeepsie. A kindly, quiet man, he rests in the Rural Cemetery, but is remembered as a hero in all Ireland. Thomas Emmet, brother of Robert Emmet, the revolutionary, had a son who married a Hosack, and was well known in Hyde Park. He came a penniless exile, and like John Scott led the New York bar. In the famous lawsuit of the tenants against "Lady Mary" Allen of "The Hill", he represented the people's party, but lost the suit.

But this is endless. The Scots-Irish gaiety, impetuousness, and spice made a good component in the decoction of the Dutchess temperament. In the Civil War Captain Auchmuty singlehanded raised a regiment of 500 engineers in 1861 at 120 Main Street.

Among the simpler folk was Henry Blair, who started the brickmaking at Fishkill Landing. He was a forerunner of the workmen, skilled and unskilled, who came from Ireland and Scotland in the century following the Revolution. It was they who laid the tracks of the Hudson River Railroad in 1847, two years after the Great Potato Blight. They were skilled in the ways of horses, too, and as all Dutchess went quietly mad for horse-racing about this time, Irish grooms were in great demand. More than one good lawyer of Poughkeepsie grew up with horses and learned to gentle them as they later gentled their juries.

When the railroad was finished the two groups merged, and went out on the lands as drainers of swamps and road-makers. According to our wonderful George Van Vliet, "the boys, however, didn't take so kindly to it; they went after something as high as the rest". Which was the Celt in them.

Van Vliet tells of a single Irish group in Clinton in the mid-century.

"Old man John Cotter lived in Ruskey Lane, his son, John, was born there. After John got older (I can remember when he worked for Joseph Arnett for eight dollars a month and his board) he finally studied medicine, became a country doctor in Jackson Corners, and then he went to Poughkeepsie and at one time was President of the Medical Society. Old man Cotter has three grandsons who are physicians: Dr. Lawrence Cotter of Red Hook, Dr. John I. Cotter of Poughkeepsie, son of Dr. J. H., and Dr. John H. Cotter in Brooklyn, son of his son James. Dr. Eddie Burns was another boy from this town that went to Poughkeepsie and made good as a physician. Patrick Lyons was another one of these first-generation Irishmen. He begot two sons, one Martin, who became the best farmer in the town of Clinton, owned three farms. Another one, John, walked every morning and back every night from east of Bull's Head in the Town of Clinton to De Garmo Institute in Amenia, for his education. At night he would thresh grain with a flail for the farmers, while the sisters held the lantern, so he could earn money to pay his tuition. That's the way he got *his* education. He went to Nassau County, became County Comptroller, and when he died he left ten thousand dollars to his native town to build the Memorial Hall at Shultzville, which is now the Town Hall."

Among the earliest colonists in Dutchess were Negroes who accompanied their masters. The first census in 1714 records 30

Africans out of 447. Approximately this ratio, or slightly less, has continued to the present since in 1749 they were 421, while in 1790 of 45,266, there were counted 1714 slaves, a little over half the earliest ratio. By 1840 the proportion had risen only slightly, with 2,270 among 52,398 (Putnam omitted). In 1950 Poughkeepsie, where the larger number of Negroes lived, there were 1,804 among 41,023, or 4.5%.

The low proportion of slaves in New Netherland is attributed by Reasly to the preference for trade as against pioneering by the Dutch. Negroes, he assumed, would be employed chiefly in the heavy forest labors. He ignores the domestic service in traders' homes, and the Negroes among the crews as well. If agriculture were their chief employment, why did the proportion not rise when all Dutchess was a great wheatfield?

A truer explanation is found in the records. Negroes in New Netherland were almost exclusively in the service of the West India Company and its officials. None of them had been brought directly from Africa. They were the prize found in captured Spanish ships. They were well treated, so far as records tell. On one occasion, when a group of slaves had killed one of their number, a lot was held, and one great chap drew the fatal short slip. Twice he was hanged and twice his weight and strong neck broke the rope, whereupon the crowd cried "Mercy", and he was reprieved.

There are records of manumission, and deeds of land to various Negroes near Stuyvesant's Bouwerie. The old governor once released three women servants, on consideration that one of them should every week "keep the director general's house clean." He lived in his retirement surrounded by the farms of Negroes.

About 1650, when the population began to increase and the West India Company bestirred themselves to save the province, efforts were made to swell the population by the importation of slaves. They apparently came to nothing, except that three hundred were found on ships awaiting disembarkation, when the English took the town and province.

To the English belongs all the credit of the northern slave

trade. They demanded and got the complete monopoly by the Treaty of Utrecht in 1713. At that time 12% of New York inhabitants were Negroes. This figure remained constant till 1790, when it fell to 11%. Thus the figure for the Dutchess amounted to less than one-half that of the province. It seems fairly clear that domestic service was their principal occupation, and that among the Dutch there was no demand for them.

One of the earliest protests against slavery is that of Van Der Donck in his book the "Representation of New Netherland," in which he inveighs against the enslaving of Christian Africans as a crime against religion. The Quakers of Dutchess followed his reasoning, and declared at a meeting in Flushing that Friends must dispose of their slaves on pain of withdrawal from fellowship.

Our ancient documents show the same absence of disorder among Africans as among Indians. Owners of slaves were held responsible for their acts, and practically all mention of slaves occurs in connection with complaints against their masters. But the number is astonishingly small against 500 that might proportionately be anticipated. There are scarcely a score of documents in which Negroes figure.

Most of them lived with leading citizens in early days, 20 of the original 30 living with Parmentier, Lewis, Van Kleeck, Le Roy, and Van Der Burgh at Poughkeepsie, and with Springsteen and Brett at Beacon. At the Bretts' the tradition holds that they slept in the attic; in all local traditions they appear as members of the family. When Robert R. Livingston set his slaves free a woman told her mistress, "I won't be free, I was born in this place, and I have as good a right as you have to live here."

Crèvecoeur, who lived in Orange but had intimate friends in Dutchess, writes, "Our Negro kitchens are always built adjacent to our dwelling houses, with a door of communication into the room in which we eat, that we may inspect whatever passes there . . . Nor are the joys and pleasures of the season confined to the whites alone; as our blacks divide with us the toils of our farm they partake also of the mirth and good cheer of the season. They have their own meetings, and are often indulged with their Master's sleighs and horses. You may see them at particular places as happy and merry as if they were freemen and freeholders. The sight of their happiness always increases mine, provided it does not degenerate into licentiousness, and this is sometimes the case, though we have laws enough to prevent it."

Crèvecoeur always looked on the rosy side; there certainly was another. Yet the absence of riots, insurrection, and violence leaves a favorable picture.

Francis Filkin, J. P., the storekeeper, had seven slaves in 1736-46. The two men served him and his neighbors in all the heavy farm-work, the five women in the house and garden. The men also fished and hunted. Negroes attended white churches in sections set aside; they were buried in special burial-grounds.

Robert, a runaway, took his fiddle with him; "Zack" played the fife and flute. They liked to gather in social places.

In 1742 there had been a panic resulting from a scare involving Negroes. This happened in New York, where thirty years before another panic had happened. In both instances the Negroes suffered through the most outrageous miscarriage of justice, far worse than the witch hangings at Salem. Unlike the repentant Sewall in Boston, Chief Justice Horsmanden of New York gloried in his shame, and published it in a book. Nothing of the sort happened in Dutchess County; the case just cited probably resulted from the law passed not long before, by which the presence of more than two Negroes in a public place constituted a felony. A Negro convicted of arson in Red Hook was burned at the stake. A white man would certainly have been hanged for the same crime.

On the other hand, the law sometimes operated in favor of a Negro. In the following old document, a Negro manumits his own son, since by law in slavery a child followed his mother's status, and in this case the mother was a white woman. The £100 bond given by the two white friends was substantial in amount.

Cornelis Jansen's Manumission

Know all men by these Presents, that I the subscriber hereof Francis Jansen of Mombaccus Township in the County of Ulster, Inhabitant, being a Mulatto of Colour, but a Free Man, by reason being born by a white woman, at the request of my Son Cornelis Jansen, and for the Love and Respect which I have and bear towards him, he being now a dweller and Labourer within Rhinebeck Precinct and Dutchess County, Have, and by these Presents Do for Love and Fatherly affections Sake, give my said Son Cornelis Jansen afores'd free so far as it Lyeth in my Power, and Possibility that he is and shall be no Slave, or, Servant during his good Behaviour and Lawfull Carriage to no Person, or Persons whatsoever, or my account In witness whereof I & Francis Jansen have hereunto Set My Hand and Seal this 21" Day of August, Anno Domini 1756

Witness Francis (his mark) Jansen
Johanness Weller
Christian Schultz

A second document is a bond for £100 by Col. Peter ten Brook & Johannis Feller both of Rhinebeck precinct—in Jansen's support.

The Dutchess jury that indicted Joseph Rykert, a Palatine, of Rhinebeck insisted on condign punishment in another case, which probably cost the courageous constable his job. Isaac, belonging to Peter de Witt, had committed some offence for which whipping was the penalty. Rykert refused to obey the Sheriff's order to take Isaac to the whipping post at Rhinebeck, and on being commanded under penalties to obey, he took the Negro, but casually allowed him to escape on the way. This bold act, characteristic of unruly Rhinebeck, occurred Oct. 27, 1762.

Two cases of slander indicate the strong public feeling against sexual relations. In one case a father sued on behalf of his daughter because she had allegedly become "familiarly acquainted" with a Negro slave; in the other case a young man, a minor, through his next friend sued to recovery against the loss of his good name and consequent inability to secure a marriage with a well-to-do young woman, because he allegedly had gotten a Negro woman with child.

Arie Hendrickse of Rhinebeck gave bond for the good behavior of the Negro, Harry, who was ordered to remain on his master's place. Mink, an Amenia Negro was arrested for stealing a little hay, as was Isaac, belonging to Isaac Delamater. Mary Jackson of Dover confessed to having run away from Rhode Island, and having taken a small "peticoat". Two or three men, one of them a Quaker, were indicted for harboring Negro slaves.

In the May Court of General Sessions 1769 before 9 Justices of the Peace including Mathew Brett a Grand Jury headed by John Rutsen presented that Johannes Radcliff of "Rynebeck" Precinct did "On Monday the 15 day of Instant May late in the night time of the same day entertained and harbour in his dwelling house in said Rynbeck twenty Negroes Slaves belonging to his neighbors and permitted and encouraged the said negroe slaves in drinking to excess and in riotous and rude behaviour to the great disturbance of the neighbours of him the said Johannis Ratcliff and also that the said Johannis Ratcliff at diverse times before did entertain and harbor negroe slaves at his said house to the great injury to the owners and masters of said slaves and also greatly tending to debauch the morals of said slaves and to excite said negroe slaves to commit assaults and batteries on each other and the breaking the peace of our said Lord the King and that the said Johannis Ratcliff have often times suffered and encouraged numbers of negro slaves to bring mutton and veal to his said house to cook the same in his said house and to tarry at his house at unseasonable hours in the night feasting and drinking spiritous liquors till they were drunk greatly tending to cause the said negroes to steal and commit many enormous crimes to the great damage of the owners of said negroes and against the peace of our Lord the King his crown and dignity."

Two serious cases are listed, complaining of white men who

encouraged Negroes in disorder, "frolick", and rioting. Here again the story follows the well-known pattern of Indian relations. In New York City Indians had been forbidden to associate with Negroes. There on June 23, 1712, two patentees of Dutchess protected their Negroes and won acquittal for them. Twenty Negroes were executed at the city for riot and arson; some burnt, others hanged. One was broken on the wheel, and one hanged alive in chains in the town. This fell in Hunter's time.

In October, 1777, two women are recorded in the book of heroism. Norma, a slave in the Van Voorhis household, stayed in the cellar with her master while British fired on the house. The rest of the family had fled. Dina, in the Anthony family at Poughkeepsie, stayed behind to finish her baking when British soldiers landed and burned the mill, but spared the dwelling. According to the tradition, her good bread softened the British hearts. Dina is buried today with the family in their plot in the Rural Cemetery.

After the Revolution, by various and too deliberate stages, Negroes finally achieved freedom in 1827. It was neglect and indifference, we may hope, that caused the freed Negroes in many instances to drift away to more friendly regions. Today only six are listed among our farmers. Seasonal workers have come and gone, among the "pickers" in the orchards, the workers at the boarding-houses in summer, and crop harvesters.

In the town of Clinton the Central Baptist Church was founded and built by a group of families; Hills, Hancocks, Braddocks, and Hohnans, who have worked as hands and in some cases as owners on farms for nearly fifty years. They are highly respected, and live on friendliest terms with their white neighbors. Their children attend high school, and are fine citizens. Brickmaking brought many on a partly seasonal basis, to live near the yards below and above Beacon. These suffered intensely after the closing of most of the ovens. Relief was afforded them in the depression, when most of them moved away, some to Poughkeepsie.

Unfortunately, until very recently the community has been slow to recognize the abilities of trained and educated Negroes. Some industries, notably the International Business Machines, have given full employment. A few professional men have made their way. Teachers have been accepted in predominately white neighborhoods. Biracial centers have been developed, notably at Lincoln Center in Poughkeepsie, where citizens of all ages have proved the possibility of social intercourse, and in Catherine St. Center founded in 1920 by the YWCA as a sewing center, where similar conditions prevail. In residence the problem is acute though less so than in past years.

In education there is little discrimination. For many years Negroes have attended Oakwood School and Vassar College. Public schools have admitted Negroes since 1875. The first private school for Negroes was in a rented room of the Primitive Methodist Church in May, 1844, when 35 colored pupils attended. The Ebenezer Baptist Church of Poughkeepsie held its centennial in 1937, when Helen W. Reynolds celebrated the occasion in a scholarly historical sketch of the Negro in Dutchess in the Eighteenth Century.

# 13. The Treaty of Dover

THE TREATY OF DOVER, signed on May 14, 1731, by commissioners representing Connecticut and New York, determined the continental boundary of the two provinces on the present line. It added some fifty thousand acres to Old Dutchess. But the event marked much more than a local transfer of land.

It brought to a legal end the Oblong controversy, which had plagued both provinces for a hundred years. It introduced principles of conciliation and humanity in intercolonial relations. It turned the key which opened the door to the Great Expansion of New England. It provided the legal basis for the case of Johan Peter Zenger that established the American law of libel and freedom of the press, a quarter of a century before the Wilkes case in England. It furnished the training for a whole school of lawyer-diplomats in New York, whose defense of provincial autonomy successfully withstood the assaults of a governor and his coterie, a powerful company of English millionaire peers, and the whole English chancery.

Again, by ending the chief cause of dispute between New England and New York, it inaugurated, and none too soon, an era of colonial cooperation that led to union and independency. Without the Treaty of Dover, Putnam County would never have been named for a Connecticut general who had commanded New York troops in defense of "Old Dutchess". Sybil Ludington, our Dutchess Revere, might not have ridden through that night to rally her father's militia to the defense of Danbury, nor men of Danbury marched away to fight at Saratoga.

Jealous of their prerogatives as all but sovereign states, the commonwealths of New England learned by the Treaty of Dover that there were other dominions than their own, with common interests, with whom peace and a good understanding would come handy in times that tried men's souls. The lesson was needed.

Finally, the terms of the Treaty of Dover gave precedent to the later negotiations of Massachusetts and New York for the extension of the boundary northward, and eventually for its continuance as far as Canada. In the agreements with Massachusetts and Vermont the lawyers and surveyors of Dutchess played the leading roles. The effect was to shut off New England domination of western expansion, so far as continuous dominions went. New Englanders became Americans, a consummation devoutly to be wished.

With the claims to history thus staked out, this chapter will endeavor to set forth their validity. The Oblong squabble was both long and obstinate. It remained on the Connecticut docket of unfinished business for two hundred and fifty years, for though the New Englanders signed the treaty, it was in a Pickwickian sense, and not until 1881 did an act of Congress signalize their final acquiescence in the terms of settlement.

The history of the Oblong reads like an adventure in Lilliput. Its stony hills and barren cliffs hardly deserve the trouble they caused; but for them diplomatic conferences were summoned and statesmen argued, protested and adjourned. Lawyers worked out their fees in land, only to be embroiled in costly suits of their own. Tenants burned one another's barns, or tossed a bum bailly in a blanket to show their contempt for law. A village in Dutchess still stands, mute witness of the controversy. Its street is split down the middle between Connecticut and New York. Ironically, its name is Amenia Union.

But the amenities are again united; the squabble is forgotten. You may flit across the state line through Bog Valley and lovely Chickadee, famous for Rex Brasher's paintings of birds at his hermitage,—you will never guess where one state ends. Ten Mile River blends with Swamp Creek and flows through Webatuck to the Housatonic—fishermen cast their lines from state to state. No one will threaten to brain you with his axe, lead his neighbors to raid your loghouse, or drive his cattle into your wheat. Farmers from Oblong no longer drive to Cart and Horse Inn to vote their share of the expense of having their liberties. Time has washed it all downstream; but the old strip carried a lot of trouble for its width.

Sixty miles long and a mile and four-fifths wide, the Oblong, or the Equivalent Land as it was called, runs north-northwest from Norwalk to Ridgefield, then almost due north to the Massachusetts line. Approximately fifty miles of this lay in Old Dutchess—the Dutchess before she trimmed her Putnam flounce off her skirt.

From Norwalk for twelve miles south-southwest, the Horse Neck Equivalent stretches along the Sound to the Great Stone at the Wading Place in Byram River near Rye. The Horse Neck is eight miles wide, and includes the prosperous and immensely valuable towns of Stamford, Greenwich, and New Canaan. Connecticut drove a bargain when it traded the Taconic Hills for all this, and the Sound, too. But they were far from satisfied at the time; and Yorkers called themselves lucky that they had hit upon anything so heavy as the Great Stone of Byram River for their bound. Otherwise the Yankees would have moved it to Hudson's River; they were on their way when Dongan stopped them.

The Connecticut point of view on all this was well put by Governor John Haynes. When in 1639 David De Vries sailed up the Fresh River to Hartford and protested, under instruction, against the English usurpation in Connecticut, Haynes answered "that it was a sin to let such rich land, which produced such fine corn, lie uncultivated, and that they had already built three towns upon this river, in a fine country". Naturally the Yankees were against sin.

Eleven years later, at the same place, Governor Stuyvesant concluded a treaty with Connecticut, in which, though he surrendered much, he thought his border troubles were ended. Long Island was to be shared by a division line running south from Oyster Bay to the ocean. The "bounds upon the main" were to begin four miles west of Stamford, and "so to run a northerly line up into the country, and after as it shall be agreed by the two governments of the Dutch and of New Haven, provided the said line come not within ten miles of the Hudson River; and it is agreed that the Dutch shall not hereafter build any house or habitation within the said line". In return the Dutch gave up all claim to the rest of Connecticut, except the garrison and fort above Hartford. Bradstreet, Prince, Willett, and Baxter solemnly signed the agreement, the latter, though Englishmen, signing for the Dutch. In Stuyvesant's latter days fully half the government of New Netherland was managed by Englishmen.

But though solemnly signed and sealed, Connecticut had no intention of observing the treaty. They furnished no copy of it to the Dutch and they kept "crowding in" westward, until they were less than seven miles from the Hudson. On the shore they reached Westchester, which the Dutch called Oostdorp, in the Bronx.

In April, 1662, King Charles II in one of his most extravagant moods gave John Winthrop a charter for Connecticut that ran "in longitude as the line of the Massachusetts colony running from East to West, (that is to say) from the said Narragansett Bay in the East, to the South Sea, on the West part, with the islands thereto adjoining" etc, etc. Thus Charles wholly wiped out the New Haven colony, which was faced with an ultimatum from Hartford and surrendered at discretion. He also coolly gave half of Rhode Island to the unscrupulous Winthrop, starting a fight to the east as well as the west.

Two years later, forgetting all about the South Sea, Charles granted to the Duke of York all New Netherland as far east as the Connecticut River. On these two ridiculous documents hang all the law and the profits of the Oblong.

When Connecticut heard of the York patent, they immediately sent an embassy to congratulate his Majesty's Commissioners, who had come with the Duke's Fleet to settle the bounds of his patent. The Hartford men succeeded in averting the worst, by surrendering any claim to land within twenty miles of the Hudson, *except* that those settlers in the Horse Neck could be granted five miles further. To make matters worse, the Commissioners, with Governor Richard Nicolls at their head, then made the boundary from Mamaroneck Creek, a bare eight miles from "Hudson River, *North-northwest* to the line of the Massachusetts . . . and all plantations lying eastward of that creek and line, to be under the government of Connecticut".

The report certainly reads as though written by Connecticut agents, for no mention is made of the twenty-mile line. A year later, however, Colonel Nicolls wrote the Duke referring to "about twenty miles" as still in the Duke's patent. But the north-northwest line crossed the Hudson below Peekskill and reached the Massachusetts line somewhere along the Delaware River, near Margaretville!

Connecticut thereupon appointed a commission in 1674 to run the line "from Marmaroneck River to Hudson's River". The colony was determined to push its case. In April, 1675, the Duke wrote his new governor, Edmund Andros, that he did not have the papers about him, but recalled that the bound was "soe as it is not to approach nearer than 20 miles". But "my opinion is 'tis best only to make accomodations of the kind temporary, soe if possible to preserve the utmost limits that my patent gives me a title to".

Accordingly, Sir John Werden at St. James expressed satisfaction that the twenty-mile claim had been revived. This was confirmed by the Duke in January, 1676. The following year Sir John wrote again to Andros giving it as his belief that since Connecticut insisted upon her pound of flesh his Royal Highness would some day retaliate by taking all as far as Connecticut River.

Connecticut remained obdurate. When the Lords of Trade wrote to ask Connecticut what her bounds were, the curt reply came:

"Our Boundaries are expressed in our Charter. As to the number of acres settled or unsettled or how much is manureable we cannot guess; the country being a mountainous country full of rocks, swamps, hills, and vales. Most that is fitt for planting is taken up. What remaynes must be subdued, and gained out of the fire as it were, by hard blowes and for smal recompence."

A cold war ensued. Governor Lovelace in 1670 forbade "strange" sail to navigate the Hudson on any errand. If they brought upriver cargo they must transship to safe sloops. Massachusetts asked leave to ship colonists to the Berkshire by way of Claverack, but Lovelace knew a trick worth two of that. He agreed to ask the Duke's permission!

Nothing happened till May of 1682, when the General Court at Hartford sent word to the Governor of New York, "to signify our dislike of (settlers) in trenching upon our Charter limits", and asking for a survey. Mr. Frederick Philipse's mill, and other improvements, along the Hudson near Tarrytown, were strongly objected to. The Yankees avowed that they had never been so unhappy as to differ with Governor Lovelace.

Governor Dongan was of another color, quite. He brought with him definite instructions to obtain a true and exact map of the Duke's territories. At once things started. John Pell ordered the constables of Westchester to appear at the New York Assizes. Connecticut remonstrated by the hand of the Secretary of the Court, not the Governor. He was taught his manners.

"Itt is the usuall way, when one Government writes to another, for the Chief and Principall to signe it, but since the Gentlemen have not, 'tis to you, Sir, that I addresse this answer."

Dongan said that whatever his predecessors had done, he was not obliged to confirm it. "Some of your colony have come to settle within six or eight miles of Hudson's River, and that without any leave of this province, as I am informed.

"If it be so, I take it to be my master's opinion, that you have abused the former contract, if any such was, and therefore you cannot blame me to take notice of it, and make claim to the whole from Connecticut River."

To this neat note the Governor and General Court, assembled, responded in a soft answer, but maintained their claim, and Dongan answered that he must then claim "to the River Connecticut. There is land enough for us all, and I love not to do my neighbors ill offices." He further expressed a wish to shake hands, "and that we may lay a foundation that we may allways live like good neighbours".

Taking the hint, Connecticut's Robert Treat appointed a commission with Major Nathan Gold at its head, and within three days articles of agreement were signed, on Nov. 28, 1683. This pushed the western limit at the Sound four miles up, from Mamaroneck Creek to Byram Creek, where it begins today as "the common road or Wading Place over the said River is," and to go eight miles north northwest, thence parallel with "the general course of the sound" twelve miles eastward to meet a line running up eight miles from the Sound. From the east end of the twelve-mile line was to be run a line northwards "in every place twenty miles distant from Hudson's River".

Now came the Oblong. If any part of the rectangle thus formed, (Horse Neck, so-called) should be found within twenty miles of the Hudson (as it all was, of course) then an equivalent amount was to be added to the east side of the boundary "the whole length of the said Parallel Line and in such breadth as will make up quantity for quantity what shall be diminished as aforesaid".

This treaty was signed by Matthias Nicolls, Speaker of the N. Y. Assembly, and George Brewerton, and by Robert Treat, Nathan Gold, John Allyn and William Pitkin. Honorable names all. The Hartford men sadly wrote the people of Rye: "We are forced to part with you and could not help it." The governor had promised he would change no man's property.

In 1684, the Great Stone at the Wading Place was hit upon as the beginning of the bound. It is now covered by the dump from a filling station on Route 1. It was a mile and a half from the Sound and six miles and a half from three white oak trees which they duly marked, seven miles and a quarter from Hudson's River. They then ran the base line twelve miles and found its eastern end twelve miles from the River.

This gave 61440 acres from the twenty mile distance in the Connecticut quadrangle. This gave 305 rods as the width along the Oblong, of the equivalent land, which "We deemed one hundred miles from our Eight Mile Line." Nathan Gold again headed the commissioners.

In spite of all this, Connecticut in 1698 instructed her London agent to continue his fight for the 1664 agreement of Nicolls; and this he did most strenuously. But in 1700 the King in Council confirmed the 1683 agreement, though James Stuart was now in exile, and Lord Bellomont had taken Dongan's chair.

In October 1707 the General Assembly granted to Captain Nathan Gold and others a considerable parcel of land which lay actually west of the Oblong boundaries. This was a plain defiance of the King's decision of 1700, but sales were made nevertheless, and farmers lived side by side with others who leased their land from the Philipse heirs. Among the farmers holding lands from Connecticut deeds were Samuel Munroe, David Aikens, Christopher Dickinson, Sylvanus Cole, Noah Smith, William Gray, Isaac Chapman, and Josiah Robbits. No doubt because of the activity of some of these in the sale of Indian deeds, a group of men, Willet, Brown, Sackett, Smith, Marsh, and Thomas, brought suit for the lands of the Yankees. Marsh was the only one dwelling in Dutchess at the time. This was in 1765.

A board of arbitrators was appointed, consisting of the Philipse attorney William Alexander (Lord Stirling), and the great landholders Watts, DeLancey, Rutherfurd, and Cruger. The conclusion was foregone. The titles to the lands were all adjudged to the Philipse party.

It was, no doubt, this controversy that made Samuel Munroe and his friends such enemies of the Philipse heirs. It was probably in the making several years before the actual lawsuits, which synchronized with those of Nimham and Prendergast.

During the four years between 1696 and 1700, Rye and Bedford had been in active revolt against New York, and Connecticut had accepted them within her jurisdiction. She now, in October, 1700, gave up this part of the contest, and signified that the inhabitants of Rye and Bedford "are freed from duty to this government".

For ten years nothing was done. The line was not run. Then from 1710 to 1718 Connecticut made moves to run the only part she then took up, that about Bedford, but gave no authority to run north of it. New York retorted by passing an act in 1719 to run the whole line. In 1720 Connecticut finally agreed to start the northern survey from "the Duke's tree", a bound at the north end of Horse Neck. No such tree was found.

In 1723 Connecticut finally acted to give surveyors the necessary authority, but her acts were based on false assumptions. New York's committee reported in June 1723, that Connecticut's west line was about fifty-three miles in length, not one hundred, and therefore the Duke's tree could not be the starting place. They accused Connecticut of "unfairly and untruly representing the facts."

Up to this time, or forty years after the Dongan treaty, Connecticut had remained in full possession of her Horse Neck, but New York had not received one acre as yet, as her equivalent. It was time to act. The new statement, one may guess, was prepared by Cadwallader Colden, the last to sign. With him were Francis Harison, Adolph Philipse, and others.

In January, 1724, the King approved New York's Act of 1719 for running the line and gave New York authority to run the survey. In February, 1724, the New York Commissioners went to visit Connecticut by appointment, but after a week of waiting returned. Connecticut sent word bad weather had prevented them, but New York ironically observed "a funeral passed from a place further in Connecticut than some of the Commissioners lived". There ensued a year of stalling by Connecticut, while its London agent resisted with all his might at court. Nevertheless since for the third time the King had acted on New York's side, New York and Connecticut once more appointed commissioners to run the line. To show his good faith Governor Burnet thereupon instructed his constables to stay further proceedings against the constable and tax collector of Greenwich, who had been arrested at Rye for trying to collect local taxes there.

There followed, April 3, 1725, a royal commission to Harison, Colden, Johannes Jansen and Isaac Hicks, authorizing them to run the line. Armed with this power the New York men met their opposite members at Greenwich, April 29, 1725. It was at this conference that Cadwallader Colden proved his statesmanship. In a letter which he wrote many years afterwards he amplified the report which he made at the time. Noting the evident desire of Connecticut men to prolong and if possible to nullify the deliberations, Colden took occasion to draw to one side the leader of the Yankee group. He then in full confidence asked him what lay behind the apparent obstructionism of his collegues. In a burst of frankness the Hartford man told him that he desired to save the people of Ridgefield from losing their improved lands, which might fall within the Oblong. Colden reassured his companion, by promising that no Ridgefield settler should suffer. He thus made good in full Dongan's pledge of forty years before. In entire good faith on both sides the agreement was reached, certainly the first of its kind in New York's history, and a precedent for many other disputes settled by equal magnanimity. Colden agreed to consider their land by "measuring the twenty miles to Hudson's River without any allowance so far as they are conserned. The yielding these small things as a favor to their settlers made them more willingly agree to other things which has given this province twenty times the quantity of land which may be supposed to be lost by strict measure in this part."

As the New York-Connecticut boundary had never been surveyed the Commissioners first ran the original line "at random", as engineers say, and then ran perpendiculars from it every two miles to the new boundary. The new line thus established became the official boundary although it was not the straight line it purported to be, by distances varying from one hundred to three or four hundred feet. In all, New York profited by 2500 acres, and the Connecticut commissioners accepted the line at the time, though trouble was to come from it a hundred years later.

Governor Burnet was so delighted with the outcome of the Greenwich meeting that he asked Harison and Colden to withdraw, and then proposed the thanks of the Board, "for their prudent proceeding upon the said survey".

It was now Connecticut's turn to press for early completion of the full survey, but in fact five more years went by before the survey was made. Poverty was the plea. Then in October, 1730, Connecticut gave permission to run the lines, and on May 14, 1731, there followed what I make bold to call the Treaty of Dover. The indenture names Cadwallader Colden, Surveyor General of New York, Gilbert Willet and Vincent Mathews commissioners for New York and Mr. Jacobus Bruyn of Dutchess, Deputy Surveyor, on New York's part; and Samuel Eells, Roger Wolcott, and Edmond Lewis, Commissioners for Connecticut. The complete survey was then detailed, and deeds for the land given by Connecticut. It was signed at Dover in Dutchess County.

The length of Connecticut's western line along the straight course was found to be fifty-one miles, and not the hundred as originally assumed. As a result the Oblong was widened from one mile to one mile and three quarters of a mile, and twenty rods, or 9570 feet.

On June 15, 1731, deeds for 44250 acres were given to the representatives of the Hawley company, Adam Ireland, John Thomas, and Benjamin Birdsall of Ridgefield, all of whom appear later as Dutchess residents. Jacob Haviland, Jr. comes under the wire separately on June 30 for lots 23 and 10.

And here we pause. We have completed the first phase with the Dongan treaty, affirming New York's right to compensation for the loss of land in the Sound. The second, or Colden phase, carries us to the actual survey and transfer of the land in the Oblong, equivalent to Horse Neck. The first honors of the Oblong go to Governor Thomas Dongan. The second chapter properly belongs to the Surveyor-general, Cadwallader Colden. The stage now widens for our third act.

A whole group of leaders enter the scene, who take the Oblong out of its rural setting, and precipitate it into the colonial struggle. As these men were most of them Scots, with a sprinkling of Dutch spice, and of the Reformed religion, I dare call them the Session. Their critics have called them a Junto, but the word suggests illegality and collusion, things foreign to this remarkable group of well-educated lawyers and merchants, who used the floor of the Assembly, and the bar of the highest court, to win their victories.

Governor Montgomerie, a good Scot, died in the spring of 1731, and Rip Van Dam, President of Governor's Council, assumed office. He it was who duly transferred to Hawley and Company the deeds for the Oblong. Actually, they left out ten thousand acres of the rockiest hillsides and rough valleys as worthless. These soon became known as "The Hoveout Land", and as such became the residence of squatters and penniless tenants who sometimes asked for the crumbs from the masters' table. With the Treaty of Dover, the Province of New York had won its case against New England. Connecticut would continue to hive out, but it would have to do it under the laws of other provinces.

Though the Treaty of Dover marked a setback, it did not divert Connecticut from her manifest destiny of peopling the continent. All would have gone peacefully, and these pages would not be written, if as in the fairy tale one member had not been forgotten in the invitations to the wedding of the Dutchess with the Oblong.

So little did the British government think of their North American provinces, that they had great difficulty in filling colonial offices. Many of the lesser posts went to men who were hardly above the ticket-of-leave level. Among these was

Francis Harison, an ambitious and active clerk, who had by various means obtained half-a-dozen lucrative posts, including the customs and the admiralty. He had served on the commission of 1725, which brought about the agreement at Greenwich; but according to Colden had had almost nothing to do with its success. Nevertheless he considered himself entitled to more than an ordinary share of a council member in the lots of the upper Oblong and on being refused further grant than the two thousand acres voted, he cast about for revenge.

How he came to hit upon James Brydges, Duke of Chandos, remains a mystery. Chandos had supplied Marlborough's army in the Peninsular campaign, and had amassed a great fortune. A born gambler, he even got out of the South Sea Bubble with more than he risked. Francis Harison suggested to him the untold riches of the ore-laden hills of the Oblong. Chandos jumped at the bait, and took it whole. He got his friends, the Duke of Montagu and the Marquis of Halifax, almost equally excited. Chandos got hold of William Cosby, on his way to replace Montgomerie as governor, and enlisted his enthusiastic support. He approached George Clarke, the Secretary of the province with less success, the gentleman seeing no need to give up two thousand acres for a doubtful grant of a higher bribe conditioned upon winning the suit. Clarke decided to play with both sides, and to keep out of the main quarrel.

Meanwhile the Chandos ring won their plea to the King-in-Council. On May 15, 1731, the day after the Oblong transfer was approved, the Council granted to Chandos' dummies, Sir Thomas Eyles & Co., the entire 61,400 acres of the patent. In New York, all unaware, Rip Van Dam for the Governor in council executed the deed to Thomas Hawley & Co. on June 8, for their 50,000. Now let the best men win!

In the Duke's corner we have the soon to arrive Governor William Cosby, an English refugee from debts and other things, among them an unsavory deal in ten thousand pounds of snuff. Francis Harison is his sly second, but Clarke, though friendly, is not to be trusted. But though a weak contender,

Cosby has the all-powerful British backing. To further their cause, young Daniel Horsmanden comes out with a letter of introduction from Chandos, to help them in law. He has great connection; his father is the brother-in-law of William Byrd of Virginia. Horsmanden will soon be Chief Justice.

In the other corner we have James Alexander, heir to the title of Earl of Stirling, to which he would have succeeded if he had not fought for James Stuart the old Pretender. He flits a "wild goose" to America, and being a trained engineer soon becomes surveyor-general, then in the same day he is admitted to the bar, is made Attorney-General of New Jersey. A scientist, correspondent of Colden and Franklin; the latter will win his approval for the Albany Plan of a Colonial Union. A rare soul, witty and wise, and a dangerous foe. One of the Upper Nine Partners, owner of extensive lands in Dutchess, attorney for Beekman and others, no man is better known in Dutchess. His son William "Lord" Stirling of the Revolution was Washington's right hand man, and husband of Sarah, daughter of Philip Livingston. His daughter Mary married Peter Van Brugh Livingston.

His second is William Smith, Treasurer of the Province, an English Presbyterian with a DuBois grandmother. Graduate of Yale, incorporator of Princeton, promoter of the first public school in New York, historian of the Province, Smith adds a wide knowledge of all factors in dispute.

Cadwallader Colden, Surveyor-General, who has carried through the Oblong Deal, is one of the most interesting figures of the century. Graduate of Glasgow, he shares Franklin's interests, but is too much immersed in law and surveys to take a broad view of the popular cause. He takes no part in the fight, but votes with Alexander, whose friend he is. Physician, philosopher, mathematician, physicist, he is the most learned man in the colony. His son-in-law is James DeLancey.

Archibald Kennedy is the third Scot on the Council. He married a Schuyler widow, his son was a Livingston ally. Kennedy once said "nor will any country continue their subjection to another, merely because their grandmothers were acquainted." His own birth was not without rank; his son became Earl of Cassilis.

Two Dutch leaders, Chief Justice Lewis Morris and Council President Rip Van Dam, have been mentioned. They are both extensive holders of Dutchess lands, both opposed to English governors and their arbitrary ways. Van Dam has a personal feud with the new governor, because the salary paid Van Dam after Cosby's appointment but before his arrival is in question.

These men will not be intimidated. They will fight until a party will be formed, which in good time will bring New York into the War of Independence. The Oblong is the symbol of their stiff backbone.

A year passes in preliminaries. We hear from dissatisfied men of Ridgefield, who were not included in the original Hawley group. Apparently Harison works on them, but loses them when Hawley arranges with the town of Danbury to give them a gore to the north of Ridgefield. Harison appeals to Colden but gets nowhere.

Cosby constitutes himself a court of equity to try the case in chancery. Smith denies his right and legality, and Alexander joins him. For this they are disbarred, and Lewis Morris who supports them is dismissed.

Meantime the Duke of Chandos indulged himself in daydreams. He pictured himself as governor, but thought better of it. A principality in the Catskills among the Indians sounded more promising for Chandos fancied his patent ran from East to West. His daydreams persisted until 1735, when a long legal paper from Colden proved a dash of cold water in his face, and the English litigants gave up their case in 1739.

The real battle had got completely out of hand, and no longer concerned the Oblong except as a base of operations. Smith and Alexander had started a weekly paper in New York, printed by John Peter Zenger. Zenger's friend and associate in business, Henry de Forrest the bookbinder, lived near the Cart and Horse Tavern. There Alexander and Wm. Smith met the members of Thomas Hawley and Company, and set up their organization. The company's books of account are still among the sixty boxes of manuscript at the New York Historical Society. For a whole generation the Company was carried on, until all the lots were accounted for. Baptists poured in at the north, and Quakers at the south. The Ridgefield men bought more lots for themselves and their children. In 1743 the Oblong was in its various sections annexed to adjoining towns of Dutchess, and became part of it.

But at first they had to meet Harison. Baulked in every legal way, with the prospect of endless lawsuits at vast expense, and lacking any support from the people of New York, Harison stirred up petitions of protest against Alexander and Smith. They replied with most effective satire. Harison's effusive praise of his own friend, the governor, was ridiculed in an advertisement:

"A Large Spaniel, of about five feet five inches high, has lately strayed from his kennel with his mouth full of fulsom Panegyricks, and in his ramble dropt them in the N. Y. Gazette."

Harison could not take it any longer. He went to Ridgefield and employed William Truesdell to create an incident that might terrify the settlers from their grants. At Harison's expense, according to Truesdell's affidavit, some twenty men were entertained with shelter and sustenance, while they entered fields, trampled crops, and pulled down a house. On the way through Bedford they had "tossed a bum bailey in a blanket".

Apparently, then, Harison wrote an account of "The riots at Ridgefield" to Chandos, complaining that they had been perpetrated on him. Professor Andrews accepts his story, but the writer could find no corroboration of it elsewhere. The upshot was, that Truesdell went to New York to collect from Harison, and the latter, at the end of his tether, and probably threatened by Truesdell, had him arrested at the suit of a Boston creditor. The complaint was a forgery, as James Alexander soon learned after Truesdell got free. With the whole story on the verge of disclosure, Harison threatened Mrs. Alexander with destruction of her house, by an anonymous letter. As Alexander then wrote Morris, "He found himself so pushed in Truesdell's two cases that there was no averting the disgrace but by mine or Smith's ruin."

The Session now fired their toughest shots; they accused the governor of "destroying men's deeds", and of other outrageous acts. But the deeds came first. Property was sacred in those days. If it was not safe, nothing was. Alexander was accused of rousing mobs to action, and things looked threatening. Cosby acted, imprisoning John Peter Zenger, the printer of the paper, by demanding £800 of bail, when his whole estate was not worth £40. Partly as result, the eighth amendment to our Constitution enacts that "Excessive bail shall not be required".

Smith, for denying the right of the governor to appoint a justice "during the governor's pleasure", instead of "during good behavior" (for life) as in England, was debarred from the trial, as was Alexander, who persuaded his brother Scot, Andrew Hamilton, to undertake his glorious defense, and win a unanimous verdict of acquittal, and a most powerful precedent at law for freedom of the press.

A few weeks later Harison left the country, never to return. Chandos turned him a cold shoulder, but finally honored a draft for £200 made by Harison upon his credit. The Marquis of Halifax was kinder, for Harison's daughter married the Marquis' son. The councillor's two worthy sons remained in New York, and had honorable careers. The affair, no doubt, was soon forgotten by all but the Ridgefielders. The Truesdells became residents of Old Dutchess. James Brown, one of the Ridgefield men, followed the case energetically, and helped pacify the disturbed neighborhood. The full story of the Hawley Company would equal in interest the other cooperative venture of Old Dutchess, the Frankfort Storehouse of Catharyna Brett and her partners.

Poor Chandos! All that remains of his grandiose ambition is the immaterial: The Chandos Anthems of Handel and the music the composer prepared for performance at Cannons, his country seat; and a savage attack by Pope, whom he patronized, in the Essay on Taste.

At Timon's villa let us pass a day
Where all cry out, "What sums are thrown away"!
So proud, so grand: of that stupendous air,
Soft and agreeable come never there . . .
Who but must laugh, the master when he sees
A puny insect, shivering at a breeze.

The Chandos claims troubled the Oblong settlers for a few months in 1753. William Kempe, who had won an election as an agent for the Duke of Newcastle, was rewarded in good English fashion with the office of attorney-general of New York. The "Hoveout Lands" caused the trouble. Residents of Hoveout Mountain Land, threatened with eviction, appealed to Kempe for protection. The Attorney examined the records, and scenting a chance at lucrative litigation, he revived the Chandos suit. He did more; he issued a proclamation demanding that all residents of the Oblong apply for licenses under the Chandos Patent. A few, something over a score, of the farmers were scared into applying, thus giving him a cause to plead. Others applied from the "Hoveout" territory, and still others from what Kempe calls the gore,—small bits of land lying west of the new Oblong west line, but not in any other patent. To a Mr. Parkins, representing twenty signers, Kempe asserted the validity of "an undoubted good patent to His Grace the Duke of Chandos of all that tract of land called the Oblong . . . . I shall prosecute according to law all people that have settled except it be under the King's said Royal Patent, and such as will attorn tenants to the said Royal Patentees . . ."

In a long letter to an inquirer in England, William Kempe expanded his views further. He had found that Alexander and Smith had hove out 12,000 acres, some of which turned out better than they had thought. They therefore issued licenses for it, evicting poor people who had become squatters. This had brought threats of violence upon Kempe, but he stoutly said he would defend himself. He also would sue for the "gores", and urged that the heirs of the English patent put their claims in trust for him to defend.

No more has been heard of this suit. His son, John Tabor Kempe, succeeded him, as attorney general, and did not prosecute it. Alexander in a letter to Colden surmised that there was a gentleman in the woodpile, but offered no guess of the identity.

Meanwhile settlers streamed into Dutchess, not stopping at the Oblong. A tripartite division in 1737 of the large Beekman patent was accompanied by the opening of the Lower Nine Partners, and in 1744 of the Upper Nine. The Chandos suit had been given up in 1738, and patents seemed secure. Until that happened, all patents were in danger. From 2,259 in 1731 the population increased to 8,806 in 1746, fourfold; ten years later it increased 60% to 14,148, and fifteen years later still to 22,404, over 50% gain. From the lowest upriver county it was now highest. Nearly all the increase came west into the woods.

There occurred lesser troubles. Richard Sackett of the Upper Nine Partners had settled on his putative "Wassaic" Patent (1703), but could not defend his purchase against the company of Lower Nine. Some of his land ran along the Rombout Patent and caused further trouble. Sackett was very active, as became a New Haven man. In 1704 he was permitted to sell his lots by a lottery. In 1705 he secured a patent for a monopoly of the "Navy trees"; in 1711 he made tar for Governor Hunter. But he died in 1746, and his son, Dr. John Sackett of Amenia, inherited his troubles. When Thomas Woolcot became Colden's tenant in the Oblong Dr. Sackett broke in upon his field, trod out his corn and injured his house. Colden threatened him, but he persisted and got Woolcot lodged in jail for trespass. The net result seems to have been that Wolcott married his sister Margaret, while John sold 3,497 acres to Moses Harris and moved on. Dr. John, one of our earliest physicians, died in Stephentown, but Ezekiel, one of his ten children, served in a Dutchess company in the Revolution.

In 1767 William Smith, Jr., wrote Colden that a new suit had been entered by Philip Livingston against Oblong titles, claiming that the Livingston patent ran to Connecticut, and therefore that the "Back Chimney" belonged to him. Colden replied, perhaps facetiously, that in that case the Oblong should sue him for the whole of his patent illegally taken from the Indians. Livingston at the time had a renewal of his troubles with his own tenants, and did not press the matter. The "Back Chimney" still sticks out defiantly.

In February, 1767, Robert Leake, who had served as quartermaster in General Braddock's fatal campaign twelve years before, appeared before Governor Moore and his council as a petitioner for 20,000 acres of Dutchess land, some of which evidently lay in the Oblong. The Memorial, preserved in the county clerk's office, is a glorious piece of bluff. According to Leake's modest estimate, Henry Beekman and his sisters had 49,000 acres more than his patent called for.

For four years Leake kept his memorial active before the Council. On March 19, 1767, he asked for a survey of the Oblong piece. Unfortunately for him, part of his claim was well settled, in the east part of Poughkeepsie, and many owners petitioned in 1771 against him. He had stirred up the hornets, and the council had too many other worries, to wish to precipitate more ridings and risings in Old Dutchess. After Sept. 10, 1771, nothing further appears for Robert Leake. He apparently contented himself with his large claim on West Canada Creek, one of the loveliest streams in the land.

Ironically, Leake's name is preserved in the Leake and Watts Orphanage, founded by his eccentric son.

The year of this writing marks the centennial, if such it deserves to be called, of the reopening of the Oblong controversy by the State of Connecticut. The best summary of the question appears in a report signed by Isaac Platt of Dutchess as chairman, and by his associates Messrs. Vrooman and Brown, in June, 1860, five years after the new controversy had started. Connecticut continued to dispute, however, until 1881, when the original survey of 1731 was confirmed.

Connecticut insisted upon a wholly new line, on the ground that 2500 acres belonged to her, by the excess in the twists and turns of the "straight" line. New York demurred, because Connecticut had agreed to the line with all its twists in 1731 at Dover, and because if a wholly new line was to be made, the starting point on the Massachusetts should be moved east, since it was manifestly short of twenty miles. By the existing exchange, moreover, Connecticut had received *in fact* 73,000 acres, while New York had received 68,000. Honors were easy.

New York Commissioners found the nineteenth century Yankees no less subtle than their ancestors but like Tam Lyn they held on to the Oblong of 1731 through all her Connecticut transfigurations, until she came back to her original Colden shape.

Interestingly, the final opinion on the legitimacy of the Cadwallader Colden survey was made by New York's eminent counsel John L. Cadwalader, while Connecticut's team of commissioners was headed in 1860 by the Hon. Joseph Hawley. Isaac Platt wrote an opinion as epitaph:

"That the original exchange of lands was proposed by Connecticut.

That all the difficulties respecting it originated on her part, as well as the delays that were most unreasonably and unnecessarily protracted.

That the proposal to run the lines anew, as it had become obscure and in dispute, was made by Connecticut in 1854.

That since its acceptance by New York in 1856 the Commissioners of Connecticut have constantly thrown obstacles in the way of a fair adjustment, by repudiating the original line, and their own proposition, and insisting on a new line.

That three fourths of all the expense, except that of the survey only, has arisen from this cause alone.

That our final efforts to get the Connecticut Commissioners

to unite with us in the survey, were met by a proposition that would have complicated the controversy more than ever.

That we have finished our work in such manner that the rights of both parties have been rigidly respected and there now remains nothing that can form a legitimate object of dispute."

The courageous men of Ridgefield, who entrusted their fortunes in good faith to the New York Session, and who withstood the arts of Harison, Truesdell, Chandos and Co., Kempe and Leake and all the rest, deserve commemoration. With them we add Colden and Wolcott, Isaac Platt and Joseph Hawley, for the peace that now dwells in the quiet and lovely Oblong.

# IV. THE INCREASE

## 14. Blue Laws over the Border. 1735

"NEVER SWAP horses with a Deacon," said Josh Billings. When Josh penned this sentiment, he was the respectable Henry Shaw, auctioneer of Poughkeepsie. He knew whereof he spoke, all the same, for in his youth he had been a regular sledlength Podunk Yankee. He loved horses, and once wrote an essay on the trotter, printed in our local paper.

He spoke for the crowd. Dutchess folks liked the New Englanders, and welcomed them as incomers, but they kept their eyes skinned on matters of business. New words came with their friends over the border, suggestive of traits uncommon among deliberative Dutch: *common,* to denote their democratic affability; *curious* and *clever,* to hint at originality and practical use; *cute* and *cunning,* identifying shrewdness as an attractive quality, to the point of sharpness.

The Yankee itch for property seemed even greater than their own. They even swore by it: "My land," "Good land," "For the land's sake," "Land alive." Their severest critic was one of their own number, the Reverend Jonathan Edwards, who once, in a funeral sermon preached at the grave of his own cousin, a good business man, deplored "a narrow private spirit that may be found in little tricks and intrigues, promote their private interest, to gain a few pounds will shamefully defile their hands, are not ashamed to hit and bite others, grind the faces of the poor, and screw upon their neighbors, and will take advantage of their authority or commission to line their own pockets with what is fraudulently taken or withheld from others." Against such a spirit Edwards waged a concern for "the public good." "The guiding principle of this society will be its welfare, and the most valuable knowledge will be that which threatens calamity for the state."

Such a spirit, and such a corrective, are not peculiar to New England; but the contrast stood out in sharper outline there, against its theocratic view of life. Its society consisted of "the godly", the "heretics", and the unchurched, both law-abiding and law-defying. There appeared to visiting Dutchmen an intensity about life in New England.

David de Vries in 1639 had found Hartford practices "comiical". He succeeded after great persuasion in securing a pardon for the Minister's servant, who was taken to the whipping-post in front of the church for his lashes, for drinking wine with a supercargo at de Vries' invitation. The second "comical" case was that of a young married man, accused by his own brother of incontinency before marriage, who was taken with his wife and whipped, and separated for six weeks. "I frequently told the governor that it would be impossible to keep the people so strict, seeing they come from so luxurious a country as England."

De Vries was also amused to find his own countrymen classed as Egyptians, and the Connecticut people as Israelites. Over a hundred years later John Adams was gratified to find New Yorkers lacking in gentility; "I have not seen one real gentleman, one well-bred man, since I came to town."

But such pleasantries were but ripples on the broad peaceful stream of colonial intercourse. There was every reason to expect violence in this clash of cultures, but in fact the two outward incidents that plagued Dutchess were rather between the haves and have-nots than between English and Dutch. Most of the cases that came to court were between Yankee and Yankee.

On October 20, 1782, Jabez Smith, Lent Farr, Enos Jones, and Jonathan Wilber "did wickedly, shamefully, and unlawfully break the Sabbath and prophane the said day by drinking, wrestling, and frolicking, to the Common Nuisance of all the Good People of this State, and against the Peace of the People of this State and Their Dignity". William McCullough of Charlotte Precinct, who had witnessed against them, brought suit ten days later against Lent Farr, who "did beat, wound, and ill treat the said William, so that his life was greatly despaired of". Evidently the Yankees thought it unmeet that a Scotsman should inform upon them.

On another occasion a Netherlander intervened on behalf of a rollicking Yankee. In November, 1771, at a "frolick" at Sarah Lossing's, William Warren, Thomas Quick, and David Hackey arrested Henry Chase. Peter J. Lossing went after the crowd, crying out "Are you a Rogue?" Warren expostulated upon this charge, "Will you listen to Reason?" Whereupon Henry Chase broke loose and escaped.

Isaac Gage, Daniel Gage, and Joel Jones of the town of Washington, on December 21, 1791, "did agree to run their horses, notwithstanding that so doing would occupy the whole street, and did drive [each man] his two horses with great violence and speed eastwardly up and along the publick highway [between Poughkeepsie and Pleasant Valley] for more than three thousand yards, and collided with a wood slay driven by one John, a servant of Gilbert Livingston's, and with the tongue of a slay did wound a horse."

(Passing over the indictment list at this time to a brother attorney, Zephaniah Platt, the doughty Revolutionary leader, wrote on the outside of the complaint, "little bob is in briches." A human pride worthy of commemoration after 165 years!)

One of the consequences of the Blue Law spirit was the licensing of taverns. Timothy Canfield, Samuel Sutherland, Joseph Mabbett, and Samuel T. Smith were on the same day licensed, each by depositing a bond of fifty pounds, that "he shall not, during the time that he shall keep a public tavern, keep a disorderly Tavern, or permit any Cock fighting, gaming, or playing with cards or dice, or keep any Billiard Table or other gaming Table, or Shuffle Board within his said Tavern or within any Outhouse, yeard, or garden thereunto belonging."

In the many documents dealing with counterfeiting, British

names prevail overwhelmingly. According to a New York newspaper item in 1761, a silversmith named Hamilton was jailed in Poughkeepsie on suspicion of coining Spanish milled dollars, but hanged himself with his handkerchief, by making it fast to a spike in the jail wall. Hamilton was a fugitive New York artisan. As early as 1739, New England counterfeits were found in the hands of Samuel Flood and Joseph Steel. On October 4, 1768, William Stephens of Beekman was arrested for passing a counterfeit bill of forty shillings. Phinneas Miner of Beekman, on September 1, 1763, was indicted for the forgery of a bond to himself as of Stonington, Connecticut. Stephens was identified as the son of Peter Stephens of Old Fairfield in Connecticut. On January 4, 1779, Joseph Ogden was bound by warrant to appear for passing forty shillings. Some of the money is still to be seen in the County Clerk's files.

From a center somewhere in western Connecticut money slipped over the border. Sir Charles Hardy was asked by the Governor of Connecticut to permit Yankee sheriffs to enter Dutchess after the counterfeits. In one case at least, coiners were enticed back across the boundary and jailed.

British intelligence seems to have learned of this activity, and to have exploited its possibilities in adding to the embarrassments of the Americans in maintaining their currency. In one instance at least a Dutchess Tory was thus employed by a British agent. This is the case of William Ross of Dover, whose deposition, together with $270 in counterfeit money in sheets of fifty and forty dollars, and $240 in separate bills of $50 and $40, are in our County Clerk's office.

Ross had been apprehended in Connecticut by Walter Lathrop, Constable, on order of Jedediah Hubbel, Justice of Litchfield County; and had been escorted to the Division line for extradition. His confession, here first printed, is left in its own punctuation and grammar for the color of the time.

. . . "the said Ross Lift home the 10 or 12 of August last (1781) with an intintion of going to france with Doctor Lee of Windham, and Mr. Cambell of Mansfield but they was a going in a letter of marque and should not sail so soon as Expected. I went from there to Brookfield and from there into the edge of New Hampshure with some horses with three horses to make sail of two which he says he made a sale of to Capt. Cutler, from there he sot out for Bedford in Massachutes state where I had some Relations on the Rode. there met with Capt. Jenkings, Enquired of him where he knew of any Vessel that was a going to sail soon. He said Capt. Roland was a going in a letter of Mark and to sail soon. On the whole I chose an other, to sail with Capt. Simpson because I would have the priviledge of a Traght [recess, vacation] and went to Old Town in Marthas Vineyard to procure Fish there met with a man from Block Island who told me he could procure me fish if I would go for them in which I hired a Boot for that purpose and sailed. When we saw a cruezer whether British or American could not tell. She gave chace and took us and carried us on Bord Admiral Arbuthnot's Fliet & put on bord the Royall Oak. Remained there two or three days. Capt Passford the Pilot of the Admirals Ship was acquainted with some of my Relations in N York. The Fliet was under sailing Orders he obtained or interceded for me so that I got paroled & Leave to go to New York. I tarried in New York some time and applied to Mr Mabbet Caine to get my paroul up under a pretence of Carrying. They Applyed to the Commandant for that purpose and used the Arguments of my being a person that had niver ben away and a Cripple and that I might Tarry and Merchandize. The Commandant sent me to the Mayor who took up my parool and gave leave to tarry in the City. At the same time I was determined to make My Escape if I could and mentioned to the men that went with me to the Commandant. After Tarrying a few days I obtained Leave of the Mayor to go to Bargin, when I attempted to Escape but was prevented by the padrouls, from thence I Returned to York in order to attempt an Escape by way of Long Island & Obtained a pass to Lloyds Neck thru a cousen of mine, procured a Whale Boat for three pounds to put me on Connecticuts shore I landed at Stratford from thence I proceeded home

Arrived the Day before Christmas the next Day reported myself to Col Morehouse was unwell some time at the Widow Chace which was two or three weeks. From thence went to Clauverick was there some time Collecting My Debts from thence to New Concord there Contracted for Six Thousand pair Cards from thence I returned to Kent towne Two Nights went to Boston State to Town called Sutton to collect money Returned to the State of New York from thence to Kent from there to Newtown was on my way to New Concord when I was taken.

"As to the money those Bills that are in sheets I had of Bennet Beaisely of North Fairfield. Those that are cut if they are of the same Emission it is likely I had of the same man. I had between Eight and Nine Hundred Dollars of him at one time which was on Wednesday Last

William Ross."

Filed with the counterfeits is a letter to a Dutchess justice, from Captain E. Hill of the Connecticut militia.

"Kent June 3, 1781.
Dear Sir,

I understand that Wm. Ross is under Bonds for his appearance at Court and as tory measures are always pursued in a dark Intricate Manner as best agrees with their perfidious designs I should consider myself as rendering asential Service to My Cuntrey if by any means I should be an Instrument to unfold their Hellish Plots. I was a member of a Courtmartial before whom Benet Bazeley was tryed it appeared he was one of the greatest Vilians on Earth. In the course of his tryal it appeared that two horses were left with him by two men that he had Conveyed to the Island. He told the Court how he disposed of the Horses one he sold to Wm Ross having previous knowledge that Ross had been taken up. Alltho it was foryn from his tryal I asked him where Ross lived he said in Dover. And what for a Limed Man Ross was. he discribed him as being Lame, & C. By that I knew him to be the same Ross. There was also a Letter found upon one Kitty Bolewin that he was

Conveying to A person on Long Island. and I heard Part of the Letter Read. the wrighter says: there is a hell of a Rought Baizley is taken up but Friend Ross is well. I thought this might Posably be of Service when Compared with other things that might be said or done by said Ross of which you might have Knowledge. This seems to discover something of a Conspiracy between Ross and Bazley However it also seem Unlikely that he should receive Counterfeit Money of Bazley in Payment for an Horse and at the same time Purchase an Horse of Bazley. I believe the Above Mentioned Letter or a Copy of it may be had by aplying to the Honourable Major General Persons. I am altho unacquainted with your Person but not with your Caracter

Your most obedient humble servant
E. Hills, Capt."

John Chamberlin, Esq.
Oblong.

But while the lawbreakers of New England made trouble for thinly settled Dutchess, the burden was far outweighed by the great groups of peace-keeping people who crowded on from Salisbury and Kent into their fertile Egypt, the valleys of the Ten Mile and the Croton. Foremost among these were the Quakers from Purchase, New Fairfield, and Rhode Island. First on Quaker Hill in the Oblong, then hiving out into the Beekman Back Lots into Oswego, they moved steadily up the Wappingers and Fishkill valleys into Nine Partners. For a century their concerns and questions pervaded the sober minds of Dutchess people.

Next to the Friends must be enrolled the Baptists, who entered Dutchess chiefly from the north, and settled in Amenia, Dover, and Pawling. They were both of the "General" and "Separate" persuasion, but not until the rise of Methodism were the churches of a denominational character. They were all dissenters from dissent.

A third group from New England can scarcely be called a group at all. They were individual deviants, unchurched and therefore in New England disfranchised, sceptics no doubt but averse chiefly to the politics of the elect. Many of them, with Baptists and New Lights, went in crowds to hear George Whitefield, and joined willingly in establishing union churches in Pine Plains, Amenia, and elsewhere.

The Rev. Elisha Kent brought his parish over as a Presbyterian church. Of all the thousands of immigrants from Congregational New England, not a single Congregational church has survived intact.

Along with their religio-political form of government the incomers gave up several salient features of their culture. When we contrast Dutchess with the later settlement of Vermont we note that the English village names of Connecticut and western Massachusetts, so frequently duplicated in the Green Mountains, did not affect Dutchess at all. With the sole exception of Dover, the origin of which is obscure, but certainly preceded the rush of settlers, there is not a New England name among our villages dating from this period. In Vermont there are Bethel, Stockbridge, Windsor, Woodstock, Norwich, and many others, in Dutchess we have only the Dutch custom of neighborhoods named for a family: Moore's Mills, Hart's Village, Crouse's store. There was no homesickness in the settlers' minds.

The Dutchess gravestones furnish an excellent record of the church groups as they moved over the Harlem valley and slowly filled up central Dutchess as far as the Upper Nine Partners. In the south precincts, too, they followed the valleys westward, taking up land vacated not long before by Indian neighbors.

The eastward movement did not wholly cease. Palatines and Dutch entered the Harlem Valley and moved south. In Beekman, the Dutch and English strains were completely mixed. Intermarriage followed, and by 1800 the Dutch tongue was seldom used, while the Yankees were thoroughly Yorkified to outward appearance. In addition to the major services of Friends, Baptists, Methodists, and other religious groups, the New Englanders made great social and political contributions. Village and town organization developed, and greater cooperation became evident. The settlers of Beekman called for additional constables to patrol the hills and dales of that wild region. The villages of Amenia, Dover and South Dover, Pawling and Patterson sprang up. Schools rose here and there, with English-speaking teachers. Roads began to multiply, to carry the grain westwards to the river landings.

Organized resistance to bad landlordship begins at the north and south of the county, and goes so far as to imperil the entire leasehold system. Though bound up with unsavory land jobbers and unscrupulous liquorsellers, the movement is alive with bold deeds and united arms, and furnishes a shabby prelude to the Revolution.

The energy and ingenuity of the leaders in these and other protests are good auguries that leaders will not be wanting in sterner times. The names of Sackett, Platt, Harpur, Benson, Kent, Kane, and many more show which way the choice will fall. Without New England names the county might have gone Tory.

In arts, New England's wooden-house-buildings, village streets, churches, and schools have prevailed over the more artistic Dutch stone houses and Flemish barns. In industries, Yankee inventiveness brought fame to Dutchess. When the *Monitor* was launched, a Dutchess Yankee named Worden commanded it, a Dutchess builder named Winslow had had much to do with its making, and a Dutchess inventor named Timby had patented its revolving turret.

On the other hand, the slower pace of Dutchess life improved the restless Yankee temperament. Puritan ideals had already been modified; they underwent still further change. Country life in Dutchess seems to have been gayer than elsewhere. Certainly its prosperity was enjoyed but not squandered.

In contrast with western counties almost wholly settled by Yankees Dutchess kept her steady pace untroubled by the lack of increase after the county agriculture had reached saturation. It was content. It did not decrease as did the hill counties of western New England. When increased scientific techniques came, the county was ready to exploit them, well supplied with capital and with intelligent labor.

The insweep of the Yankees upon Dutchess was prelude to the westward drive. The sons of Dutchess went forward with the rest. New England men claim the making of the midwest as their triumph. But the midwest culture is a blend of many cultures, which began in Dutchess to assume the characteristics typical of the later Americans. It is less stiff, less conscious, less critical; more easy-going, trustful of common human nature. New England has made its own great contribution. It has blended well with other great cultures, by learning to adapt its eccentricities to the general welfare.

The expansion of New England began in Dutchess County. For seventy years before the Great Migration began which filled up western New York, the Western Reserve in Ohio country, a steady flow of Yankees (Dutch *Janke,* "Johnny") here made their first contribution to a "foreign" province. Taking the census at the nearest available twenty-year periods, we have:

| | |
|---|---|
| 1737 | 3418 |
| 1756 | 14148 |
| 1786 | 32656 |

Nine Partners, Beekman, and Philipse Patent were their old stamping ground. Thomas Taber sent his wife and children on a barge with household goods upriver, but himself trudged with his oxteam over the hills and was settled before 1737. Thus started the great trace that ended only in San Francisco Bay.

# 15. My Heart Is a Book. 1741

CHRISTIAN HENRY RAUCH, a young Silesian, landed in New York one day in the summer of 1740, and put up at a tavern. On July 16 he met Frederick Martin, a companion in the Moravian fellowship. Martin had bad news for him. The mission in Savannah, to which Rauch was to be assigned, had collapsed in complete disaster. Ripples from the War of the Austrian Succession, begun in that year, had reached the quiet American shores, and the English settlers had attacked the Spaniards of Florida. Between them lived the Cherokee nation, whom the Moravians had come to serve. But the Indians, with no interest in the conflict, had decamped into the uplands. The Moravians could not follow. The English, aroused, demanded of them an oath of allegiance and aid in the war. Both were completely unpalatable to the Moravians. They did not lack courage. John Wesley, their fellow-passenger during a Hatteras hurricane, had seen them quietly praying when the crew and other voyagers had panicked. But they gave no oaths, and they were pacifists.

There was nothing for it but to give up, and wait for their leader to tell them God's will for their next service. Nicolaus Ludwig, Count of Zinzendorf and Pottendorf, Dresden-born and forty years of age, educated in Lutheran universities, had created a militant order of young people ready to go where he might send them. "Will you go to Greenland tomorrow?" Zinzendorf asked a young missioner at Herrnhut. "I will if the shoemaker has finished my boots," he said.

Frederick Martin left his companion for Ally, near Reading in Pennsylvania, where a mission had begun. Zinzendorf had bought land there from George Whitefield, whose evangelizing tours in New England had sharpened differences in the Puritan world into strife. Already Moravians were viewed askance as possible allies of that dangerous innovator.

Christian Rauch lingered at the tavern. A vision had come to him. He had engaged in conversation with two Dutchess County Indians, Wasamapa and Shawash. They were Mahikans of Shekomeko, he learned, dwelling on either side of a beautiful lake, which the white men in their wisdom had split right down the middle. Its eastern bank fell with Connecticut, its western with New York. Yankees and Yorkers hated each other most cordially, but the Indians remained of one tribal government, neglected and bewildered. Just north of their little lake, across another troubled boundary line, lay Massachusetts, where their kinsmen had set up their camp-fire on the right bank of the river Housatonic. They, too, were slowly losing their land. Jacob Spoor, a Palatine whose cousins lived at Rhinebeck, lived among them.

The Mahikans were sunken in profound despair. Their Iroquois enemies, armed with Dutch guns, had driven them from the Hudson valley. Now the English from the east were taking the rest. Three years before, Shawash, or Shawasquo, had agreed to the sale of the Nine Partners tract in Dutchess. Livingston Manor was already gone. Nothing was left but a few hundred acres round the lake and Shekomeko Kill, which Richard Sackett of the Nine Partners had promised should be theirs without disturbance. But settlers were pouring in, and their livelihood seemed in danger. They had come to New York to get justice, and failing to get it, they got drunk.

Here, then, was Christian's mission, brought to his very door. Just as the light came to him, the Indians' money gave out, and they paddled back to Rhinebeck on their homeward trail. The patentees of Upper Nine Partners were about to split up their lands, and their hunting was lost.

Christian had secured from them, in a sober moment, consent to his companionship on the home trek, but they fooled him at the last, and left him in the lurch. Nothing daunted, the boy set out, and somehow made his way upriver and over Sepasco trail to Shekomeko and Indian Pond.

What he found appalled him. On the Dutchess side of the pond, in the chimney of the Oblong, a few Palatine Germans had ventured, clearing a little land, and drifting back to a life scarcely less savage than that of their neighbors, with no stores, schools, or churches. The land was still unsurveyed, and no man knew where his land ended and Indians' land began. To make matters worse, on the Connecticut lived the landmongers, refusing to recognize the boundary line surveyed only eight years before, which had taken the Oblong from them. The Massachusetts line, still completely fluid, left settlers free to plant where they pleased, so long as they signed a Livingston lease; which meant nothing to them, for they often signed a Massachusetts lease for the same land. Around Stockbridge a family called Williams had gathered like vultures, grabbing and grafting the land up and down the Berkshires. The words are borrowed from Perry Miller, the latest New England historian of the region.

The landjobbers got the Indians in debt to them for the liquor to which they were enslaved, and signed their names to false deeds. This was of course standard practice, but the Dutch and Germans did not approve it. Fourteen years later, at Albany, the Netherlander John Henry Lydius and his Yankee patrons received deeds from Iroquois chiefs to the Wyoming region in Pennsylvania by means which Conrad Weiser denounced, and which brought war and massacre later.

It was not such distant foreboding that troubled Christian, but the miserable plight of the little tribe. They were besotted and starving, in a rich and lovely scene. In their wild ragings they threatened his life, and once an Indian about to tomahawk him fell into Shekomeko brook just as the blow was to fall.

Christian could take no more. He wandered off from the hillside at Shekomeko. At the farm of a Palatine, John Rau, he found a welcome. Rau said; "I will take you in, if you will teach my children, for we white men are as vile as the Indians." So for months Christian Rauch lived with his German friends, teaching children and helping on the farm. Now and then he slipped back to the Indian village, giving lessons to some of the Indian children who had come to love him. One of his pupils, Jeannette Rau, was to marry a future fellow-missioner, John Martin Mack.

At last his patience and devotion began to win friends. His fourth convert was the chief Wasamapa. Early Moravian narratives have preserved the words in which the old man told his story. Through them something human still shines.

"Brethren, I have been a heathen and have grown old among the heathen; therefore I know how heathen think. Once a preacher came to us and began to explain that there was a God. We answered: "Dost thou think us so ignorant as not to know that? Go to the place whence thou camest.' Then another preacher came to us and began to say, 'you must not steal, nor lie, nor get drunk,' and so forth. We answered 'Thou fool! dost thou think that we do not know that? Learn first thyself, and then teach the people to whom thou belongest to leave off these things, for who steal or lie or are more drunken than thine own people?'

"And thus we dismissed him. After some time Brother Christian came into my tent, and sat down by me, and spoke to me nearly as follows: 'I come to you in the name of the Lord of heaven and of earth; He sends to let you know that He will make you happy and deliver you from the misery in which you lie at present. To this end He became a man and gave his life a ransom for man and shed His blood for him.' When he had finished his discourse he lay down upon a plank, fatigued by his journey, and fell into a sound sleep.

"I then thought: 'What kind of a man is this? Here he lies and sleeps. I might kill him and throw him out into the road, and who would regard it? But this gives him no concern'.

"However, I could not forget his words. They constantly

recurred to my mind. Even when I was asleep I dreamed of the blood which Christ shed for us. I found this to be something different from what I had ever heard; and I interpreted Christian's words to the other Indians. Thus through the grace of God an awakening took place amongst us. . . ."

The tribe's hostility melted like ice in the spring. Within a few weeks most of them professed conversion and reformed their ways. The news spread that something wonderful had happened to the little village.

That Indians were a religious people some Netherlanders had learned. Here and there, and especially among the Mahikans, religious expression had been manifest. Jasper Danckaerts the Labadist had written in 1680: "I was surprised to find, so far in the woods and among Indians—but why say Indians? Among Christians ten times worse than the Indians—a person who should address me with such affection and love of God." He had also reported the lowest depths: "We heard a great noise, shouting and singing in the huts of the Indians. They were all drunk, raving, striking, shouting, jumping, fighting each other, and foaming at the mouth like raging wild beasts."

We may have here a clue to the alcoholism of the first Indian relations. Liquor induced in a moment the frenzy akin to religious exaltation of the dance. It restored to the Indians a sense of possession by a spirit, of defiance against the destruction wrought in their life.

But Wasamapa kept faith with himself. "Your Bible is true, I am sure; the experience of my heart tells me the Bible is true, for my heart is also a book." He said this at a meeting on Buttermilk Pond, where his friend Christian Rauch and a newly-arrived colleague, Godlob Buettner, attended. Frankly as a child Wasamapa told his friends that his wife's mother was his chief opponent. "She told me I was worse than a dog if I believed no more in her idol, but my eyes being opened I understood that what she said was altogether folly, for I knew that she had received her idol from her grandmother. It is made of leather and wampum, and she being the oldest person in the house made us worship it, which we have done until our teacher came."

At the end of 1741 Rauch and Buettner took the first converts to Ally for baptism by Zinzendorf, who had come to America. The Shekomeko mission was strengthened; Martin Mack worked at Kent (Schaticook), Joseph Shaw worked with him. Pyrlaeus and Senseman prepared themselves to become apostles to the Iroquois, some of whom lived at Stockbridge.

Next year Zinzendorf and his beautiful daughter Benigna visited the Taconics. The Count described the Sepasco trail as dreadful, but he found a wigwam "the most pleasant dwelling I have ever encountered". He returned to Bethlehem in September, taking two more Indians with him, whom he baptized on his arrival. Wasamapa lost his own beautiful name, and became John. Shekomeko Indians assisted the Moravians in the conversion of the Delaware nation, which had been unfriendly.

At Kent John preached by symbols. Mack tells how John took a piece of wood and with charcoal drew a heart upon it. Strings and points proceeded from it in all directions, indicating the temptations. "With the Indians this simple figure tended more to illustrate his discourse than the most elaborate explanations". It must have delighted the Moravians, educated by the *Orbis Sensualium Pictus* of their great teacher Comenius.

The Christian townsfolk anxiously questioned John about the prospect of war, now threatening from Canada. "There are tidings enough", said John, "but the tidings that interest me are the tidings of our Lord Jesus Christ."

Under the shadow of Poconnuck Mountain, above Indian Pond, a white church sprang up, and white converts joined. Other white Christians held Moravian services along Sepasco Trail. Godlob Buettner married a Palatine girl, Pyrlaeus an Indian girl, who joined Jeannette Rau in a little colony.

The good news spread to Stockbridge, Sharon, and Salisbury. Congregational clergy became alarmed. Spurred by the landgrabbers and liquor-dealers (if we may trust Zinzendorf) a persecution began.

Perhaps if the communion of Brethren had been a little worldly wise they would have listened to the ancestral voices prophesying war, that had not interested John Wasamapa.

For the Third Intercolonial War now fell upon the provinces. King George's War, they called it. The English king took the field in Germany bravely enough, but he did little to aid his American people. New York militia embarked on the unlucky expedition to Cuba, and few of them returned. Others fled from the fiasco at Savannah. Albany was threatened, and Algonkians invaded the Berkshires.

It was not unnatural to suspect that this strange man Zinzendorf, with his German speech and secret sway over Indian hearts, was venturing near the frontiers of war with no good purpose. It was not difficult for a few agitators to create something akin to panic among the people of New England and the Oblong.

One Thomas Lamb of Sharon led their forces. He claimed lands on the Indian Pond, now called Gnadensee (Wechquadnock, in Mahikan). The town of Sharon in 1742 reported that Lamb asked more land than he had contracted for, and suggested a Christian mission to the Indians. The Williams family at Stockbridge were quick to act on the suggestion. In 1744, at the house of Rev. Solomon Stoddard in Northampton, Stoddard's grandson Jonathan Edwards helped to found the mission at Stockbridge which his cousins the Williams then used as an ambush in their landgrabbing. Edwards himself, driven from Northampton, ministered to the betrayed Indians at Stockbridge. He would have loved Wasamapa, who had departed for Bethlehem.

Zinzendorf wrote in 1749: "Some years since, (by an almost evident instigation of the Colonial clergy and a mean sort of people who through their ignoble disposition easily take occasion thereto) there has in the American colonies arisen an evil custom of disturbing and burdening honest men of all sorts who have settled there, hoping to enjoy an unrestrained freedom of religion."

This is fair enough. Baptists and Quakers, New Lights and Presbyterians could certainly subscribe.

But if the Moravians knew this, why did they not arm themselves accordingly, seeking the defences of the law?

Speaking German, crossing from colony to colony without local license to preach, dwelling in Pennsylvania in the style of the early Christian community of goods, obeying a leader with unparalleled devotion, acquiring the Indian tongues, initiating new white churches—all this was enough to alarm the clergy of the Housatonic Valley. Their priests had no salary, no home; they planted corn and wheat like the Indians, or St. Paul. From the common stock at Bethlehem came their clothes and other necessities. What was to become of the parson's lot in the village, his house and tithing?

Indians were beginning to gather from points a day's journey distant, to attend their meetings. Wamponoags and Pequots were among them. The year 1743 marked the height of interest and acclaim among the visitors.

In the spring of that year the first communion was held at Shekomeko, in a ritual of the first century that must have pleased the Indians' poetic sense of nature. The love-feast preceded it, and washing the believers' feet followed. Three months later, in July, a new chapel was consecrated at the village, now named Bethel. Sichem was near it. With exquisite tact, the Moravians finished the house of God with a bark veneer, though it was of permanent construction. Thirty by twenty feet, it was overcrowded from the first, nearly two hundred standing where a hundred had room.

Here old Wasamapa John preached. He is described as having looked more like a wild bear than a man, but now stood majestic and tall, still the trusted counselor of the tribe in all things. "I am like a piece of wood in His hands. He may force me according to His pleasure. His word is sweet to my taste. There are men who say the Bible is a hard book, but I have not come so far. It is all sweet and easy. I am waiting patiently till I shall come to the hard part."

John Weiser, Conrad's father, who had been justice of the peace at East Camp, in his old age had returned to spend his last days among his old friends of the Palatine pilgrimage. But his son Conrad was now a prominent and successful leader in Pennsylvania. He journeyed one day in 1743 on a visit to the old Palatine, and spent some time at Shekomeko. His testimony is of great value, for Conrad, the skilled interpreter and Indian agent, was then the best informed man in America on things relating to the Tawny People. He was so greatly impressed by what he saw, that he joined the Moravian Church.

"Their old people sat in the assembly, some on benches and others for want of room, on the ground, with great gravity and devotion, and harkened to Brother P-(yrlaeus), as if they would *hear* the words out of his very heart. The saying 'Jesus Christ the same yesterday, today, and forever', came quite fresh and alive in my heart when I saw the patriarchs of the American church sitting there as so many witnesses to the atonement of our Lord Jesus Christ."

Some memory of Shekomeko lay thereafter in this great man's labors for peace between the colonists and the Indian nations. Through the long and troubled story of twenty years Weiser stands almost alone to redeem the stained honor of the European in his ruthlessness.

There came at this time also young Teedyuscung (who-makes-earth-tremble). A Delaware shoemaker from New Jersey, he was to become famous as "King" of the Delawares and leader in their war to wipe out the stain of "women" that had been put upon them by the Six Nations. He professed his conversion and was baptized as "Gideon", though afterwards he was known to the Quakers as "Honest John". Tall and handsome, he put his education to account in developing his oratory, and in strengthening his body for the great trails he made among the Lenape nations, building up a confederacy in Pennsylvania. It was Teedyuscung who welcomed the Mahikans later when they came to him in their wandering. The Munsis of Orange and North Jersey also found him their protector. His story is a tragic one; if the Shekomeko mission had survived it might not have been so.

There was no more reason then for the destruction and expulsion of the Indian than there is now. When we talk of eighteenth-century enlightenment let us remember that men like Philip Schuyler and Conrad Weiser, whose houses were open to the tribesmen day or night, were rare exceptions.

Another witness to the influence of Shekomeko comes from another direction. In April, 1744, Josiah Ross, of Mt. Ross on Roelof Jansen's Kill, in his bill for services as surveyor of the Upper Nine Partners patent, wrote "to Mr. James Alexander and Company: after I came from New York last winter, hearing that the Indians would not Suffer the Lands to be Surveyed, I went two days to know and speak to the Indians, and found to the contrary as [to what] Mr. Sackett informed me". Ross's statement precedes a bill for petty items furnished by John Sackett for the survey. Sackett's father, Richard Sackett, was then still living, but his son represented him on the Upper Nine Partners committee that affixed their signatures to Ross's account.

All the more significant is Ross's further statement:

"There is several other small articles Mr. Sackett just put me to it, but I scorn to take it."

Again at a later point in the bill: "Mr. Hoffman (Martinus Hoffman, J P and a leading man of the district) asked me for the money what Mr. Sackett had of him in rum and Blankets and Sundrys for the Company which Mr. Sackett has not payed, and when I do not know."

Along with the bill of Josiah Ross in the ancient documents lies the only local accusation against the Moravians and their converts that has been found. It confirms the statement of Ross that in 1743 John Sackett was spreading false rumors that the Shekomeko Indians were in a riotous and dangerous state, making the neighborhood unsafe even for a party of armed surveyors. As these documents have been hitherto unknown no apology is needed for their publication in full.

"Be it remembered that on the Twentyeth Day of June Anno 1744 Personally appeared before Lawrence Van Kleeck Esqr one of his Majesties Justices of peace for said County Mr Richard Treat of Dover in said County being Sworn on the Holy Evangelist of Almighty God Decleared,

That he that Deponent sometime last Novr- had some considerable discourse with a white man unknown to the deponent who told the said deponent that he was one of the Moravian Instructors of the Indians at Checkomecho. The said Deponent declared that among other things he told the said Moravian Instructor that he had heard that the Gouvarnour of New York was about to take Cognizance of them the Moravians. He the said Moravian reply'd what have I to do with the Govr- of New York? I have nothing to do with the Gover*nour* of New York, nor has the Gover*nour* of New York anything to do with me. The Said Deponent further asserted that he the Said Deponent said there to the Said Moravian That is strange. What? have you nothing to do with the Governer of New York nor has the Govourner of New York any thing to do with with you? would you not be glad of the favour of the Govenour of New York? Said the Said Deponent I am sure I should be glad of the favour of the Govourner of New York. and why should you not be glad of it as well as I? The Said Deponent declared that the said Moravean replyed thus I am authorized by the ArchByshop of Canterbury and therefore I have nothing to do with the Governer of New York nor has the Govourner of New York any thing to do with me and further saith not

Richard Treat

Sworn before me the<br>
day above<br>
Louwerens Van Cleeck—"

"The Day and Date above written Likewise appeared Mr John Sackett who deposeth that the person unknown is to the Best of his Knowledge & by all probability his name is Joseph Shaw and knows him to be a Moravian Instructor and further saith not.

John Sackett

Sworn before me
Louwerens van Cleeck"

Dutchess ) John Sackett of Dover in said County of full age
County ) Deposeth on the Holy Evangelist of Almighty God that he the Deponent Some time last winter heard one Hatchetoussick and one Young Poney and a squaw named Hannah say that the Moravian told them that they expected a fleet shortly and Expected 5,000 Moravians & Irish would come over to settle some where on Delaware near the forks and that the English and Dutch had Cheated them of their lands and when that fleet did come there would Come an Army from the West or South West from the flatt heads & another from the North & would drive the Country before them & then they would be masters of their Lands Again and further saith not.

John Sackett

Sworn the 20" day
of June Anno 1744
before me
Louwerens Van Cleeck"

"19" day of June 18" yr.
Hendrick Joachim Senseman of the North East Precinct in the County of Dutchess and Province of New York yeoman personally came and appeared before me Francis Filken Esq One of the Justices of our Said Lord the King the Peace in the County aforesaid to keep assigned and acknowledged himself to be Indebted to our said Lord the King George the Second Forty pounds current Money of the Province of New York and of his Lands and tenements goods and Chattels to the use of our

Said Lord the King his heirs and Successors to be made and Aviese if it shall happen the aforesaid Hendrick Joachim Senseman to make default in the underwritten condition. The Condition of this Recognesance is Such that if with the above HJ. S. shall personally appear at the next General Sessions Here soon to be holden for the . . . at "pogh (keepsie) in the said County on the . . . of October next to and receive what shall . . . be enjoyned . . . by the Court and in the meantime . . be of good behavior towards our Soveraign . . King and all other his Lieje people then the above recognizance to be void and of none Effect or else to Stand in full force and virtues

Taken and Acknowledged the )<br>
day and year above written )<br>
Before me — The King )<br>
Frans Filkin. — v )<br>
Hend. J. Senseman )<br>
verso )<br>
discharged and my fee paid."

A second recognizance, identical with that for Senseman, was issued against Godlob Buettner on the same day. It is in better condition, and names "the third Tuesday in October next" as the date of the hearing.

The Rev. Richard Treat is here named for the first time as the "Dover clergyman" who wrote the letter mentioned in Moravian sources as the main charge against them. He was in sorry company when he leagued with John Sackett in his attack on Shekomeko. His own story may explain why he chose to do it.

Richard Treat (1694-1759) was an itinerant preacher in that age of revivalism. In 1728 he had married Susanne Woodford of Hartford, and had a son who became an early settler of Sharon, and later settled in Spencertown, to which John Sackett also retreated after his failure in Dutchess. It is interesting that the family association lasted so long between the physician and the minister. Undoubtedly they looked on themselves as benefactors of humanity in their slanders on Shekomeko.

Richard Treat taught Indians in Middletown in 1735, and left for Brainfield, Mass., and was dismissed there, unpaid for his services. Between 1742 when he was at Glastonbury and 1748 when he was in Sheffield, his later career has not been traced hitherto. He can now be placed in Dover during the last part of that period, in 1743 and 1744. He received a grant of land in Sheffield in 1751, but did not remain there, for he appeared in Charlemont near Norfolk in 1759.

A grandson, Cornelius Treat, was the hero of a fight against Indians at Ft. Schuyler, (Utica) in 1781. Another grandson Richard, sixth of that ilk, was one of the founders of the Shaker Colony with Mother Ann Lee in New Lebanon. He wrote hymns for their dance ritual in 1784.

Leap and shout, ye living building!
  Christ has in His glory come.
Cast your eyes on Mother's children,
  See, what glory fills the room!
Full of glory, all in motion,
  Skipping like the lambs in May,
Dancing in their sweet devotion,
  How the blessed virgins play!

John Sackett, "practitioner of physique", did not bear a good name in Dutchess courts. He was sued perhaps more often than any other citizen. Cadwallader Colden sued him, as we know, for his violence in breaking in upon Colden's tenant Thomas Wolcott, his neighbor at Wassaic. He was sued for slander by Jacob Van Campen in 1739, and was sued by a woman, Mehitabel Watson, in 1741. His testimony against Hatchettoussick is therefore suspect. Perhaps the poor Mahikan was repeating something he dimly remembered out of Jeremiah. It is true, however, that more Germans did arrive in Pennsylvania during those years.

Sackett was always hard up, never paid his bills, was in trouble year after year. Treat could not find a permanent place for his pulpit. Both men were clever. Treat had been a teacher of Indians; he naturally disapproved of the invasion of Moravians upon the Indian mission field at the Kent reservation so near Dover. His testimony was skillfully planned to excite the anger of Admiral George Clinton, the stiff old blimp who turned out a lieutenant and twenty-six soldiers to stand at dress-in-escort every time he left or entered his stone house at Ft. George in Manhattan.

There can be no doubt that the Dover revivalist was aware of the stir along the Housatonic. He had perhaps instigated it. It needed little enough. The time was explosive.

At Sharon, near the Indian Lake, a woman reported that some Indians in the woods near her house had frightened her. Her shrieks aroused the neighborhood and for a week Sharon men went armed. Such fears could not be brushed off. When the fatal year 1744 began, the French alerted their Indian allies from Maine to Niagara. Saratoga was burned, and Stockbridge threatened. Remembering our own Nisei, we can hardly censure the Valley folk at Housatonic for deciding that the troublesome Moravians must go. At Pechgachgoch (Kent) Martin Mack and Pyrlaeus were arrested by the people, and dragged up and down the river valley for three days, to answer at hearings before justices and their associates the ministers in their civil capacity. The Governor of Connecticut heard of the tumult, and after inquiry ordered them to be honorably dismissed. The Moravians were however put under heavy bond to keep the peace. Already at Catteraugus among the Iroquois, an English clergyman had denounced Pyrlaeus for preaching. Buettner wrote from Shekomeko to Peter Pratt, minister of Sharon, denying that the Indians had arms, and affirming the Moravians' intention to live in peace.

But their very sobriety and poverty were an offense to the Yankees. They needed the Indians to fight for them. Indians from the region had been with them before. Stockbridge was to furnish several hundred in the final struggle twenty years later. Praying Indians were all right, but not the pacifist kind. The murmurs swelled.

By March 1 of 1744 the situation seemed to threaten the peace of Dutchess. Connecticut men never stopped at the border when they had a righteous cause. In New York City during the Revolution they had the nerve to invade the town and destroy a Tory press, long before war was declared. No freedom of printing for them.

Henry Hegeman, justice of the peace of Filkintown in Nine Partners, visited the village. Like Ross before him, he found no truth in the charges flying about. He assured the missionaries that the exemplary lives of their Indian converts put the Christians of the county to shame. He offered beyond the letter of his duties, to help them by a detailed examination of their affairs, with the view of silencing their adversaries. As a justice six miles from Dover, he knew who they were. Unfortunately for Shekomeko, Buettner was absent on a mission, and the younger men did not dare to accept the responsibility. Hegeman took his leave, asking to be informed when their leader should return.

But the storm worsened. The Dover letter was abroad. It charged the Moravians with entanglement with George Whitefield, hated by the Old Light clergy. Whitefield had, it's true, sold Zinzendorf an estate in Bethlehem.

Rumor spread that 3,000 stand of arms were stored at Shekomeko, ready to fire at the helpless Sharonians. On the eighth of June, George Clinton the admiral (never to be confused with the patriot George Clinton, soon to be surveying in York Province) ordered Colonel Henry Beekman, commanding the Dutchess militia, justice, and assemblyman, to go to Shekomeko and make a full examination, and to jail vagrants or other disturbers of the peace. Until the governor's pleasure was more fully known, he was "to cause the said Indians to be dispersed".

Possibly the same instruction was sent to other justices. Before Beekman could make the ride, the Poughkeepsie justice,

Francis Filkin, with his brother the Sheriff Henry Filkin and a posse of eight armed men clattered into bewildered Shekomeko. In spite of their consternation the Moravians received the judge civilly. Filkin "upbraided the priests that they were suspected to be disaffected to the Crown". The Moravians denied it. Like others, they were afraid of the French, for they were Protestants. Their only duty "was to gain souls among the heathens". For this they had a commission from the Archbishop of Canterbury, which they offered to show. Filkin refused to look at it, and cited them to appear in Poughkeepsie on October 16th. This done, "with great civility" the justice took his departure with his eight courageous constables.

Next day Colonel Beekman arrived. Although Poughkeepsie had stolen the march on Rhinebeck, the good man felt bound to make an independent search. He reported to the governor that all he found were four priests and many Indians. No arms, no ammunition, no whispers of any.

In his turn the assemblyman cited the Moravians before him at Rhinebeck for further questioning. Thither went poor Buettner, already ill, and with the rest was courteously entertained by Beekman at dinner. He did not, however, use the Governor's implied wish and authority to put them in jail, or to disperse the Indians. On receipt of Beekman's report the governor ordered the Missionaries to be brought before him the following August. The hearing was before the governor's council. It was a browbeating performance, but the Moravians stood their ground. They turned out to be very simple men, indeed, not even gentlemen like Mr. Treat. How dare a mere carpenter, a baker, and a tailor come into this royal province and start teaching Indians about God, without his Excellency's permission? Poor Joseph Shaw, the carpenter, an English convert, (the same that had told Treat he was authorized by His Grace of Canterbury) announced boldly that he thought New York gave liberty of conscience to all.

When Buettner, the tailor, was asked how he dared go, he said "compassion in his heart for the ignorance and condition of the Indians moved him to come and preach to them". The council minutes suppress the fact, recorded by the Moravian historian Loskiel, that Henry Beekman of his own motion and expense appeared at the trial for the defense, and gave testimony as to the high character of the Mission. "The good done by these men was undeniable", he said.

It is probable that Beekman's word carried weight with the governor's council, for they advised the governor merely to send the Moravians back to their homes to practice their religion according to their tenets "and to conduct themselves in such a manner as not to bring suspicion on themselves".

The Moravians were emboldened to ask the governor for his certificate in writing and this was given them. It was sorely needed, for Hegeman had haled them to Filkintown in July. Dr. Alexander Hamilton's narrative of his day in Poughkeepsie, June 24, 1744, when he met Col. Beekman and Godlob Buettner, on their way to New York, recites for us the popular opinion. The young snob gives us a good glimpse of the public mind.

"The Taylor's phizz was screwed up to a sanctified pitch, and he seemed to be either under great sorrow for his sins or else a hatching some mischief in his heart, for I have heard that your hipocriticall rogues always put on their most solemn countenance or vizzard when they are contriving how to perpetrate their villanies. We soon discovered that this taylor was a Moravian. The Moravians are a wild, fanatick sect with which both this place and the Jerseys are pestered. They live in common, men and women mixed in a great house or barn, where they sometimes eat and drink, sometimes sleep, and sometimes preach and howl, but are quite idle and will employ themselves in no useful work. They think all things should be in common and say that religion is intirely corrupted by being too much blended with the laws of the country. They call their religion the true religion, or the religion of the Lamb, which I believe is true in so far as some of them are wolves in sheep's clothing. This sect was first founded by a German enthusiast, Count Zinzendorf, who used to goe about some years agoe, and persuade the people to his opinions, and drop a catechism which he had published upon the highway."

In February, 1745, Godlob Buettner died at Shekomeko. A monument to his memory stands on the mission site.

On September 21, 1744, the New York Assembly had passed an act, to be valid for one year only, requiring "all vagrants, Moravians, and other suspicious persons" to desist from teaching the Indians and preaching, and to remove themselves from the province. Specifically exempted were all Quakers, Anabaptists, and other sects. Sheriffs were ordered to enforce the law. Our Nisei two hundred years later will understand.

On December 31 Count Zinzendorf addressed the Lords of Trade. He rehearsed the story of persecution. "I petition for two declarations: The one, to keep honest people, as well strangers in, as inhabitants of America, from being chicaned with and plagued, without the least reason. . . . The second, that nobody in the colonies but least of all the Indians shall be hindered from joining any Protestant Church."

The Lords of Trade demanded an explanation from Clinton. His reply is a masterpiece of falsehood and evasion. The Lords thereupon ordered that Moravians be restored to full York privilege. They were so restored, and in 1749 New York City witnessed its first Moravian Church.

But it was too late. Two weeks before Zinzendorf wrote the Dutchess sheriff had already warned the Moravians to leave the county. The Sheriff had delayed for three months before acting, and had then received a direct order from the governor to execute the law at once.

A local sheriff—of "Milsy", in the Moravian narrative, probably Mill Hill, or Hammertown, a later name—dwelling "about four miles from Shekomeko, declared that he would rather suffer his right arm to be cut off, than treat the brethren conformably to the act passed against them, for he was thoroughly convinced that the grace of God had by their means brought miracles in that place".

When the Moravians reached Kingston, on their way to

Tulpehocken, an ugly mob awaited them, and a justice, perhaps for their protection, arrested them. Colonel Robert Livingston, Jr., who came up at the time, ordered the justice to set the Moravians free, and rebuked the mob.

Except for the testimony of Treat and Sackett, Dutchess is not guilty of innocent blood. Livingston, Beekman, Ross, Hegeman, Filkin, and "Milsy", all bore witness to truth and decency. It was not enough.

As Joseph Shaw had predicted at the New York inquisition, the Mahikans wished to follow their teachers into exile; but the governor had forbidden it. In spite of him some families departed, and settled Gnadenhütten in Pennsylvania. Five hundred Indians joined them later. Others led by Martin Mack went further west to Shamokin (now Sunbury).

From time to time, as people returned to their senses, prohibitions were relaxed, and Moravians resumed their visits to the few who had remained. On Indian Lake David Bruce of the mission labored for two years, serving Westenhuck (Housatonic, Stockbridge) also. When the French and Indian War began in 1755 the Sharon people made an end of Gnadensee, and the Indians at Kent suffered with them. A barren strip remained on the river's right bank, where the last indweller died a few months ago.

Abraham Reinke served the white people on Indian Pond, west side, where a monument stands today. Joseph Powell and David Bruce continued at Sichem and Gnadensee. The curtain slowly descended. Persecution and massacre attended the doomed Mahikans in Pennsylvania and Ohio, the last safe haven being at present Fox Lake in central Wisconsin.

# 16. Travelers on Truth's Account. 1750

THE STORY of religion in our county would fill volumes. From its beginning there was never uniformity, the Lutheran Church at Rhinebeck being the earliest, while Calvinist Reformed Churches were starting in Poughkeepsie and Fishkill. The people did not come by congregations, with a minister at the head. Even the Friends' Meetings were at first only missions of a larger group. Churches sprang up, flourished, and came to an end when the neighborhoods went back to woods. Old neglected cemeteries of families and lost churches lie scattered over the county. There were very few settled preachers and these were seldom of any quality. People met as they meet now in the mountains, when a minister came their way.

Missionary enterprise was the chief characteristic of New York, in this respect our province taking its place with those of the Alleghanies rather than New England. "Enthusiasm" was denounced from one end to the other of New England, and the discontent of enthusiasts became a major cause of the Great Expansion. Dutchess County, on whose threshold the expansion began, received the first fruits of this movement.

Baptist, Quaker, and Methodist filled the eastern and central valleys, meeting the Lutheran eastward thrust on friendly terms. Presbyterian and later Episcopal enterprise pushed up the Hudson with increasing population, their strong central organization creating stable churches that often fell heir to the embers of enthusiasm. Their leaders championed Whig and Tory sides in the Revolution, while the others were often against all war. Leaving that story for a later time, this chapter follows the "Travelers" through the woods on their Mission pilgrimage, a not unworthy group. The Dutchess's County has been hospitable to religion. Although this record will mention strife and division, the accent has been chiefly upon harmony. Here the Quakers found welcome and thrived, though they suffered disabilities from the state. Here they first spoke out as a body of believers against slavery in their midst. Here the breach between old and new in the Reformed Church was permanently healed. Here Union churches flourished, one of them occupied each Sunday in the month by a different denomination. Here a great Lutheran healed a sore spot in the primitive churches. Our patentees won the first great legal victory for freedom of religion in New York. They encouraged churches, often giving the land on which the church was built, and not infrequently the church itself.

When the Methodists were building their church in Red Hook, the Lutherans invited them to use their own church. They did so, and the Methodists in thanks gave the pulpit which the Lutherans use today. Such incidents are not infrequent in the history.

In no single element of life was the frontier more limited than in religion. The many Catholics who lived in Dutchess had no regular place of worship for a century. Many churches had no pastors because their church rules required ordination of ministers in Europe. The Episcopal Church was managed from England as a missionary enterprise, and was much involved in the politics of colonial government. In consequence, its churches were closed during the Revolution. Yet one Dutchess Episcopalian took the Continental side and preached to the Congress.

Probably the first regular minister to preach in the county was the Rev. Joshua Kochertal, who preached in 1711 to the Palatines at East Camp. The first Lutheran pastor in America rests under a stone at the foot of the Overlook Mt. not far from West Camp. He was the father of Newburgh, naming it for the Palatine Elector who was of Neuburg in Germany.

"Under this stone rests, alongside of his Sibylla Charlotte, a true pilgrim, who was the Joshua of the High Germans in America, and a pure Lutheran preacher to them, both on the west side and the east side of the Hudson." So runs the epitaph.

To the Lutherans Beekman and Alexander gave land for churches; they were one of Dutch Reformed, the other of Presbyterian religion. Conrad Weiser, the Rhinebeck boy who became the most famous of American envoys to the Indian Nations, had a son-in-law even more famous, Heinrich Melchior Muhlenberg, the founder of American Lutheranism. He, too, came to Rhinebeck in 1750, though but for a short time, in the course of his ministry to the struggling country churches of the provinces.

Muhlenberg's mediation between the austere young minister of the Rhinebeck Lutheran Church and his rebellious parishioners was so far successful as to tide matters over for several years. The great Lutheran church-builder had gone to Rhinebeck with Weiser. In his journal he left a lively account of the ride. The hot days and cool nights brought on a summer chill, and his oversolicitous wife Anna Maria had let blood from two deep incisions. "All in all, a speechless rider with a swollen hand on an old stiff horse presented a sorry figure."

The travelers put up with a Dutch justice of peace who might have come from Dutchess. His custom was to send the litigants out of doors to settle matters with their fists. Further on, in Ulster, they put up with a rude pioneer "of Spanish nation" who refused them supper and told them to sleep in the straw. "He sat in his armchair with great gravity, his six grown sons sitting around him, all of them smoking tobacco with the father and looking like chips off the old block. Weiser's name was held in great esteem wherever we went on this whole journey, but this Spaniard depended only on the wilderness where he lived, and cared for no man but himself."

Dinner in the Catskills consisted of raccoons and pumpkins. Resting a day at Kingston, Weiser pushed on to Rhinebeck with his missionary son-in-law. He was eager to see his old friends of the village where he and his parents had lived when they first arrived. Muhlenberg testified to the cordiality with which they greeted the now famous Indian envoy.

They were no less eager to greet Muhlenberg, and they gathered in a crowd to question him, and to express their hopes for a solution of their problems. Through no fault of their own, the Lutheran Churches of Dutchess had gone through deep waters. In the Rhinebeck region an impostor who called himself Prince Carl Rudolph of Würtemberg had for two years gained their support. At the same time another unfit German, Hofguth, was endeavoring to install himself as the regular minister at Poughquag, and was ousted only after three petitions to the governor for legal protection. At this time there was no general Lutheran organization, no regular supply of ministers from Germany, and no place for the training of ministers. Red Hook and Rhinebeck, and the little groups in the Harlem Valley, Wappinger, Poughquag, Hackensack, and Newburgh were without regular pastors. They met only when Michael Knoll of the New York church came to preach.

In 1750 Pastor Knoll's church in New York was split by a secession, and he resigned. The same group whose names appeared in the petitions soon barred their doors against the new pastor from Rhinebeck, who had taken on the charge of the Lutheran groups in Dutchess.

A document in the County Clerk's office relates that in February or March, 1750, a riotous group including Nicolas Emigh, his son Nicolas and his relatives Philips and Hendrick, and Johannis Berger, David Ballard, Christian Sackrider, Jacob Hass, George Addam Apler and George Johannes Wager, all of Beekman Precinct, had broken by force into the Poughquag church and hindered their minister from preaching. This rumble of a winter storm in southern Dutchess was a forewarning of troubles to come in the north.

John Christopher Hartwig, the center of the controversy, had come from Germany to Rhinebeck at the call of the Lutheran churches in Rhinebeck and Red Hook (Camp). Unfortunately he had sought counsel of Muhlenberg, who was in unfriendly eyes suspect because his wife's father had once been a Moravian. The success of the latter in New York had excited great jealousy, and a late German preacher, Berkenmeyer, had attacked Hartwig both in print and pulpit.

Thus when Hartwig came to Dutchess, where memories of Shekomeko still lingered and Moravian groups worshipped, the congregation divided, with the majority against the pastor. The real trouble lay in the whole situation, where groups of newcomers augmented the Palatines, who spoke neither Dutch nor English, and who without any supply of pastors were trying to preserve the religion in which they had been brought up. It was not, primarily, though it became the point of difference, that any stigma attached to Moravians since Shekomeko. But Muhlenberg, who was one of the most perspicuous travelers for truth that ever lived, analyzed the true root of trouble in the young Europeans' ignorance of America. "Young beginners in this important office of the Ministry do not have sufficient experience and possess more efficiency than insight. They start out vigorously and use European standards which do not always fit the complicated conditions in America. Then the diabolic comes along and begins to use his diabolatry, and the result is a Gordian knot that cannot be untied in many years." Parenthetically, exactly the same words could after two hundred years be applied to most European visitants in ministry, science, and learning today.

Muhlenberg visited Livingston Manor, being well entertained by its lord, but disappointed to learn of the disaffection of the northern Indians whom Weiser now set off to visit. The minister preached at Red Hook, which had suffered from the ministry of the imposter, Carl Rudolph. "I prayed the blessed God to purify this house, to reunite the poor scattered sheep, and to forgive those who had brought in such a blemish and servant of Satan." Those were days when spades were spades. Next the traveler preached at "Tar Bush", evidently one of the old "camps" in tarmaking days of thirty years before.

On his return to Rhinebeck he preached to a large congregation, and held a full conference. He concluded that while Hartwig had been hasty and in error, he had also suffered from great and unfair hostility. He wisely suggested that Hartwig should return with him to Pennsylvania for a six months' leave, and that Muhlenberg's young candidate Rauss should replace him. The suggestion was accepted by the church, and harmony reigned.

The incident is instructive to anyone who wishes to understand the problems of the pioneer church. Hartwig had felt it his duty to forbid marriages between a Lutheran and a Calvinist, though the Huguenot and the German of necessity worshipped together in the wilderness. He preached so long that members who rode home at night could not finish their chores. He enacted obeisance from his people, but gave no friendly salute in return to Rhinebeck "peasants". He refused all advice: "he had come to teach, not to learn." How familiar it sounds! Such a spirit could not thrive in the free-spoken frontier. The people in Pennsylvania objected with equal vehemence to Pastor Hartwig. Those at "Old Goschehoffe" frankly said that he was too strict and hottempered, and they did not want him as their pastor any longer. He had made everybody sign a pledge that "at the beginning of the New Year they would forswear shooting, horse-racing, boozing, and dancing".

"I told Dr. Hartwig that his action was doubtless well intentioned, but . . . that one should first lay a foundation of true Christianity in the hearts of the people." But Hartwig would not learn.

He returned to Rhinebeck, and the inevitable occurred. Unfortunately Muhlenberg's journal for 1754 is very short, but the Rhinebeck documents are explicit. On April 14, according to a grand jury indictment, the Rev. John Christopher Hartwig "did assault, beat, pushed, and kicked out of the church Martin Sitcher of Rynbeck, labourer", and also one "Margert File" of the same place. On April twenty-first in the same church Elizabeth Rykert, wife of David Rykert, swore that she was "at the Lutheran Meeting House" "assaulted and beat with a horsewhip by Johan Christophel Hartwig the Minister of the said Meeting House without any cause as she know off". Her witnesses, and those of the other deposition, composed a goodly number of the respected members: Nicolas Bonesteel, Eva Barberkleinen, Johannis Korns, Susanna Zeberlen, Heinrich Wuderwap, Jeury Tecter, Johannis Klyn, Frederich Scheever, Johannis Toevelt, Wilhelmus Feller.

In 1752, while still at Rhinebeck, Hartwig had endeavored to circumvent the efforts of Orange County men, no doubt aided by Colden, to gain entrance on the Wassaic Patent, originally granted to Kochertal's Palatines for a Lutheran Church, school, and glebe. But the Palatines of Orange fell away to Dutchess and Pennsylvania, and the other settlers took possession of the five hundred acres in Newburgh, and even the church and its fine bell, given them by Prince George. Hartwig's English lawyers advised him to plant secretly a few German settlers who would return and fight for bell and church; but Colden was evidently beforehand with this somewhat questionable project.

Our later views in Muhlenberg's journals picture poor Hartwig in "supply", not in any regular charge. The quiet church at Rhinebeck dwelt in peace thereafter. Pastor Muhlenberg's son Peter became the famous general of the Revolution, and later U. S. Senator.

Freeborn Garrettson of Rhinebeck was the husband of Catherine Livingston of Wildercliff, one of the sisters of Chancellor Robert R. Livingston. Their home on Hudson shore was a haven of Methodism for over thirty years, from 1793 to 1827, when the great preacher died. Catherine lived till her 98th year, one of the best loved of the famous sisters. It was due to their united efforts that Methodists stood first in Dutchess with two-score churches in 1875. For nearly twenty years before their marriage Freeborn had been a circuit preacher chiefly in the South.

But if Freeborn Garrettson was a Dutchess man only by courtesy of marriage, he became a loyal and devoted son. No man did more than he to build up his church in the county. It was his preaching that swelled the little congregation at Rhinebeck until the church could not hold them all, and then set about to build a new church. He preached everywhere in the district, in churches or in the open air to overflowing meetings. It was the time of the Great Awakening, and Garrettson's voice was raised throughout the land, until he was laid to rest on Rhinebeck Flats.

Methodism was started in the English provinces by some Irish Palatines in 1766 (there are, near Limerick, Palatines still to be found). Nine years later Garrettson, at twenty-three, began his ministry, two years after Francis Asbury and Richard Wright had begun their work. In all America there were less than a thousand members of the young denomination. When he preached his semi-centennial sermon there were more than half a million by his count, though he does not specify their bounds. His own choice was simple and unspectacular. "In the forenoon I attended Church, but I could not find what I wanted. In the afternoon I went to hear the Methodists; and something told me, 'These are the people'."

His printed journal is a document in the "varieties of religious experience." We seldom stop to reflect that scenes like that recorded in the page which I copy from the "Life" by Nathan Bangs (1829) were taking place at the very height of the American Revolution, and within sound of the battle.

"As I entered the door (at Ellis Chapel, in the Essex Circuit, Virginia) I saw a man in the pulpit dressed in black, engaged in prayer. I soon perceived he was a man bereft of his reason. I went into the pulpit and desired him to desist. After he ended, I gave out his text, and began to preach. But I had no other way to stop him, than to desire the people to withdraw. His testimony was that he was a prophet sent of God to teach the people; and that it was revealed to him a person was to interrupt him in his discourse. After a few minutes the people returned, and all was still. I then gave out, Feed my sheep; John xxi, 17. I had liberty in showing, I. The character mentioned in the text, sheep; 2, why the followers of our Lord might be called sheep; and 3, how the sheep are to be fed. I. The Shepard; 2, the food; and 3, the manner of feeding the flock. The prophet returned home, and that night he told his family, at such an hour he would go into a trance; and that they must not bury him till after such a time, should he not survive. Accordingly, to appearance he was in a trance. The next day I was sent for to visit him. Many were weeping around the bed, in which he lay like a corpse, for I could not perceive that he breathed. He was happy in God, and a sensible useful man. About the time of which he spoke he came to himself. Satan was partly disappointed; for in some measure he was restored to his reason, and I took him part of the way round the circuit with me. What was the cause of this? Satan prompted him to think of himself more highly than he ought to think; and so he fell into the condemnation of the devil. I had a hope before we parted that his fallen soul was restored. Some time after this he began again to preach Christ; and I trust was more humble than ever."

"I continued on this circuit about three months, had many happy hours, and some distressing ones. Two things were a great distress to my mind: I. The spirit of fighting; and 2. that of slavery, which ran among the people. I was resolved to be found in my duty, and keep back no part of the counsel of God. Day and night I could hear the roaring of the cannon, for I was not far from Yorktown during the siege and the surrender of Cornwallis. Many of our pious friends were absolutely against fighting, and some of them suffered much on that account, for they were compelled, or taken by force, into the field; though they would sooner have lost their lives than taken the life of any human creature. I saw it my duty to cry down this kind of proceeding, declaring that it could not be justified in the oracles of God.

"I was, in a particular manner, led to preach against the practice of slave-holding. Several were convinced of the impiety of the practice, and liberated their slaves: others who did not liberate them, were convinced that they ought to use them better than they had done. Had it not been for these two evils, I might have been more popular among the people.

"I preached at a quarterly meeting at Mabery's chapel, where there were about two thousand present of all ranks; and, being pressed in spirit, I cried, "Do justice, love mercy, and walk humbly with thy God". There were more than a thousand people who could not get into the chapel, and some of those without called for an officer to take me. After meeting was ended, I walked through the midst of them, but no one laid hands on me."

Garrettson was the true circuit pioneer, who preceded that picturesque figure, the circuit rider. What an entertaining contrast he affords, to his Livingston brothers-in-law! Mr. Garrettson's meeting must have been pretty lively at times. "I am never offended at hearing convinced sinners cry aloud for mercy; neither do I doubt but that the children of God are so happy at times, that they are constrained to shout the praises of God." Sometimes, he tells us, there was so much "wild fire" among the people, that the voice of the teacher was drowned. But he preached on, "with strength and freedom", as he expressed it. For the latter phrase he was roundly taken to task by John Wesley, who wrote him in 1789, "There is one expression that occurs twice or thrice in yours, which gives me some concern: you speak of finding *freedom* to do this or that. This is a word much liable to be abused. If I have plain Scripture or plain reason for doing a thing, well . . . I regard not whether I had *freedom* or no. This is an unscriptural expression, and a very fallacious rule." One recalls that the founder of Methodism wrote vigorously against the American cause at the time of the Revolution, but the spectacle of an Englishman, in 1789, telling an American not to use the word *freedom,* because it is "fallacious", is stimulating.

A favorite text of his was: "O my dove, which art in the

clefts of the rock, etc." He says often that he was "sweetly drawn out". But life was not always easy for him. He was stoned, beaten and jailed, and once at Albany only escaped being poisoned by his host's wife, through a presentiment that he should not drink her ale. She wanted to poison all Methodists, she said.

His greatest physical suffering came from a horse, however. It was at Sharon, where he had preached to a thousand souls, and no doubt had had "a weeping time". He went out to the pasture to saddle his horse, and as he grasped the halter-rope the horse jerked his head up, and managed to catch the preacher in the rope-loop, around the waist. He was terribly constricted, with broken bones and contusions, and was for a long time unconscious. This is the first record of a horse's lassoing a man, so far as I have read.

Again and again in his journal Garrettson refers to his happiness at Rhinebeck. "During this tour of about two weeks I had great sweetness in preaching the word. I am now officiating in my little congregation. Here I am pleasantly situated, an agreeable family with everything necessary to make life desirable. This makes it the greater cross for me to leave home." Indeed, he once pleaded with the Lord to let him off, because he was old and deaf. The Lord promptly healed him of his deafness, restored him physically and spiritually, and told him to go on with the work. And on he went, to the very week of his death, in 1827.

In the new church at Rhinebeck he had preached morning, and afternoon, and night, during the revival, until a strong congregation was gathered. He seems really to have loved the place, but he was never happy except when riding the circuit. For fifty years he traveled on horseback through the states, his journeys averaging a thousand miles a year. A nephew took care of his business affairs, for he was not able to cope with them. His portrait at 73 is that of a vigorous, intelligent, and benignant man. Certainly in the later days of the Great Awakening there was none more eager to serve his Master.

The Reformed Church, often called the Dutch Reformed,

ministered at first chiefly to the Dutch-speaking incomers from Long Island at Fishkill and from Albany and Ulster at Rhinebeck and Poughkeepsie. In 1730 Henry Beekman gave two acres for a church-yard and forty acres for a glebe and cemetery, the latter property comprising most of the original village of Rhinebeck and thus answering most effectively the charges of those who thought of him as a landgrabber. About the same time, or perhaps a little earlier, Mrs. Brett and Johannis TerBoss gave a glebe land at Fishkill Village. Poughkeepsie's congregation was organized by the pastor from Kingston on October 10, 1716. The first regularly appointed minister, however, did not arrive till 1731, when Domine Cornelius Van Schie came from Holland to assume charge of both Fishkill and Poughkeepsie. Ordination in Holland, together with the restriction to preaching in the mother-tongue, proved the stumbling-block to expansion. The first recorded deed in the County states the problem unequivocally. Jacobus Van De Bogaerdt gave the church lot into the keeping of Captain Barendt Van Kleeck, Myndert Van De Bogaerdt, Peter Velie, and Johannes Van Kleeck. The deed prescribes that the gift is "for the proper use, benefitt and behoof of the Inhabitence and Naborhod of Pochkepsen aforesaid, to Bild and Maentaen a proper Mietinghouse to worship the one and onely God, according to the Rule and Mathodes as it is agried and concluded by the Sinod National kept at Dordreght in the year 1618 and 1619 and that in the Nieder Dutch Lingo and Manner as it is now used by the Claasse and Churche of Amsterdam: with the banefitt of the Mietinghouse yard for a bureall place of Christian Corps to the same belonging." But by 1740 preachers sometimes spoke in English, although the last sermon in Dutch was not pronounced till 1794.

This colonial relationship involved control from Amsterdam, and created the "Coetus" party in the church, as an American reaction. Domine Schoonmaker, the first Coetus preacher in Poughkeepsie, found himself barred out from his pulpit, and was ordained from a wagon under the apple-trees. The irreverent derive the heavenly flavor of Dutchess apples from this source.

For a time the two parties each sustained a clergyman officiating at both villages, but the Conferencie withdrew to the Fishkill region, including Hopewell and New Hackensack. On April 21, 1765, the Coetus at Fishkill appealed to the Attorney-General of New York for aid. Isaac and Direck Brinckerhoff, Coert Van Voorhees, Gysbert Swank, Hendrick Philipse, Rodolphus Swartwout, Obediah Cooper, and Coenrad Rapalje complained that they had been kept out of their church. "The Conferency have attacked the Coetus, because we of the Coetus Party say for Consiens Saike we cant Soberdenate under any farren Ecclesiastical or Spiritual Power." A dozen years later the sons of these men were the Revolutionary leaders of the district.

John Brinckerhoff was not of his kinsman's opinion. "These people are eating themselves with rebellion, it seems to me, by acting so direct against his Majesty's good laws."

To the honor of the Poughkeepsie church, it was the Rev. John H. Livingston who brought the reconciliation about, and restored peace to his communion. Dr. Livingston later became president of Queens College, later Rutgers University. The Reformed Church was unique in this period, in healing an ancient cleavage.

Among those who suffered persecution in New England none had a harder time than the Baptists. There were many, however, who declined the cordial invitation of the Simple Cobbler of Agawam to depart.

"I dare take it upon me to be the Herauld of New England so farre, as to proclaime to the World, in the name of our Colony, that all Familists, Antinomians, Anabaptists, and other Enthusiasts shall have free liberty to keep away from us, and such as will come to be gone as fast as they gan, the sooner the better."

But when Dutchess was the place of refuge they hesitated no longer. Fishkill in '45 for those who came by water, Northeast in '51, Dover in '57, Stanford in '59, and Separates in the City at Amenia at about the same time, prove the rapid growth of Baptist churches. The later one in Rhinebeck about 1800, was led by Elder Robert Scott of Norfolk, England, the friend and companion of the Vassar family, with whom he came to America in 1795.

Scott had been a Methodist preacher, and served at several English churches from 1782 to 1789. He wrote M. D. after his name, and translated Greek and Hebrew for the Methodists, but he sought America for civil and religious liberty as a dissenter, and for a safe haven from the wars of the day. Landing in New York, he worked as a cabinetmaker until Mrs. Margaret Beekman Livingston chanced to talk with him at his shop, and joined in a theological discussion. She urged him to start a school in Rhinebeck, to which he came in 1795. In a short time he started a boarding school that became famous. James Stokes and Robert Colgate were among his pupils.

At the same time Elder Scott became a Baptist and preached at Rhinebeck and elsewhere. A church grew up about him, the building dating from 1825, on a lot given by Mrs. Montgomery, Margaret Beekman's daughter.

Scott designed his own seating in the church, placing himself between the men's and women's entrances, with his back to the front porch. The people face the doors. He killed many birds with this stone. Every one could see who came without turning around. When a bride entered the whole church could see her. When anyone left he did so confronting the minister. No scurrying at the close of service by the minister, on the other hand. He had merely to step from his place to greet his parish. Why was it never thought of, before or after?

Scott wrote his own funeral sermon, and planned the ceremony. From it one sentence stands in golden letters: "To you who have been my pupils: God is my witness, and you, also, that I never used any means to forestall your judgment, nor to make proselytes of you: but my aim was to lead you to regard the word of God: to act honestly: to speak the truth: to be slow to anger, and not to avenge yourselves. I pray you to think for yourselves, and then act as the Lord has directed."

Robert Scott was offered the presidency of Colgate University by his former pupils the Colgate brothers, but declined it, to stay in his church and school at Rhinebeck.

The Friends, entering Dutchess in an organized body, soon surpassed sister churches in strength of discipline. The individual congregation is the opposite of the Congregational church. It is called a Preparative Meeting, because it merely prepares business for the Monthly Meeting which is the executive branch. It holds property, appoints officers, exercises discipline. The Quarterly Meeting is supervisory over common enterprises of Monthly Meetings, but is chiefly advisory in policy. The Yearly Meeting, like a State Synod, is the only legislative body in faith and order. Thus by a series of steps the individual's responsibility is chiefly for his own life and conduct.

Oblong Monthly Meeting, to which New Milford Preparative Meeting belonged, was from 1731 to 1800 a part of Purchase Quarterly Meeting. Harrison's Purchase, called Purchase for short, included the present village of Harrison on the Sound. To it Quakers had been coming from their spreading settlements in Long Island, and from it they went up the Byram and Croton rivers to Quaker Hill. From there they hived out to Quaker City, or Oswego, near Moore's Mills, then up Quaker Lane to Clinton, and along the Fishkill Valley to Nine Partners Meeting which grew until it absorbed the Oblong in its own Monthly Meeting.

Three major steps distinguish Dutchess Quakers in the Dutchess. In 1755 they were by act of the New York legislature exempted from military service in the impending war against the French. Their names, which Quakers hereabouts hold as the cabin list of their Mayflower, have been printed in one of the numerous excellent brochures that have come from Quaker Hill. But a still more select list has not been printed. It is that of those choice spirits who, exempted on the payment of an exemption or commutation of 40 shillings a quarter, refused to make even that allowance to the gods of war, and were subjected to arrest and distraint of goods in consequence. Their names, listed in a County Clerk's document were: Samuel Russell, Philip Allen, Timothy Dakin, Jonathan Hoeg, Elijah Doty, Daniel Chase, Isaac Haviland, Jonathan Dakin, Judah Smith, Richard Smith, and Matthew Wing, all of the Oblong; Silas Mosher, William Parks, Jesse Irish, William Irish, Josiah Bull, Josiah Bull Jr., William Gifford, all of Oswego Meeting; and John Wing, Joseph Smith, Daniel Shearman, Moses Shearman, Joshua Shearman, Sylvester Richmond, Eliab Yeomans, Zebulon Ferris of Beekman precinct; Elijah Doty of Oblong House. Justice Louerens Van Cleeck (as he spelled his name) signed separate warrants for each offender, reciting the Act of February 19, 1754, which exempted both Moravians and Quakers, and ordered the sheriff to distrain for £ 3 and 21 shillings costs of service.

The second outstanding act of the Friends was the proposal from the Oblong, made in 1767 at Purchase Quarterly Meeting in session there. "If it is not consistent with Christianity to buy and sell our fellowmen for slaves, then whether it is consistent with a Christian spirit to keep in slavery those that we have already in possession by purchase, gift, or any other ways." At the Yearly Meeting in Flushing to which this leading question was addressed, the query was laid over till the following year, when action in the affirmative was taken, though with consideration of the possible harms from immediate freedom to certain groups. From 1778 on, Monthly Meetings disowned those who continued to retain slaves.

In fairness to other groups, it is noted that the subject was widely discussed at the time and that Baptists as well as Quakers spoke bravely out. The Oblong action, however, must be granted its historical moment as the first formal step of an organized group of citizens against the laws recognizing slavery.

The third action of the Friends, less spectacular, is no less significant in the light of later events. The New York State Legislature, in February, 1786, passed an act abolishing quitrents upon equitable terms. Freeholders subject to quitrents unpaid might commute indebtedness by paying 14 years of back rents, less 8 years for the war period, and by paying in full for 14 years in advance.

In action striking by contrast with the antirent riots of the years of "Tin Horns and Calico," about 1840, the Quakers of Quaker Hill paid in full for their Oblong Lots in 1786.

Although the Friends in later years suffered losses, both by dissension and by rigorous disownment of those who fell away, their influence still remains strong in the county. For many recent years Henry Allen represented it in the legislature, and today Poughkeepsie Meeting has a strong place in local affections.

# 17. Tidewater New York. 1742

*Dread God, do law, love truth and righteousness,*
*And wed thy people again to Steadfastness.*
CHAUCER, 1390.

NO PEOPLE EVER SET more store by order than did the English. When Chaucer prescribed the king's duties, he wrote for all England. But the scribes who copied this poem in later years were not sure that Chaucer's gentle method would work. Some wrote for "*wed* thy people", "*bring* thy people". Others wrote "*lead* thy people". Still others, and these perhaps of the higher class, "*drive* thy people". If England's eighteenth century governors of colonies had been of diplomatic Chaucer's mind, they might have kept their colonies. When General Gage rode down Rhode Island way, his troopers tried to drive a teamster off the road, to make way for his Excellency. "I vow, I won't be druv, that I won't", quoth the teamster, as he blocked the whole highway.

On order, all were agreed. But to be wedded to it, there's the rub. Theoretically England's order was static, like the heavens. Each rank kept in its degree, as was divinely appointed. Respected and respecting, with due deference to every estate, the English world of the later middle ages was to wag on for ever.

Conservative Shakespeare loved the stable country-side, and hated the upstart townsmen, the unruly city mob. His plays are all of gentry. But in fact a great new class, the yeomanry, was rising all around England, who would join with the crafts and trades to put the gentlemen down. And that is exactly what happened in the colonies. Distinctions of rank disappear, even in the old legal records which are the strongholds of old custom. Men at the end of the colonial period are either classless or known by their calling only. No wonder Englishmen at first thought the young Republic would not outlast their generation, and did their little bit to help Providence push it over the dam.

The order and degrees of men in England ran thus: King, nobles, knights, gentlemen, esquires, franklins, yeomen, farmers, tradesmen, craftsmen, apprentices, laborers, bondsmen.

The order in Dutchess differed only slightly. The King (in documents, shadow more than substance) the governor and council, gentlemen of estate, of office, of blood, of calling, yeomen, farmers, trades and crafts, apprentices, laborers, bondsmen, Indians, slaves.

In England the yeomen soon swallowed franklins and farmers. In America farmers took over the yeomen. The effect was the same. One strong agricultural element replaced the gentlemen of estate, with their rents and tenures. The orders passed into history.

In America the change was more complete than in England. Laws abolished many privileges after the Revolution, but in fact the obliteration of the hedgerows of privilege had begun long before.

On one matter the people of both countries were agreed. Land was King. English hunger for land was not confined to the colonies and conquered lands. It infected the whole kingdom at home. Yeomen fought gentlemen for it, yeoman fought yeoman, for every slice, gore, patch, common, and waste. Noblemen entered the race as avidly as the rest. The story of land-grabbing is not a pretty one, anywhere. Human nature is at its worst about it. Land was capital, land was office, land was property, land was gentry, privilege, degree; in a word, land was life. As Roger of Sicily remarked, "nothing is worth fighting for but land". It has remained so, down to our "Westerns".

Try as they might to deal land out fairly, the governors

of New York could not enforce their own laws. There is no better instance than that of Richard Coote, Earl of Bellomont. Historians have been kind to the bluff old Irishman, chiefly because he wrote a picturesque style, but also because he was honest, and his heart was on the side of order. But he did no better than the rest.

"Send me a good honest judge and a sharp attorney, and I will turn the rascals out, who have stolen his Majesty's province." This was his constant plaint. He never trusted any colonial. So the Lords of Trade sent over the best men they could find, Sampson Broughton to be his judge, and Leigh Attwood to be his attorney on land questions.

And what did *they* do for Old Dutchess? Broughton became one of the Upper Nine Partners, and had thousands of acres for his unlawful share. Leigh Attwood manoeuvred Heathcote of the Lower Nine Partners out of a great part of his Scarsdale patent, and tried to cut a big slice out of the Lower Nine Partners as well. In the last raid he failed, and many a good Dutchess farmer breathed the easier for it. These were the model gentlemen by whom Bellomont hoped to reform his landstruck people.

But the struggle for land was waged for the most part behind doors, in the law courts and land offices. Though society was built upon it, men and women went quietly about their business. They were reminded of it when the law spoke. Juries were drawn in the early days (1739) from "twelve free and lawfull men of the neighborhood of which each of them shall have in his own Name and Right a Good House and Messuage with Ten Acres of Land of Freehold in the County".

In later days this was broadened: (1774) "Twelve free and lawfull men of the Said County of which Each of whom shall have in his own Name or right or in trust for them or in their wives' right a Freehold in Lands, Messuages, or Tenements, or in rents, or fee, Feetail, or for life, of the value of sixty pounds free of all reprizes, demands, and incumbrances whatsoever."

Still later, in the New York Constitution of 1776, the qualification was reduced, at the suggestion of Gouverneur Morris at Fishkill, to thirty pounds.

These were the definition of the yeoman; but in fact men of every sort might be yeomen, not merely those of ten acres. "Jacob Sanders of Poughkeepsie, Yeoman." The Sanders, patentees of Poughkeepsie might surely claim to be "gentlemen of estate," but did not. "Cornelis Van Der Bogard and Francois Van Der Bogard, Yeomen;" these were among the best and wealthiest citizens. "Leonard Lewis, Merchant," was also an Esquire, and being judge, a gentleman of office; but he never claimed the honor. Sanders had an English father, Lewis an Irish, but both spoke Dutch.

"John Gay of Dutchess, carpenter," is an early example of the numerous craftsmen of every quality through the country. In our machine age it is hard to realize how many occupations were needed to outfit a community. For lack of them in most neighborhoods men and women were Jacks and Janes of all trades. A visit to one of our wayside museums of old times, such as that at Monroe, or Cooperstown, with their innumerable tools and wheels, would soon have one bewildered. New York City's artisans and their many crafts are well described in the two volumes of that title published by the New York Historical Society.

But these men were merely classified by calling, not actually ranked. They were in trade, but so were many gentlemen and yeomen. Blacksmiths were numerous, but they bought their iron of Philip Livingston, Gentleman, Lord of the Manor of Livingston, who got most of his ore from Salisbury. And all the gentry were in overseas trade, including on occasion privateering or its shady cousins, piracy and smuggling. Even Frederick Philipse, Gentleman, got tangled up in these affairs.

In Dutchess the ironmongers who dealt with the first blooms of the iron were called "Bloomers," though the term is not in dictionaries. What a "Masener" is, who knows? The word occurs several times in documents, spelled also "Masender." Other crafts are less remote. All sorts of tailors and dressmakers, cordwainers and haberdashers drifted through the countryside, outfitting whole families at a time. "Chapmen" peddled their wares from door to door.

Schoolmasters were more or less itinerant. Theirs was a craft. "Diniss O'Reily of Rumbout precinct, schoolmaster," and "Mathias Cooke, yeoman" also of Rumbout, were cited together for breach of the peace.

Edward McGregor, a laborer, sued Simon Milkan for £ 2 14s. for "stubbing two Morgens" (four and a half acres) of woods. Ten acres were regarded as the work of a whole winter. But neither "laborer" nor "servant" is frequent in the old records. The writers evidently tried to avoid the words as distasteful. "Slave" was even less common. Slaves were called "man" or "wench"; neither term was derogatory. "Hired Man" and "hired help" are used in letters but not in court.

Laborers fell in three categories; casual, seasonal, annual. "Hired help" were more often on the permanent basis, practically of the family. Most of the Negroes seem to have been house servants, very few families having more than one or two. They were known only by given names: "Ebenezer Hurd of Pawlings Precinct, yeoman, and Jonathan Cutler, of the same place, yeoman" served as bond for the court appearance of "one sartain Negro man belonging to Ezra Rutty".

Through all the eighteenth century documents there runs a strong ferment of leveling, in which title and degree come to mean less and less, and would die out altogether were it not for the attorneys themselves.

Thus ran the legal style, as late as 1786: "Henry Livingston Gentleman Clerk of the Inferior Court of common Pleas of the People of the State of New York for the County of Dutchess for inrolling Pleas in the said Court complains of Jonathan Landon Gentleman one of the attornies of the said Inferior Court of common pleas according to the Liberties and Priviledges of such Attornies hitherto used and approved of in the same now here present in Court in his proper Person: For that, to wit": etc. Again "Henry Livingston, Gentleman, &c.,

puts in his place Gilbert Livingston and James Kent, his Attornies". June 1, 1786, for £ 50.

Lord Bellomont set out mightily to be a scourge of the patentees, but compromised for two of the greatest villains, Captain Evans of Orange and Domine Dellius of the Adirondacks. The rest slipped through his fingers; Henry Beekman, Adolph Philipse, Robert Livingston, the Nine Partners, Schuyler, and Van Cortlandt all of Dutchess, as well as those in other parts. Chiefly, I think, he hated them because they upset the order of things, in setting up to be gentlemen.

"I would complaine to the Admiralty Board of the insolence of that fellow if I thought they would do me right. 'Tis wonderful to see how insolent men of mean beginnings can be. This man's father was a shoemaker, and turning grazier has got into a good estate".

Bellomont looked with a newcomer's contempt on the colonials, and they responded with fury. "The angry people", Bellomont always called their party, forgetting that he had himself spread slanders abroad about them. Of Augustine Graham of Upper Nine Partners and his father James Graham, Attorney General, who might claim to be gentlemen by blood, being lineally descended from James Grahame, the great Marquis of Montrose, Bellomont sourly wrote, "He will be sober when his father is honest."

But he reserved his choicest epithets for David Jamison of Nine Partners, as an upstart Scots rebel, who from being an indentured transport, sold in the public square, had in a few years bought his freedom and become Attorney General of New Jersey and a member of the governor's council in New York. This was not to be borne. Yet in two generations Jamison's children were among the gentry on our Hudson Shore.

Bellomont came late in the day (1697-1700), though he pushed through the fight against Connecticut and saved Rye and Bedford to the province. But he forgot, if he ever knew, that the great grantees, Van Rensselaer, Schuyler, Livingston, were the only people with stake enough in the land to think it worth their while to stick it out at Albany among the Mohawks, and to fight the French year in and year out. He denounced them even while he used their services among the tribes. Yet he had deeply engaged himself in Livingston's project of Captain Kidd and the "Venture Galley".

The governors blamed the patentees of Dutchess and elsewhere for the slow growth of population in early days. Yet where were the people to come from? Not from England, certainly. From Scotland?

In 1698 two Scottish ships called the *Caledonia* and the *Unicorne* came to New York in a miserable condition "having lost a great number of people by famine and sickness". They applied to Lt. Gov. Nanfan for leave to buy provisions which might be thought a reasonable request. But that timorous gentleman decided he must write to Governor Bellomont, then in Boston, who ordered that no more provisions should be sold them than would carry them back to Scotland. They were turned away, no doubt, because to land there would upset the town's economy, or spread disease. Nanfan reported to the Earl that "the Scotch were very insolent in their demand for food".

Perhaps it was not wholly the fault of the low-born patentees that the Scots sought Boston, Philadelphia, and Baltimore thereafter. But Bellomont was correct in his diagnosis, though "insolence", perhaps, did not quite fit the facts.

When John Arthur impleaded Stephen Thorne in 1737 for a debt of £ 237, neither of these substantial citizens was described by any rank or title. When Asa Potter sued Robert G. Livingston for £ 500 for slander, no "conditions" were named. Livingston, it was alleged, had accused Potter of running off to avoid payment, and urged John and Philip Pink of Pinks' Corners to arrest him, if they ever expected to see their money. The Pinks were of that well-known and respected calling, tavern-keepers. Asa Potter was a busy trader following "the business and employment of horses, mares, and geldings, and Exporting them to foreign markets for sale".

Henry Beekman himself, though a judge, assemblyman, and owner of vast lands, put on no airs. His descendants used a Beekman coat of arms, claiming that an English queen had plucked two roses and given them to a Beekman who had fought on the English side against Spain, upon which the roses of gold were set in the coat.

But Janet Montgomery tells that when his wife, the Gertrude Van Cortlandt of older days, and a beauty at Lord Cornbury's court, boasted of her lovers, her old grandfather replied, "And yet you took up at last with an Esopus farmer".

Janet herself was not free of pride of gentry. When her grandfather's agent whose office room she had preempted ventured to speak to her and her friends, "it was not to be endured". Yet she was proud to say that her grandfather's tenants "to this day give him as a toast, and talk to us of his goodness". In their place and order, well enough: not as equals. Mrs. Brett thought otherwise, and so did Henry Beekman.

The Dutchess gentry belonged to the country party, but the marriage of Frederick Philipse's daughters with the English army officers, Beverly Robinson and Roger Morris, brought that family into the Tory ranks, while the DeLanceys' long struggle with the Livingston group carried them along with Philipse. Thus in southern Dutchess and central Westchester Tory squires and Whig people created a No Man's Land of guerilla raids and reprisals, embittered by tenants' riots. In the rest of Dutchess the gentry were Continental for the most part.

Tory groups among the people gathered round Episcopal clergy, or spread from tenants whose landlords were unsatisfactory. Chief of these were the tenants of Gilbert Livingston in Beekman precinct, and of Philip Livingston in the Manor.

The fight with the mother country brought about a closer relation with gentlemen and yeomen, and did much to remove the old barrier. Leveling ideas spread among the people, while government remained largely in the hands of the landed gentlemen. As time went on, a new split occurred between the people and the gentry; and once more a powerful section of the gentlemen espoused the people's cause and won a victory.

The people of New York have always followed their well-to-do leaders. George Clinton built the handsomest place on the River in Dutchess, but he led the popular party for more than a generation.

The compromise by which the gentlemen gave up the shadow of superiority, in degree and title, to preserve the substance, of property and inheritance, has worked exceedingly well. America gradually gave up the forms of monarchy, but kept its respect for position.

Thus when along the River shore the places of the well-to-do began to rise, people took pride in them as reflecting the general prestige of the county. For five generations, from 1730 to 1880, the Livingston family produced leaders of their party, and most of the time gave the general color and tone to society. As James Parton once remarked, "the Clintons had the power, the Schuylers had the money, but the Livingstons had the sons". None of the three groups was unworthy to lead, though there was a great variation in ability.

Amateur students of heredity have noted that some families produce leaders today, but only through the female line, and claim that this is due to excessive in-breeding, which they say affects the males. Chancellor Livingston's two daughters married Livingstons, though he had designed one of them for a son of Jay. But certainly few families have stood the test of time better than the gentry of River Row.

While there was in-breeding, so that the Livingston line made contact with almost every other prominent New York family, there was also much exogamic drive as well. Livingston men married Creole and French, Polish and Irish, English and Scot. In their own heredity the Dutch predominated, though they are usually called "straight Scotch".

French Huguenot families like the Valleau, Bard, de la Bigarre, and de Cantillon joined the Stoutenburghs and Beekmans on the River. Scots like Allen, Johnstone, and Armstrong joined English like Huntington and Rogers, and Germans like Astor. The River society was never exclusive.

Houses were simple enough, some of them larger than the large farmhouses, but not by much. Their "places" were farms, well tended, where orchards abounded, and experimental planting was carried on. Livingston lands kept tenants, and something resembling English county life of a century later sprang up. Chancellor Livingston's correspondence with his farm agent, Dr. Wilson, shows a generous and understanding spirit in human relations.

In 1935 Helen W. Reynolds listed the "country-seats on Hudson's River in Dutchess County". She recorded eighty from 1742 to 1925, all of them separate and distinct places, though many of them produced by division of the older estates. Thirty-one of the eighty places were connected with the Livingston family on one side or the other. Of the thirty-one created before 1812, one-half were of Livingston origin.

These Places, as they are locally called, have given the county its reputation of being a pleasure seat. River steamer guides for decades pointed out the fine estates, and claimed that the drive from Poughkeepsie through Hyde Park to Rhinebeck was "the finest in the country". Few of the places, however, were ostentatious, most of them no larger than the ample farmhouses on the Back Lots.

Most of the builders were gentlemen of estate or calling, some also of office. The first of them, Henry Livingston, Sr., was Clerk of the County, and one of its busiest citizens for many years. He called his place Linlithgow, after an ancestral Scots seat of the Livingstons, where once a certain Lady Livingston was solemnly excommunicated for too frequent "dealings with midsummer fairies". His son Henry, an equally busy man, built the third. Charles Crooke, an active dealer in real estate, purchased the second for the residence of his blind son, with his tutor. The next dozen places were almost all of Livingston creation, after the dispersal of entail by Chancellor Livingston. Montgomery, Armstrong, Lewis, Tillotson, and Garrettson, were all married to the Chancellor's sisters: a Revolutionary general, a Secretary of War, a New York Governor, a Surgeon General of the Revolution, and a Methodist circuit rider—not exactly idlers. Doctor John Bard and his grandson William, Dr. John Masten, Governor Clinton, Nathaniel Pendleton, and Judge Brockholst Livingston of the Supreme Court were other residents. Others like Daniel C. Verplanck had great landed estates in the county, that required supervision.

From the beginning, then, the Places were not merely country seats of men primarily engaged in city life. Here their owners resided for great periods of the year, with many interests. The Bards, and Dr. Hosack after them, were absorbed in landscape gardening, their work of infinite benefit to the art. The politicians and statesmen of New York City knew very well how important to their political career was a place in the county, where they could hold caucus unobserved with men of the great estate above the Harlem River. Some of them, like Nathaniel Pendleton and Maturin Livingston, held local office. And more important than all this were the lifelong active citizens among them, Dr. John Masten, Peter De La Bigarre, Gerardus Duyckinck, Rev. John McVicker.

Children of the Places loved the county, and frequently found local matches within the families of county yeomen. Four of Maturin Livingston's children made such marriages, thus spreading the heredity of Robert Livingstons, both uncle and nephew, abroad through the county.

If the builders of the Places thus brought prestige, experience, skill, and education to the county life, they gained from it infinitely more. If they also had houses in New York City, they turned to the country in escape, and thus initiated one of America's greatest industries, the summer resident. Down to the days of Franklin Roosevelt, the best of the Places have sheltered men who valued the friendship and life and color of the county, and felt the richer for the exchange.

There is of course in all social change a "last leaf upon the tree". In Rhinebeck there used to walk in its shady lanes an old gentleman in knee breeches, silk stockings, silver buckles, and well-powdered wig. He was Goldsbrough Banyar, formerly secretary of the governor's council, and one of the most active speculators in New York grants. He seemed the very image of Dr. Holmes' famous sketch in "The Last Leaf".

But the people of River Row had long outgrown whatever nostalgia afflicted them. They were building steamships, racing an *America* for a Queen's Cup, cutting ice on the Hudson to cool a fevered city, founding banks and insurance companies and railways, teaching in the universities, writing history and watching birds or sailing the Atlantic in a ketch, or climbing Kilimanjaro. To tell their whole story you would have to tell all these and many more. Some of it, we hope, will crop up in these or other pages.

The Livingston type was, and still is, long and lanky. The women have beautiful swan necks, but one of the men was called "whipping-post". When a Livingston was shot in the nose in a duel, George Washington exclaimed with a hearty laugh, "You know his nose, how could one miss it?" Franklin Roosevelt, in shipping cordwood to New York from his upriver dock, was only keeping up a custom of Mrs. Roosevelt's ancestor, Judge Livingston.

"I desire also you would hire a Pokeepsie sloop if possible to go to my farm for a load of nuttwood, I'll give bushell a Cord as also to bring down some provision from thence - - - Van Worme would be a very proper persone. I have 25 cord lying at my landing".

R R Livingston.

He asks also for "a good Dutch farmer".

In the public papers of New York's first governor, Vice-president George Clinton, is correspondence with seventeen men of the Livingston name, as well as with husbands like Wm. Smith, Tillotson, Jay, and Duane.

At the first Inaugural in New York, General Washington was smothered in Livingstons. Chancellor Robert administered the oath of office, John R. was the general's assistant, Morgan Lewis was Grand Marshall, others led the parade, while eight matrons and many Misses Livingston were duly noted at the inaugural ball on May 5.

Yet one cannot pass off all Livingston attitudes as snobbish. William Livingston wrote powerfully for the people. When a Tory clergyman delivered a sermon on the text "Touch not mine anointed", William wrote a gay reply, arguing that the people were the Lord's anointed, and should not be touched. He thus anticipated Abraham Lincoln's aphorism, that "the Lord must love the common people, because he made so many of them". Certainly the Lord seems to have loved the Livingstons, for the same reason.

There are those who still begrudge the Livingston fame, because here and there among the landlords there were unmerciful ejectments of tenants. The Tory Robert G. Livingston had unenviable fame. Much research is needed to place blame, if blame there be, upon the guilty parties.

But to blame the Livingston name for all the anti-rent feeling is absurd. Colonial boundaries and Puritan aggression were largely responsible, and there were many other landlords, some of them yeomen, that dealt in ejectments of their tenants. There are still tenants in Dutchess, and even four sharecroppers. The system works, in the right hands. The assumption that every Livingston election was rigged, and others were fair, is a bit on the partisan side. Some, in so numerous a family, erred, no doubt. But few groups can match this extraordinary circle in the variety of their interests, their zest in life, or their proclivity for the right, or at least the winning, side.

Yet the real eighteenth century story in Dutchess is that of the yeoman who shakes off his English rank and becomes an independent citizen, who struggles with the forest and learns to live with it and to take his toll of it, who works his way through the no less perilous swamp of debts and obligations, and becomes a free man among free men. Of a substantial farmer's housekeeping one may get glimpses from the old records; but a visit to the Hasbrouck or other houses at New Paltz would repay a visitor. Much of the furniture is from Dutchess County, as many descendants of the New Paltz patentees moved east into the woods.

Daniel Babbitt of South East precinct made claim for the complete spoliation of his home while he was in service, apparently.

July 6, 1779

"A True Account of goods taken from my family while I was absent.

1 Yoke of Oxin
11 Milk Cows—3. 2 year Old huffers
1 2 year Old Bool 2 yearling huffers and 1 Dtto Steer
28 hed of sheep, 2 horses and 11 Hogs
1 Cart 3 ploughs 2 harrows
2 Cyths & tackling 2 axes 3 Broad hoes
2 Ox Yokes & 2 Chains 1 Ox Sled & 1 horse Sled
1 hunting Side Saddle & 1 Man Saddle
2 Setts of Blacksmith Tools
100 wt. of Iron & 50 wt. of Steel
100 Bushels of coal
2 Feather Beds & Beding
1 Sett of curtains & 4 Table Cloths
6 Pare of Linnen Sheets
8 woolen Blankets & 8 towels
3 Tables - 5 cheers & 2 Bedsteads
1 large Brass kittle 2 Iron pots & 1 Dtto kettle
Shovel & tongues 1 pare of hand Irons & 1 frying pan
3 pails & milk cellars
1 Grindstone & Crank

4 aker good weet 434 corn groing
1 hay cart 2 sets of hay tacklin

Daniel Babbit"

"At May court, 1769, John Langdon impleaded Robert Patton in a plea of Trover and conversion of his property. Two Feather Beds, one green rug, one flowered coverlid, one white blanket, one streaked blanket, five pillows and two pillow cases, two straw beds, one Bedstead, one Cord, seven chairs, two chests, one trammell, one tongs, one pair of hand irons, one Iron pot, one copper tea kittle, one plain Table, one Dresser, one Churn, two bags, one Pewter platter, one pewter Bason, eleven Pewter plates, one Pewter teapot, one Green earthen Tea pot, one Green earthen plate, six cups and saucers, two earthen Basons, one bowl, three tin cups, one Stone milkpot, one earthen platter, four forks, & six knifes, four large pewter spoons, six tea spoons, two shoemaker benches, two pales Iron hoops, two wooden dishes, one old pewter Bason, one old Trunk, one Cedar tub, two oak tubs, one Looking glass, one barrell, one barrell of Beef, half a bushell of Flower, one bushell of Indian meal, half a pound of Tea, one spinning wheal, one sugar box, one frying pan, one book called the Young Mans companion, one psalm book, and one brass Candlestick, all of the value of £ 50 currant Mony of New York.

Bartholomew Crannell served as Attorney."

This is the story that comes through the scanty documents, with all its failure and all its victory.

One poor yeoman, who however has many descendants in these parts, had not much left in his bankruptcy.

Christian Sackrider had "One Tea Kittle, one Iron Tramel, one Slawbonck, one Shovel and Tongs, one Cheast, one Two-gallon Keg, 1 Bed Stead, and Beading, one Taylor Gous & Large Taylors Shears Two Teables 6 Chears Chamberpott one Large Chear. 1773." He owed nearly £ 200.

A pleasanter picture is painted in this little idyll of 1797, in Poughkeepsie. It comes probably closer to the average small place than could be found elsewhere. Who would not snap it up today?

"*Notice*

I want to sell the Place where I now live, pleasantly situated a little south of the court house in Po. The lot has 280 feet front on the post road and contains one acre—on the same is a house convenient for a small family; a pretty good barn, a good well of water, a large and very good garden, with a fine asparagus bed in it,—I believe I may say that there's no place of its size in this county that has more and greater variety of fruit on it than this has, consisting of apples peaches pears plumbs cherries and quinces—etc. in the garden raspberries, strawberries, gooseberries & currants all in their prime for bearing.

John Davis
Jan. 30 1797."

In 1724 three wolves were killed by the Indians Pesewin and Kriches, at five shillings apiece. Later heads, of which there were many, were paid for at 10 shillings if killed by white men, 5 if killed by Indians. "Young Nimham" however received 12 for two wolves' heads, while 5s. 9d was paid for rum to Nimham and other Indians, in 1742. Indians were also hired for road work and 7s. paid them. The law lasted till 1780.

The worthy supervisors registered earmarks for wandering pigs, as "halfmoons, slits, crops, nicks, triangles, tip cuts" and the like. Brands on horses and cattle were customarily by owners' initials. Henry Van de Burgh's was a cross in a circle.

By the end of the century, a little village like Red Hook may boast a notice like the following:

"Horses for Sale.

A pair of Dapple Grey Horses, about 15 hands high, handsome, and move well, broke to a Phaton and Sulkey, and are Good

Saddle Horses, price £ 100, apply at Red Hook Landing to Sylvanus Bliss. Dec. 24, 1795."

The French traveler Chastellux records his talk at Rhinebeck with a prosperous exporter of horses to Canada. Only seventy years before, fourteen proprietors paid forty per cent of all assessments in the county, the largest £ 60, being paid by Widow Brett. The supervisors in the same year 1717, paid one pound four shillings to the tax assessors "for to Vew the Palentines and rate them".

From frontier life to a well-tilled landscape, beautiful in its rich fertility and cropped pastures, all in one lifetime. From the neglected corner of a great growing realm, to the position of Empire State, its first governor vice-president of its nation, all in one man's lifetime. From a polyglot province to a common new dynamic American speech.

Within the memory of man, William Smith wrote, and as treasurer of the Oblong company he knew it well, scarcely a dozen families inhabited, and now by 1760, twenty-five hundred fighting men could spring to arms. The guess was accurate enough; it was soon to be tested.

It is characteristic of the cosmopolitan Hudson shore that the best account of its early life was written by a Frenchman. St. Jean de Crèvecoeur spent twenty years on river farms, first in Ulster, then in Orange. He had many contacts with the Dutchess. Robert the Chancellor got new ideas from him; among others, the improvement of City Hall Park, and better grass for American farms. He advised William Livingston on a new botanical garden in Jersey. When Peter V. B. Livingston's daughter died, her husband married Crèvecoeur's daughter Fanny.

But his closest contacts were with Fishkill. There lived Samuel Verplanck, his very good friend. Samuel's cousin, Daniel Crommelin, sold Crèvecouer his farm "Pine Hill", near Goshen. There was visiting to and fro. The "Letters from an American Farmer" described life in Dutchess as well as Orange—the two being identical to start with, with Palatines and Huguenots and Dutch the prevailing tone.

Crèvecoeur suffered, too, for his loyalty, in Dutchess when during the Revolution the courageous Frenchman sought to return to France. He was imprisoned first in Fishkill until he could be conveyed south, then in New York by suspicious British. His wife died, and children became barefooted runaways in the woods, when the Indians raided in Orange. Two years later, on his return, St. Jean heard of them through a Fishkill Continental officer who had found the children wandering near his farm in Orange, and taken them in.

So we may claim his classic as in some degree our own, and urge readers to include its reading among their musts. He was a master of description, with a fine feeling for effects. Free of all nationalistic jealousy, he could see with open eyes the wonder and beauty of the vast woods. He wrote a whole essay on the acacia (locust-tree) and made it popular. He praised the maple, and extolled its beer, wine, and vinegar as well as its sugar. Most of all, he was the first to put into words what the woods had done to the American farmer. He saw the farmer replace the yeoman, and take his place among equals in the new world.

On his return to France he brought about a packet service through government encouragement of commerce. His praises of the States, read in Britain, helped to swell emigration to the west. This brought a bitter attack upon him, and he was called a liar and a myth-maker. Thus the half-century-long campaign of abuse of everything American began in Britain, while eager Britons thronged the harbors, and crowded the steerage, a paradox of which the Dutchess author, James K. Paulding, took gay advantage in his "John Bull and Brother Jonathan".

In significant extracts reprinted in No. XXIV of the Dutchess historical series, the high lights of Crèvecoeur's descriptions are summarized. The choice of land, the log-cabin, and the pioneer's arrival with his family begin the new life. The husband enters the Do-it-yourself stage, and becomes an "intuitive" carpenter and shoemaker. He prospers and gets help, but soon becomes a slave to his farm. "The number of debts which one part of the country owes to the other would astonish you," writes Crèvecoeur, who is well sustained by the Dutchess records. But we recall that the Father of his Country, who was also one of the richest and most provident men of it, was also apt to be without funds.

It is possible, however, to waste a lot of misplaced sympathy on the American debtors against whom thousands of warrants lie in the great cartons of the County Clerk's office at Poughkeepsie. The eighteenth-century consumer was merely forging a substitute for the installment-buying of today. Instead of purchasing "with nothing down" and $2 a month for the rest of his life, the consumer merely bought and failed to pay at all. Year after year new warrants were issued against him, when he would make some token payment to keep out of jail. Then, after five years or so, the creditor would get tough and jail his man, after which judgment would be confessed and some compromise worked out. Jails grew slightly larger, but not more so than the population; and it is evident that the innumerable warrants were not really intended to imprison. In a depreciating currency like that of the period the way to riches was by keeping progressively deeper in debt.

More seriously, the lack of commercial credit was keenly felt, and imprisonment for debt was one of the first abuses in English common law, to be amended by the new State of New York. All that is argued here, is only that if a fifth of the warrants had been executed, the jails of the whole province would not have contained the debtors of Dutchess.

Crèvecoeur is no less realistic in outlining the many chores on the American farm. The cares of the orchard, the barn, and the pen; the wagons and ploughs, the firewood and the preserves are not overlooked in his generally rosy picture. Nor does he omit the civic duties of the farmer: the drainage of swamps, the care of roads and dams, are included along with the accounts of barn-raisings and frolics. He admits that there are poor to be cared for, and sick to be nursed.

But all this is set against the liberty of the woods. He is endlessly charmed with the endless hospitality of the forest.

Farmers on their way to market come in at any time of night and sleep on the floor beside his bed. The French gentleman often watched his house fill up while he lay abed.

A hard but a happy life, he thought. He wrote for his age, but his book is a classic of the period, and still sells in the cheap editions, part of every American's reading. It is the pride of the River farmers, that their life, so like the rest of America, should in this way have become part of the great American dream.

# V. LEVELERS BY PRINCIPLE

## 18. Ferment. 1755

NOTHING IN THE OUTWARD appearance of Dutchess prepares us for the summer cloud that overcame us. From a quiet countryside, harvesting fine crops from its fertile fields, with scores of mills cheerily splashing, and every sign of peace and plenty, Dutchess suddenly becomes the scene of riot and rebellion, its citizens under martial law with heavy fines and prison terms. If we look below the surface, however, we shall find ample evidence for the existence of deep-searching roots of discontent.

Hardly had the war smoke drifted off the Plains of Abraham, when a new and unpleasant sense of change hung over the Valley. Only too mindful of the united efforts of the colonials in troops, supplies, and funds, the British government viewed the prospective union askance. They had no mind to add to the growing provinces the Ohio lands for which Weiser had sought so long. He and his diplomacy backed by arms and supplies had reduced Fort Duquesne to an empty shell into which General Forbes was carried on a litter. But that was forgotten.

Instead of expansion into Canada and the Mississippi, the colonials found themselves hemmed in by a rival state, and themselves treated more like the conquered than the conqueror. Hungry English veterans, "reduced" after their service was no longer indispensable, clamored for land grants, in many instances "jumping" claims long established by custom if not by full legal protection of patents surveyed and registered. Poughkeepsie went into a tizzy when Robert Leake, Commissary of General Braddock's army, demanded 5000 acres of the Minnisinck patent, covering most of the unbuilt part of Poughkeepsie. In the scurry that ensued to get the uncompleted sales of Thomas Sanders rectified and recorded, it did not please everybody that the Episcopalian church got many acres of it, and their rector another big slice.

Indeed, the curse of the fathers' careless purchases of land unsurveyed or inaccurately measured now began to come home to the children. "Gores", those narrow strips or pie-slices of land between two patents, were turned up and squabbled over in long suits at law. Between Dutchess and Albany at the river, between the two Nine Partners Patents, between Beekman and Lower Nine Partners, between Philipse and Rombout, Minnisinck and Schuyler, and all along the Oblong's lines, west and east, the troubles began. The total effect was a profound sense of insecurity, and a deep prejudice against the lawyers who pressed the suits.

Impairment of a right tight title was not the greatest cause of worry in Dutchess. Evictions raised their ugly heads in the lands of Robert Gilbert Livingston, and, less frequently, elsewhere. John Den complained of Richard Fen, James Jackson of Thomas Stiles, John Right of James Wrong, and John Apple of Thomas Pear, in the inhumanly cruel jocoseness of the satirical lawyers' actions. Incredibly mean in its callous disregard of the suffering involved is the letter of Richard Fen that is copied in dozens of documents preceding an eviction of a tenant, for any one of many causes or for none.

Mr. Benajah Millard
Sir
I am Informed that you are in possession of or claim title to the premises mentioned in the Declaration of Ejectment, or to some part thereof, and I being sued in this Action as Casual Ejector, and having no claim or title to the same do advise you to appear at the next Inferior Court of Common Pleas

which is to be held at Pokeepsie to and for Dutchess County on the first Tuesday of January next by some attorney of that Court and then and there by a sale to be made of the same court to cause yourself to be made defendant in my stead, otherwise I shall suffer judgement to be entered against you and you will be turned out of possession.

I am Your Loving Friend
Richard Roe

October 5, 1773.
James Livingston against
Benajah Millard

No wonder that not only the victim of this oppression, but his neighbors up and down the lane, failed to see anything humorous in the situation, and began to say, as they soon did openly, that they must do themselves justice, if they could not find justice in court. Lawyers who had a monopoly of the "dogget" of cases were themselves landholders, and disinclined to oppose the landlord's advantage at court. No Dutchess attorney in the eighteenth century stands out as the friend of the oppressed.

When Indian deeds were in question not a Dutchess lawyer could be found to defend them.

So widespread, on the other hand, was the farmer's sympathy for poor tenants that sabotage began to occur. Constables were hindered in their duties. They "failed" to collect their taxes, or were intimidated on approach, sometimes even attacked. In turn, they let prisoners escape on their way to jail. So numerous were escapes and jail breaks that connivance on the part of officials must be presumed. Of the leaders in the River riots, Hallenbeck, Noble, Prendergast, and Munroe all escaped from their captors.

At the height of the hubbub the militia and the posses were ineffective, and British regulars first mingled with the local authorities, then by companies assaulted the tenants with arms. All this, of course, meant the complete breakdown of law, and its restoration by force gave it no standing in public opinion.

Riots and assaults were the order of the day up to the Revolution and even later, as the evil fruit of this resort to foreign arms.

The brutality of rural oppression offered a most unfavorable contrast with the cowardice and restraint of the military in the face of New York mobs. The same John Morin Scott, who would soon lead the Sons of Liberty in New York City, defended the Philipse heirs in their rapacious evictions of Indians' tenants. He was himself a large holder of patents in Dutchess and elsewhere. William Livingston, the host of "Liberty Hall", who stood for "the people" in New York, and insisted that it was they who must not be touched because they were "the Lord's Anointed", was himself a colleague with Scott and James Duane in the initial Philipse suit. "Liberty and Property" was the radical slogan of the day, not "Liberty and Equality".

There were some who harbored runaway slaves, and others who entertained them and incited them to riot. Still others encouraged slaves to engage in illicit trade in land, by getting drunken Indians to sign their false deeds to land.

It was not enough for the Yankee landlookers that Ridgefield had possessed their Oblong, or thousands of their fellows crossed the boundary to buy farms in Nine Partners and the rest of free Dutchess. They coveted the tenants' lands of Philipse and R. G. Livingston, while they rejected the theory of rent, especially when it got in their way. Rents were not unknown in Benning Wentworth's New England, or Ethan Allen's either, but it made a difference when "evil men" held title to pleasant little farms tucked away in the protecting hills of the High Land. In every instance of the rent hubbubs in Dutchess, the chief leaders had come from New England.

Abettors of this insecurity were the numerous impecunious Scots, Scotch-Irish, and Irish that now began to settle in Dutchess. Noble, Munroe, and Prendergast are of like origin. Macdonald, McPheeters, Campbell, all became leaders along the eastern border. Against the poorer and more disorderly strong prejudices arose. Dick Cain, though an anti-rent leader under Prendergast, was sued for cruelty to his poor workers, and was heard to say "that every Irishman should be hanged".

Worse than border disputes and hostile courts across the New England border was the ineffectiveness of their own New York government. During the hundred years from 1670 to 1770 there were no less than fifty separate appointments to the office of Chief Magistrate, whether governor, lieutenant governor, president of the council, councillor, or commander. No less than seven terms of lieutenancy were authorized, because England saw no need of promptly filling a vacancy. One governor committed suicide, and several died in office after a few months. The office was not sought by the best men.

"After all" said one of them "the governors of the Queen's Plantations must have a fine time of it, if every private man is allowed to meddle in the affairs of their governments, and upon this foot no man of honor would accept of such tiresome places."

The effect of poor government was disastrous in the county. Many titles to land were not registered, and many patents were illicit in intent if not in form. Quitrents were not collected, and uncollected taxes are the sure sign of cancer in the commonwealth.

The colonists were certainly an unruly lot, justifying Samuel Johnson's low opinions in a hundred ways. But their defiance of the governor and his party was not all rascality, as was alleged. They practised piracy and smuggling partly because they thought navigation acts unjust. Some of the chief promoters of "privateers" were Dutchess landlords.

They harbored deserters from British regiments, because they sympathized with the vast neglect of the army shown by the home government. They passed counterfeit money, because they did not have any sense of loyalty to its legal authors. They nullified law after law, by the simple process of forgetting it. Morale has a fluidity of transit, and when the wealthy are permitted to break the law with impunity, the poorer people catch on.

There is no record that any governor or other chief magistrate, during his term, set foot upon Dutchess soil. Traders, pedlars, and gentry visited New York frequently, but in most of Dutchess the sights of Albany and New York were unknown. Upriver and down were two separate provinces in general opinion, and when the governor wrought his will through New York authorities he was resented. The higher courts in circuit were no part of the local mind.

Yet by proclamation and by act of assembly Dutchess grew to feel that it was integrally bound up with its province. The wars at least did this much good, that they brought men to a sense of the common weal. The supervisors willingly voted sums in contribution to the cause of protecting our frontier. Their volunteer companies marched off to the defence of Albany. The storekeepers went to New York to replenish their stock. It was there that storekeeper Nate Sackett heard of the battle of Lexington, and hastened home to Fishkill to organize the county.

The history of the landlords strikingly refutes the theory of economic determinism. Rather, it illustrates the permanence of family and childhood experience. The most active and persistent leaders were Scots of impoverished and exiled families having a score to settle with the English government that had marooned them in New York. Next to them, and more direct and obstinate in their resistance, were the representatives of old Dutch lineage, and the French Huguenots.

These groups naturally took issue with the governor's party whenever they felt the country's interests suffered by his actions. Gradually they came to be known as "the country party." After the mid-century the governor's clique took the stump against them in the interest of what they thought national policy. As time went on the country party gathered round the Livingstons of Albany and northern Dutchess, while the court group fell in behind the De Lanceys, whose alliances with Colden and the Van Cortlandts and Philipses for the first time put power behind an English governor.

Twice the tenure of office in the governorship was so

short that leadership of the court party fell by default in the local families. Among them was every shade of opinion, from Colden, who held a realistic philosophy of the state, and did his best to stand by law and order, to James Watt and Oliver De Lancey, who were aristocrats of fine feeling and faith in the crown, and to Beverly Robinson and Roger Morris, army officers on the lookout for their own personal fortunes and nothing else. They all wound up in the loyalist camp, joined by wiser men who admitted the justice of the American side, but not to the length of what they deemed disloyalty.

Most of the time fortune favored the country party because they excelled in leadership, knew more law, and fought their causes through with better timing.

In the development of this "country party", as Colden so often called it, the Dutchess played a not inconsiderable part. We may surely claim for the county the patentees who invested in it, and whose families came to live upon its shores. We may also claim a share of pride in those residents of other river counties whose financial and political interests extended across Dutchess, and who spent much of their active life in its promotion.

Colden, of Orange, not the most sympathetic but in many ways the best of them, surveyed the Rombout lands in person, brought peace to the Oblong, and perhaps regretfully sided with the landlords against the Indian deeds, which as he very well knew were purloined in Connecticut.

Alexander, skilled and capable lawyer, watched over the purchasers of the Nine Partners and Beekman, and fought the executive for a whole lifetime by legal obstruction. With Colden, he saved the Oblong. His children married Livingstons, his son William became "Lord" Stirling of Washington's staff.

These and many others came of the Scots or Scotch-Irish. With Wm. Livingston and William Smith they formed a Presbyterian group that stood for equal rights in religious liberty and the disestablishment of education. They opposed the sanction for Episcopal Kings College, and their descendants founded New York University, one of the first

American colleges free of all sectarianism. Without their Dutchess background it may be doubted whether they would have sensed the popular trend of their state toward the broader foundation. Less conservative than they, perhaps because free of entanglement in the affairs of New York City, were the Clintons and the Poughkeepsie Livingstons, Gilbert, James, and the two Henrys. They cast in their lot with upriver entirely, finding their happiness in the promotion of the River folks on both shores. George Clinton helped his father, no doubt in his Dutchess surveys. His residence here during many months in the Revolution renewed his love of its countryside. He retired to it in his last years. The three Livingstons settled in Poughkeepsie and served the county with over a hundred years of devoted work.

Clinton, perhaps unfortunately, inherited the Dutchess distrust of Yankeeland, though not of individual Yankees. He prolonged the Vermont squabble unconscionably, though the law justified his position at long last. Similarly, his strong reaction to the Dutchess experience of quartered troops, undue fines and jailings, and tyranny by governor and council, confirmed his opinion that the Federal Constitution provided insufficient protection for the unprivileged. But he was no sulker, and served long and honorably as vice-president, thus healing our first deep breach.

All these men, with Egbert Benson, John Jay, James Kent, Robert R. Livingston Jr., Edward Livingston, and Melancton Smith, make a most honorable list at law, and go far to redeem the bar from the charge of subserviency to privilege. Essentially however, they are all undeniably conservative. They created a great tradition at a rural bar of justice, and trained a younger generation almost equally brilliant. But they took almost no part in the troubled years before the Revolution, or in the particular troubles that are told in detail in the pages that follow.

The real leader of the "country" or "popular" party during the quarter-century before the Revolution was Judge Robert R. Livingston, son of Robert of Clermont; grandson of Robert first lord of the manor; and father of Chancellor Robert R. Livingston Jr., and nine other useful citizens, three sons and six daughters. He is not to be confused with his contemporary Robert Livingston, third lord of the manor, who was concerned with "Hallenbeck's Hubbub", later described.

The Livingstons were too parsimonious in bestowing baptismal names. We are dealing here with Scots clannishness in a family whose only Scots claim is in the family name, since nearly all the wives were of Dutch lineage.

Our Judge married Margaret Beekman, daughter of Judge Henry Beekman, Jr. Both his father and father-in-law had vast possessions in land, though not too much ready cash. They both lived to extreme old age, Robert of Clermont dying in 1775, Beekman in 1776. Judge Robert, too, died in 1775, and thus lived in very limited circumstances, according to his daughter Janet. A great inheritance was always imminent but never realized.

He is often referred to as of great possessions, quite untruly.

Though somewhat less famed than his sons, Judge Robert R. (the "R", being merely patronymic, never written in full) Livingston was a leader in his own right. Elected by Dutchess County to the Provincial Assembly for the ten years 1758-1768, Livingston stood stoutly for the popular prerogative. In 1762, when the costs of the Canadian war were mounting, he effected a compromise by which New York lent Parliament funds for the bounties promised to the American soldiers requisitioned by Sir Jeffrey Amherst. In 1759 he was appointed judge of admiralty, and in 1763 junior (associate) justice of the supreme court, "at the king's pleasure". This brought radical criticism against him, but did not affect his independence. On the main issue of the mid-century, the encroachment of the governor upon legal rights, Livingston was independent, and refused to allow appeal from the judges to the governor-and-council on questions of fact. Thus he sided with John Morin Scott, and opposed Cadwallader Colden, who strove in vain to remove him.

Colden remained his friend, however, as did his other opponent, James Watts, leader of the "Court" party in the Assembly. When the mob ruled New York in Stamp Tax days, the Judge saved his rival's life by making an oration at the angry people on the steps of the courthouse in New York, while Watts was escaping from a window. Later Watts met him, and embracing him said, "God bless you, Robert; I do not believe you have an enemy in the world." His daughter Janet tells the story.

William Smith, another leader of the day, once said, "If I were to be marooned on a desert island with one book and one friend, I should choose the Bible and Robert R. Livingston."

But his constituents, after ten years of re-election, changed sides after the Prendergast trial. He had not acted in that case, but the Judge was, after all, in favor of property. "If that goes, everything falls," he told his son. He was defeated in 1768, and therefore re-elected as the Assemblyman from the Manor district, his election being five times rejected on the ground of his occupation as judge. Governor Sir Harry Moore thought highly of him, and appointed him to the council, but that body rejected him. Led by Watts, they were all intransigent Tories, and would not forget Judge Livingston's part in the Stamp Tax affair of 1765.

He was chairman of the New York committee of correspondence that arranged for the Stamp Act Congress. The letter sent by the New York Congress to King George III was written by him. Though conciliatory in tone, it was firm, and hinted that the ties with Britain were not insoluble.

The Judge led the debate through this Congress. He proposed to it a resolve for a plan of confederation with a permanent national congress that should assign quotas to each colony for the purposes of the whole British Empire. Each colony was to raise the money in its own way. The articles of Confederation in later years contained a similar plan. At the moment, however, it was not pressed.

In 1775, not long before his death, Judge Livingston, in

anticipation of the possibility of bloodshed, had built a powder mill at Clermont, and had secured a quantity of saltpetre to begin the manufacture. The mill, under the supervision of his son, John, was later an important source of supply for the Congress forces. It was burned by Vaughan, but soon reopened.

Among Judge Robert's services were his appointments on the Massachusetts-New York boundary commissions of 1757 and 1764. As will be seen, New York played its part fairly, but final settlement was reached only after the war. The line adopted, however, was that of '73.

Robert's daughter Janet (Mrs. Richard Montgomery) was passionately devoted to her grandfather, and has left a most pleasing picture of the family life. She wrote of him, "My grandfather alone foretold war with England, at that distant day in 1773 who could allow him to talk of it as a certain matter? One day after some disputation there was a pause. He turned to my father (the Judge) and said: 'You and I will never live to see this country independent; Montgomery, you may, but (speaking to his grandson Robert) you will.'" The prophecy came true.

# 19. Riotously and Routously. 1760

THE IMPACT of new ideas from centers of learning was not difficult of translation into violence. From men like Thomas Young of Yale and Edinburgh came political and social theory as well as scepticism. Livingston and others learned to push forward the legal barriers to aggression. John Morin Scott and William Livingston, busy in Dutchess law cases but even busier with the Sons of Liberty in New York, were definitely intellectual liberals with a Scots burr in their wits. Young Dutchess attorneys read law with them and imbibed their ideas as well as their books. Under their direction the Stamp Act was defeated by nullification and riot, while the principle of property was maintained in all relations unaffected by British exaction. Such a situation could not appeal to poorer people who suffered as much from American as from British unfairness. Nor did it appeal, of course, to the Tories who thought the American wrongs could be righted by less violent means than riot. Colden and William Smith, Jr., outstanding defenders of Dutchess liberties, pointed out quite truthfully that the Sons of Liberty broke the law of peace with entire impunity in New York City, while the courts dealt harshly with the same kind of rioting in Dutchess County. Such inconsistency lent color to the claim that the threatened war would really be between the British governors and the rich merchants and richer landholders. It explained why so many of the farmers turned up Tories in the Dutchess valleys.

Five years before the Revolution a Palatine of Rhinebeck

was tortured by burning, by a group of his neighbors. He survived to plead his cause against them. The case of Peter Lodowick is typical of a number of assaults and riots in the county. The full court included the best justices, and the indicting jury reads like a Who's Who of its citizens. The whole presentment deserves record.

"At a Court of General Sessions of the Peace of our Sovereign Lord the King held at Poghkeepsie in and for Dutchess County aforesaid on Thuesday the fifth day of January in the Thirteenth year of the reign of our Sovereign Lord George the third by the grace of God of Great Britain France and Ireland King Defender of the Faith SS Before Beverly Robinson, Nicolas DeLavergne, Henry Van Der Burgh, Bartholomew Noxon, Ephraim Paine. Lawrence Laurence and Thomas Barker EsQ. Justices of our said Lord the King, the peace of our said Lord the King in the County aforesaid to keep, and diverse fellonies and other misdemeanors in the said County and perpetrated to hear and determine assigned.

The Grand Jurors of our said Lord the King and the body of Dutchess County to wit Zephaniah Plat, John Bailey, Timothy Doughty, Elias Van Bunschoten, Isaac Hagaman, Jacobus Stoutenburgh, Arie Van Der Bilt, Mathias Luyster, George Freligh, Moses Ver Veelen, Isaac Storm, Wilhelmus Hermanse, Daniel Ter Boss, William Gay, Jacobus Freer, Jacobus De Graft and Barent Von Benthuysen being duly sworn and charged upon their oath do present that Henry Levy of Rinebeck Precinct in Dutchess County and Province of New York Yeoman David Marte of Rinebeck aforesaid Yoeman Gerardus Van Steenbergh of Rhinebeck aforesaid Yeoman Francis Busherone of Rhinebeck aforesaid Yeoman on the Tenth day of December in the thirteenth Year of our Sovereign Lord George the Third now King of Great Britain France and Ireland King Defender of The faith & others with force and arms at Rinebeck precinct aforesaid in the county aforesaid did *unlawfully riotously and routously* assemble and gather togather to disturb the peace and so being then and there assembled in and upon one Peter Lodowick in the peace of God and our said Lord the King then and there being unlawfully riotously did make an assault and the said Peter Lodowick then and there *unlawfully riotously and routously* did Burn with live coals of fire and did beat wound and ill treat so that of his life it was greatly despaired and other wrongs to the said Peter Lodowick then and there *unlawfully riotously and routously* did to the great damage of the said Peter Lodowick and against the peace of our said Lord the King his crown and dignity. The King vs. Henry Levy, David Marte G V Steenbergh & Francis Busherone.

Witnesses: Henry Teater
David Beninger
Wilhelmus Becker
Peter Ludowick

A true bill
Zepha Platt Jr."

If one may judge anything by the number and the nature of the cases in Dutchess County courts, the period of the Revolution witnessed a conflict in society beginning twenty years earlier and lasting ten years longer than the actual hostilities of war. While material conditions improved, population increased, and the Dutchess overtook her sister counties both of the Hudson and the Sound, she was not entirely sound at heart. Over and above the mobbish outbreaks of Hallenbeck and Munroe there is ample evidence of misrule in other areas that seem to indicate a rather general deterioration in human relations.

A brief review of matters already touched upon will bring out some of the sources for this loss. Most important are those which bring out the falling away from cultural groupings and the consequent retreat into isolation. Chief among these are the church and the school.

We have seen among the few members of the Connecticut clergy that have entered our story good ground for belief that all was not well in the home church. Rev. Peter Pratt of Sharon was removed for drunkenness and land grabbing. He later drew up deeds for the Indian Nimham and sold him out to the Philipse heirs. Rev. Richard Treat of Dover and Sheffield was among the rioters arrested in the Hallenbeck Hubbub. A letter from him, languishing in the Albany jail, begs for freedom after eighteen months of prison. Rev. Cyrus Marsh of Kent was removed on moral grounds. His successor, Asa Spalding, was denied confirmation, and soon left the ministry for law practice, as did Marsh. If conditions in central Connecticut affected church life as did those on the western border, the old Puritan church was in a bad way.

But matters were no better on the Dutchess side of the line. Conditions in the Lutheran church have been fully treated. In the Dutch Reformed churches the split over ordination embittered many good folks, and replacements from Holland became difficult of procurement. Old Light and New Light in other denominations caused harmful weakening. Presbyterian groups were forming out of New England and Scotch incomers, especially in the Nine Partners, but these were still small in number. The Hicksite controversy had not begun to trouble the Friends, but their concerns over partaking in war and slavery, and particularly in severance from the meeting of those who intermarried with communicants of other faiths, had led to serious doubts. Some were stirring for removal to Vermont and northern New York. The Church of England, through its Society for Propagation of the Gospel and through strong leadership under Samuel Seabury and others, attracted membership among the more conservative groups of other religions, to a point where Toryism and Anglicanism came to mean much the same thing to many people. Christ Church in Poughkeepsie subsisted during the Revolution only upon a system of supply. The acquisition of the glebe property, and the dabbling in real estate of the rector, were subjects of criticism that broke into open hostility against the church as soon as war began.

All this was not without its effect on the unchurched

groups, which grew bolder in their language. Blasphemy as a civil offence appears in several cases. Ribaldry offended church members, as well as blasphemy. The good wives of Crum Elbow coming to church one day were outraged by a vile bill nailed upon their church door. It burlesqued the notice of banns of marriage, and announced the intention of the writer to unite with an Indian squaw. The language of the "pestilent pasquil" makes it unprintable. This was not the only instance.

Education in colonial days followed the fortunes of the church. John Rau of Pine Plains told the young Moravian Christian Rauch that his children for lack of schooling were growing up like wild animals. At the opposite end of the ladder sons of the gentry enjoyed private tuition and read scripture and law at Yale College. Livingstons were listed at the head of the registry because of their gentle birth. More than in any other sphere, education was the touchstone of aristocracy.

Without a printing-press until 1776, with intermittent schooling by ill-taught itinerants, with only one grammar-school of account, (Chauncey Graham's in the Fishkills), with religious ties weakened or decayed, the county was slipping back into a half-barbaric culture, credulous, panicky, and mobbish, the prey of rabble-rousers. In the midst of a growing farm economy and a budding industry of mills and mines, rebellion lay in the way of anyone that might find it.

The breakdown showed itself most clearly in the administration and execution of law. In January Joseph Sheldon, a constable of Pawling, refused to assist another constable in retaking a prisoner who had escaped from him. At the same time Constable Marcy was indicted by the grand jury for assaulting Eli Burton. On the other hand there are numerous complaints against constables, for failing to collect taxes, for letting prisoners escape, and for absence from duty. Representatives of Beekman Precinct allege that there is not a single constable in an area of fifteen miles.

One letter is both comic and pathetic, as showing how a

jail was managed in colonial days. With a considerable part of the population hostile to the current justice, escapes were made easy. James Johnson, Thomas Richardson, and William Moore appealed to the Attorney-General May 16, 1754, because "the jailer will give us no more food. We are put in the Back room and our window openeth into an orchard where there is no passing except men at work—pray, sur the prisoners that are in the same jail with us, who are prisoners at large and have liberty to go all about there and stand the dore as much as they plese have the Rooms next to the strete and we are in the back gail. . . ." Evidently prisoners were supposed to beg their food, and starved if people brought them none, while well-to-do prisoners might go at large.

The familiar list of petty crimes and misdemeanors increased with the population. Drinking was so universal that it went unmentioned in the indictments; but it must have been a frequent cause, for Dutchess legends point to the use of hard liquor and apple jack. The cocktail was invented here or hereabouts. Tavernkeepers abused their position, and a licensing system was begun. As leaders of the farmers, often Justices, centers of information and discussion, the taverners were of great influence. Apparently they met the demand of the community with fair success, for few offenders were charged. One of them gave drink to a minor; another permitted the playing of cards "in an outhouse"; a third kept a billiard table, which was specifically forbidden along with shuffle-board and other games. In Prendergast's troubles, the taverns were invariably the rioters' rendezvous.

Although the Dutch citizens of New Netherlands had quietly submitted to the overwhelming force of arms, and remained in submission as the years passed, they never gave up the liberties they had won as Hollanders. Dutchmen like Samuel Staats had joined Leisler's cause, and Rip Van Dam of Upper Nine Partners had valiantly stuck to his guns in resisting Governor Cosby's bullying. In the era of riot and rout, however, they are conspicuously absent from the records, if we except the Hallenbeck family. English names from New England furnish the greater number, while Scots and Irish are common.

The Scot Edward Noble supplanted Hallenbeck in the bloodier riots, while the Scot Munroe and the Spanish-English Gunsaulus followed the Irish Prendergast to the Philipse riots. These people found the more aristocratic and dominating influence of privilege harder to bear than did the Hollanders. As hired men, competing in low pay with bound-out men and slaves, they felt at a disadvantage, and engaged in laborers' riots. Their lawbreaking cannot be ascribed to the system of land-tenure, except as that feature contributed to the general condition of inequality. Such riots kept on long after the Revolution. It is to be noted that the farmer Hallenbeck was himself an employer of labor, as he was harvesting with seventeen men to help him when found by the sheriff.

Daniel Mills, of Charlotte Precinct—Dec 16 1784 was "attacked by Knap, David—Nelson Francis & John, & Edwards Emanuel, & others unknown". "Forceably took & carried him to house of D. K. & then & there assaulted & beat the deponent & cut off some of the hair of the deponent & besmeared him with tar & put feathers on the tar: & obliged him then to dance around the room in Which they then Were & threatened to kill the D unless he would so dance . . . & threatened that unless he would remove out of the precinct they would ill treat him again in the same Manner. Ezra Mills, his brother they also stripped & tied to a tree with design to Whip him".

On the problem of Colonial wars and conflicts something must be added to reference elsewhere. Those who dwell only on the picturesque and romantic aspects of colonial life unfairly sketch the landscape. To the hardships of stubbing and planting, fencing and building must be added the worry of war. Four long and disastrous conflicts led up to the Revolution. The periods of peace were all too short, and were disturbed by border troubles with other colonies that came near to them.

England's tradition of losing every battle but the last has been rather costly in the long run. Unfortunately there have risen other traditions less widely celebrated by witticisms. One of them is the ignoring, in the peace settlements, of the interests of her partners in war. This was notably true of her colonial wars in America. Worst of all was the English policy after the last Canadian war, when her troops on their return from the capture of Quebec and Montreal were kept as garrisons in New York and Albany, and treated the province as though it had been recently conquered.

The Cassidy case, already widely known from its inclusion in the Colonial Document series, can now be supplemented by a half-dozen additional documents which throw an entirely different color upon the screen. What has hitherto been portrayed as a riotous treatment of unoffending British troops who were merely doing their duty, now becomes an armed resistance to the illegal quartering of troops, and their brutal treatment of Dutchess County households.

The truth must lie somewhere between the two versions. This is not the only document in which Dutchess men are accused of harboring deserters, but it is interesting to speculate as to the cause of desertion. It was about this time, or a year or two later that the four British companies which had been stationed at New York for over half a century had been dissolved because of their utter failure in recruitment, discipline, and efficiency. About this time, too, at the height of Britain's conquest, a recruitment campaign in England brought only 15% of the enlistment sought.

Captain Paul Rycaut of the British army took an examination of Sergeant Philip Cassidy, who went Sept 29, 1761, by command of Col. Darby of the 17th Regiment to Dutchess in search of deserters. When the sergeant came to "The City", a neighborhood of the Nine Partners Patent, he received information that a deserter named McIntosh was working for

Justice Bockee. Sergeant Cassidy divided his forces, seven going under a Second sergeant of the 55th regiment to Bockee's while he kept on to "The City". Unfortunately he gave his fellow-sergeant his pass and authority. Learning that Charles Lee, John Bravington, and Joseph Roberts, whom he knew as deserters from the 17th had been lately at Jonathan Mead's the Blacksmith, near Southerland's Mills, he inquired of Mead, who answered in a most unBritish fashion, that "he did not know, and if he did he would not tell". Cassidy went on to the Mills and learned from Mr. Southerland that the three men had been there a few days before, apparently with "coined" dollars. Freeman, another man interrogated, also reported the same story, and went next day in search of his coat which the deserters had stolen. At Driskill's house the master confessed his daughter was married to a deserter. Going with Driskill to another house and getting into bed he was dragged out by Jonathan Mead who had thirty others with him, and "drag'd the Serg't and Allan Cooper a Granadier into different rooms and beat them in a most cruel manner, saying "Damn the King and all such fellows that were after deserters." The people kept them prisoners all night, then took them to the house where the other soldiers were quartered. Next day they were carried before Justice Roswell Hopkins "who abus'd them very much" saying they should be hanged, and committed them to the common jail. The Justice refused to take any cognizance of the charge of harboring deserters.

Mr. Bartholomew Crannell told Cassidy that Hopkins would not have treated them so if the sergeant had kept his pass. He was told they could not be released but "by order of the Governor or a letter from him to ye Justices".

"By what information I could collect from the inhabitants" remarked Rycant naively, "those of the Nine Partners are a riotous people and all Levellers by principle."

The new documents following give an entirely different picture of the Cassidy Case.

(1) "By John Darby, Esq. Lieut. Colonel
of His Majesty's 17" Regiment of Foot
Commanding at Albany

PERMIT the Bearer Serjeant Cassidy of the 17" Regiment with ten men and a Corporal of the above-mentioned Regiment to pass and repass in quest of Deserters wherever they may get intelligence of them

Given under my hand and Regimental Seal
at Albany this 27" day of September, 1761.
John Darby."

To Whom it may concern

"By His Excellency the Commander-in-chief's orders to me, You are to Apply to all Justices of the Peace, Constables &c., and to all Troops Regular or provincials You may meet with for their assistance for the Apprehending the Deserters or any others you may get intelligence of whether Regulars or provincials

Dutchess County John Darby"

The effect of this peremptory intrusion upon the privacy of the individual appears in the following documents, which may be allowed to tell their own story.

(2) "The Examination of Jonathan Mead the third taken upon oath before me Roswell Hopkins Esq. one of his Majesties Justices assigned to keep the peace in said County on the Second day of October in the first year of our Reign. This Examinant saith that on the thirtieth day of September last past as he was at work at his Smith shop about his lawful Business and in the peace of our Sovereign Lord the King Sargent Philip Cassidy came to his Shop and without any provocation Bound him with a small Rope Round his arm and then one of the party with Cassidy run up to him Cocked his Gun and swore he would Blow out the said Examinant's Brains if he would not tell where was any Strangers or Deserters. they also told this Examinant they would carry him to New York and hang him and that they with force and arms

did greatly terrify this Examinant Contrary to the Peace of our Sovereign Lord the King and further saith not

Sworn before me the day and date above
Roswell Hopkins"

(3) "The Examination of Caleb Thomson taken upon Oath Before me Roswell Hopkins Esq. one of his Majesty's Justices assigned to keep the Peace in the County of Dutchess on the second day of October in the first year of our Reign—This Examinant says that on the 30th day of September last as he was a plowing in his feild Sargent Philip Cassidy, Joseph Robertson, Allen Cooper, John Roeth, and Thomas Lacock Came to him while he was in the peace of our Sovereign Lord the King and in a Riotous and Inhumane and Barbarous Manner with force and arms did seize this Examinant and Bound both his arms and Protested they would Shoot out his Brains with some of their Guns and told him they would carry him to New York and hang him without any Provocation and this Examinant further saith that he see them use his Brother Ezra Thomson in the Same manner Except Binding him

and further saith not

Sworn and taken Before me the day above written
Roswell Hopkins"

"Dutchess County

(4) Deposition of Timothy Driskill of Crum Elbow Precinct in said County of full age. Taken this fifth day of October One Thousand and Sixty One As follows that on thurs. last five men who are Confined in Poghkeepsie Goal, by virtue of a Mittimus from Justice Roswell Hopkins, the Deponent having just now viewed and seen the persons—they in company with one John Freeman, in the morning of the said Day, the Deponent being in Peace in his own house, Suddenly and at unawares, one of the said five men seized him by the shoulder, another went in the Deponents celler another in his Storeroom, the Deponent asked the reason of this proceeding and what they wanted, on which immediately two others ran up to the Assistance of the person who held him, & they three

hauled him out of his door and Pinioned him with his hands on his back and one struck him with his Gun on his head and one (who they called Lieutenant) pushed him Violently with the butt end of his Musket against his breast, the bruises whereof still remain, the Deponent's wife making an Outcry, one of the five presented a musket to her breast, (she being big with child) swore he would kill her in an Instant, if she spoke another word, his Daughter also Crying another Stept to her and presented a Pistol at her breast, and threatened to kill her and fire the house about their Ears, if she spoke another word—They Ordered his Son to go Immediately and fetch a horse, upon which he went and brought a mare from the plough, when one came to the boy and took the mare out of his hand and made him go in and fetch a Saddle out of the house & lay it on her back. Then one went in the Deponent's house, and fetched out the Deponent's gun & Delivered it to the person they called Lieutenant, who took the Gun and Dashed it all to pieces Except the barrell then the Lieutenant ordered the Deponent on the horse, two of them helped him on, he being so bruised & fatigued as not to be able to mount alone & ordered his partner to go in & destroy everything in the house. they went but broke only a Bayonet as he knows of. then they Carried him backwards and forwards Several miles about the Country, one of the persons signified to this Deponent that if he gave their Lieutenant some thing he would release him, he said he had nothing to give. they continued this usage almost all day, When they Released him & told him they Intended to go to John Albrage one of his Neighbours, and Tie him, but as the Deponent was Informed this Neighbour got Intelligence and Escaped, and further this Deponent saith not, only that John Freeman did not do any hurt Except helping to hold him while the others Tied him.

Timothy his mark Driskell

Louwerens Van Kleeck
Justice of the Peace."

(5) Dutchess County Jacob Klinck of full age being sworn Declared, that Last Thursday in the morning five persons now in goal by order of Justice Hopkins Came to his father's house Enquired for three Deserters, but were answered they know of none, upon which one of them took a saddle out of the house and Laid it on a horse belonging to his father they presented their Muskets to five persons' breasts, two of them being women, and threatened them with Death if they spoke a word. the Deponent finding they wanted to carry every thing away, he took hold of a Gun from the beam. & was goeing to Convey it away, when one them tore it out of his hand and Examined it, and finding it unloaded, took it and broke it in two pieces across a fence Just by the lock, came in and struck and bruised the Deponent in a Violent Manner, his Eye being much hurt now, then went and struck his sister Three blows, then took away the horse saddle and bridle & went off, and further saith not.

Sworn before me
Louwerens Van Kleeck
Justice of the Peace Josam Berg Klinck"

Not all offenders were gentry, or British recruiting officers. Jacob Everson, the defendant in another case, was a substantial farmer and landlord of Amenia.

"Common Pleas January Court in the year of our Lord One Thousand and seven hundred and sixty-seven.
Dutchess County. Samuel Beman Complains of Jacob Everson in custody of the high sheriff of Dutchess County for that to witt that the said jacob the fifteenth day of Aprill in the year of our Lord one thousand seven hundred and sixty five the Close and Dwelling of him the said Samuel at Amenia Precinct in the County aforesaid and within the jurisdiction of this Court with force and arms &c did Break and enter and Divers Goods and Chattels of him the said Samuell then and there being to witt two chests, full of wearing appearell, two Beds, two Bolsters four Pillows, two Beadsteads, six sheets,

one Cupboard, three large Pewter Dishes, four Pewter Basons, Nine Pewter plates six knives, six forks, One Iron Kettle, one Iron pot, six chairs, one Iron trammell, one fire shovel, one pair of Tongs, one bag of Flower, and two Meat Barrells, of the Value of one hundred pounds, in the House and Close aforesaid Being, did take, carry away and Destroy, and the wife of the said Samuell and his five children, being the servants of him the said Samuell in the House and Close aforesaid Being, did beat, wound, and evilly entreat, so that of their lives it was greatly despaired, and them out of the said House did eject, expell, and remove, by means whereof the said Samuell the service of his said wife and children for a long time did loose and other harms to him the said Samuell he the said Jacob then and there did, Against the peace of our Lord the King now, and to the damage of the said Samuell one hundred pounds, and thereof he brings this suit. Bartholomew Crannell"

Dutchess County Samuell Beman put Bartholomew Crannell his Attorney against Jacob Everson "In a plea of Trespass &c."

Considering the number of slaves in the county—about two thousand at the Revolution—their offences were few. Some of them ran away, a few committed violence, or gathered to frolick at a tavern. But they appeared more sinned against than sinning. One of them was sold to a trusting farmer, and then proclaimed himself a free man—under what threats or bribes is not known. In an amusing series of letters R. G. Livingston tries to pass on to Brother Henry the care of a slave woman of whom he is obviously afraid, because of her "opstropalous" behavior. In general, references to slaves in wills are with affection. Many were set free, or given a choice of masters among the heirs. Care of aged slaves was often made a condition of bequest.

A sinister sidelight in the riots of the time is afforded by a letter to the Attorney-General, February 22, 1754. The "blacking up" of the riots suggests the Indian warpaint of Big Chief Thunder of a century later.

"To the Atty Genl of New York

May it please your worship When the late ryot was here in Duchess County I was a stranger here and then falling into the mob they Blackt me by violence & then I wipt it of again as well as I could I went with them and when the complainers made up with Mr. Haveland then they told me that I need not fear for they had made up for me & I paid them £ 1 10s and now your worship informs me that they have made up a Complaint against me etc—

Samuel
Stringham"

Stringham's Mills were in Rombout, and Havilands lived in South Precinct. Otherwise there is no clue to this riot, which may long have antedated Prendergast's rout. Personal assaults were numerous. Even women were not exempt. Brutality is common enough today certainly, but colonial days were by no means exempt.

"People vs Holloway Affidavit.

Sarah Holloway, being duly Sworn, deposeth, that in consequence of The Assault and Battery committed upon her by Joseph Holloway, her husband, and by reason of some other circumstances, she is unable to attend at The General Sessions to be held at Poughkeepsie on Tuesday the 15" of May Inst.

Sworn this 14" Day of
May 1792 before me
Mathew Paterson
Justice of Yr. Peace

Sarah her mark Holloway

Oct. Court—1770."

David Webb complains of Daniel Parish in custody of the high sheriff of D. C.—"on 25 day of December 1770 . . . with force and arms to witt with swords clubs and knives . . . upon him the said David . . . an Assault did make and him the said

David . . . did beat wound and evilly entreat and a stab with a certain Penknife through the Privitus and into the thigh of The said David he the said Daniel then & there did give so that The said David fell to the ground and by reason of the said stab and the loss of Blood thereby occasioned he The said David then & there for Dead did lay by means whereof the said David for a long time to witt for The space of Three months the next following Remained under great anxiety Pain and Distress & in greatest danger of loosing his life and became Mahimed................100 pounds

Crannell Livingston—Att'y for David Webb . . . in Plea of trespass in Assault & Battery."

In 1746, for example, the New York legislature passed an act authorizing bounties of 20 pounds for adult French or Indian scalps, and bounties of £ 10 for the scalps of children sixteen years or younger. It does not make matters better that the act was in retaliation for the Saratoga Massacre.

In the later war of 1754 slaves were requisitioned as laborers with the British Army, and heavy taxes were imposed to support the war and the 2600 soldiers who formed New York's quota in the colonial force of 20000 men who marched under Lord Amherst's orders. Wolfe did not take Canada singlehanded, though English histories overlook our share.

Requisitions were also heavy on the farms, and must have caused great discontent. Some of them were paid for, years later. William Prendergast was paid £ 5 10s for a horse "lost" in his Majesty's service. This was the highest price paid among many Dutchess horses taken. The current price was much lower. Wagons, too, and equipment were taken throughout the county.

In 1755 Quakers and Moravians were required to pay heavy fines for their exemption from service, giving these good citizens great concern and a discontent that may have been a most fruitful cause of the purchase of Vermont acres. Quakers were also required to serve in labor battalions, and to come equipped with spade and shovel, and each with six empty bags. Registration of the whole Quaker population was also enacted. The original law, passed in 1754, was renewed for several years.

By an act at the end of 1756, quartering of British troops was authorized in all public buildings, inns, and taverns, and where these were not available, in private houses, as many as four to a house. These were to be selected by local justices. But if the Cassidy case is any evidence, the tough sergeants did not wait for justices' consent to carry out their orders.

Search for deserters was authorized, and heavy penalties imposed for harboring them. In effect, the colonies were put under martial law like the subject provinces they were, under arms which to them were foreign, and which accordingly were resisted.

One evidence of the times is the act to authorize control of the poor in Dutchess County, Dec. 7, 1754. The poor were to be worked for their keep, and their children taken from them and bound out to service.

Debtors became so common that an act was passed allowing the juryroom in the new courthouse to be made over into an additional jail. As another means of relief to the overcrowding, insolvent debtors were allowed to petition for liberty from imprisonment after certain periods: after three months if debts not over £ 50; after two months, if debts not over £ 25, after one month, if debts not over £ 10. Relief was granted, however, only in case most of the creditors agreed to it, and the debtor agreed to a sale of his assets to pay them. The many inventories in Dutchess records furnish pathetic witness to abject poverty of some debtors.

The years leading up to the Revolution were thus preparatory to the coming struggle, so far as Dutchess was concerned. Their conclusions were negative in character, but they laid the groundwork of the Dutchess position during the war and the Constitutional struggle that followed.

# 20. Conspiracy. 1760

FOR HALF A MILE, at the northern end of our Back Chimney, the boundary of Berkshire County, Massachusetts, marches east-west with that of Dutchess. The joint line once ran the full width of the Chimney, 1.8 miles, but when "Hell's Acres" were ceded to New York, Columbia replaced Dutchess for most of the way.

The lay of the land takes the line over a "hideous steep mountain", as Benjamin Wadsworth called it. Rattlesnakes are still the only occupants. But something very like their venom poisoned relations between Berkshire and Dutchess for a score of years after 1750. It is one of the most sordid stories in colonial history, one of which no one has any reason to be proud, or to cast the first stone. The real trouble with Massachusetts arose because Indians did not accommodate themselves to colonial boundaries. The Mahikans' hunting ground in the Taconics lay in both New England and New York. When the Dutch made a treaty with the Mohawks, its echoes woke the Rattling Hills of Berkshire County.

Dutch preference for peace with the Mohawks had provided that warlike nation with more than their fair share of guns. Thus armed, they fell upon their eastern neighbors the Mahikans, and drove them from the Hudson. The Mahikans' Council fire at Schodack was exchanged in 1724 for a new camp on the Housatonic, and this in turn was sold in the Westenhook Patent, in exchange for the township of Stockbridge in 1736. Peace ensued with the Mohawks, and friendly relations brought about some more or less permanent visitors from their former enemies. Hence the "Mohawk Trail" from North Adams to Greenfield, today.

At Stockbridge occurred the only extended effort to "civilize" an eighteenth century tribe. Some of their members built good New England homes, and planted, while others kept up their old ways of hunting and trapping in the hills.

The Stockbridge experiment soon got out of control. Without the strictest enforcement of justice there has always been deterioration of both Indian and American cultures, when in contact. The praiseworthy efforts at conversion by Jonathan Edwards and his predecessor John Sergeant were ruined by the criminal conspiracy of the landjobbers to get possession of the Indian lands.

At the head of this conspiracy was "the Family of Williams", as Edwards called them. The great man fought his relatives to a standstill, but when he left in 1757 the family of Williams resumed its predatory way, until by 1762 there was almost nothing left of Indian Stockbridge. In 1762 the Indians through their chief Solomon appealed to the General Court of Massachusetts, which ruled that Indian land could be taken for debt like any other. This, of course, meant final destruction, and Solomon with two other chiefs, Jacob and John, went to England to plead the Mahikan case. With him went his friend and fellow-chief of the Wappingers, Daniel Nimham, upon the same errand. The mission proved fruitless for both tribes.

Philip Livingston of the Manor of Livingston was ambitious. He threatened suit about this time for the whole of the Back Chimney, alleging that his patent to Ancram ran "to the line of Connecticut," and that the Back Chimney, though in another county than his Albany patent, must be annexed to his land. William Smith, Jr., was very much worried over this, as it might invalidate the ownerships all along the Oblong. But suits in chancery dragged along, and nothing came of it at last.

Our Manor Lord had other plans of aggression. He invested

heavily in Salisbury and Sharon, perhaps hoping to get these villages under his patent as well. At any rate, when Salisbury celebrated a two hundredth anniversary a newspaper article declared in its headline that sharp Salisbury men had stolen the village from him. It was alleged at the time also, that much of the Sharon common was in the hands of Philip Livingston.

What is certain is that Philip Livingston joined with several men of Massachusetts and Connecticut in obtaining Ore Hill. This famous open mine lies one mile east of Millerton, just below Lakeville. Daniel Bissell of Windsor obtained a grant of it, but Livingston's company persuaded Connecticut that the title was invalid, and took possession. Ore from this hill furnished Livingston with fine quality iron for his furnace at Ancram.

It also furnished ore for the New England furnaces of his rivals; and the wrecking of his forge and the kidnapping of his best workmen must have convinced Livingston that "you can't swap horses with a deacon". One of these men was Elisha Williams, then rector of Yale, and next to brother Elijah, also an ironmonger, chief owner of the Berkshires. Another partner was John Ashley of Sheffield, next door to Ancram of the uncertain boundary. Thomas Lamb, perhaps most unscrupulous of all the sharpers of Salisbury, and involved in the theft of Indian Lake, had got possession of the Davis Mine, another outcropping. His forge was at Lime Rock. With Williams and others Lamb created Lakeville, then called Furnace Village. Its lakes include not only the two beautiful sheets of blue water with long Indian names, but also the two ponds that now occupy the two abandoned ore deposits. Sharon protested against Lamb's depredations, but with no effect. He kept his gains.

Samuel Forbes, a late comer in this deal, brought in two other men of the region, Ethan and Heman Allen. Chard Smith calls their works at Lakeville "the first real furnace as distinguished from a mere forge". Altogether a million and a half of tonnage poured out of these works. Some thirty odd enterprises are listed by the historian of the Housatonic, the biggest one upon Mt. Riga, where the charcoal was brought from all the pits on the mountains. Half a dozen of the forges were on the New York side. There lay the rub.

Heman Allen and another Allen brother, Levi, who had been living on a farm in Dutchess near the border, now set up "in company" in Salisbury. There is good evidence that Ethan Allen visited in Dutchess, and met there his famous friend Dr. Thomas Young of Amenia, who had married a daughter of a Dutchess pioneer in Salisbury, Gerrit Winegar A good deal came of that friendship, as will be seen.

But Ethan had begun to think of wider fields. His heart was not in the smelting of iron, but in what we now call "merchandizing". He was a born salesman, the first and one of the greatest in American history. His capital was too limited, and his influence in Connecticut too weak, to attempt a pitched battle with the well intrenched gods of the valley: Williams, Ashley, Forbes, and Lamb. His were the gods of the hills, where men were as yet self-employed, and willing "to listen to reason", of which Ethan proclaimed himself an oracle.

Ethan sold out in 1765 after three years of puddling, and presently departed for the upper valley of Vermont. Heman and Levi were left behind, though Heman and Ira, a fourth brother, soon joined Ethan. Levi, after a shorter stay in Vermont, became a Canadian Tory. They left debts behind them in Dutchess County, as the following document proves. Andrew Hermanse of Rhinebeck wrote Henry Livingston, clerk of Dutchess County, about a writ.

Rinebeck, Sept. 18, 1769.

"Mr. Livingston

Sir.

The writt I took the other day at your office for Heman Allen was wrong. It must be against Heman Allen and Levy Allen, in company. I did not know that they were in company when I was in Poughkeepsie. You will please to let the Bearer have a writt against Heman and Levy Allen of Salsbury Merchants, and the Bearer will satisfy you for your Trouble.

I am your Humble Servant

Andrew Hermanse."

With new villages springing up around Ore Hill, and laborers in iron filling Sheffield, Barrington, and Stockbridge as well as Lakeville and Salisbury, it became obvious that the most natural outlet of the product ran westwards to the broad and quiet Hudson, through Livingston land. Once over the hump west of Millerton, a level road, well made, led to tidewater. Nothing like it existed on the New England side. Nowhere in America was it more evident that intercolonial commerce was a necessity. But the evil land-itch had possessed the inholders, and they opposed hatred with hatred, to their own great loss.

There were great natural affinities between the Dutch and Yankee traders and artisans. They were living peaceably together in Dutchess. Dutch settlers in Salisbury had surrendered their rights as Yorkers after a few protests. Yankees were crossing into Dutchess and Albany counties. The Yankees were the adventurous, the young, and, many of them, the unchurched. The Lambs and Williamses were not the best of examples. On both sides of the border the more radical people had come, to get free of clerical interference with their loose living. Drunkenness, violence, and counterfeiting were endemic along the line. Each side accused the other of lawlessness; a pot-and-kettle affair.

These conditions in Massachusetts and Connecticut would ripen in thirty years into Shays' rebellion and the riots of the river towns. There were signs of disorder already. Why not employ these restless people in an attack on the Livingston fortress so thinly held by right of paper patents illegally obtained from trusting Indians? Why not, indeed, make common cause with the poor cheated natives, by honoring their putative grants through approval of the General Court of Massachusetts? It might be possible, in the present disturbed state of things, with the French threatening the Yorkers' northern frontier and with the eastern boundary unset, to fulfill the old dream of a Yankee port on the tidewater Hudson.

The Indians were soon won over. Col. Elijah Dwight, husband of Abigail Williams, was the storekeeper and general manager at Stockbridge. He was quite ready to dispense liquor to the Indians. Massachusetts appointed this worthy gentleman to the boundary commission, from which point of vantage he could view the land and make out his deeds. A cousin of his wife, Joseph Hawley, an honorable but stubborn man, was head of the boundary commission, and was so committed to his own notion of a Massachusetts boundary that he refused to accept the evidence of his own surveyors. The boundary was left unsettled till 1786, as a result. But Hawley, who was the nephew of Thomas Hawley, was waiting for some such compromise as that of Ridgefield. It did not come, but his position thus gave him a perfect point from which to act at the right time.

Robert Livingston, son of Philip, tried to persuade his manor tenants to take out his deeds, and when he was refused, called on the sheriff to evict them. Thus began in 1752 the so-called Anti-Rent Wars, which were nothing of the sort at first, although later the cry of "No Rent" was raised when radicalism got into the picture, and riots were spirited up to win what the law denied.

# 21. Hallenbeck's Hubbub. 1753

WHY IS THE PERSONAL stand of a single Hudson River farmer possessed of historical significance? The answer lies in the words of loyal Cadwallader Colden, Lieutenant-Governor of New York, historian and scholar: "The Eyes of the other Colonies were on New York, and were at a stand still till the most daring insults upon the Government there encouraged them."

Another acute observer, and, like Colden, most hostile to the current turn of affairs, was the merchant and provincial councillor John Watts, leader of the Court party. "For my part", he wrote at this time, "I really believe some new constitution will be found in time, between the Mother country and the colonys. Nothing similar to the present State appears in History."

These are Loyalists speaking in criticism of their home government. We make a great mistake if we think that Whig and Tory in New York were wholly opposed in principle. On the contrary, they were united in most affairs that concerned the welfare of the colonies. Only when it came to the crown's ultimate prerogative did they part company. It was John Watts the Tory, not his opponent Robert R. Livingston the Whig, who predicted independence and its cause. Speaking of England's refusal to permit the use of paper money in New York, when the province was under financial strain from the wars, Watts observed: "to throw the Burthen off their own shoulders upon those of their absent, unrepresented, and of course unheard fellow-subjects, must not unless the Nature of Man is changed such a Government end in oppression? Then, what follows?"

The crisis was approaching, and clear-headed men were aware of the signs. That is why a small cloud over a distant hill might presage the deluge. And when, to change the metaphor, the valley of Ruliff Jansen's Kill "drank the deepest of the baneful cup of infatuation", as they said, the wise man inned his money.

Michael Hallenbeck, of Dutch Albany stock, dwelt at Taghkanic in Albany County, now Columbia. He was kin to Jan Casper Hallenbeck, whose name adorns the Casper Kill in Dutchess. Catryna Hallenbeck, wife of Pieter Lassen the brewer, lived by the kill, and through her line the heritage is widespread in Dutchess in the clans Lawsons, Lassens, and Lossings. Michael, in fact, had two sons, Jan or John, and Casper Hallenbeck, who appear in this story, as does another Hallenbeck, William by name.

Historians, I find, like to get at what they call the "basic" element in the composition of any historical event. To some, the Hallenbeck Hubbub is "basically" a proletarian uprising of an agrarian nature, an "anti-rent war". To others, myself included, it is "basically" an incident in the dashings of New England waves against the Dutch dykes along the rim of the Hudson valley. But certainly to His Majesty's Government at the time it was an intolerable insult, because it set at naught the instructions of the colonial office. Here were colonies, in such legal matters as titles to property, practically at war with each other as if they were independent states and not the meanest subjects of the Crown! On the part of New York the rebellion was the more flagrant, because his Majesty's troops were actually ordered into action in defence of one of the landlords, Robert Livingston.

But as Dean Swift remarked of another matter, "if a man makes me keep my distance the comfort is that he keeps his at the same time." The determination of Mr. Pitt's government to keep two brawling provinces from going to war over

Michael Hallenbeck's crops not only saved the Hudson from Massachusetts, but kept Britain in ignorance of the larger issue, until the smoldering resentment found time to gather and burst into more open flame. They were too far from the scene to realize that the same troops that suppressed Hallenbeck and his friends were stirring the hill folks of the Berkshires into anger. It is no accident that Joseph Hawley, commissioner in 1758 on Massachusetts boundary commission, was the first man in his colony to proclaim for open war with England. "I am of that man's opinion", said Patrick Henry when John Adams read Hawley's letter to him in 1774. In open defiance of the instructions from London, Hawley pulled up the surveyors' stakes and declined to go further, thus throwing the whole question over till after the Revolution.

Michael Hallenbeck had been a tenant farmer on Livingston lands for thirty years and more, when he started his rebellion. His farm in the valley of the Taghkanic Kill lay a few miles north of the parallel valley of Ruliff Jansen, on the road that led through Ancram to the Salisbury mines and Ore Hill. There were deposits of ore scattered all through the Livingston patent, as the neighborhoods still bear witness on today's maps of Columbia County: Ancram Lead Mines, Weed Mines, Copake Iron Works, Spaulding Furnance, and New Forge. These, and the prospects of rich ore on Mt. Riga in the Dutchess Back Chimney, were no doubt the exciting spurs in the activity of the Berkshire landgrabbers who interested Hallenbeck in the flattering prospect of leading his fellow tenants in exchanging Livingston leases for Massachusetts titles backed by Indian deeds from Stockbridge. The pretext, of course, was the high rent.

The conflict of claims reached as far back as 1705, when the Westenhook (Dutch for Housatonic) Patent was granted by Lord Cornbury. It extended vaguely into the towns of Sheffield just north of the Connecticut line, and Stockbridge, north of Sheffield. Some Dutch farmers had settled upon it, but the Indians gave deeds to the land along the river in 1724, and reserved a part for themselves. Apparently the Yorkers then obtained Massachusetts deeds, for both in Sheffield and Salisbury to the south, old farmhouses still bear the Dutch stamp.

In 1734 the Stockbridge mission school was started by John Sergeant, and continued in 1751 by Jonathan Edwards. The latter saint struggled manfully to keep his relatives of the Williams and Dwight families from the double graft of sales to the Indians, and of purchases of land from the Indians through deeds for land included in Governor Hunter's patent to Livingston.

Massachusetts on its part laid claim to a line five miles from Hudson River, while at the same time stating, truthfully enough, that her colonists had once a hundred years earlier surveyed the river on both sides and picked sites for settlement "with grants of land and privileges of trade" upon the Hudson's shores. The Yorkers stood out for twenty-five miles, after giving up the claim to the west bank of Connecticut; then they came down to twenty-five miles east of Hudson. But both sides knew well that the twenty-mile limit on the Connecticut boundary would be the ultimate point of compromise.

Why then all the delay, all the letters and instructions, meetings and arguments? In the vain hope of somehow taking advantage on one side or the other, of some crisis of helplessness, when one's own side, ready to spring and establish possession, might take over the mine fields, and the growing iron industry.

The boundary commissioners for New York were connected with Dutchess; William Nicoll of the De Lanceys, William Smith, Jr., of the Oblong, and Robert R. Livingston. On the Massachusetts side, besides Joseph Hawley, were the land dealers Elisha Williams of Pittsfield, Oliver Partridge of Salisbury, David Ingersoll and John Ashley of Sheffield, and Major Joseph Dwight of Stockbridge. Through Ingersoll they dealt with the settlers, through Williams and Dwight with the Indians, and through Partridge with the governor and the General Court of Massachusetts. They constituted a most formidable organization, predecessor of the predatory gangs of grafters that have more than once laid hands on oil domes, forest reserves, and railroad lands.

Our stage is now set, with this long preamble of a tale. Tempted by the prospects of ore lands as yet unpossessed, Michael Hallenbeck, with other tenants of the Manor, applied for Ingersoll's Indian deeds and leases, and refused to pay Livingston further. He had been, as some said, sixty years a tenant without complaint. But thirty or sixty, he succumbed all too soon to the Yankees' sales talk, as many a man had done since. With him went Josiah Loomis, an ore-digger, whose knowledge of the region was important. A number of others joined them.

Robert Livingston defended his manor. He acted now with promptness, taking up Loomis' one-year lease, and turning out the Hallenbecks in 1753 after the usual notice.

The Bay State crowd at once forbade this. The connivance of the Massachusetts plotters appeared at once in Partridge's letter to Livingston forbidding him to oust his "Massachusetts" tenants at Taghkanic. Livingston promptly referred the letter to the New York Council, whose committee report reached Lt. Governor Phips of Massachusetts. The upshot was that Massachusetts authorized their own commissioners to grant titles to Livingston tenants, or to others if they refused. New York then appointed its first commission to negotiate. Some New York tenants were seized; and a proclamation was issued, calling for the arrest of the aggressors.

It soon appeared that many Livingston tenants had been deceived by the landjobbers who had told them that their new lands lay outside of the Livingston patent. Ingersoll quickly covered up this discovery, which might have led the tenants to reconsider their position in so directly challenging Livingston ownership. Ingersoll's surveyors appeared, and soon persuaded the doubters that New York lay in New England. New deeds multiplied, and Massachusetts officially surveyed several townships on York land.

In July, 1752, Livingston burned one tenant's house and

reaped Loomis' wheat. This brought reprisal from Hallenbeck. Two Livingston tenants were driven out, and a Yankee tenant replaced them.

Next year, Livingston evicted Jan Hallenbeck at Taghkanic, and arrested his father, Michael Hallenbeck, involved in the events of 1752. Hallenbeck was taken to Poughkeepsie jail, where he became for a time the center of the controversy. The Colony of Massachusetts in its most official hectoring tone, demanded his immediate release and complained of his sufferings. Governor George Clinton in his reply admitted that Hallenbeck had not been long in escaping. As for the evil treatment while in Poughkeepsie jail, Admiral Clinton said rather naively that he could not believe such inhospitality had occurred. No doubt Hallenbeck's Lawson connections had arranged things in jail very comfortably for him, including his escape.

Meanwhile in the field of conflict both sides were getting bolder. Massachusetts sales were being carried into Rensselaer's Manor, where the argument of illegal Indian purchase did not obtain. Robert Noble of Claverack now joined with Hallenbeck, who had returned. With their band they caught two deputies and deposited them in turn in Springfield jail. Honors were even now, and one can see a grim smile on Michael's face as he bade his prisoner rest easy!

The Albany sheriff, Yates, next arrested a Yankee and was himself caught and added to the Springfield jail-boarders. Michael Hallenbeck was soon officially appointed to protect Yankee rights, and Noble made a captain of militia. Open warfare resulted. New York's De Lancey took up the fight as Lt. Governor, realizing that all this was linked up with the Philipse Patent and its troubles.

He conferred more authority upon Sheriff Yates, who with a larger force put Noble to flight, and captured Loomis. William Rees, Yankee tenant by attornment, was killed. Massachusetts offered a reward of £100 for the arrest of his "murderer".

A month later, in May, 1755, John Van Gelder, son of an Indian and a white woman, joined Noble in a raid of revenge at Ancram, where the whole force of skilled workmen were carried off from Livingston's furnace and kept as hostages. On this occasion they came up the Dutchess Chimney and assaulted Ancram from the south. Jacob Spoor's house suffered there. Ancram had been in Old Dutchess until 1717, as it lay south of Ruliff Jansen's Kill.

Both sides now armed for real conflict. The Governors were impressed with the dangers involved. Public affairs further north demanded attention. The French war had not gone well. As a result, and to ensure cooperation in the war against Canada, both sides forgot their quarrel for a few months. Prisoners were finally exchanged, and De Lancey asked the Lords of Trade to intervene.

Once more the Berkshire gang tipped over the apple-cart. Noble kept on selling Indian deeds, Van Gelder wounded a Dutchman and was later caught. Troops were ordered from the English army to protect Livingston, whose life had been threatened. The next Governor of New York, Sir Charles Hardy, renewed the appeal to England, and in 1757 the Lords of Trade at last set up the twenty-mile limit as the boundary between the provinces.

Again the frontiersmen took matters over. Van Gelder, released as an Indian by Sir William Johnson's request, killed two Yorkers. Livingston obtained a secret order, and rounded up the offenders, keeping them in prison for a year. But the sales kept on. Reference by a Livingston man to "the rioters' Club" indicated, if such were needed, the organized nature of the conspiracy. But York had the whip hand, and a double purchase including York grants was sought by many Yankee tenants lest they should be driven out.

From 1758 to 1766 Hallenbeck and Noble kept fairly quiet. These were the crucial years of the French war when conscription was high and discouraged a domestic Kilkenny.

In New York, according to John Watts, one man in five was taken in the draft. Dutchess alone sent half a dozen companies. The Indians whose deeds were sold had all joined the army. But when the Indians returned in 1762, things started all over again. Walter Livingston, Robert's son, led forty armed tenants and drove off a threatening mob that had been collected. The odds would indicate only a half-hearted attempt, and some collusion with similar mobs raised by Munroe and Gunsaulus in southern Dutchess is suggested.

At Poughkeepsie in 1766 it was rumored that a house had been seized and fortified by the mob, imitating Noble's style of invasion. Poughkeepsie experienced her second visitation of regular troops. The Twenty-eighth Regiment then in pursuit of Prendergast was followed by the Forty-sixth. Another company, the Nineteenth Infantry, shipped to Claverack and from there marched rapidly inland, capturing Noble and dispersing his followers, and sacking Egremont and Barrington.

It was Lt. Governor Colden who authorized this action, though he commented sourly on the fact that public opinion sanctioned this attack on rioting country mobs, while in the same province city mobs roamed the streets unpunished, with soldiers closely confined to barracks, lest outbreaks occur. Unfortunately, Colden had incurred universal condemnation in the town, for appealing against the contention of John Morin Scott, hero of the mobs, that jury's verdict was final as to facts, and no appeal lay to a higher court. Once more the executive was crippled by its invasion of the judicial function.

Shelburne's warm heart was moved by compassion for the Massachusetts victims. A dispatch favorable to them was printed in an English newspaper. The London Chronicle of August 25, 1766, detailed the British soldiers' excesses in terms that suggest that the dispatch was at least semi-official with the Massachusetts government.

"By an express from Pittsfield last Wednesday we have further accounts of the distresses of the inhabitants at the western parts of the province who are at their wits' end, being afraid to work in the fields in the day, and of having their houses burnt or robbed in the night:—a number of armed men, who call themselves the King's troops, but conduct themselves like a number of banditti or collection of robbers, not content with their daily ravages in Nobletown (Hillsdale), have extended themselves into Egremont in the province, broke into and robbed the house of one Bunts, in the night of the 13" instant, bound the old man, etc., then went to another house and took off another man and carried him with them: the night following they were again in Egremont it is said those armed men give out they will clear all the inhabitants off from the river (Housatonic); they are in fears of a visit from them at Great Barrington, as they wrote to them that they should come. Major Williams and Capt. Dwight went to Nobletown to solicit the officers of the party for liberty that Sheffield and Barrington people might come and reap the grain that was not destroyed, and afterwards Col. Ashley went upon the same errand, and were refused.

"It is said the basis of L----n's and R-N-'s invenomed treatment of these people is, conscious of the weakness of their title to these lands, and that they never obtained the Indian title in a just and equitable manner, and that Jacob, Solomon, and John, who were the proper owners of the land, are gone home with Mr. Griggs, nephew of General Conway; they imagine they shall not hold any of these lands unless they so distress the present occupiers, who have bought the Indian title, to come in and take leases under them. This is the stimulus that actuates them at the present day!"

The "stimulus" of this propaganda was, of course, to take the onus from the Indian plea against themselves. Williams, Ashley, and Dwight knew very well that the Indians had "gone home" to England to complain of the loss of Stockbridge of over 10,000 acres, and of the Massachusetts law that took from them all protection of law against these hungry landsharks. Solomon, Sachem of the Mahikans, fought later at Bennington with the Americans. Jacob and he were at Boston in 1775, with Nimham. The riots and raids by Noble and his gang all over Livingston Manor are blithely passed by, and sympathy given to the Yankee cause alone.

Finding that the Yorkers meant business, the Bay State resentfully quietened down. Some guerilla riots followed, but the back of the invasion was broken. Hallenbeck returned to

Salisbury, where the beautiful Hallenbeck Brook and Valley join the Housatonic. The name of the old rebel now adorns the most peaceful of countrysides, where by a grim irony an exclusive club of New York fishermen holds sway over the lovely brook and its lively trout. The old man must have turned in his grave.

Robert Noble settled in Massachusetts. Some of the land-grabbers transferred their activities to the Wyoming, where Connecticut was presenting its claims to Pennsylvania. But most of them went to Vermont, where the free-for-all was now under Allen's rule. They carried their Tory predilections there, and some of their clients from Dutchess as well as Columbia followed them. But the northbound trend cannot be wholly attributed to their skill as Yankee salesmen. Something of allure must be allowed the Green Mountains.

Meanwhile, in spite of the absence of the salesmen, and in spite of the historians, too, Dutchess and Albany continued to flourish, both counties reaching the mark of 50,000 population about the same time, 1800. The Hallenbeck Hubbub revived in 1790, but was quickly put down by Governor Jay.

The Livingston title in Manor lands,—no longer a manor—was more fully disputed by a claim to its northern gore in 1811 and 1812. "Lady Mary Allen" Livingston, widow of Henry Walter Livingston, defended the suit, which had been carried on by the Attorney General Van Vechten of New York, at the direction of Governor Daniel D. Tompkins. Yet with all this weight of counsel she won the suit by a directed verdict of the Chief Justice. An entry of Lady Mary reads like an extract of the Hallenbeck times. June 1812.

"A villainous plot has lately been discovered, as was formed principally by . . . to burn several houses and to kill Mr. J. S. Livingston. These three men are the ringleaders in this lot, in the Commotion which exists; they engaged to pay largely one . . . if he would destroy by fire Genl Livingston's works at Ancram & my house and barns &c. Van Gelder employed . . . Kline to assist him . . . is lodged in jail. Very soon after this viz on the 3 of July my house was discovered to be on fire at the roof. . . ."

"Lady Mary" may fittingly close the story of the Hallenbeck Hubbub. This is a different story from that of the Van Rensselaers, which wound up at Hudson in the 1840s with tin horns and calico, the Ku Klux paraphernalia of night-riding. Some of this originated in real grievances, which law or economics could properly settle; more often in mere violence for its own sake; and part of it in that element of romance which seeks the irony of turning the tables upon the rich, fortunate, and vindictive, by exalting the poor and illiterate.

# 22. Daniel Nimham of the Wappingers. 1762

AT WICCOPEE, along the northerly slopes of the Fishkill Mountains, there dwelt in 1700 the principal tribe of the Wappinger Indians. The word Waban means east, and applied to the whole confederacy of nine tribes on Hudson's eastern shore, all the way down to the Manhattans. These had local names, such as Nochpeem in the High Lands, Sint Sing and Kitchawonk in upper Westchester, Weckquaesgeek and Siwanoy in the lower county. But in 1700 only the tribe at Wiccopee survived in any numbers, although goodly encampments dwelt in the Highlands at Canopus and Peekskill Hollows.

The number of these River Indians, as the English called them, was then about 300 fighting men, perhaps 1,800 in all. But these included also the Mahikans, who lived north of the Wappingers. Thus the Wappinger tribe could hardly have amounted to more than a thousand. Some of them, as our early deeds and maps prove, dwelt in little groups along the major kills, with good-sized units at their mouths.

When Roger and Catheryna Brett came about 1710 to develop their estate at the Fishkills, they very wisely befriended the Indians, and were loyally repaid. The Indians continued their hunting and fishing on unoccupied lands. Their deeds of sale they regarded as permits of habitation, and though they came in later years to a notion of the white man's sense of property, their ideas of it were vague.

When Mrs. Brett, in return for some signal service, assured the Wappinger tribe that she would not disturb them in occupancy, and that they might dwell in Wiccopee "during her pleasure", they were no doubt pleased but puzzled. They had never intended to live anywhere else.

The Indian Sachem Nimham is usually described as native of the county or as "of Wiccopee", never of "the Fishkills" or of Rombouts Precinct. As Sachem for his nation his "land" extended to the whole watershed of the Wappings Kill and Fishkill, as well as the High Land. He was born about 1700, and probably grew up as a companion of Mrs. Brett's three boys, Francis, Robert, and Rivery. The last named did not reach manhood. Some knowledge of the Indian tongue was valuable, and many Dutchess men spoke it fluently, serving as interpreters. Judge Jacobus Ter Boss, a contemporary at Wiccopee, testified he knew the Algonkian well.

It is thus quite a matter of fact to picture the Indian youth as guide and teacher of the white boys at the Fishkills. At the Wappings Creek nearby dwelt another Indian boy, with a Dutch name, Couwenhoven. He may have come by his name in the way of nature. In 1663 Lieutenant Wolfertse Van Couwenhoven was in command of the West India Company's yacht during the second Esopus outbreak, and passed extended periods at the Wappings, with supplies for soldiers and settlers on the west shore as the quarrel dragged on. The young sailor made friends with the neutral Wappingers, and persuaded one of their Sachems to undertake a mission for the return of white captives, which proved successful.

The perpetuation of his name in the tribe strongly indicates that the Dutch commander, politic in all ways, had been afforded the hospitality of the tribe, and that a son had been born to him. In 1702, forty years later, a leading Wappinger, Kowvenhahum, signed an Indian deed, and in 1729 a young hunter Kounham, was rewarded by a bounty of the Dutchess supervisors for bringing a wolf's head. Nimham had already won this honor, his reward being included in a group of four payments aggregating £1 15s. The other three were white men.

Evidently Indians and whites made common cause against the wolf-packs in 1721.

By this time the young warrior had been chosen Sachem, or Sakemaker as the old deeds read. At least in October, 1730, he was selected in a lawsuit to testify concerning the sovereignty of the River Indians. He stated in his deposition that "the Wappingers were the ancient inhabitants of the eastern shore of Hudson's River, from the city of New York to about the middle of Beekman's Patent; another tribe, the Mahiccondas (Mahikans) were inhabitants of the remaining eastern shore of Hudson's River; and these two tribes constituted one nation".

How shall we interpret Nimham's testimony? Beekman's Patent was the popular name of the great Back Lots Patent, preserved today in the town's name. At no point did it touch the river shore. The upper Beekman's Patent is more commonly known as Kipsbergen.

If we observe that the Rombout purchase was defined in terms of the two interior waterways, the Fishkill and the Wappings Kill, I think we shall have our answer. The Indians bounded by streams. These streams and their water-shed extend across the county to the east but do not include the eastern ridges or the Harlem Valley, as does the Beekman Patent. Thus the Wappingers hunting grounds went halfway toward Connecticut, while the Mahikans owned the watershed to the east, including those that flow to the Housatonic, on which they were also at home. By this explanation the Wappingers "owned" the whole Wappings Kill watershed, which rises in the Upper Nine Partners near Milan. Along the shore of the Hudson fishing was doubtless in common.

The white men followed Indian preference in buying "east into the woods". When the Nine Partners bought their land, they secured their purchase from both Wappinger and Mahikan sachems. Their tract extended from the Hudson to the Connecticut line, and both tribes were involved.

The usual explanation, which divides the court between the two tribes by an east-west line near Poughkeepsie, does not fit the facts, since Nine Partners precinct lies wholly north of this line, and Wappingers would certainly not be entitled to half the payments. Nor can it explain why the Wappingers did not invite Mahikans to share in their sale to Rombout.

Nine Partners Patent had been licensed in 1697, but not until Nimham's time, October 13, 1730, was valid payment made. Nimham joined with Acgans as "Principal Sakemakers and Proprietors" for this Lower Nine Partners land. The deed, printed in 1923 in our Historical Society records, names fourteen Indians, apparently seven each from the two tribes. With true Indian courtesy, Mahikans are recorded first in signatures, Wappingers named first in the body of the deed. Among Nimham's associates were Pechewyn and Taquehamas, two of his comrades in wolf-hunting a dozen years earlier.

When Acgans and Nimham receipted "for all the rest" in accepting goods of £150 value, all specified, they specifically reserved and excepted for certain "North Indians" who had not yet been paid. Seven years later these Mahikan chiefs, Shawanachko and Shawasquo, receipted for their special gifts. They include "ten striped blankets, ten duffle blankets, twelve dozen pipes, thirty knives, seven hatchets, two strands blankets, twenty-four pounds of powder, twenty eight pounds of lead, six white shirts, two guns, and a half-barrel of strong beer". If Shawasquo is our Shawash of Shekomeko, his alcoholism may not have been helped by the sale.

The well-known Charles Clinton surveyed the tract. No doubt here, as elsewhere, he was accompanied by Indian guides, whose payments he records in his accounts. It is probable that Nimham went with him, both to protect his party from wandering hunters, and to make certain of the bounds. As Clinton's sons were often with him, Nimham may have known both James and George, leaders of New York in the Revolution.

In 1721 Mrs. Brett complained to the governor that her surveyors had been obstructed and driven off by drunken Indians, and that on another occasion they had come to her house, shouting that they meant to kill her. This occasion, the only violence by Indians reported in all Dutchess history, fortunately passed without harm. Mrs. Brett's escape may be attributed to Nimham's timely warning. At all events, she did not lay the blame on the Indians, but on Judge Leonard Lewis, who with George Clarke, of the governor's council, was trying to jump her patent to the Rombout tract on the western side.

In an Indian suit, the Wappingers declared that they had often served their white friends in war. One such period was 1689, when Arnout Viele, owner of a putative Dutchess patent, was a recruiter. Another period was in 1745, when the colony's volunteers were called out. As the conflict with the French rivals deepened the local tribal hostilities weakened, until Mohawk, Mahikan and Wappinger gathered in friendly fashion at Stockbridge, in Massachusetts, and on tracts in Mohawk country in central New York. Others of the Wappingers had joined some of the Mahikans who followed their Moravian friends to Pennsylvania.

At this time, it is probable, Nimham became a Christian. He was baptized Daniel, his son was named Jacob, and his friend became Stephen Kownham. Leaders of the Mahikans at Stockbridge were named John, Jacob, and Solomon.

When the French and Indian war had reached alarming proportions, in 1756, Sir William Johnson, Superintendent of Indian Affairs, summoned all the River Indians to join him. Nimham led the Wappingers to Stockbridge and deposited there his aged, and the women and children, and then marched off to the war with his friends, three hundred strong.

Captain John Montresor relates that one dark night in Canada, on his round, he heard a stir in the bushes. "Give the countersign" he shouted. "I cannot" was the reply. "O John, it is you! Don't shoot. It is Solomon".

Stockbridge, to which place Nimham had entrusted his weaker people, must have been well known to him. He had perhaps gone to school there, though he always signed with his mark N, an N reversed, as on a seal. Perhaps, after all, he could read. He may have attended Jonathan Edwards' lectures on the geography of Palestine, for Edwards was there when Nimham left his people.

The warring colonies must have set him thinking. Perhaps he had known of Noble's work from the first, for some Indians, seduced by liquor, had already practiced Noble's tricks in Rombout precinct. It may, indeed, have involved Nimham himself, for he was Sakemaker; The Wappinger Indians are not known to have acted in anything without their leaders' authority; and certainly it was Nimham who managed all the later sales which have come to light. But if it was Nimham who erred, it was but for a moment, and he strove to repair the wrong he had done.

"Letter to John T. Kemp, Atty. General of N.Y., July 29, 1755. We, the undersigned subscribers, understanding that one Jack, a Negroe fellow, formerly being slave to William Green of this place, had made application to your worship in respect of lands from the Indians, which by him and others of his accomplices and by that most wicked and dishonest seducement has we understand obtained a lease of said Indians by deluding them with strong liquor and making them drunk in order the better to obtain his lacivorous ends which after these Indians getting sober and considering what they had done by the crafty and subtel intreague of the fellow, they then with terror made the whole matter known to me Cth Brett who am the right and lawful owner of said land, which may appear evident by my patent. I only gave these Indians a verbal promise (as they were friends to me in a time of difficulty) to live upon my lands as long as I should think proper. Judge Chambers, I question not, knows very well how and for what reason I came to give these Indians liberty to live upon my land.

"To describe this fellow according to his deserts is more than tongue or pen can express or do. He has been whipped at the public whipping-post several times by order of the authority, which no doubt this fact can well evidence. He lived with his master borne Greene having companies of his neighbors' Negroes rendevezing with him etc. The authority thought proper to banish him and he has lived with Samuel Bayart at New York.

Catharyna Brett
Robert Brett
Theodorus Van Wyck
Henry Terbos
John Bayley"

William Green, mentioned in Mrs. Brett's complaint, may be William Green of Long Island, who came to Dutchess from Suffolk County before 1765 and died there in 1775. He was a Quaker, and lived in Amenia. A son, Augustus, also lived in Dutchess, serving in the 7th New York Regiment. His third son, Ambrose, married the daughter of a prominent Amenia settler, John Lester, and had children as early as 1767. But another William Green is also recorded.

It is worth noting that while the complaint of Nimham issued later mentioned Brett land as well as Philipse land, no charge was ever brought against the Brett family, and the trial specifically exempted that part of the complaint.

Of the service of the Wappinger company in the Canadian War we have no adequate record. Sir William Johnson evidently approved of it, for he continued the tribe in his friendliest protection, and sent his son to act as their protector. But when the tribe returned, soon after 1760, they found that what little remained of hunting land to them was endangered by the lawsuits instituted over the Gore dispute.

Not content with the two hundred thousand acres in their patent, the Philipse heirs laid claim to land that had been regarded as part of Dutchess, lying in the north slopes of the Fishkill Mountains. Although the Rombout Patent read "easterly into the woods", it also mentioned the Fishkill with the low lands about it, as part of the south bounds. This emboldened the Philipse family to claim up to the banks of the kill, except for lowlying meadows. The result was a compromise, by which the boundary ran East 6° North instead of directly East. Beekman had already settled the eastern part, but the Brett heirs did not settle till after the Revolution. Thus Wiccopee, the real home of the Indians, was in dispute at this time, and might be taken from them. This was the last straw. The enraged Indians fought back by the only means in their power, private sales of their own along the Gore, and perhaps further south.

Public opinion, if the phrase fits, had been aroused by the arbitrary actions of the parties at law. In 1762, as was testified by a well-known Connecticut attorney, James Brown, both Beekman and Philipse agreed to determine their bounds by a law suit over a tenant's deed. The tenant selected for the trial was Moses Northrup, a Quaker of good standing, whose farm lay in the eastern part of the Gore, next to the Oblong. Beekman won the suit, and Northrup was evicted, for no purpose except to fix the bounds.

This flagrant injustice appears to have given the spark that set off the conflagration. The angry Indians were at hand to face the flame. Without them, there would have been some rioting. With their aid, the whole province was to threaten its masters with revolt. As in Boston, British troops were used, and only good discipline and restraint on the part of leaders of both sides prevented a "Dutchess massacre" from entering the record as a cause of the Revolution.

As it was, the fire was checked from spreading, but its coals smouldered in the ashes.

Fortunately for the welfare of the colonies, and postponing actual rebellion for a decade, the Pitt Ministry led by the Earl of Shelburne suddenly switched to conciliation. The Stamp Act was repealed, and orders went out in every direction to cease illegal land jumping, the intimidation of Indians, the boundary fights, and unjust evictions. But the Whigs were tied up with slave trade and greedy commerce, and wealthy men who demanded that the colonies should "pay their share". Shelburne was only two years in office, the old theory of dominance was reaffirmed, and new winds began to rise.

News of the settlement of the lawsuit concerning the Beekman-Philipse gore may have reached Nimham during the war. On July 3, 1758, the Wappinger Indians Hendrick Wauman, Arie Sawck, Out Quamos, and John Backto gave Nimham their power of attorney to act for the tribe. In other letters, Mektoos, One pound Pactone and Stephen Cowenhum gave their own powers of attorney to their friend. The procedure is unusual, and suggests the legal guidance of white men.

Of these the most active up to the final trial was Samuel Munroe. He seems to have been the grandson of one William Munroe, a tough Scot who had been captured by Oliver Cromwell at the battle of Worcester, and deported along with thousands of other Scots to be sold into slavery at Boston. We learn of his imprisonment for Anabaptist tenets. His family tree claims that sixteen descendants fought at Lexington.

Samuel, a born trouble-maker, infested Dutchess from the early seventeen-thirties. He lived in Beekman, and most of the charges against him were for unpaid debts. One was for another violence, and is a charge brought by a woman. A certain John Munroe is also charged with violence, and a Jean Munroe is found with child by Archibald Campbell, who is mixed up with Munroe in another affair. Both Munroe and Campbell turn up in the list of loyalists whose property was confiscated.

In spite of his ill-repute Daniel Nimham was persuaded to put his case in Munroe's hands. On November 6, 1764, the five Indians Stephen Kounhum, Daniel Nimham, one Pound Pocktone, Jacob Aaron, and Jacobus Nimham affirmed their choice and election of Samuel Munroe as "their attorney and Guardian of their estates for them, to enter upon and take possession of their messages, etc.", "that they shall be better capable of better managing their own estates". This instrument was acknowledged before Judge Jacobus Ter Boss of the Court of Common Pleas, and John Akin, a Justice of the Peace for Dutchess. Both men were well known; their courage in sanctioning a transaction of this kind speaks for itself. Ter Boss' evidence at the 1767 trial was equally bold.

Nimham had begun to follow the Stockbridge precedent in the sale of deeds to lands of dubious title, even before he was thus protected by a white man. Since it has been stated that no examples of these transactions have been found, we give one document copied in full.

We give below, as nearly as we can, the copy of a document written in 1764.

"This Indenture, made in Dutchess County, in the Province of New York, the twenty-fourth day of July, in the fourth year of the reign of our Sovereign, Lord George the Third, by the grace of God, of Great Britain, France and Ireland King, defender of the (Faith) Ann Dominie, one thousand seven hundred and sixty-four. Between Daniel Nimham, (Indian) Native of the county and province aforesaid; in behalf of one pound. Poktone, and Stephen Kounham, (Indians) Natives of the county and province aforesaid, of the first part, and Nathaniel Worden Cordwainer, of the same place and county aforesaid, and province aforesaid, party of the second half, witnesseth: That the said Daniel Nimham by virtue and force of a power of Attorney from said Poktone and Stephen Kounham, well executed, dated the 21 Day of this Instant July, Being fully Impowered in my legal manner to dispose of the land of them or either of them, in the county of D, for and in consideration of thirty pounds Lawful money of New York already in hand paid, the Receipt wherof the said Daniel Nimham here-by acknowledges, and in consideration of the Rents and reservations hereafter mentioned and hereinafter contained, are reserved on Behalf of the said Nathaniel Worden, his heirs Executors, and assigned to be paid, observed and performed, hath granted to farm let unto the said Nathaniel Worden aforesaid, all but part of land aforesaid lying Being in Dutchess county in a place called Beekmans *** (Thence follows the description of the reserve.) from thence running east to the top of the mountain to a heap of stones; thence a northwesterly line along said mountain to the southwest corner of Thomas Worden's lease; thence alongst said lease North to the Northeast corner of the same; thence due west to the great pond called [Whalley] pond; thence alongst said pond to the south end of the same; thence a Direct course to the rocks called the Indian Rocks; thence a southerly line to a certain white oak tree, and so to the place of beginning. The same together with all and singular, the Improvements, Income, advantages, profits and appartnances of wood and under wood upon land, and meadow, streams, water course, and all priviliges thereon being thereon arising, proceeding of any Name, Nature of Kind whatever, thereunto belonging an any wise appearing, to Have and to Hold, the same lands and premises afore described the same Nathaniel Worden, his heirs, Executors and Administrators, and assign from the Day of the Date hereof, for and during the term of Nine hundred and Ninety and Nine years, full if to be completed, Ended, Expired and finished; yielding thereof Besides the thirty pounds already paid, yearly and every year during the said term unto the said Poktone and Kounham, their heirs, Executors Administrators and assigns, or to the said Daniel Nimham for them, two Pepper Corns in and upon the feast of St. Michael, the Arch Angel, if demanded, as a yearly Rent and Reservation for the premises, and the said Nathaniel Worden for himself.

his
Daniel N Nimham
Mark

The Wordens were a most acceptable Quaker family. Another deed, in the Palmer papers of the New York Historical Society, describes the sale between Daniel Nimham, Indian of Dutchess County, New York, and Stephen Kounhoun of the same, to Benjamin Palmer of Pelham Manor, for land in Dutchess County, dated Dec. 19, 1765. This was made after the first trial; the sale was clearly in defiance of the governor's order.

Meanwhile Captain Robert Noble of Massachusetts was continuing his own depredations on the same tack. In 1763 he wrote from "Barrington" to Sir Wm. Johnson advising him of his intention to purchase from the Indians a tract "now claimed by Mr. Renslear" (Yankees never recognized the honorific "Van") and referring to a Mr. Bostwick, apparently as attorney. The letter is lost.

On July 28, 1762, the New York Council were informed that "Daniel Nimham, an Indian, claims lands in Dutchess County in possession of Col. Frederick Philipse' heirs and of Mr. Brett." The Attorney General was ordered to examine the case. Like the other officials of his day, John Tabor Kempe, the Attorney-General, was heavily involved in land-schemes of his own.

"Mrs. Catharyna Brett to Sir William Johnson

Fishkills August ye 26" 1762

Having been Informed by Mr Van Wyck when Your Honour was there Last Capt Nimham had Informed You that he had Land here and was kept out of his Right Sr I should a thought my Self happy to have waited on your Honour at Mr Van Wycks had I known on it and Given You a true Account of the whole Affair which I have Many Evidences to prove; Sr I must Trouble You with the foundation of the Affair, Upwards of Thirtie Years Ago Sr I met with a vast Deal of Trouble by Some white people at Poghkeepsie, Sr wee having the Oldest Patent of any Round us, the Poghkeepsie People Getting on that part by Division was allowed to me and Sold part of it I Sr Endeavoured to convince them in a Kind Manner but there was no Convincing of them and Sr there lived a Vast many Indians in this place, when we first Came here and this Company my adversaries Began to threaten me and I was Advised to Aject two of the white people they never Apeared but let Judgment go by the fault, I received the Writts of Possession, this Enraged them, to Sett up the Indians Against me telling them that I had stollen their Land, and they would but (y) it, but Old Nimham and two of his Sons Remained my friends, the White People Could Not corrupt him he was an Honest Morral Creature, as ever I knew for he was an

Instrument to protect me for I was in Danger of my Life, and I was obliged to Complain to Governor Burnet, who sent for the Ring Leader one Lewis, and also the Indians called a Councell on purpose, and Ordered an interpreter, had Our pattent and Indian Deed Read to them, the Indians Owned the Indian Names in the Indian Deed to have been the First Proprietors, the Governor Reproved them and made them Decease, and the Governor desired me to have that part Surveyed so that the Indians might be convinced of the Bounds. He gave a Special Warrant on the Late Governor Colden who was then Surveyor General, who came himself in Order to do it, but was Soon Repulsed by a Company of Drunken Indians who were sent by them, who threatened to Break his Compass and was stoped. He Sent for me and I went too him and found Old Nimham and his two Sons With Mr Colden, Persuading of them to lett it be Surveyed but in Vain and then I agreed with them, to pay them if they would see it Done, and with much Difficulty Mr Colden proceeded and after it was Done, the Governor ordered the Indians to Appear before him, and Convinced them. And that time there was Mr Philip Cortland and Mr Guyline VerPlank present, and the Governor desired to make a present being they were Indians, and we the Pattenties Mr Cortland Mr Verplank and myself, promised we would but not as a Debt but to renew friendship. I Waited a Considerable time for my partners to join with me, and the Indians were uneasy and they Neglected so Long At Last I went and Paid my part which amounted to Seventy Pounds, and I had Carried to Judge Swartwouts when Nimham came with the Indians and they were fully satisfied. then this Nimham put me in mind of a promise, that I had made him, concerning a place where he lived, that he and his children might Live on it as long as he Lived, that neither I or my Children Should molest them I Did in gratitude to Old Nimham, being he was a friend of Mine, he never Asked me what quantity of land he should have but the place were he lived. and when ever he went off the Land was Mine. But Sr in a Little time after, Some mischievious white people went to the Indians and hired Little Bitts of land and made them Give their Leases, then they put in what Quantity of Land they pleased and made their Leases for Ninety Nine Years. And this Old Nimham has been dead about Twelve Years but his Children might have stayed on till this day but his oldest Son one Shake Came to me and Asked me Liberty to Sell the Improvement to one Capt Swartwout I opposed it at First and a Little after he came down Again with Seven or Eight more Indians for Liberty to Sell the Emprovement. I give him Leave to Sell the Emprovement, and he sold it for Twenty Pound. It being a Precarious time, I suffered all this, for fear of their setting up the Indians Against me. About a Year Ago Capt. Nimham was last with me, And I told him if the Whites owed him Any thing by promise he might Set it if he Could, I have Nothing to do with it, but from that time forward he should make no Demands there, and he Seemed to be Satisfied and thanked me and I have not seen him since. Honoured Sr I am Ashamed to Trouble your Honour with such a Long Scraul but hope you will Excuse me for Necessity Obliges me to it to prevent Trouble Sr I have heared that he has made a Complaint to Governor Monckton and he has ordered the Attorney General to Enspect into it; Sr if Your Honour would be pleased to Order Some One to Enquire of the truth of what I have Wrought as there are many Evidences to proof it.

Sr I Remain with my most
Humble Regards Sir/Your most
Obedient Humble Servant
Catharyna Brett"

On Sept. 20, 1763. Sir Wm. forwarded this letter to Lt. Gov. Colden.

Colden counted the River Indians in 1763 at 432, scattered about.

"To the Honble Sir William Johnson Bart.

Spring Hill Oct. 8" 1763.

Sir

I have your favor of the 20" of last Month by the Indian

Hendrick Wamash who says that several people at Fishkill and Poughkepsey owe him for some peices of Land in several places. I told him that near 40 years since the Indians of Fishkill and Wappingers were heard by Governor Burnet on a like complaint at the House of Mr Haskol near the place since called New Windsor, that then everything was settled to the content of Nimham the Grandfather of this Man & of the other Indians to which this man had nothing to reply, but owned that he was then a boy and present at that meeting.

I told him that I could do nothing without hearing the Parties concerned for the doing of which he said he could not stay, and therefore I advised them to lay before you what they have to say upon that Land & on your writing to me I would call the parties concerned before me if there appear any just reason to you for believing there is anything still due to these People, & shall if the Council agree to it summon the persons indebted to the Indians to appear before the Council.

But I must desire you not to send the Indians to me without necessity, because it occasions an expense to me, for which I have no allowance.

I gave directions to Mr Banyar to make out the Commission for Mr Johnson as you desired. Why he has not don it I know not. As to the Blank Commissions he told me it had allways been refused by former Governors as those can be no necessity of doing it. As soon as you shall send me the names the Commissions shall be made out.

You may assure yourself that no man can be more desirous to comply with your desire than Sir Yr &c

C. Colden"

On every hand arose the complaints of Indians cheated of their lands. A certain Robinson wrote to Sir William Johnson of the vile treatment given in Rhode Island. Cherokees complained in the South. The threatening war-clouds broke into storm in May, 1763, and did not clear till peace was signed in 1765. Johnson had his hands full with Teedyuscung and other troubles. He had no chance to force compliance with

King George's proclamation of December, 1761, though Lieut. Governor Colden had given it currency in his own proclamation on February 17, 1762. It required "persons having seated themselves on land claimed by Indians to remove therefrom on pain of being prosecuted with the utmost rigor of the law." Officials were forbidden to pass any land claimed by Indians, without a proper license from a lawful authority. The proclamation was very strongly worded, but it did not daunt the ragged Scots who settled Red Stone, nor the Tory landlords of Dutchess. On this matter Tories and outlawed tenants were at one.

Glimpses of Nimham's great activity at this time turn up in the archives. On September 18,1764, he sued Philip Griffith for £50, and on September 19, 1764, he sued Isaac Chase for payment of £10. On December 9 an indictment was sworn out against him by Richard Cain (living at Pawling) before Judge Henry Van de Burgh. Nimham was sworn in £50 and his bondsmen Isaac Perry and John Ferris (Quaker names) £25 each.

Since Nimham's name appears in no suits before this date it is clear that these relate in some way to the sales, and that the Indian Sakemaker had free access to Dutchess Justice in the courts. Two of the most interesting cases are those of Nathaniel Sackett against Daniel Nimham in 1764 for a total of £50. Sackett became a Revolutionary leader of the best repute. He was the son of a famous minister, a prosperous merchant of Fishkill. That he gave credit to Nimham at this time is significant.

We learn from court records that Nimham issued leases also to Stephen Willcox, a respected citizen (one of that ilk served in the 4th New York), to Joseph Craw, and Daniel Munroe, son to Samuel Munroe. All these were linked by the Governor's Council as implicated in the case, because their names had been reported by Philipse Counsel, William Livingston and James Duane. A third attorney, John Morin Scott, later joined them. All three were Whigs, perhaps purposely chosen, though Livingston had long been attorney for Philipse.

Duane, Mayor of New York after the Revolution, and Scott, a leader of the Sons of Liberty, are in strange company here. Both, through their wives, were interested in Dutchess lands. Property may become a paralytic prison.

On receipt of the attorney's report, Beverly Robinson, Roger Morris, and Philip Philipse petitioned the Governor for a hearing. A Committee was appointed, of which Daniel Horsemanden, Tory lawyer introduced by Chandos, was chairman. They reported that the tract in question belonged to the proprietors, who already had a considerable number of tenanted farms and possessions. They recited the organization of the Indians, and Munroe's election as guardian, and sales of the land.

At the trial March 6, 1765, Nimham under interrogation claimed the lands in question, amounting to all the lands except the original purchase. He was too modest.

Few properties of the size were held in flimsier titles. Nothing but interest preserved it.

The original purchase by Jan Seybrandt and Lambert Dorlandt had never been consummated, though licensed for purchase in 1691. Adrian Philipse bought them out in 1697, but his deed describes the land differently and is therefore highly questionable. Seybring and Dorlandt had purchased "to a marked tree" along the Rombout Philipse line. Philipse omitted the mention of the tree altogether and extended his line to the whole length of the Rombout Patent (16 miles). Governor Fletcher then, without further warrant, extended it still further to Connecticut (4 miles further). No further payment was made for either extension, nor was the amount of payment given. The Indians therefore, in law, were entitled to the deed under the proclamation of 1761.

At this point in the trial, when the above deeds were in question, Beverly Robinson suddenly produced a deed dated August 13, 1702, and signed by Tackquararas (Tochquamas) Cowenhahum (Couwenhoven), Sungham, Shawess (Shawash) Sipowerak, Crounatacht, Wassawawogh, and Mecopaas. Two of these were certainly names connected with Nimham, but of an earlier generation. Two others had signed the original deed.

This deed granted all the land mentioned in Governor Fletcher's Patent, and to the extent justified it. But the Indians present objected that the names were not those of a whole council, that the deed was totally unknown in the tribe's history, and that all Indian history showed the greatest accuracy in such matters. One Pound Pocktone, Nimham's associate, a man eighty years of age, exclaimed that he recognized some of the names. A later account adds that he had never heard of the deed, however.

The case at law turned on the validity of the three documents: the purchase of the original Indian title, the Fletcher Patent, and the Robinson deed of 1702 (produced in 1765).

Of the first, it must be added that while it describes the river line from above Verplanck's Point to the Rombout line, and the Rombout line to the marked tree, it does not describe either a western or a southern line. It has therefore no value.

Of the second, there is no indication that the Indians at the time ever sold their land as described in the deed.

Of the third, there is some doubt that it may be a forgery. Professor Oscar Handlin so describes it, in plain words. But Cadwallader Colden examined it carefully, and pronounced it genuine. The signatures of several well-known men figuring in government in 1700 were recognized, and the handwriting was affirmed to be that of William Sharpas, a clerk of the Council, and an attesting witness. The quality of the paper was challenged; but this, too, was found genuine.

Forgery may therefore be dismissed. The Governor's Council were not in such straits as to descend so low as that. But Robinson's conduct in keeping the document in his own hands, and the refusal at the later trial to permit the defendants counsel to peruse it for more than a few minutes, render it subject to justifiable suspicion that the deed was false, in that it was obtained, as so many other deeds were, by seduction and bribery, and thus would fall under the condemnation of the Shelburne Ministry, if carried too far.

Certainly none of the Sakemakers had signed it, nor was it known to the tribe. It had never been recorded, but the Council averred that this was not a law. In this they quibbled, for it was a regulation, and was regularly insisted upon. When Arnout Viele was granted land in Dutchess, he lost it because the deed had not been recorded; and a later deed displaced it.

The weakness of the Philipse case lay in this fact. It was glozed over by the Council decision that the Robinson deed was valid, and that it was superfluous, because the Fletcher Patent already covered the same land. The Council carefully omitted the fact that the governor's Patent was a complete violation of all rules laid down for other patents. If governors could do this with impunity, let each man look to his own!

As if conscious of the dangerous nature of their procedure, Beverly Robinson and his friends used every means to browbeat and intimidate Daniel Nimham. He had no counsel to advise him. Samuel Munroe, who attended him, was threatened with the charge of maintenance, and was actually arrested and imprisoned immediately after the trial, by the Attorney General. "Maintenance" is a legal term, "an unauthorized and officious interference in a suit in which the offender has no interest, . . . to assist with advice . . . to defend the action." But as Munroe had been appointed guardian by the tribe, acknowledged before two justices, this charge savored of Star Chamber proceedings. This again the Council perceived, and therefore preferred charges against the two judges, citing them to appear and show cause why they should not be dismissed. This was, indeed, high-handed, and must have aroused the people of Dutchess to a feeling that the landlords would stop at nothing to maintain their titles. The Council adopted the Committee's opinion "that by reason of the said Samuel Munroe and the Indians, and his abuse and perversion of the proclamation a great number of persons are deluded into a belief of the validity of an Indian title . . . which by stirring up the Indians and similar claims may be attended with dangerous consequences to the peace and tranquility of the whole province and greatly discourage the further settlement and improvement of the country."

This was the crux of the matter. The settlement of the country had been attended by such dishonesty and graft in the land-grabbing, that any verdict which set matters right would be sure to furnish a precedent for upsetting other patents, and the whole rotten edifice would tremble.

The Council members were all "Gentlemen of estates", and were acting in panic. The number of Philipse tenants who had turned to Indian deeds had grown so large as to constitute a real threat. The authority back of Robinson and Morris was the fact that they were veterans of Wolfe's army, and with many veterans already settled as tenants, that hundreds of other veterans were at the moment clamoring for land with which to pay their debts, so that Colden was issuing titles to 2,000,000 acres of Vermont land alone to meet their maws.

It was a dramatic moment in colonial history when Robinson offered his deed in evidence. It lay upon the Council table. Samuel Munroe got hold of it, and had started to read it, when it was snatched from his hand by a member of the Council, who told the Indians to go home, their case was lost.

Poor Nimham, daunted, but still hoping in white justice, said he would only accept that from the lips of the Lieutenant Governor. Colden, (in the later account: "after a time of hesitation and after urging by some members of the Board") then said "the case was so; they must go home like good children and accept the verdict." The deed was valid.

So the Indians, whose expenses had been mounting while they awaited the court session, went sorrowfully home. Munroe was imprisoned, but soon escaped and put new forces into motion.

There now enters into the case a fresh figure: that of a "next friend", who prepared a legal statement of the case called at the time by its first words: "A Brief State". It was used in the second trial as a source book. Oddly enough, at the second trial two years later, presided over by Governor Moore, this document was seized by him, while the Robinson deed remained in Robinson's pocket, Sir Harry Moore saying that he could not invade a gentleman's privacy.

But the "Brief State" was probably widely read. As was intended, the injustices of the trial were spread abroad, to alarm the remaining tenants, and to excite the whole populace of the court. Out of this alarm came the Prendergast case, in the following spring. Munroe, it was asserted, was at the bottom of it. If so, he certainly used the document. Its authorship is therefore a matter of some interest.

A study of the document involves a comparison of it with a second document: "A Geographical Historical Narrative of the case of Daniel Nimham against the heirs of Frederick Philipse" etc.

The two documents are clearly by the same hand. They are by a New Englander, since the writer speaks of evicted persons flying to New England as the more hospitable parts of His Majesty's Provinces. They are by one who attended the second but not the first trial, since the detail is entirely different in the two. They are by a person of legal training, of academic background, and of religious vernacular. The writer speaks of "clouds of witnesses", for example.

Finally, the attorneys in the second trial, acting for Daniel Nimham as plaintiff, were named Spalding and Marsh "of Connecticut". A great part of the second document consists of the entire closing speech of Spalding in verbatim style, identical in general purport, with the remainder of the 90 page document.

A careful search has revealed only one possible author, and one possible associate counsel for the defense. Asa Spalding, Yale 1752, and the only Spalding of the period with a Yale degree, studied theology at college, and prepared to enter the ministry. He succeeded Rev. Cyrus Marsh at Kent in 1755, for a short time. The Litchfield Association declined, however, to sanction his permanent appointment. He left in 1756, and two years later served as chaplain with Connecticut troops at Fort No. 4, now Charlestown, New Hampshire. He settled in Fairfield as an inn-keeper for a short time, which of course implies an interest in politics. The General Assembly of Connecticut appointed him Surveyor of Lands, and in 1765 by request of the assembly he acted as chief surveyor to prepare a new map of the Colony, which was to be forwarded to England. In 1766 he was lieutenant of Militia, and in 1768 deputy for Norwalk in the General Assembly. He then removed to New Haven as lawyer and surveyor. In later years he returned to Fairfield. Though known as a sound lawyer, he was reported to be intemperate in habits.

The Rev. Cyrus Marsh may with equal confidence be named as the "Mr. Marsh" who served with "Mr. Spauldin of Connecticut" as the attorney for Nimham. Marsh was pastor at Kent from 1741 to 1755, when he was removed from his pulpit on the charge of immoral conduct. During the first years he took an active part in opposing the Moravian Mission to the Indians at Pishgatigook, or Schagticoke as the Dutch spelled it, the Kent encampment of the Mahicans. In 1766 he secured a testimonial of good conduct from his ministerial association, and was restored to communion, though not to his pastorate. He had devoted himself to legal business, and between 1761 and 1767 he represented his town of Kent in the General Assembly. From 1764 he also served as Justice of the Peace. He died in 1771, at the age of 51. No other man of the name, with legal experience, dwelt so near the Indian lands as he, and none is described as having any interest in their life.

It was stated in the verdict of the Governor-and-Council that some affidavits submitted by the attorneys in their evidences had been taken before officials of another province. Judge Marsh would have been the logical agent to secure such depositions in Connecticut. The one contribution to the argument made by Marsh was to the point, and must have been the subject of a ruling before any impartial judge. This was that the Philipse heirs could not both deny that Nimham lived on their Patent since he dwelt at Wiccopee, and in another suit pending at the time claim Wiccopee as legally included in this patent.

With Samuel Munroe either in jail or in flight, and with the Dutchess justices indicted for exceeding their offices, Nimham must have turned to New England for aid, "The more hospitable of His Majesty's provinces", as Spalding neatly termed them. He would naturally have gone to Schagticoke, or Kent, and there have learned of Marsh, and through him, of Asa Spalding. The latter is careful not to disclose the source of income that paid for Nimham's next move, the journey to London. It may have been the same that paid for his companions for the Mahikans, John, Abraham, and Solomon.

With them went a letter from Sir William Johnson, wishing them a prosperous journey, calling them his children, and expressing his concern for them. Spalding in his plea tries to make this an official sanction, but Sir William Johnson was probably not eager to cross swords with the whole Council on so obscure a case. He gave the excuse of illness for not attending the trial—no doubt a good one, and sent his son Capt. Guy in his place, with orders not to intervene in the case.

From the time of his landing in Britain until his return at New York, Daniel Nimham was the guest of His Majesty King George the Third. It is pleasant to relate this personal act of kindness, recorded by Asa Spalding. In another of the Shelburne Manuscripts the authorized Bill of the entire expenses is given, for one white man, and the seven Indians. Possibly the white man was Mr. Griggs.

The Earl had secured for his Indian guests a private interview with His Majesty, and a referral to the Lords of Trade. Shelburne's letter is very direct and explicit upon the thing.

"To the Lords of Trade. Whitehall August 16, 1766.

My Lords:

Four Indian Men (one of whom is their Sachem) and Three Indian Women, belonging to the Tribe known in America by the Name of the Wappinger Tribe, have been brought from thence, without the consent of the King, or any Recommendatory Letter from any of the Governors, in order to Petition His Majesty in Council for the Recovery of a Tract of Land, which, they complain, has been unjustly taken from them; I send your Lordship enclosed, by the King's Command, all the Papers which have been put into My Hands, by those Indians, upon the Subject of their Complaint, & am to Signify to You, His Majesty's Pleasure, that, after taking the same into Consideration, you do Report to me your opinion upon the Contents of them for His Royal Information.

I am, at the same time, to signify to your Lordships His Majesty's further Pleasure, that you do consider of the properest Method of having these Indians taken immediate care of here, and of sending them back to America, and as in a former instance, it was thought proper to order the Agent for the Colony of Virginia to take care of three Cherokee Indians who were brought to England in the same manner these People have been. His Majesty to prevent Inconveniences or loss of Time, desires your Lordships will immediately settle with the Agent for the Massachusetts Bay (to whom I have in the meantime given proper Notice) and Report to me (for His Majesty's Information) an Estimate of the Necessary Expences of their reembarkation, Presents, &c, as in the case of the Cherokees; But I am commanded to acquaint your Lordships, that as these Indians have been brought over without any Authority, His Majesty does not think proper to re-imburse Any Expences, which may hitherto have been incurred, for their Passage and Maintenance.

I am &c
Shelburne"

According to the itemized bill for the expenses incurring in hospitality to Nimham and his group, from August 20 to September 26, £40 were paid for lodging and £83 for wine and liquor. Such bills were never seen since Sir John Falstaff's pocket was picked by Prince Hal!

A later bill for liquor was for £127, 2 pence. Twenty-five

pounds were paid for the return passage, £53,8s for wine and brandy for the voyage.

To make the Indians ready for presentation at Court, "lace coats", "silk ribbands", "colors of cloth", linen, and "Hats" were purchased, together with buckskin for making sandals. The combination of buckskin Moccasins with full court regalia must have been stunning.

Eight pounds were paid to an Apothecary; no wonder, after all the liquor! Fifteen pounds went for silver arm-bands suitably engraved. Twenty-six pounds were set out in presents to take home.

They sailed for New York some time after the end of September, and must have arrived in October or November.

It was later reported that at a meeting in Philipse Patent on his return, Daniel Nimham was asked by Philip Philipse why he had engaged in the voyage. He was alleged to have replied that it was none of his making; he had been led into it, as he had been in the whole matter. The story rests on ex parte evidence. It is hard to believe that Nimham did not look back to the day when he gave homage to the English King as the proudest of his life. It would be some time before another citizen of Dutchess would have the opportunity to greet an English Monarch as his *own* guest, and repay Nimham's call on George III.

Nimham got to England in the nick of time. Six months later he might have been jailed. William Pitt became mentally ill toward the end of 1766, and Shelburne, then Secretary of State, was thereafter continually thwarted by his colleagues and the King, and finally dismissed in 1768. It is not unlikely that the Tory Council in New York had some inkling of how things were running "at home", and felt they could defy the Secretary's orders with impunity. The Earl of Shelburne wrote to Sir Wm. Johnson:

"If you find cause to believe that these people have been ungenerously treated and deprived of their Lands by fraud and Circumvention under pretence of undue and unreasonable grants on pretended or inequitable purchases; you will doubtless take every measure that lies in your Power Towards procuring them such a satisfaction as the nature of the thing will admit of, and afford them, in general, the benefit of your Countenance and Protection."

Sir William could not go along with his Excellency. It was not as simple as that. It was no longer justice, but the state itself that was threatened. If mobs like those in Dutchess should rise in every county, what might not the Indians do, in emulation of Pontiac? Let sleeping dogs lie, and growling dogs be silenced.

Spalding is careful to avoid any reference to William Prendergast, so that it is difficult to say whether the scene of eviction he depicts is connected with the troops called out to suppress the Irish leader, or whether it is, as Spalding represents it, an entirely separate incident. He narrates it as a sequel of the scene just described.

## Bloody Sunday

"This affair, however, has been lamentable in its consequences. The said Mr Robinson (as it is confidently Reported) without any manner of legal Warrant, or authority for so doing; thereupon having collected a Body of upwards of two hundred soldiers, consisting partly of Regular Troops, and Partly of the Militia of said Province, all well armed, and supplied with ammunition, and other warlike Aparatus, besides Waggons and Waggoners, in a warlike Posture marchd up against that poor defenceless People under a Pretence of subduing the Rebels, giving out, that they had acted in open Rebellion to the Crown of Great Britain; that they were a Pack of Rebels! Rebels! and Traitors! and upon a Sabbath Day, long to be remembered, arrived among the Inhabitants aforesaid, and in a Hostile Manner, drove them out before them, burnt and destroyed some of their Houses, pillaged and plundered others, Stove their Cyder Barrels turned their provisions (such as they did not see cause to use otherwise) out into the open street, Rift open their Feather Beds, laid open their Meadows and Fields of Grain, and either took or destroyed the Greater Party of the Effects of this poor but loyal people."

While Nimham was on the ocean the Earl of Shelburne addressed a letter, his first, to Sir Harry Moore, just arrived as governor of New York.

"Whitehall, Oct. 11, 1766

Sir: Application having been made to his Majesty in Council by four Indians of the Wappinger and Stockbridge Tribe complaining that they had been deprived of the property and possession of about 204,800 acres of land, between Hudson's River and the Line which divides the Province of New York from that of Connecticut, His Majesty, as well from the consideration of Justice as in tender compassion to those people, whose distresses have driven them so far to seek his Royal Protection: has been pleased to refer their cause and the vouchers they brought with them to the consideration of the Lords of Trade and Plantations, who have reported their opinion, that there is ground for further examination into the state of the Tracts and Proceedings upon which the complaints of these Indians are grounded, and observing in particular that the prosecution directed by the Lt. Governor and Council of New York against the guardian, agents, and protectors of those Indians carries with it unreasonable severity, the colour of great prejudice and partiality of an intent to intimidate these Indians from prosecuting their claims; it appears extraordinary that these Indians, having continued in uninterrupted possession of their land and in the actual improvement and possession of a great part of it, should whilst they were fighting under his Majesty's banners be deprived of the possession of it by persons claiming under a grant made by the Governor of New York of as old a date as the year 1697, or by any pretence of a purchase made from the ancestors of those Indians by the original grantees.

"The small and inadequate consideration usually given on occasion of those purchases and the arts and management by which they have generally been acquired seldom entitle these claimants to an equitable Relief, and render the Indians the object of attention and humanity.

"The principle of equity and justice cannot be dispensed with in any country, or considered upon a footing with instructions merely local, altho those principles may chance to oppose the temporary policy of a public place they will notwithstanding be found to be the only basis of lasting power and prosperity.

"His Majesty has therefore directed me to recommend to you in the strongest manner that you will take under your most serious consideration the case of these distressed people and turn your thoughts to every possible measure that may obtain for them a just and lasting satisfaction and that you will take on yourself as far as justice and the reason of the thing shall demand the office of their advocate and protector. I am, Sir, with truth and regard, Sir,

your most obedient humble servant

Shelburne."

Matters in Dutchess County had been going from bad to worse. The affair of William Prendergast in the year 1766 was an outgrowth of the same quarrel. Because of its interest it has been given separate treatment.

According to Spalding, it became dangerous even to speak of Indian leases in Dutchess County. Sales of land continued in secret, however, and Beverly Robinson, sensing the drift away from Philipse deeds, decided upon a bold step, that of issuing one-year leases, to be executed at once, with a notice to leave at the end of the year, to all reported to be on the point of signing up with Nimham. Fifteen tenants were singled out for this summary treatment.

Robinson came upon them at some place on the land. The tenants had chosen one of their number to speak for them. Robinson rushed upon this man, threatening him with a charge of "Champerty!" The terrified tenant was unable to speak for some time, and the evictions proceeded. Spalding expressed his opinion that these evictions were carried out in "a somewhat Mobbish Manner", as were the replacement with more obedient tenants. "Champerty" is the agreement of a party with some one party in a suit to undertake the suit on the promise of a share in the award if successful. Americans call it "ambulance chasing."

When Nimham presented a new petition on his own arrival, Sir Harry could not refuse it. He appointed the following January to hear it, and later set March 1 as the date. Meanwhile Nimham, unable to find a New York attorney, had turned to "Mr. Spalding", the young gentleman from Connecticut. At the hearing on March 1, Sir Harry Moore demanded an immediate trial. Spalding pressed for the attendance of Sir William Johnson. The Governor was willing, but objected that he would not be able to come at that time of year. The Council, however, pressed for immediate trial, and March 6 was set. Spalding had but a week to prepare and bring his witnesses.

Under the circumstances his performance was amazing. To gather such a "cloud of witnesses", as he called them, on such short notice, in the very face of their landlords, and so soon after the Prendergast trial, would be thought impossible. But Dutchess men were of stouter stuff than some others. Against Nimham's complaint only three witnesses were called, and two testified, neither of them at the time a Philipse tenant.

We learn that the Wappinger tribe at the time consisted of two hundred and twenty-seven persons. Spalding urged the governor to try the case alone, since all the Council were interested parties; but this was rejected as reflecting on the honor of its members.

Of the several lists of witnesses, that of Spalding's Narrative is given here: Deacon David Paddock, George Curry, Peter Angevine, Captain Guy Johnson, Samuel Drake, James Philips, John Buoys (Buys), John Dupee (Dupuy), Nehemiah Horton, Joseph Crane, Samuel Astin, George Hughson, William Hill, Joseph Traverse, John Van Tassel, Daniel Townsend, and Bartlet Brundage. Judge Underhill and Joseph Merrit were not examined because objection was raised that they were too much interested.

Samuel Munroe was also served with a warrant and came to town, but before the trial took place was committed to jail, "where", Spalding remarked sourly, "he appears likely to pass the remainder of his days". Actually, he was in Dutchess within a few years, and sued a debtor in good form.

Other names appear on the Council's list: Samuel Field, Henry Van Amburgh, Richard Curry, James Dyckman, Esq., Dan Cornwall, Gilbert Bloomer, William Ogden, Samuel Hozer. These were on the list served with summons.

Spalding gives some interesting details of the "evidences". James Brown, an ancient gentleman and a celebrated Connecticut lawyer, (undoubtedly he of the Oblong business) testified that he had defended Moses Northrup unsuccessfully in the put-up job of eviction between Beekman and Philipse. Brown testified that he told tenants that Adolph Philipse himself had told him the land was never owned by the latter. Brown looked into the title and found this was true.

Daniel Townsend told how when he went to live on the land years before in 1738 he had to agree with the Indians before they would let him live on it. He finally signed up with them, and agreed to make a new deed with them in case he signed with Adolph Philipse.

David Austin deposed that in 1730 he had cut and stacked hay which the Indians burnt, and insisted on his making payment to them. On his complaining to Adolph Philipse, the latter told him that the area was the Indian Hunting grounds and he must come to composition with them.

James Philips, formerly of the Philipse Patent, found a Wigwam on his land, and was forced to agree with the indwellers.

"In short", concluded Spalding, triumphantly, "clouds of witnesses have been adduced, whereby methinks it hath been fully, clearly, and absolutely proved, that almost every Person that ever settled himself upon said Lands before 1756 did it only by permission of Said Tribe."

In written depositions Jacobus Ter Boss and James Philips

testified that Indians had already maintained their claims; that they never sold their land twice: Judge Ter Boss affirmed that he understood the Indian language well; that he had lived nearby them for thirty years before the settlers came. Adolph Philipse had told the tribe they must all meet him, but they never did.

Spalding added: "Samuel Munroe, I am credibly informed, will testify that Adolph Philipse and he had agreed upon a deed for the Indians to sign, but Philipse was on his deathbed and died before he could sign it." "I have heard the said Munroe give the same account of the matter," he added.

Peter Angevine testified that all Tenants "bought their peace" with the Indians, prior to the going off to war.

This the Philipse attorneys did not deny, but claimed it happened only once, and was merely a bribe to keep the Indians quiet. Matthew DuBois of Fishkill testified to the same effect, alleging that he had been employed by Philipse to go around among the tenants, and bring all to an agreement under the patentees, and all but one had so agreed. The Indians were then given presents.

Timothy Shaw for the defendants gave the names of forty tenants who had always paid the Philipse family their rents. The names were certainly of bona fide tenants. Shaw had moved south, to Westchester.

During the trial the governor observed some writing in the hands of Nimham's attorneys. He demanded to see it, and it was surrendered under protest. Beverly Robinson and others read it and were much disturbed. Springing to his feet, and pointing out Bartlett Brundage, he cried out: "There! there's the man." Another cried: "Swear him!"

"The harmless old gentleman was brought forward and suddenly qualified. "Now" (said one of the Honorable Council) "What say you? Dare you say upon oath that the Complainants have not had a fair trial? Was there any browbeating? Instead of any such treatment were they not treated with the utmost tenderness? Did not the Council appear as mild as they do now upon their present trial? What say you? Remember you are upon oath? Dare you say they have not had a fair Trial!"

"The Good Old Gentleman now a little Daunted with great simplicity and deliberation made a low bow and said he did not think they had a fair trial, that he thought the Parchment that had just been read contained a just and true account of the matter."

Mr. Robinson demanded to know who had drawn up the document. Brundage asked whose property it was, referring to Robinson's keeping his own deed in his pocket. The parchment was however delivered, and its contents duly denounced by the Council in their verdict.

Spalding, suddenly required to sum up, did the best he could, after having been given a few minutes to peruse Robinson's deed of 1702. His summation occupies twenty-five pages of the "Narrative", and is a well written brief.

The Wappingers' land, he claimed, had never been purchased. If land could be transferred without purchase, why not any man's land? The Indians were still a nation, in treaty with the King of England. Philipse's disuse of the land for so many years proved that he knew he had no title to it. No ex post facto law can make anything lawful which is unlawful ab initio. Smith's History of New York stated flatly that no purchase without a previous governor's license was valid. By testimony of both James Brown and Captain Johnson a great concourse of Indians is necessary to validate a sale. The 1702 deed had been executed in New York, and had never been acknowledged before a legal authority. Enrollment was required under English law. How could a governor's doing what he was forbidden to do make the enrolling unnecessary?

As to the conduct of both parties, he urged the preponderance of credible witness. Both Adolph Philipse and Frederick Philipse his nephew and heir had been heard to admit they had not purchased the land. Thus a strong presumption had been made.

Then in a moment of Connecticut cuteness, he committed

an error that lined the Council as Yorkers up against him. He made the point that Philipse's deed read from the east side of the Hudson east to the Connecticut line; whereas in 1702, before the Treaty of Dover in 1731, "the Connecticut line in law" ran at that time (1702) on the west side of the Hudson! This piece of egregiousness went unargued.

John Morin Scott, in his rebuttal, took Spalding's case to pieces, but Spalding did not preserve what notes he took, if any. He recalled, however, that he hammered away on just one point: the effect on the province if the verdict should run against the patentees. The question at issue was, in effect, the divine right of Property.

When the others had withdrawn the Council considered their verdict. Their Committee had again reviewed the case, which was unchanged. They added a scurrilous libel upon the Indians; that they were the lowest and most degraded of their race, the proof being that they had no property. No mention was made of their war service.

The Council forthwith pronounced for the defendants. The Indians had no title whatever to any of the land.

Spalding states that he received no notice of the verdict, but read its publication in the public press. There it appeared on March 17 and 26 in the New York Post Boy. No other comment on the trial has been found in the papers of the day.

In their own minutes, the Council recorded their judgment that the deed of August 13, 1702, was entirely genuine. Settlements had begun in 1727, with forty families by 1740, and three hundred by 1756. Nimham had never lived in the Patent, unless Wiccopee be in the Patent. Other Sachems controlled that land, of whom two had died, and the third fled to Delaware, where it was suspected that he had joined the enemy. The tract was deserted.

Matthew DuBois' testimony was accepted, as proving the settlement of tenants at 1740, except for one troublesome one, who was later accommodated.

By 1745, all save a small part, rocky, mountainous and unfit for cultivation, were inhabited. In every instance, at that time, the Indians were again "satisfied". Adolph Philipse approved the payments, to keep the Indians from becoming troublesome.

The trial in 1765 was entirely fair and impartial, false and scandalous statements in the Parchment to the contrary notwithstanding.

The court defended Robinson's ejectments, the tenants being ruled to have failed to enter a plea, when they refused the new year leases. All Nimham's witnesses gave ex parte evidence. Some depositions were executed in another province. One was made by a person of disordered mind.

Lastly, Beverly Robinson was entirely cleared, as "a man of Character, of Prudence, and of undoubted Loyalty".

Captain Guy Johnson asked only whether the Attorney General thought all needed evidence had been submitted. Mr. Kempe said he thought it had.

A copy of the judgment was sent to Sir William Johnson. We hear no more of Indian deeds in Dutchess County.

The tribe of Wappingers returned to Stockbridge and then scattered. When Ethan Allen made his rash expedition to Canada he was accompanied by Indians of Caughnawaga headed by Captain Nimham who had attended the School at Stockbridge. This is apparently our hero. After the Battle of Lexington, the Stockbridge Indians were invited to join the Congress forces. Under Captain Jacobs they fought in the siege of Boston. Under Nimham they fought in New York, in Pennsylvania, and finally at Kingsbridge where Captain Nimham was killed.

# 23. William Prendergast, Agrarian. 1765

AN AGRARIAN is one who advocates by agitation or political dissension a redistribution of the system of land tenure in the direction of greater equality. Alone among the "rioters" of '66 William Prendergast stands out as the true agrarian because of his single-minded devotion to the farmers' cause. He never bought nor advocated the purchase of Indian deeds. He had never paid rent, and had no personal grievance. He never advocated, as did the Connecticut radicals, the cancellation of all debts. On one occasion, as a conspicuous example, he paid off a small debt at a country store, while leading his followers against the landlords. He wanted one thing only: justice for the farmer; reform of the courts, an unprejudiced judiciary, and a land tenure inviolable so long as a fair rent was paid and the farmer treated the land well; with no more cruel evictions by a conspiracy of sheriffs and landlords.

In a word, William Prendergast was a crusader, fighting for a cause every item of which has been enacted into law in England since 1875, and most of which has been won in these States, where more than a third of the land is held in tenancy. Prendergast is a hero of the farmers' cause, and deserves to be remembered by some monument in our famous county.

Where did Prendergast find his principles and his practice? In Ireland, his native country, where Presbyterian Protestants like him suffered almost as cruelly under the Anglican tyranny as did the Catholics. So heavy were the taxes, and so harsh the penalties, that only two courses were open to men who refused to conform, outlawry or emigration. Prendergast probably tried first the one and then the other. Certainly his friend and neighbor, John Kane, had done so. "Kane was Prendergast's good friend" Seth Lovely testified, "for he was his countryman and also traded with him a hundred (pounds) a year." On one occasion, when the mob fell to quarreling as to who should occupy the house from which a "replaced" tenant had been forcibly evicted by them, Kane's advice was asked. "Damn it", cried Kane, "you will bring yourselves to nothing yet by having so many disputes among yourselves." He never knew but one mob succeed yet, he went on, and that was in his own country; they did not go on contending, but what they did, they did quickly. "They destroyed or tore down gardens and made Gentlemen get out of their coaches and swore them on their knees."

It was Kane, not Prendergast, whose fiery eloquence fired the mob. Simon Lovel testified: "If it had not been for Kane's persuasion the mob would never have risen." Neither in the field nor in the "Notes" of his trial is there any suggestion that Prendergast was an orator. What is quoted of him is succinct and pithy.

His role in the conspiracy was rather like that of Brutus. A man of integrity, quiet and law-abiding, well-liked by his neighbors—so the testimony ran. As he had taken no part in the plot to sell the Indian deeds, which had been engineered with Nimham by Samuel Munroe, Stephen Wilcox, and Dr. Charles Peck of Danbury, so he took no part in the organization of the purchasers of Indian deeds as substitutes for Philipse leases. It was Dr. Joseph Crane who like Cassius persuaded our Brutus "to go over to Van Wyck's as an advocate of the mob before the Congress." Our information comes from a deposition of the excellent Jonathan Dakin, well-known Quaker, who adds: "I have often heard of Isaac Perry and others say that Dr. Joseph Crane was a very good head-piece to consult with, and to write for the mob, and that they made great dependence upon him." With Munroe as original agent for the Indians, and John Kane as Clerk, Dr. Crane served as Treasurer, receiving all funds for the maintenance of the tenants' cause, and paying the expenses of meetings.

All this suggests a full incorporation of some kind, and in fact such has been found. At a meeting in the summer of 1764 Eliphalet Peck of Pecksville on the Beekman-Philipse Gore was elected Moderator, and a committee chosen to further the interests of the thirty-four signatories at the meeting. Elisha Baker was sworn as Clerk of the meeting.

A committee of Samuel Munroe, Benjamin Weed, John Ferriss, Isaiah Bennet, Jermiah Fowler, and Daniel Palmer were chosen. An office was set up at the house of Edward Rice, and an underwriting trade "to insure the lands at 25%," drawn up by Samuel Johnson as Attorney. But although the association had agreed to assume charge of further selling of leases, Samuel Munroe "continued to take Bonds to himself", while Joshua Baker, "an Incendiary", offered to take them at eight shillings the lease.

Such is the picture of the troubles in Philipse Patent. Our source is not too trustworthy. It is our old friend ex-Rev. Peter Pratt, who will be remembered as the first minister of Sharon, who had apparently gone into business along the Oblong. By his own testimony it was he who wrote out the leases for Daniel Nimham. He became an informer and spy for Beverly Robinson, who received from him ten documents, among others, which Robinson in turn sent to Attorney-General Kempe as material to set up the trial of Munroe for disherison and maintenance.

The documents were:

1. A petition from Squire James Dickinson and thirty others in November 21, 1764, asking aid against the competing leases, "in very reasonable terms", for 999 years, then being issued by Nimham, Pratt, Wilcox, and "Dr. Charles Peck" of Danbury.
2. The power of attorney from One Pound Pocktone and other leading Fishkill Indians to Daniel Nimham as Sachem.

3. An advertisement from Nimham, reciting the Indian claim, and urging settlers to come in attornment to him.
4. Bounds of the Indian leases to Munrow and Joseph Crane.
5. Deposition of Jas. Sackett to the lease taken by S. Willcox.
6. Power of Attorney and Guardianship to Samuel Munrow from the Wappinger Tribe.
7. Joint advertisement of Munrow and Nimham.
8. A letter from Daniel Prindle (signed Pringle) giving information. Prindle was a witness at later trials, evidently in Robinson's pay. He joined Pratt in sending the deed of Nimham to Daniel Munrow.
9. An original lease from Nimham to one Hobby. Also to Daniel Palmer of Pelham.
10. A long letter from Peter Pratt, written after the first Nimham trial of March, 1765, but relating details from the beginning. In this letter Pratt points with pride to the suspicion held by some settlers that he had been the forger of Beverly Robinson's deed of 1703. If he was not, his letter lends some color to the possibility that some one forged it.

All these documents, save the last written before March 1765, show clearly by the fact of omission that William Prendergast was no party to the early agitation.

What brought Prendergast into the fight, and with him his adviser John Kane, was probably the cruel evictions and the forced one-year leases carried forward by Beverly Robinson in the summer of 1765. It is this action and not those of a year later, to which Asa Spalding referred so feelingly in his "Historical Narrative" of Nimham's case. If so, then Spalding was only echoing and exploiting the wave of indignation that swept over the county and its Connecticut border. One can imagine now John Kane's fiery eloquence, no doubt exceeding that of his grandson James Kent, that spirited the mob up to the point of violence.

As early as April of '64, Moses Northrup had joined Munroe and Willcox in guaranteeing the validity of Indian deeds, for which, or a similar action, Robinson had expelled him from his lease along the Oblong. It was this "gore" on which Munroe and Willcox lived, as Prendergast lived in the "debateable" Philipse-Beekman gore. Such dry details must be insisted upon, as showing how completely the so-called "anti-rent" period was initially a question of title rather than of rent.

Prendergast, however, was perfectly clear in his own mind as to his course of action. Asked what his purpose was, he replied quietly: "to restore poor people to their possessions". He never varied.

Some time in the spring of 1765 a riot occurred at Fishkill. The Widow Clarke and her son William were assaulted by rioters. Complaint was made to the Attorney-General, who responded promising to try the case at Poughkeepsie on June 11. The rioters named on this occasion were Isaac Lent, Peter Vandewater, John Van Vleck, among others. Prendergast's name does not appear, but he may have attended, for his entrance into the trouble is stated to have occurred "after his return from the Fishkills."

A year later "the common talk was that all the tenants would join, and it was high time the great men such as the governor and the lawyers should be pulled down—there was some discourse among the mob to suffer no person to be arrested for debt, but to turn out effects to the value."

But at this time, June 1765, such views were far from the thoughts of the Indian-leaseholders. They were all separately searching for allies. Confederates were stirring in Connecticut and New Jersey, as well as in Albany and Westchester Counties in New York. In April, 1765, Mahikans at Stockbridge petitioned Governor Sir Harry Moore for the return of their land on the Hudson shore between Claverack and Kinderhook. Obviously, this barefaced incursion was timed carefully, for the Stamp Act riots were in progress in New York. What better chance to get to the Hudson!

In Westchester County active proselyting went on, so that by the following spring mobs were ready for riot, and some of their number had been arrested in April. The situation had become so serious that Governor Moore issued a proclamation against them, naming Prendergast among a group of a half-dozen agents from Dutchess at work in Westchester in expelling replacers. By June Connecticut farmers of Wallingford were bold enough to demand a moratorium on debt actions.

But these, though undoubtedly linked up with the Prendergast mob, found no leader like him. He first took "office" in November, 1765. The Dutchess lawyer Moss Kent, who had married John Kane's daughter, testified to the effectiveness of the "General Combination'" among them. He had read on November 12, 1765, a paper ("advertisement") "inviting all persons having regard to their Tenements (tenures) to assemble in a few days to do justice to 'em." Their motive was that of Prendergast, "that none should be arrested for debt; that they would stand with lives and fortunes by each other; that they would suffer none of their party to be arrested for what they did as a mob; to resist all officers of justice; and that none should agree with landlords till the whole did. The combination existed in all the counties to support each other." Kent often reasoned with them, but was threatened and insulted. He had gained his knowledge of their General Combination from Dr. Stephen Crane, among others.

At Malcolm Morrison's tavern on November 19, 1765, Kent watched Prendergast enter the room and walk about. He had already "opened his Commission" the week before, and had told Kent his purpose was "to restore the people turn'd out of possession". Now, however, for the first time he "swore he would head the mob".

On November 21, Gideon Prindle at Fredericksburgh (Patterson) watched a hundred farmers march past his door on their way from Towners to Morrison's. They were headed by Samuel Munroe, his son Daniel, Isaac Perry, Philip Philipse (no relation, I think, of the "heirs") and William Robellier. "Samuel Munroe took William Prendergast by the shoulders and told him he must be the captain or leader. Prendergast at first declined, but it being insisted on by Samuel Monroe and two or three others, he told them if he must be their captain they must obey him and do no mischief, nor abuse any person, but be very civil; and told them to fall in line and follow him to Sam Towners tavern.

"In the afternoon, after he had gone home to dine he went to Towners and found all the above, and Benjamin Gifford, Daniel Townshend, Hope Covey, Samuel Goodspeed, Joseph Dowe, clothier, and many others, about 200. (He) asked what they were doing and Samuel Munroe replied they were oppressed by landlords. (He) asked if they would consent to arbitration, and Munroe said no. They would have the terms mentioned in the advertisements. John Cane of Beekmans precinct got on a table to read a paper he proposed to send to Landlords. Some approved, some disapproved. He (Prindle) and Malcolm Morrison dissuaded some from turning out of possession. Isaac Perry proposed to go to Beverly Robinson. A majority approved by holding up hands, and he and Malcom Morrison went off. But William Prendergast went off with the mob to Edward Rice's (the Combination's "officer"). Perry said (to him) 'after you left Prendergast went off. Several farms were dispossessed, among them Amos Willcox and Ebenezer Weed.'

"Some of the mob asked where Beverly Robinson was, and one (Dr. George) Peck of Danbury asked him (Prindle) that question, and said they would see Robinson that night. Daniel Prindle said he had set off for New York, they could not see him. Peck said they would see him before they dispersed if they had to go to New York for it; they had gone so far Beverly Robinson must take their terms. The mob lay overnight in a valley near Morrison's."

Thus the die was cast. According to Justin Dickenson of Fishkill, the Sheriff, James Livingston, with two or three companies of militia "desired an interview with Prendergast. It was had and after some conversation between them he agreed to discharge his company which was done."

At some time Prendergast succeeded in obtaining an interview with Beverly Robinson. A petition, probably Kane's, had been prepared, but the Committee of Twelve had not approved. The Committee apparently was elected to control the "government" on the Combination and to prevent Prendergast from coming to an agreement with the landlords. The Captain had answered that he was willing to treat with them. In return Robinson notified him that if the Tenants would not rise he would "make them any condescensions that were reasonable."

Justice Samuel Peters told of the interview between Robinson and Prendergast at Robinson's store. Prendergast told the Colonel that largeness of rents and shortness of leases was the cause of his rising. Robinson asked him whether he had ever paid any rent, or any was asked of him. He replied no, "but I do it for the good of the Country and am so far engaged that I will not draw back."

Later, Peters and others obtained a conciliatory letter from landlords "which pacified a number of them." At a meeting at Hasels' store, probably in December, Justice Peters read the letter, in which Prendergast said: "If this is all we will bring them to our own terms." Unfortunately Peters, the most courageous of the officials, bade the crowd to disperse. He probably threatened the mob with warrants, for Prendergast issued an order forbidding the serving of warrants on "Mob's days." The mob, however, dispersed after "three Huzzas."

There ensued a busy time of planning. Contacts with other counties were made, and meetings held. Towards spring the governor got wind of the goings-on, and on April 2 issued a proclamation. When Timothy Shaw, a former loyal tenant of Philipse, endeavored to circulate this in Dutchess, Prendergast caught him and kept the proclamation.

Our Captain next appeared at Westchester, with several of his lieutenants. Riots followed in the lower county against Van Cortlandt and others. Cooperating with them, Prendergast went to New York to rescue two Westchester tenants. They were halted at Kingsbridge, where the leader made a law "that recalcitrant officials who persisted in serving warrants or in spying on the tenants should be dragged and ridden on rails." Soon after his return Justice Peters fell in his way, and with a subordinate was given the works. Half strangled with the mud and sore from his ride on a rail, he had to swear on a Bible produced by Prendergast that he would give no evidence against his captor.

The New York march had produced alarm in the city. Governor Moore ordered out the militia, and commanded the rioters to disperse. In face of these actions, the local Sons of Liberty saw no reason to risk their necks, and Prendergast, who had proposed the march to his committee, and who expected a general uprising to join him, returned in great disappointment. He called his men Sons of Liberty, but the men of York were after the British, not the landlords, some of whom were their leaders.

On May 6 Governor Moore issued a second proclamation offering £100 for the arrest of Prendergast, and £50 each for Munroe and Wm. Finch, who had apparently led in Westchester. The Captain's lieutenants in Dutchess were besides Munroe, Jacobus Gunsaulus, Michael Vail, and Isaac Perry, all of them elected by their companies in March, 1766. The twelve "judges" or committee men were, in addition to these, James Hulings, Jacob Brill, James Jenkins, Matthew Coon, John White, Caleb White, Oliver Astin, and Israel Vail.

None of the better educated instigators were chosen, such as Kane, the two Cranes, Stephen and Dr. Joseph, and Dr. George Peck of Danbury. There was need of this officer material, for the farmers were never more than the mob they called themselves.

In addition to the eviction of Robinson's "replacers" on the farm, the most notable performance of the mob was the rescue from jail of John Way, a Dutchess tenant who had been arrested on the complaint of Colonel Ten Broeck as executor of the estate of "Mrs. Paulding." On June 10 a mob headed by Gunsaulus, but under Prendergast's direction, came to Poughkeepsie and forced Ten Broeck to open the jail and release Way. Sheriff Livingston stood helplessly by as Gunsaulus under Prendergast's constant prodding terrorized the Colonel. Poughkeepsie militia were present, but Justice Van Kleeck and his colleagues refused to permit them to fire on the mob. This was a courageous act. Doubtless on this account the governor's council cited them in an action against all the justices of the county.

The justices were right, however; blood would have blood, and guerilla warfare would follow. Livingston had some experience of this when after the "dragging" of Peters he went to arrest Prendergast and found him, sword in hand, at the head of his company. He drew off in good order.

Dutchess was now in disorder, half in revolt. Neither militia nor sheriff, judges nor constables, had authority. In the emergency Moore acted promptly, though it brought him great unpopularity. On June 19 the Council advised military succor from the British forces, and next day the Twenty-eighth Regiment sailed from Albany for Poughkeepsie. On the 26th Sheriff Harmanse Schuyler of Albany fought the battle of Nobletown, with several killed and many wounded. Robert Noble, who had thus joined Prendergast at his return, was defeated and escaped, only to be captured later.

Captain Prendergast, however, had lost heart, as did Brutus before Philippi. His captains quarreled among themselves for command. His Twelve Men disputed his authority. The mob went here and there at will. Worst of all, radicalism was rising and violence was spreading. The Prendergast code was forgotten. The attack was now on all law. The Sons of Liberty had disowned him.

In his distress he got into touch with Robinson's agent, Gideon Prindle, and employed him to go to Robinson and "make it up for him." According to Prindle, "he said he was afraid of his life from the Mob, and therefore applied to him in a secret manner."

Samuel Munroe, his aid, had probably been arrested, also, for he does not appear in any of the numerous reports of witnesses and others. Munroe's movements are, however, somewhat difficult to follow. After appearing as guardian for the Wappinger chiefs on March 6, 1765, he had been arrested, and escaped. He was soon recaptured, however, and by early autumn was safely lodged in the "New Gaol" at New York, from which he kept up a lively correspondence with the Attorney General. His legal arguments and threats are amusing enough, and so clever that a lawyer's aid may be suspected. Robinson's demand for his prosecution had not been followed up by Kempe, who wrote Robinson that he had no cases on the convict's charges of disherison and maintenance. Doubtless for this reason Kempe released Munroe, for by November he was promoting Prendergast, and claiming that he had been the first promoter of the riots. But he disappears from the story with a pathetic plea in October, 1767, asking for release from prison because he has "made it up" with Judge Horsmanden and Col. Robinson. His wife and two children are penniless and destitute and he himself in despair. Apparently he was released, for in 1770 Isaac Crow sued him for failure to pay for a silver watch. He was back at his old tricks again.

On June 28, the Twenty-eighth Regiment marched off for the South Precinct. Everything was in disorder there. Prendergast had gone, apparently to his home near Quaker Hill. A few followers were with him, according to Peter Terry. Apparently he had marched from Fishkill after the Militia had been disbanded there. Stephen Crane told Terry they were on their way to Quaker Hill to meet the regulars.

But at the same time—June 26—Mical Vail, one of Prendergast's officers, was still at Fredericksburg, completely ignorant of his Captain's whereabouts. He asked a witness where he was, and one "person said William Prendergast had skulked off in the woods, and many others were with him. Mical Vail asked if there was a road to Quaker Hill." Daniel Prindle said "yes, back of the mountain, where they would not meet the Regulars." At Malcolm Morrison's they heard that William Prendergast's house had been pulled down (this was not true) and that 30 troopers were coming. They went towards Quaker Hill but came running back and ran up a lane into a bushy place.

Then Regulars came. One of the mob called: "Don't run, turn and fire!" One of the mob did fire. The officer cried:

"Now, they have fired, fire!" Then a firing ensued on both sides and a soldier was shot in the face by some one in the mob. This soldier was not George Henry, whose death was the only one reported. Wounded in the leg, he died a month later of blood poisoning, at New York.

Of the fight at Quaker Hill we have no direct report. D. Akins testified that two days before the fight he had told Prendergast that the Regulars would come; he had replied they should never get across the mountains. But apparently he never was able to carry out an ambush on the West Pawling Mountain such as he planned. He was caught at Pawling without a shot, and his troop dispersed. Taken to York to prison, he was brought back for trial at Poughkeepsie.

There, from July 29 to August 14, the Supreme Court under Judge Horsmanden held a special session. Prendergast's trial took only twenty-four hours. Many other rioters were tried, but his was the only one on the charge of high treason. He was convicted and sentenced to be hanged with the usual pretty details customary in British law for traitors. A recommendation to the King's mercy was included in the jury's verdict, and joined by the judges in their sentence.

The "Notes" on the trial, taken by a reporter who leaned toward the side of the King, and the News reports of Weymann's Gazette contrast with the report in the Weekly Gazette, which dwells on the sufferer, the fairness of the judges, and particularly on the newsworthy and unprecedented participation in the trial of Mehitabel Wing Prendergast, the defendant's wife. Dr. Mark, to whose careful reprint and still more valuable study of the whole period I am indebted, notes that in the copy of the Post Boy on file in the New York Historical Society, Thomas Jones, a leading attorney and of counsel for the King, says the account of her intervention is false. His word has weight, though Jones was ultra-Tory.

Nevertheless there must be more than a grain of truth in the story, for it matches with the undoubted fact that the young mother of five on the completion of the trial speeded on horseback to New York and returned from the Governor, Sir

Harry Moore, with the reprieve and "good hopes" of pardon, which duly came in the following December. Fortunately for Prendergast the Earl of Shelburne was still in office, and the policy of conciliation and a wider justice prevailed.

Dutchess owes much to Shelburne: Nimham's retrial, the restraint of intercolonial conflict in Vermont acres, the request for an inquiry into the acts of reprisal at Nobletown, and now Prendergast's pardon, all came about within a few weeks of one another. With the repeal of the Stamp Act, they set the pace for further steps which if followed up, would have delayed if not forever disposed of the division of the Empire.

Of Mehitabel, who at this moment shares our attention with the despairing Prendergast, the Post Boy wrote in glowing terms. The whole item must be quoted, in order to understand how completely our poor William was overshadowed by Mehitabel.

"At the Special Court of Oyer and Terminer which began at Poughkeepsey on the 29th of July, and held till the 14th August, for the Trial of Persons concerned in the late Riots in Dutchess County, several indictments were found, one for high treason, one for burglary, a large number for Riots, a few for Assaults and batteries and other trivial Offences.

"William Prendergast, after a Trial of 24 Hours, wherein every reasonable Indulgence was allowed him, was by a Jury of some of the most respected Freeholders, found Guilty of High Treason: ('tis said in this, they differ'd from the opinion of the Court, and were sent back, but persisted in their Verdict.) He was sentenced and ordered to be executed on Friday, the 26th of September Instant. Several of the Rioters, more ore less according to the Nature of their Offenses, two stood in the Pillory, and two were ordered to Imprisonment for a Trial. They all expressed much Penitence, protested against such Riotous Proceedings for the Future, and exhorted the Bystanders to take Warning.

"The Sheriff of Dutchess County, Mr. James Livingston, has offer'd a Good Reward to any Person Inclin'd to assist at the Execution of Prendergast, and has promis'd to disguise them so that they shall not be known, and secure them from Insults.

"(We hear that on the Trial of Prendergast, the Behavior of his wife was very remarkable, and greatly attracted Notice of the Audience. During the whole long Trial, she was solicitously attentive to every particular; and without the least impertinence, or Indecorum of Behavior, sedately anxious for her Husband, as the Evidence open'd against him she never failed to make every Remark that might tend to extenuate the Nature of the Offence, and put his Conduct in the most favorable Point of View; not suffering one Circumstance that could be collected from the Evidence, or thought of in his favour, set out for York, to solicit a Reprieve, and tho' above 70 miles, returned in three Days, with Hopes of success—the Prisoner having been recommended by the Court and Jury to the King's Mercy. In short the whole Behaviour of this unhappy woman was such, as did Honour to her Sex and the Conjugal State.)

"When the terrible Sentence was pronounced upon the Prisoner, he utter'd an ejaculatory Prayer to God for mercy, with such Earnestness, and looked so distress'd, that the whole Audience, even those least susceptible of Compassion, were melted into Tears."

The Prendergasts returned to Pawling after the trial. No objection to his tenancy came from the Philipse heirs. In 1771 William obtained title, and in 1774 completed purchase in fee for £137. Quitrents still hampered him, however. The first represented the original Philipse quitrent of twenty shillings on the first patent; the second was based on the Colden formula of two shillings sixpence for each hundred acres, and was assessed on 4725 acres of the second patent. Thus by 1784, according to the reckoning of Humphrey Slocum, "yeoman" of Pawling, when Prendergast sold the farm to him, he was indebted in the sum of £62. 16s. 10d. This was one-third of the quitrents for fifteen and twenty-five years respectively. Morris and Robinson shares being confiscated, and quitrents abolished by law on such estates, only a third remained to pay.

But Prendergast, as stated in this document, had removed to "Scatacook", near Saratoga. Slocum's bill may have had something to do with our hero's trek to the west, for he certainly would have died rather than pay a cent for quitrent. He joined the great migration, at one time getting to Kentucky.

The family finally settled on the southern end of Lake Chautauqua, where his son James is celebrated as the founder of Jamestown. There was good stock in the family. The history of New York would have contained brighter pages if all its Irish Presbyterians had married all its Quaker maids. There were not enough Mehitabel Wings to go round.

On June 4, 1786, Colonel Robinson, whose sons were knighted for their service, wrote to Frederick Philipse that Prendergast had agreed to pay the whole quitrent for the entire Philipse patent, and £160 18s 7d in addition, for his three hundred acres. Robinson added airily "as this was a very advantageous bargain for Pendergrast, and gave his bond for that sum, 14 April, 1774, not a farthing of which has ever been paid. Pendergrast sold his lease to Humphrey Slocum for a very great price, four or five times as much as he was to give us for it, and therefore ought to pay off his bond . . . Pendergrast moved above Albany upon Hudson's River, I think, but what is become of him since is impossible to tell. He was always a very industrious saving man, and I have no doubt is able to pay you." Our hero's agrarianism seems to have been somewhat more thoroughgoing than the orthodox variety. He believed in paying nothing for land. His westward trek may have been hastened by a threat to make him pay up. Under the circumstances, Colonel Robinson's tribute to our William's industry and thrift was very handsome. Robinson, by the way, had received over $140,000 for his losses by confiscation, from the British Government. Thus in a sense Britain paid for Prendergast's agrarian propensities.

Col. Robinson forgot, evidently, that he had signed on May 19, 1774 a receipt for Prendergast's payment of the £137 18s 1½d mentioned in the deed. He was right about Prendergast's profit; Humphrey Slocum paid £600 for the 249 acres, on Nov. 6, 1784. The property adjoined the farm of old John Kane, in Pawling.

It was politic of Col. Robinson to lease land to his enemy, for he was undoubtedly popular in the neighborhood. He is mentioned in the deed as having been a tenant "for several years past"; and it is likely that Prendergast remained in Dutchess until the Revolution, when he, Munroe, and Kane among others were listed as "disaffected persons." It is strange to find him on the same side at last as his Tory landlord.

# 24. Vermont Acres. 1761

A PARTY OF LANDLOOKERS from Amenia, exploring the valleys of the Green Mountains, were enchanted, as well they might be, by the region now called Manchester. On their return they sought out the patentees and purchased the tract. In February, 1764, they held at Amenia their first meeting as proprietors, under their moderator, Samuel Rose, and Jonathan Ormsby, their clerk.

Next spring they visited the valley and laid out 6800 acres of the 23000 acres in the whole township of six miles by six. These were divided into 100-acre lots. There Samuel Rose built the first house, and Jeremiah French was asked with Ormsby to survey the first road, which was made the next year. In 1766 came the first town meeting, with Stephen Mead as first town clerk. Purdy, Weller, Soper, Bullis, Johns: these are all good Dutchess names from Amenia.

Jeremiah French, Sr., it is probable, was the keeper of the Old Drovers Inn at Dover. He lies buried in the cemetery at Dover Plains. His 700-acre farm at South Dover was confiscated at the Revolution. Probably his son Jeremiah was leader of the committee that journeyed to New York in 1765 to labor with Lt. Governor Colden to cease granting land about Manchester that had already been purchased. Jeremiah Sr. had a daughter Sarah, who married Col. William Marsh and lived at first in Beekman. Her husband became one of the leaders of Vermont in her fight for independence. He was a Loyalist, like his father-in-law, and during the war actively collaborated with Gen. Burgoyne.

Between 1760 and 1764 at least thirty other townships were purchased by residents of Dutchess County, either in whole or in part, an area one and one-half times as large as Dutchess herself. They extended up the whole western boundary of the present Vermont line, and along the northern part as far as the Connecticut River. Many Dutchess names are repeated over and over in the lists printed by the New Hampshire Historical Society (vol. XXVI). Benjamin Ferris of Quaker Hill, for example, owned rights in at least fifteen townships, besides his own township that has ever since borne his name, Ferrisburg.

No contemporary account gives any clue to the allure that drew the swarms of Dutchess buyers to plunge so heavily in this great land speculation, the first of its kind in American history. Many facts may be advanced as likely to have entered into its composition.

Everybody was doing it. Even godly souls like Jonathan Edwards and Timothy Dwight bought rights. The great landholders of New York pushed their own claims. Boston, Providence, and Springfield sent their quotas. The speculators peddled their patents from one end of New England to the other. Nothing like it had been known. It might be compared to the sudden thrusting upon a hungry market of the shares of some great motor company, hitherto inaccessible to the public.

It was cheap. The rights went for £4 to £9, or less than ten cents an acre. For ten years the only rent was to be an ear of Indian corn, and thereafter a quitrent of half the New York going price.

The grants came directly from the Governor of New Hampshire, Benning Wentworth, and purported to be sold by direction of the British government. The townships were described in clear terms, or seemed to be; and the proprietors appeared to have self government from the beginning.

The Rev. Chauncey Graham, at the head of the Fishkill list, may be credited with the initiative in stimulating local interest. Doctor Theodorus Van Wyck, Captain Cornelius Swartwout and Col. John Brinckerhoff gave substance and leadership also. But the one name that suggests the origin of the sale is that of Samuel Averill, which comes last, and significantly, just before the relatives and friends of the Governor.

Samuel Averill was the only man who did not live in southern Dutchess. His home was in Kent, Connecticut. His name appears more frequently on the Vermont Patents than that of any other except those of the Governor's favored clique. He was a leader in organizing the Pawling Petitions. In 1766, the year of Prendergast and of Nimham's visit to London, the Boston proprietors of New Hampshire rights had decided to appeal to Governor Moore for New York confirmation. They met with others, first at Deerfield, then at Pawling in Dutchess County, at the house of Benjamin Ferris. This meeting was historic, because at Pawling the decision was made to appeal to the King rather than to Sir Harry Moore. If an Indian like Nimham could appeal to him, why not poor settlers? On November 26, by which time Nimham had returned to America and spread abroad the good news of his kind entertainment, the delegates and salesmen met, drafted and printed petitions, circulated them and obtained signatures. All the names were taken to London by Samuel Robinson, leader of the Bennington settlers. William Samuel Johnson, son of the President of Kings College, accompanied him. They were supported by the energetic Society for the Propagation of the Gospel in Foreign Parts, a Church of England semi-political body, named as beneficiaries in the Grants. Two other petitions from New York sources complicated matters, but the upshot was that while the Government suspected the validity of the Pawling petitions Lord Shelburne suspected the provincial governments still more; and the privy Council forbade any more grants whatever of lands already granted by Governor Wentworth "until the King should make known his pleasure." This did not confirm either the New Hampshire or New York grants thus far made, nor did it forbid the grant by either governor of lands not already granted by either, though that may well have been the intention.

A paragraph is needed at this point to dispel the fog, and to show how important the Pawling Petition became in the later history of the New Hampshire Grants.

The same confusion that had attended the boundary dispute of southern New York had now reached its northeastern parts. New York claimed to the Connecticut River under the Duke of York's grant of 1664; and this had been confirmed by the British government in 1764. But from 1750 till 1764 Benning Wentworth had mapped and distributed his grants under New Hampshire's charter of 1741, which extended the southern line of that province from a point on the Merrimac River "due west across the said River till it meets with our other Governments." Vague though this certainly was, the line had actually been surveyed to a point twenty miles east of Hudson's River. As soon as King George's tour had ended, Wentworth started on his grants, though the governor of New York had warned him that his territory ended at the Connecticut River. Stupidly, New York at the time ran no surveys to prevent him. It had just borne the brunt of the Canadian war.

The Pawling petition of 1766 stopped the duplication of grants that had been made under these conditions. It also provided a breathing-spell in which battlelines might form for the next assault, more settlers enter the Grants, and more leaders emerge. Of the 648 names on Pawling petitions, only 175 were of actual residents in 1766, most of them in Bennington. But a good many of the others, certainly a good many of the Dutchess names in petitions 12, 14, and 18, representing the Ferris and Averill groups, became residents soon after, chiefly from Amenia, Dover, and Pawling. The petitions no doubt confirmed their interest, as they came to realize that only by actual occupancy could they defend their purchase. The number, however, has been greatly exaggerated by some historians of Vermont. Prior to the petitions, not over a dozen families had gone. The Quaker townships of Danby, Dorset, Mt. Tabor, and Manchester undoubtedly registered several substantial groups up to 1770. The French family alone contained perhaps ten names of men. But very few of the names left the county for good. Dutchess still claims its Marsh and French, its Ferris and its Averill, its Wing and Hoag. From 1756 to 1771 Dutchess grew from 14,000 to 22,000, nearly 60%.

Among the Dutchess families represented in Vermont today is that of Canfield. Timothy Canfield of Amenia is often mentioned in lawsuits, chiefly as defendant. A distinguished Vermonter of his name is Dorothy Canfield Fisher, who brought her children to Oakwood School in Poughkeepsie, the successor of the famous Friends School in the Nine Partners.

There is a family tradition that Timothy Mead and his wife Sarah Bouton settled early near Rutland, while a relative, Zebulon Mead planted on Otter Creek west of Rutland, between Mead's Mills and Sutherland Falls. Their family record states that these men were the first white settlers in Vermont. Evidently they bought New York rights, for Zebulon, who was a Lieutenant in 1755-6, was in a York Regiment "from Vermont" during the Revolution. Both names, and those of their sons, occur frequently in our documents 1760-1769, from Nine Partners.

The New Hampshire Grants owe their present name to a Dutchess County resident. It came about in this way. When Ethan Allen was a young lad of nineteen years he marched off in 1757 to Lake George in the regiment of Col. Ebenezer Marsh. Perhaps through William Marsh of Dover, perhaps through Cyrus Marsh of Kent, he became acquainted with Dr. Thomas Young of Amenia, in the most formative years of his life. When Young died, Allen tried to get a grant in Vermont for his family, then in Amenia. Dr. Young had married the daughter of Gerrit Winegar of Salisbury, whose brother lived in Amenia on the old farm. Thus it may have been Young who met Ethan, though he was seven years older than the big fellow.

Thomas Young was a greatnephew of James Clinton of Belfast, Ireland, whose son Charles was the famous surveyor of Dutchess lands. Young was therefore a cousin of George and

James Clinton. He had more than a spark of the Clinton genius. Born at Little Britain in 1731 he grew up on a farm next to the Clintons. For his besetting trait of wildness in boyhood he was challenged by a brilliant schoolmaster, John Wilson, and set out to prove that he could learn in six weeks more than his teacher knew. The effect was just what Wilson wanted; Young became a scholar, as well as a wild Irishman.

Young studied medicine at Yale, and on his return boarded at first with the Winegars in Salisbury. His wife, Mary Winegar, gave him six children. He settled in Amenia's part of the Oblong. Ethan Allen's wife, Mary Brownson, was a Salisbury girl also.

No two young men in their twenties could have been more congenial. They were wild and gay, imaginative and keen, boisterous and bumptious, sceptical and sarcastic, drinkers and roisterers; but underneath all this frontiersman's disguise there lay a vein of serious thought, and a deep love of liberty. Thomas' wild claim that he could outlearn his teacher in six weeks was something Ethan wished he had thought of.

Both young men indulged in blasphemy, the radical thing to do in the New England of the day. As the documents in Young's case have not been printed they are appended here.

"Young, Thomas.

Indictment

That of Thomas Young late of Crum Elbow precinct in the said County of Dutchess Physitian Being a person Bred in and here to fore professing the Christian Religion the Eighth day of August in the year of our Lord one thousand seven hundred and fifty six at Crum Elbow Precinct in the said County and not having the fear of God before his Eyes but being seduced by the instigation of the devil did then and there speak and publish these Wicked false and Blasphemious Words concerning the said Christian Religion (to wit) Jesus Christ was a knave and a fool (Our Lord and Saviour Jesus Christ the second person in the Trinity then and there meaning) and that he the said Thomas Young then and there de-

clared that he meant and desired to be understood that he the said Jesus Christ of whom he then and there spoke was born of the Virgin Mary. Against the peace of our Sovereign Lord the King his crown and Dignity and so forth.
Witnesses Thomas Langdon
Henry Filkin Esqr Signed for the jury
Silas Deuell
Young. Thomas."

His answer "I plead not Guilty" was filed Dec. 1, 1756, by Francis Hull his attorney at the Court of Gen. Sessions.
"Thomas Young's Presentation personally delivered in May Court 1758.
Be it remembered that I Thomas Young Being Indicted for Blasphemous Expressions against Jesus Christ do own and acknowledge myself to have abused the person and character of Jesus Christ said such things as were unworthy of him inadvertently and in Passion and fully clearly and absolutely renounce that opinion humbly begging the pardon of God Almighty the world of Mankind and the present Court of Sessions.
Dated Poghkeepsie
May 18" 1758 Thos Young"

Ethan Allen's profanity was uttered in irritation at being threatened with prosecution for practising inoculation for smallpox without the Selectmen's certificate.

Two such convivial friends must have talked many a night through in little Salisbury. From the sceptical Thomas, Ethan borrowed his notes on his readings at Yale, and acquired a pretty thorough indoctrination in eighteenth-century "enlightenment." According to a sister-in-law of Allen's, the two young men spent a long summer together in Amenia working on a book, which they agreed to publish when they had time. The older man kept the manuscript and notes. After Thomas' death Ethan came for them, either at Amenia, or as one tradition has it, Philadelphia. He made them up into a book, "Reason the Only Oracle of Man". It reads more like the Irishman than the Yankee.

The indebtedness of Paine to Allen's book was asserted not long after the Revolution by Judge Henry of Pennsylvania, in his memoir of the march against Quebec. His vindictiveness, characteristic of the time, may be pardoned the old soldier.

"That which is very remarkable is that not long after the publication of Allen's book, which had fallen into oblivion, even with its readers, that vile reprobate, Thomas Paine, loaded with every crime, which stains and dishonors the christian and the gentleman (in addition to his shameful practices in life, Paine, as an author, superadded plagiarism) filched from Ethan Allen, the great body of his deistical and atheistical opinions."

There was of course nothing original about Young's deism, which he no doubt acquired from his reading at Yale. But the incident suggests that Paine, clever journalist as he was, may best be remembered as the man who hit the market with timely thoughts rather than as the original thinker.

In earlier years Young had bought rights in New Hampshire Grants from Col. John H. Lydius of Albany, whose claims he defended in a pamphlet of 1764. Perhaps this essay on "Liberty and Property", "the household gods of Englishmen", introduced Allen to the prospects in the north. At all events, he borrowed Young's slogan and made it the countersign of the Green Mountain Boys. Dr. Young found Allen an apt pupil in the arts of the pamphleteer.

From Albany, where Young's radicalism found little congenial soil, he went on to Boston, leaving his family at Amenia, where they joined the local church, and lived down the doctor's careless words. The Amenia Leveler found rebellious Boston most congenial, and under the guidance of Dr. Joseph Warren, Young was soon high in favor and deep in intrigue. Twice he addressed roaring audiences in Faneuil Hall and Old South Church. Member of the Boston Committee of

Correspondence, of the North Side Caucus, and of the Tea-room Group, it fell to him to lead the Indians at the famous Tea Party, though he was the only man not disguised. For this bravado he became a marked man, and was proscribed by General Gage.

He fled to Providence and then to Philadelphia, after narrow escapes. There Dr. Franklin became his friend, and Dr. Benjamin Rush appointed him senior surgeon of one of the Continental hospitals. Research has not yet identified any of the numerous pamphlets issuing from local presses as Young's work, but he was certainly active. He is credited with aiding Franklin in his sketches for a state constitution.

By this time the Green Mountain Boys were in session upon their own state government. To them Young sent a copy of the Pennsylvania model, the most liberal of its kind, and urged that they follow its lead. In the same letter the clever physician suggested the name "Vermont". Both suggestions were adopted, and thus the inventor of Dutchess' prettiest name, Amenia, became the originator of the prettiest name among the states.

Thomas Paine, author of "Common Sense", was in Philadelphia at this time. Dr. Rush turned over to him his notes and outlines for the famous pamphlet, along with the title. As true sons of the Enlightenment, Paine and Young shared identical views in religion, politics, and social ethics. So closely does "Reason the only Oracle" resemble Paine's "Age of Reason", and so probable is it that Rush's medical and political assistants knew each other, that it is tempting to look for some share by Young in the pamphlet "Common Sense."

But the wounded began to arrive in the military hospital, and Young's scientific interest was aroused by the prevalence of "putrid fever." He began a study of it, and died of its effects.

When Allen's delegates to Congress appeared to plead for the acceptance of Vermont as a state, Young had buttonholed its members to secure their votes. This aroused New York delegates to anger, and at their behest Congress passed a vote of censure on him. Perhaps Young enjoyed this little revenge for his severe treatment at the hands of Dutchess sheriffs.

His family remained in Amenia for years, respected. Young John Barr of the army used to dine and hunt with Young's son in the Oblong.

The Housatonic and Harlem Valleys, linked by the Webatuck intervale, had built a social and economic region, almost independent of the three colonies under whose rule it fell. There the westward drive of New England expansion met resistance from the landlords Livingston and Beekman. There the growing iron industry met competition in Dutchess mines, and Dutchess sloops to carry their metal to market. Although the Treaty of Dover had pointed the way to a solution through considerate cooperation, the Berkshire pioneers were too aggressive, and the Dutchess proprietors too unimaginative, to realize it.

When the first Yankee assault had been beaten off, the stream of aggression faced north for thirty years, filling up Berkshire County and western Vermont. It carried with it the disaffected in Dutchess who had made common cause with the Housatonic forces.

While the peaceable families were flooding through the Webatuck gap into Dutchess, the dominant "angry people" shoved up the river, politically radical, morally indifferent, and so hostile against their own province that they kept Loyalist during the Revolution. An astute captain rode these bumptious logs down white water into the millpond, and made a sound structure of them.

They were an odd group: Whitefield dissenters from dissent; errant Quakers with money to invest; landlookers and speculators; riotous farmers from unruly Crum Elbow and Beekman; a few tough miners from the Furnaces. They achieved the "Contrary Country" of Vermont, but they left behind the men who followed Daniel Shays in Pittsfield and the radical agitators in Connecticut, with intransigents all along the Taconic ridges that made plenty of trouble for the Congress.

Yet they had real grievances not of their own making. Their church had failed them; their governments were at odds; their leaders too often sought their own profit. Out of their troubles they forged a strong and peculiar dialectal character which still colors the life up and down the Taconic System of rocks and rills.

# VI. A FIRM UNION

## 25. The Summons of Nathaniel Sackett

ON SUNDAY, April 23, 1775, the news of Lexington reached New York, four days after the fight. New York's mob at once seized arms and terrorized the town. One of the onlookers was a storekeeper of Fishkill named Nathaniel Sackett. His relative John Alsop was a leading New York neutral. His sister, Hannah, was the wife of the Loyalist Stephen DeLancey, but she was not of his mind. Neither was her brother Samuel, a captain in the militia. Her uncle Ebenezer Hazard became postmaster-general of the United States. Her father's church at Crompond (Yorktown) was burned by the British Cow Boys. Her mother was a York Lady Babbie; she wrote:

"I sigh when I look back on the time when I sparkled in the gay circles of my acquaintance; frank, easy, lively, brilliant, and innocent as gay—the darling and delight of all my numerous associates who were ready to divide me in pieces to share me among them, each contending who should have me."

Nevertheless she went to work, and her twelve children were a credit to her, spreading the Sackett name as far as Sackett's Harbor. Nathaniel had his parents' spirit. He no sooner got to Fishkill than he met with his friends, and soon there issued this appeal:

"Whereas, alarming accounts have been received of the massacre in Boston, and a resolution in Parliament taken, declaring the whole continent rebels, a number of inhabitants of this Precinct, having this day assembled at the house of

John and Hendrick Wyckoff, taking the alarming situation of this continent into consideration, agreeable to the handbills sent up from the county of New York, requesting them to poll on such measures as may be thought most necessary for the freeholders and inhabitants for their future safety and preservation, And as it has become absolutely necessary for the future preservation of our Families in this Precinct that a firm union may subsist between us and the other precincts, it is sincerely hoped that all former prejudices and party disputes be entirely laid aside and all ranks and denominations appear, and their names be taken at this crisis.

"It is therefore requested that none on any account or excuse whatever will keep back but appear at the house of Messrs. John and Hendrick Wyckoff on Friday, the 5" Instant, at ten o'clock in the forenoon, there to determine on such matters as are necessary to the present occasion."

The appeal is undated and unsigned, but the copy from which this is taken is in Nathaniel Sackett's handwriting. As the meeting was held twelve days after the news of Lexington had arrived at New York, we may assume that this handbill was issued within a week, or before May 1. Certainly Nathaniel Sackett had left New York before April 29, the day on which the "Revolutionary Pledge" with its "articles of association" was adopted in New York. Otherwise reference would have been made to it. The document bears every evidence of being a local composition. So far as known, this was the first call in Dutchess. New York had met April 29.

On May 16 a county meeting was held, and deputies elected for a six months' term to the Provincial Convention. As these men became the county leaders during the Revolution their names are recorded: Dirck Brinckerhoff, Anthony Hoffman, Zephaniah Platt, Richard Montgomery, Ephraim Paine, Gilbert Livingston (Clerk of Dutchess), and Jonathan Landon, Esquires, and Messrs. Gysbert Schenck, Melancton Smith, and Nathaniel Sackett.

The Provincial Convention or Congress met on May 22, and endorsed the "Pledge." It was immediately circulated to the counties, and committees were formed to circulate it for local signature. A photostat of one of these is in the public library at Poughkeepsie. It is for Northeast Precinct. When this list is added to the lists previously printed, the total for Old Dutchess is given as 2700. Signers, 1800: refused to sign, 900.

It is said that many militiamen refused to sign, on the ground that signature would be contrary to the oath of allegiance which militia were required to take. On the other hand, many non-signers did not stand up to be counted: for example, Rev. John Beardsley of Christ Church in Poughkeepsie. It may be assumed that at this date from a third to a half of the men of Dutchess were opposed to any united action with other counties in resisting the enforcement of English restrictions on the colonies.

The election of Nathaniel Sackett among the members of the Provincial Congress is significant. He had made something of a local name, and had served as foreman of a grand jury; but to be chosen in the crisis, in full knowledge of the decided stand he would take, was an honor not to be expected. Perhaps he had been responsible for the remarkable "Orders" for the Fishkill meeting, preserved in his records. As an example of the endeavors of revolutionary leaders to carry out their plans in a spirit of law and justice, the "Fishkill Orders" are well worth our attention.

"Fishkill Orders. May 5, 1775.

1. That a chairman be chosen.
2. That a clerk be chosen to enter all matters concluded upon.
3. That no person speak only in his turn.
4. That no person call any other person in private.
5. That all matters be debated with candor, without constraint, and with perfect freedom.
6. That all persons shall be heard, and proper weight given to their reasons, without any distinction to either rank, quality, or fortune.
7. That all persons shall be heard, and the question being put,

every person present is to answer only yes or no, as his judgment may direct, with out giving any reason.

8. That no business, diversions, stories, histories, or any other matter or thing that may divert or delay the business of the day, be mentioned or encouraged until the whole business is gone through and completed.
9. That every question put shall be carried for or against by a majority of the voices of the people present.
   1. Choose a committee of thirty to be a Committee of observation.
   2. Their power to be fixed.
   3. Some of that number to wait on Col. Brinckerhoff at Poughkeepsie, they to make a report on their return to the other members of the committee to establish their sense.
   4. To choose one deputy to the Provincial Congress.
   5. The affairs of the Negroes to be considered.
   6. What to be done with them in case of a battle.
   7. What precautions should be taken now.
   8. Enter into some resolution to be published."

Endorsed on the paper are the names of forty persons who responded to the call, including Col. Brinckerhoff. Our present legislative bodies have improved upon these rules of order.

At the First Provincial Congress Nathaniel Sackett was never absent from roll call. Others were less attentive, and on July 8 a Committee of Safety was chosen to carry on its administrative powers. Nathaniel Sackett was duly appointed to its Dutchess counterpart, and its duties gradually were assigned to him. On September 21, 1776, a year later, he became the active member of the Committee to Detect Conspiracies, which controlled the movements of Loyalists. The orders of this committee to the militia for the arrest of Tories were signed by Sackett. On January 6, 1777, the committee at Fishkill listed John Jay, Zephaniah Platt, Nathaniel Sackett, Egbert Benson, and General Morris for the army. A stronger committee could not have been chosen.

One month later, February 4, 1777, General Washington appointed Nathaniel Sackett to handle his secret service in the Dutchess area. This included counter-intelligence and the liaison between the regular army under General Wayne and the Militia levies on special duties. In a sense, the crucial civil war between Loyalists and Americans was handled by Sackett in the early period of the War—first by county choice, then by choice of the Commander-in-chief. By this date, of course, Fishkill had become a key point in the national line of defense, and the enemy was putting forth efforts to learn more about it, and to weaken it. Arnold's treachery in 1780 was but the climax of a continued effort to secure the mountain bastion of the Highlands. Sackett's appointment came just before the plans for Burgoyne's invasion became known.

General Washington wrote from Morristown:

"Sir; The advantage of obtaining the earliest and best intelligence of the designs of the enemy, the good character given of you by Col. Duer, added to your capacity for an undertaking of this kind, have induced me to entrust the management of this business till further orders on this head.

For your care and trouble in this business, I agree on behalf of the public to allow you fifty dollars per calendar month. (etc.)

Given under my hand at Morristown this 4" day of February, 1777."

Nathaniel Sackett was already at work.

"Fishkill Jan. 7, 1777.

To Capt. Goosbeck.

Dear Sir—I had almost forgotten to give directions to give our friend an opportunity to escape—Upon our plan you will take him prisoner with the parties you are now watching for. His name is Enoch Crosby, Alias John Brown. I could wish that he may escape before you bring him two miles on your way to the committee. You will be pleased to advise with

Messers. Cornwall and Captain Clark on the subject, and form such plan of conduct as your wisdom may direct, but by no means neglect this friend of ours.

I am sir your humble servant
Nathaniel Sackett

Fishkill
To Capt. Goosebeck
from Nath. Sackett member of Committee"

Enoch Crosby, the original of Cooper's "Spy", was a soldier in the Fourth New York (Dutchess County) Regiment. Sackett refers here to Enoch Crosby's infiltrating a group of young loyalists and leading them directly into Continental bounds. Sackett was soon deep in other matters than controlling loyalists. The first board was dissolved in February, 1777, and a new board chosen, on which Egbert Benson became the most active member, with Jacobus Swartwout and Melancton Smith. The boards continued their work till 1783. In October, 1776, 6000 pounds of lead were delivered to Nathaniel by Peter Curtenius, representing New York State. On January 3, 1777, Nathaniel Sackett was authorized by the Committee on Conspiracies, John Jay, Chairman, "to employ such detachments of Militia as are not on active duty as he may deem expedient for the execution of his charge."

"Dear Sir: Fishkill Landing
Aug 4th 1779

You will please order a detachment of 150 men, with ten days' provisions, under command of Colonel Butler, on particular duty. I wish you to order Major Hull, with him. N. 13. The detachment will move tomorrow morning early.

Interim believe me yours,
Anthony Wayne B. G.

To Nathaniel Sackett"

Stony Point had been taken July 15, 1779.

It is no wonder that as Mr. Sackett's "business was of a very urgent nature" the Treasurer of New York State advanced the $50 a month, since the army paymaster was apparently out of funds.

I have broken into the even course of narrative to give you Nathaniel Sackett all of one piece, as a Dutchess County Blue-skin, utterly devoted to the cause of independence. He fought no battles, led no troops, but he led his county into the cause, and wore himself out in its service, now in the Provincial Congress, now on the Committee of Safety, now discouraging Loyalists, now directing espionage for General Washington, now helping the quartermaster with the vital service of supply. He received no honors, made no fortune. He died at the home of a son in Sullivan County after the war. Of his five children, Elizabeth married a Crosby, possibly a relative of his friend Enoch Crosby, the "Spy" of Cooper's Novel.

It was because of such Americans that Washington was able to put army after army into the field, to hold his lines, and to get his supplies.

Nathaniel's sister Hannah was a chip of the block. She had refused to stay in New York with her loyalist husband, Stephen DeLancey, and lived with her parents at Crompond. Later she married a Continental officer. The British burned her father's house and church in 1777. While fleeing from the fire Hannah was overtaken in Dutchess by cavalry who robbed her of her shoebuckles and earrings. She cried to them, "Is this the way you treat unprotected females? I will inform your superiors. Where is your commander? I am Mrs. Stephen de Lancey."

Hannah's young husband had been arrested in May, 1776, but escaped from Hartford the following year. A letter from him to a friend and employe, Cornelius Steenbrun, is so typical of the aristocratic young Manor aristocracy that I cannot forbear reprinting it from the Sackett genealogy which has furnished most of this information. The book was compiled by General Charles Weygant of Newburgh, whose wife was a Sackett.

To Cornelius Steenbrun

"Ungrateful Cornelius

Why don't I hear from you? Why did you not send me a letter, or a message at least by Mr. Townsend? Where is Mother: What made her move? I hear you live there, and Mother Bostwick. Where is old Agnes, Is she alive? Why arn't you as good as your word? Why don't you send any letters? I would not that anyone else should see them. I left seven shirts and three stocks and you must bring them to that house where we were, and my trimmed jacket and leather breeches. Take care, don't take arms. You must send me a mortgage on the mill and land adjoining belonging to your son. Do for God's sake come down to Milford's and consult with him. Let me have a letter and tell me you are sorry you took a commission and was over-persuaded, and repent and ask pardon of God and the King, and I will do my best and Governor Tryon will assist me. That is absolutely necessary. I wonder you are so careless. Will you never learn wit? I could beat you, you careless toad. I have gold and silver, you rebel. Don't you want some? Read my letter to Mother Bosworth and tell her I hope that she and little James are well, and tell Agnes I will come to see them before next fall, but never to live in that hateful place again. Remember me to poor David and Esther. I will send him a line, poor David I hope he repents. I am going to live in Maronack as soon as it will be safe. Our army is going to take hold soon. Wo! Wo!! Wo!!! to the rebels. Send me a long letter to my sister and see if my Mother will consent to come down and let me know it. Do for Gods sake.

Stephen de Lancey."

This letter speaks clearer than hundreds of documents for the whole picture of Tory-Blueskin relations.

# 26. Tories and Blueskins. 1775

*James Rivington, "Printer" (of late) "to the King"–*
*But now a Republican, under your wing—*
*Let him stand where he is, don't push him downhill,*
*And he'll turn a true Blueskin, or just what you will.*

*Rivington's Confession,*
PHILIP FRENEAU, POEMS, 1783.

JIMMY RIVINGTON must have grimaced a bit as Philip Freneau pushed his jibe home. For it was Rivington who popularized the term "Blueskin" as befitting the Congress people in the early days of the struggle. His Gazette ceased publication when Connecticut rioters came into New York and wrecked his press one day. New York was as usual more tolerant and allowed the Tory journalist, in spite of all his bitter attacks, to return after the war and set up his press again. The city still has a Rivington Street.

The origin of the term is unknown. It suggests blue laws, blue Presbyterians, blue bonnets of Scotland. But the official instruction for Continental uniforms prescribed Dutch blue as the general color, trimmed with buff, green, or other colors according to regional or service wants. Perhaps the women who wove the blue cloth for Fishkill and Continental Village were the first to spead it. Every housewife kept handy an indigo pot and a crock of butternut brown. In October, 1776, five men were appointed a committee to buy cloth everywhere in Dutchess.

Captain Abraham Swartwout of Rombout had a blue cloak, which he contributed to form the field of stars in the first star spangled flag of the United States carried in battle. This was at Fort Stanwix, where the Dutchess regiment was stationed in 1777. Being a thrifty Dutchman, he decided to put in a bill of eight shillings for his cloak, "for the colors", as he put it; and thus he entered history.

More plausible seems the theory that the word described the ragged New York mob that made such trouble for respectable folks on Broadway and the Bowery, or the half-naked soldiers as they stood stiffly at present arms, and wrung Washington's heart. Chastellux did not pity, but honored them, when he saw them "at the approach of Winter" in the log hut encampment four or five miles from Fishkill. "These honest people, for I will not say these unhappy ones (they know too well how to suffer for a cause too noble) have not in fact coverings, not even rags; but their assured mien, their arms in good condition, seem to cover their nakedness, and allow one to see only their courage and their patience."

Nathaniel Sackett's concern that all former prejudices and party disputes be laid aside in favor of a firm union of the precincts was well grounded. In no county was Loyalist sentiment stronger or better organized. Philipse, DeLancey, and Verplanck in the south were powerful opponents. Crannell, Emott, and the Rev. Mr. Beardsley, the Anglican rector, held Poughkeepsie in line at first. Quakers in the east and center, and Palatines in the north needed no leaders to keep them against war.

In Amenia, in the very month of April, 1775, the vote was 140 to 35 "for the constitutional liberties" under English rule. "We are firmly attached to our most happy Constitution, and are disposed to maintain peace and good order under His Majesty's government." Earlier, at a Poughkeepsie meeting, it was declared that "our representatives, in General Assembly convened, are the only guardians of our Rights and Liberties." The language harks back to Dongan days.

In the whirlwind of Addresses and Declarations that followed the Continental Association against commerce with England under the Tea Act in 1774, this loyal counter-association in Dutchess has a modest place. It was issued January 18, 1775, and is printed without the names of the signers in the "American Archives."

"We, the subscribers, being desirous to convince mankind that we are most firmly attached to our beloved Constitution, and are disposed to maintain peace and good order under His Majesty's Government do therefore declare, that our Sovereign Lord King George the Third is the only sovereign to whom British America can, or ought to bear true and faithful allegiance, and that there is no legal power or authority but that is only derived from him; that our representatives in General Assembly convened are the only guardians of our Rights and Liberties; that without them no laws can be made to bind us, and that they only are the channel through which our grievances can properly be represented for redress; and that, to support their right and authority, we do hereby associate and mutually covenant and engage to associate with each other as follows, namely:

First; we will upon all occasions stand by and assist each other in the defence of life liberty and property whenever the same shall be attacked or endangered by any bodies of men riotously assembled upon any pretence or under any authority whatsoever not warranted by the laws of the land.

Second: that we will upon all occasions mutually support each other in the free exercise of our undoubted right to liberty in eating, drinking, buying, selling, communing and acting with whom and as we please, consistent with the laws of the land, notwithstanding the Association entered into by the Continental Congress to the contrary.

Lastly, that we will endeavour to promote, encourage, and when called upon, enforce obedience to the rightful authority of our most gracious Sovereign King George the Third, and the laws which constitutionally can, do or may extend to, or in, the British Colonies in America.

In witness we have hereunto set our hands this 18" day of January, in the 15th year of our Sovereign Lord King George

III, by the Grace of God of Great Britain, France, and Ireland, King, Defender of the Faith, &c, and in the year of our Lord Christ one thousand seven hundred and seventy-five.

(Signed by a Number of Inhabitants of Dutchess County.)"

Two months later, on March 21, 1775, a Liberty Pole on John Bailey's place in the Town of Poughkeepsie was cut down by the sheriff, in the presence of two justices of the peace, a judge of Common Pleas, and a constable, "with other good friends of common liberty and good order, as a public nuisance."

When Lexington came, the shoe was on the other foot.

By the fall of 1775 Egbert Benson was able to report that a General Committee had been chosen to administer the affairs of the county. With Benson as chairman, it included Colonel Freer, Captain Zephaniah Platt, John Child, Paul Schenck, and Dr. Peter Tappen, acting as a committee of correspondence. Their first field-officers were the Colonels Tobias Stoutenburgh, Peter TenBroeck, David Southerland, Dirck Brinckerhoff, and William Humphrey. They collected muskets from the people, agreeing to pay two pounds apiece for them, but months later Dirck Brinckerhoff was writing to the New York committee that the people wanted their money.

By April 17, 1776, Egbert Benson could write proudly to the New York Committee of Safety, that four companies were then enlisting, of Rosekrans, Swartwout, Child, and Pearse, and were being sent to the Highlands. This was in addition to the men that had marched to Canada the previous year.

There were many difficulties, among them the rumor that young men of Dutchess were enticed into Connecticut enlistment by higher Congress pay than was possible in Dutchess. Congress of course denied this. With a lack of military experience every company became a threat to good order, though General Schuyler stormed and denounced such conduct. Nevertheless, stores began to accumulate at Poughkeepsie, which became a principal depot of supply for the army, being shipped south to West Point and north to the troops around Albany.

Meanwhile the British Parliament slapped loyal New York in the face. When Edmund Burke tried to present the pacific petition of the New York Legislature to the House of Commons, Lord North first secured an amendment to Burke's motion, stating that the Assembly claimed rights derogatory to the authority of Parliament, and then defeated the motion to hear it. This was on May 15, after Lexington.

The First Provincial Congress had done little beyond advising militia drills to maintain order. Even in 1775 New York was still occupied by British troops. Faced with the loss of trade the city hesitated even after Lexington, while nearby counties like Queens were openly Loyalist. The Second Provincial Congress in November, 1775, scarcely dared meet, and a minority turned its power over to a Committee of Safety. The Amenia freeholders had protested the "Rump election" of Robert R. Livingston, Egbert Benson, and Morris Graham to the Continental Congress.

One Dutchess man wrote that of the 1800 freeholders of Dutchess at least 1200 were opposed to any abandonment of the legally chosen assembly. Yet when Governor Tryon of New York tried to reestablish the outworn Assembly in the following February he was beaten by the prompt action of upstate New York.

By December the County Committee were at work, and the Tories began to leave the county. Peter De Witt wrote that the Berghs and Timothy Doughty at Rhinebeck were shipping volunteers to the British in New York. Doughty was arrested and jailed in Poughkeepsie, but in January 1776 on the eve of the election of the third Provincial Congress, Egbert Benson had him transferred to Kingston "because a vast number of people would attend the election in Poughkeepsie."

Some of the Scots colony at Paterson's were in the game. The Dutchess Committee of Safety wrote Peter VanBrugh Livingston, president of the Provincial Congress, on August

3, 1775, that Lachlan Macdonald was taking people from Fishkill on Peter Bogardus' sloop. They added, "we are in so much danger from the disaffected persons in the county that we shall be obliged to take some spirited measures concerning them."

The mob actions feared by Egbert Benson did not materialize because the Tories, sobered by the war, did not appear at the polls. They were on their way out of the county, those at least who had the will to fight. The rest stayed at home.

The Dutchess delegation to the Third Provincial Congress was headed by Robert R. Livingston, who was also a member of the Second Continental Congress. Thus, though appointed on the committee to draft the Declaration of Independence, he did not sign it, because the Provincial Congress was sitting in New York, at a most critical time. It was sharply divided, even as late as this, over the question of all-out war. When the Declaration came out a Fourth Congress had been elected, and on July 9 came out for independence. This Fourth Congress then constituted itself a constitutional convention, and fled to Fishkill to prepare it. The rash of Congresses was at an end. New York was a state, of its own sovereign people.

Looking back at this chaotic sequence of events, New York's handling of its internal affairs, though it displeased John Adams, seems not inefficient. The people were exercised in free elections, with ample time to debate and make up their minds. There were no bloody clashes with the Tories. Law prevailed.

The successive Congresses were so many responses to the changing moods of the people. The difficulties of New York were inherent in her history. Her composite and tolerant people became proper custodians of the gateway to the new world.

The Committee of Safety in New York City voted to send to Dutchess County 150 soldiers to put down the Tories. There is no record that it was sent; the County soon proved able to take care of herself. A Committee of Observation began the work in Rombout Precinct. It included several militia officers and other strong leaders who saw the thing through. There were the Brinckerhoffs, Direk, Abraham, John G., John A., Sr. and Jr.; Theodorus, William, and Richard Van Wyck; Elias and Matthew Van Benschoten; Thomas and Joseph Storm; with Jacob Griffin, Jacobus DeGraaf, Henry Godwin, Isaac Hegeman, John Myers, Henry Rosecrans, Henry Schenck, Isaac Ter Boss, Henry Godwin and John Langdon. Dutch and Palatine names ran three to one.

The Committee held its first session July 13, 1775. They examined the militia, of which seven companies had been created three months before the muster rolls began. Three captains, Luyster, Bedell, and Southard, were deranged because of suspicion of disloyalty, and replacements were commissioned. Thus the recruiting of Tories was pinched off, and just in time. At the first census of Bedell's company the vote had been 82 to 18 against signing the Association. By September the same company elected its own officers with the others. At these elections two Committee members attended to observe.

On one occasion a member of this Committee was arrested and ordered in jail by James Smith, a justice of common pleas, on the charge he had required the disarming of loyalists. This "enraged the people so much that they rose and rescued the prisoner, and poured out their resentment on the villainous retailer of the law." Judge Smith and his relative Coen Smith were "very handsomely tarred and feathered for acting in open contempt of the resolves of the County Committee."

Washington, who had taken command in July, visited Dutchess in August, 1775, to study the defenses of the Hudson. He liked the position of Constitution Island, and drilled upon it in later days, so that its flat came to be called the Washington Parade. It was on Constitution Island that the General mustered out his bodyguard in 1783.

From concern with immediate defense the Committee of Safety could turn to a second problem no less pressing, the Loyalists. For their protection as well as for the country's defense, the Congress policy was to deport the disaffected to the enemy's lines, whenever their actions were beyond the line of neutrality. Thousands of Loyalists, it should be remembered, stayed quietly on their farms, unmolested. Only a third of the New York Tories, 35,000, sailed for Canada and England at the close of the war. The great majority, Verplancks, Emotts, and all, remained and became "true Blueskins", like Jimmy Rivington.

But the active one-third were indeed a thorn in the American flesh. Dutchess men, DeLanceys, Crugers, and even some Livingstons, officered the Loyal Regiments, some of them making brilliant records, like that of Cruger at Fort Ninety-six in the Southern mountains. But it was not only the landlords. The disaffected tenants of patriot landlords made more trouble than anyone else. Livingston Manor was a Tory hotbed. The Scottish plantation of Archibald Campbell in Beekman was equally troublesome. Most of the Prendergast company turned Tory. Even good Stephen Willcox got into trouble up in Albany County, to which Prendergast and most of his group emigrated.

Although nothing is heard of Michael Hallenbeck, other Hallenbecks were active Loyalists. Three of them are mentioned in Albany records. Robert Hallenbeck, alias Moses Akins, apparently posing as a Quaker, was removed from Poughkeepsie to the New Jail in Amenia, 1778, but escaped December 10, and was concealed and harbored by Zeckariah Flagler in Charlotte.

Dutchess and her neighbors had difficulty with her conscientious objectors during the war. David Darrow, for example, "derided" all civil jurisdiction for this state. Jonah Case of Litchfield got into trouble for dissuading Quakers from their civil duties. One of the most troublesome was Mother Ann Lee of the Shakers, who spent some time in Poughkeepsie under duress in December, 1780, "on account of her Influence in bringing over Persons to the Persuasions professed by People called Shaking Quakers . . . having a tendency to alienate the Minds of the People from their allegiance to this State." She was put under bond of £100, paid by Ann Lee and her associate, Whitacre. Further North, at Lebanon, the Shakers were accused of harboring disaffected persons.

It was natural that the frequent voyages of boats downriver with refugee Loyalists should become the avenue of espionage. Women seem to have been participants in this traffic.

Early in the war Wm. Livingston, Governor of New Jersey, warned President Reed of the Continental Congress that assassination was threatened against Washington, and others. On Long Island and about Kingsbridge in Manhattan bold marauders managed attempts at kidnapping, at times successfully. The most notorious instance in the Hudson Valley was the attempt in 1780 by Hans Woltimyer with a gang to kidnap General Schuyler at Albany. Woltimyer was one of the most successful Tory spies. His story would equal that of Enoch Crosby on the Congress side. He was active too, in Dutchess County, for a grand jury in May, 1779, found Henry Sleght of Charlotte Precinct guilty, "for that he did on July 1, 1778, at Charlotte consent, advise, and excite the said Johannis Woltimyer and others to go to the city of New York and join the troops of the King." For the same offence Samuel Smith was fined £100 at Beekman Precinct. The minutes of County Committees are full of references to Woltimyer, who issued from hiding places along the Taconics and Helderbergs upon his raids. So bold was he that the Albany Committee appealed to the regular troops for help against him.

Next to Woltimyer, perhaps, a man of Nine Partners named Isaac Huddlestone seems to have been regarded as the most dangerous Tory at large. In June, 1778, he was indicted for murder and other crimes, but escaped and joined the enemy forces. Returning as a spy, he was reported as having enlisted under an assumed name in the American cavalry. On December 4, 1779, Governor Clinton wrote a letter about his activities to General Heath commanding in the lower Highlands. A plan of detection was arranged, and Huddlestone was captured on Wild Boar Hill, near Yonkers. He was listed as imprisoned for felony in Poughkeepsie jail in May, 1780. This seems to contradict Lossing, who says he was convicted and hanged in April of that year. The tradition of his hanging on Forbus Hill, where the gallows stood at the time, seems well established. A great crowd is said to have gathered.

Colonel Lewis DuBois of Dutchess presided at the trial of Daniel Taylor, the British messenger who carried the silver bullet containing Sir Henry Clinton's letter to Burgoyne. Governor Clinton examined him at Poughkeepsie, when he suddenly swallowed the bullet. An emetic soon restored it, but Taylor managed to conceal it a second time. Clinton coolly issued an order to disgorge the man, and he produced the bullet. He was convicted and hanged by order of the DuBois military tribunal, at New Windsor.

Walte Vaughn of Pawling Precinct was another famous outlaw, who terrorized the South-east until Capt. Pearce, on a furlough, organized a chase and shot him.

Among the active Dutchess patriots was Robert Harpur, who after two years on the County Committee was appointed Secretary of the State under Governor Clinton. To him in later years have been attributed the classical names of New York's towns and cities. But as a classic era swept over the world at the time, resulting in classic costume in France and classic revival in architecture and painting, and as other states have their Athens, Rome, and Cicero, Harpur's influence may be overstressed. Harpur College at Binghamton perpetuates his name more justly, for he exerted much influence in starting public education.

The story goes that two Dutch farmers bet their farms on the outcome of the Revolution. Gideon Oosterhout won Derick Dutcher's farm when peace was declared.

William Haff of Poughkeepsie town is said to have been brought to the whipping post for some youthful escapade. When set free, he thrashed the justice who had sentenced him, and ran off to the enemy. Returning later to see his girl, he was caught and sentenced to be hanged. During the exercise period, he would stand at the open window of the jail and sing. His fine voice attracted not only an admiring crowd of Poughkeepsians, but the guard at the rear of the jail, who came around to Market St. to enjoy the concert. Failing to make the circuit of the jail after a particularly good number, they waited for the encore, which never came; Billy had jumped out through a back window.

After the amnesty for Tories, Billy came back in full British uniform and married his girl.

Every jail must have one such story; usually the lover carries off the jailer's daughter.

August 28th 1776—newspaper extract

"A few days since, about 100 women inhabitants of Dutchess County, went to the house of Colonel Brinckerhoff at Fishkill, and insisted upon having tea at the lawful price of six shillings per pound and obliged the gentleman to accomodate them with one chest from his store for that purpose. Shortly after he sold his cargo to some Yorkers who for fear of another female attack forwarded the nefarious stuff to the North river precipitately, where it is now afloat, but the women have placed their guard on each side."

The County Committee soon became a committee on Un-American Activities. In December, 1775, Samuel Dodge of Dutchess reported that witnesses were refusing to testify in regard to accusations of treason. The Congress then passed a law making such persons accessory to treason and authorizing their imprisonment.

In addition to the openly active loyalists, the Whigs recognized three degrees of sentiment with which they had to reckon: the "equivocal", the "suspected", and the "disaffected". In the first degree were those who professed good will to the cause of liberty but sold their wheat only for hard money; in the second, those who consorted with active loyalists, but concealed their own motions; in the third, those known to have violated the rules of the County Committee. The last were warned, fined, or imprisoned. But the Dutchess Committee were men experienced in the law, and their minutes show no undue severity or retaliation. After 1776 life on the county surface was tranquil as compared with the days of ferment, and the night watch was relaxed.

In Dutchess, Harpur signed the documents controlling Loyalists. Many young Dutchess loyalists, heartily sick of the thankless service, and eager to see home again, deserted from the enemy. These, after a while in confinement, would be released in care of some relative or friend, or if still suspected restricted to "one mile from the courthouse or other limited area."

In Philip Smith's history are many anecdotes of the Revolution. Some of them refer to the use of caves by Tories. Confirmation has been found in at least one case.

"The Jurors of the People of the State of New York for the body of the County of Dutchess upon their Oaths Present that Samuel Tid and Solomon Baker disaffected persons did lurk secretly in Pawlings precinct in Dutchess County being lately from within the enemy's lines; and that Ichabod Prosser of the said Pawlings Precinct owing ellegeance to this state, little regarding his duty as a subject of the state, wickedly and Maliciously with force and arms did on the tenth day of April 1781 guide and conduct the said Samuel Tid and Solomon Baker to a cave in the woods in said Pawlings precinct frequented by Enemies to this State as a hiding place &c." Mr. Julian Hunt, of Oblong Lot 41, possesses two muskets of the period, found in a cave near by.

Misprision of treason was charged against Myndert Vielie of Beekmans Precinct, who refused to take the oath of allegiance, was deported to the enemy's lines, and later in 1778 was found in Beekmans. The suit was filed in 1784. Deserter's recognizances are numerous in the records. One of them may be quoted. The distance from the point of report varies widely, apparently based on a faithful study of each applicant. Bonds went as high as £1,000.

With it is printed a "Certificate of Attachment to the United States," also a common document toward the end of the war and later. Whether the document could restore the individual to good standing is questionable; at least he lived in peace.

"Be it remembered that on the 11th day of October in the fourth year of the Independence of the United States of America, James Boyce a Deserter from the Enemy and Henry Boyce of Charlotte Precinct in Dutchess County Yeoman, have each of them personally come before us Cornelius Humfrey, Thomas Moffat, and Robert Harpur, Esquires, Commissioners for enquiring into, detecting and defeating all conspiracies which might be formed in this state against the liberties of America, and acknowledged themselves to owe to the people of this state each the sum of five hundred pounds of good and lawful money of this state, to be levied of their goods and chattels, lands and tenements, respectively, to the use of the people of this state, if the said James Boyce shall make default in the condition following—

"*The Condition* of the above Recognizance is such, that if the above-named James Boyce shall depart by the most direct road from Kingston in Ulster County to the dwelling house of the above-named Henry Boyce, and then not depart more than four miles from the said dwelling house (except for the purpose of doing Militia duty) till the further order of us, or any three Commissioners appointed for the purposes, and shall be of his good behaviour during the present war—Then the Recognizance to be void, otherwise to remain in full force.

Acknowledged before us<br>Cornelius Humfrey<br>Robert Harpur<br>Thos Moffat

Oct. 11, 1779,<br>James Boyce<br>Deserter<br>Henry Boyce<br>Surety<br>£500<br>N. 150

"Dutchess Co. We Cornelius Humfrey one of the Judges of the Inferior Court of Common Pleas of the said County of Dutchess, and Joseph Balding both Freeholders of the said County of Dutchess, do certify that William McNeal who resided in the said County during the late war with Great Britain, is well attached to the Freedom and Independence of the United

States of America, and has taken an active and decided part therein.

Given under our hands in Dutchess
County aforesaid the twenty-fourth
day of June in the year of our Lord
One thousand seven hundred and
eighty four
Cornelius Humfrey
Joseph Balding."

Escapes and jail breaks added to the committee's troubles. In May, 1781, Joseph Thurston and Samuel Coffron assaulted Constable Reuben Allerton of Amenia, thus enabling a prisoner to escape. Four men in Fredericksburgh, in November, 1780, set free Daniel Parish, an old offender. Silas, Zeporah, and Peleg Ballard also escaped, along with a Westchester man named Webb.

But considering the times, the whirl of war's surprises, the area controlled, and the enemy so near, one wonders that the cases are not more numerous. In the maintenance of popular morale, the Committee acted promptly to circumvent the Tokyo Rose of the day.

On March 15, 1781, John Allen, Jr. of Charlotte and Purdon Burlingand were indicted for "giving force and countenance to a certain proclamation signed by the officers of the King, tending to disunite and discourage the people."

While New York contained more Tories than any other state, and while Governor Clinton and the Legislature were most relentless in deporting them, it is also true that two-thirds of the Loyalists remained unmolested on their farms, and that many exiles returned to have their properties restored to them, after the first heat of resentment had passed. Several leaders in Dutchess, among them Robert R. Livingston Jr., opposed the severity of the legal measures taken.

An example of the reconciled Loyalist is Peter Mesier, whose house is now situated in the park at Wappingers Falls. He was one of the wealthiest men in New York City. On his return his property was restored to him, though his Toryism had been so strong as to cause the sacking of his store by the Sons of Liberty. Mesier sold out in New York City and came up to the Falls, where he purchased the four Red and Yellow Mills, and other land in the county.

The manorial system and leasehold tenantry have usually attracted the greatest censure for New York's high Toryism. But many other causes enter into the picture. The activity of the Church of England heads the list. When the Rombout Committee of Observation met in 1776, their principal business was the case of Captain Leyster, who had spoken "disrespectful" of the Congress. Capt. Leyster said "The Boston People were all a parcel of Cromwell's People, and hanged the people along, as they could in former times. After they were tired of hanging the Cromwelians the Remainder were sent to Boston." He was quite vulgar in his reference to the paper with signatures of the Association. Captain Cornelius Leyster in his defence made complaint of Dr. Theodorus Van Wyck who at a tavern had proposed the toast Damnation to the Church of England "(the said Dr. Van Wyck having a bowl of Tody in his hand)."

The Rombout Patent had had its ecclesiastical troubles in the Reformed Church, and the Episcopalians had profited by it. Samuel Seabury had been successful in starting new churches in Dutchess. Bartholomew Crannell of Poughkeepsie, an active church member, testified in later years that he and his friends had been the means of preventing Dutchess from sending delegates to the Provincial Congress.

But the chief cause lay in geography and history. British policy, for all its weaknesses, had succeeded in pacifying the dangerous Six Nations, and with them had conquered Canada. Upstate New Yorkers had already crossed the line and were beginning to open a wider trade. Dutchess horse-dealers were actively engaged in this trade. No longer did Albany and Schenectady have to fear destructive raids. A war with Britain, on the other hand, would certainly renew these panics in a higher degree, and bring Canadian Indians again upon them, to add to the loyalist Senecas and Mohawks the horrors of desolation. On the whole, also, the governors themselves had been conciliatory. Moore and Colden stood shoulders above other colonial governors. They had not only supported a successful war; they had sided as far as they could with the people, in the matter of Vermont, in pardons to rebellious tenants, and in support of New York's eastern frontier against Connecticut and Massachusetts. Shelburne's policy had borne fruit. The Stamp Act repeal had come before matters were as violent as in Boston. The best citizens were not at first among the Sons of Liberty. They were looked upon as aliens. The Dutchess tenants did not forget that the Sons of Liberty had taken a dim view of their march to New York and appeal for help.

As for Long Island, it was completely under sea power. War would devastate it. New England and upriver had their hills, but the clamdiggers were defenceless.

The wonder grows, indeed, that New York, a conquered or "regulated" province, had succeeded in maintaining its love of liberty and its power of action. Under Clinton's vigorous rule at Poughkeepsie the state without access to the sea, with a mere strip of river counties as its sole territory, with the Five Nations to the west, Canada's highway to the north, and the British fleet and army seven years at its capital, met its problems manfully, fought what Thomas Campbell called "The American Civil War" with courage and moderation, and yet contributed much to the general cause of independence. The long years of resistance to court-party aggression, the skill in law and in argument, the effective local government, were the real causes. As General Washington explained to his young guest Niemciewicz, a Polish visitor who married a Livingston and settled down, the secret of American success was the "town", the local and almost self-governing unit, ready at any time to defend its liberties. This it is that justifies the pursuit of local history for one who would understand the springs of American action.

# 27. Our War Governor. 1777

"BROTHER JONATHAN" TRUMBULL of Connecticut had a worthy rival in his record as war governor, in the record of George Clinton of New York. The Clinton House, our best preserved mansion of Poughkeepsie war days, keeps green his memory. Clinton Point, where he built his fine river mansion, no longer remembers him; but Clinton Town, with its Hollow and its Corners, has taken the old fellow to its heart.

During the Revolution he stuck to Poughkeepsie, as unyielding as the Kaal Rock itself. His first Poughkeepsie letter is dated January 24, 1776. Beginning in December, 1777, after his fight at Fort Clinton, and his escape and furlough to catch his breath, he lived at Bartholomew Crannell's house, now 448 Main Street, while his friend and associate in state business, Col. Udny Hay, lived in the "Clinton House." Crannell of Crannell Street was our leading Loyalist, a good man and honest lawyer, and large landholder. His daughter Elizabeth married young Dr. Peter Tappen, of the County Committee, whose sister was Mrs. George Clinton. Elizabeth's sister Catherine of Catherine Street was Mrs. Gilbert Livingston. These ardent whigsters at their father's tea-table flaunted aprons embroidered "Liberty" and "No Tea".

During his seven-years-exile in Dutchess, George Clinton came to know the county well. He made several judicious purchases of land here, and was a tax-payer as well as a war guest. He had, in earlier days, practised in Dutchess courts. No doubt he had "carried chain" for his father on his numerous surveys in Dutchess. At all events, Dutchess is proud to shine in the reflected luster of the great citizen of Ulster and Little Britain.

July 19, 1776, Poughkeepsie.

"Almost every Tory in the County was hunted up by the Yankie's & Brought to County Committy, then we had news of the ships moving up the river, Troops flocking in here like swarms of Bees, People that live at the river moving everything away, . . ."

"Your loving wife".
Elizabeth Tappen to
Dr. Peter Tappen.

(This is probably the earliest recorded use of "yankees" in this sense).

"I hear they are all well at Clinton's we hear nothing of Toryism since independence was read to them at Carpenters they seem to be as much distressed about the ships coming up as the wigs I believe they have given over all their lead & give up their tools for the purpose of intrenching at shipyards, they as well as wigs are at work there it seemed the lot fell most on the tories, there was in our neighborhood coll. Van Kleeck, Snediker, Hair, Emot, Fisher, John Davis, Dick Everit."

On Oct 26 Peter Tappen wrote that the ships had gone down again. He rejoiced to hear that "Gen How has lost one of his legs by a Shot from our People". He described "Brother Clinton (General, later Governor) as "very harty and in high spirits."

Mrs. Tappen in 1783 went to New York to bid farewell to her loyalist father, Bartholomew Crannell, then sailing to Nova Scotia. The Governor occupied his Poughkeepsie house on Main Street, No. 448, through the Revolution, except for absences in the field. No other governor equalled him in combining the official with the officer.

He led the state troops in 1779, and expressed to John Jay of the County Committee his satisfaction with the conduct of the Dutchess Militia. The British captured Verplanck's

Point and Stony Point; the latter, recaptured by Anthony Wayne, was soon recaptured and again abandoned by Sir Henry Clinton.

In 1780 the Governor again led his troops to the field, this time near Lake George against the northern Indians. His correspondence is full of military affairs. He suggested the fortification of West Point in preference to sites further south, and his advice was taken. He urged activity upon Putnam, of whom he thought little as commander of the Hudson defences. He urged Gates to examine the forts; their capture cannot be blamed on Clinton's overconfidence. He urged the new chain at the Point.

He knew the County. In May, 1776, he wrote of the half-pay veteran officers that Robinson had settled at Fredericksburgh. These Scots were "of course disaffected." Of one Scot, Duncan Campbell, he wrote with grim irony. With a pass issued by General Schuyler this "ministerial Major" had left his luggage deposited at Wiltse's store in the Fishkill. There some little boys in play untied the ropes of one box and discovered arms enough to equip a couple of companies.

While he defended against the British diversion upriver, his brother James led Dutchess men to the Genesee to punish the Iroquois for their raids on the settlements of the frontier from Wyoming to Crown Point. Cherry Valley had been but one of many destroyed settlements. Sir Henry Clinton feinted against the Highland walls, capturing forts and raiding villages as far as Bedford. Tryon got as far north as Danbury and threatened Dutchess. The Americans lost Stony Point. Both winters were exceptionally severe. To add to New York's troubles, Massachusetts begged for permission to buy flour, and when that was not forthcoming, it was smuggled. Burgoyne's veterans paroled in Canada broke parole and led raids in the north. Loyalists increased their efforts, spreading counterfeit money, buying food and smuggling it to New York through Long Island. With a depreciated currency and pay in arrears the officers in Clinton's New York Regiments suddenly resigned in a body, while the soldiers sent a committee to treat with the Legislature for a redress of grievances. Nothing went right, everything went wrong. A friend wrote to warn the governor that assassins were on their way to Poughkeepsie to make an end of him.

Yet through his hundreds of letters he remained the same unbowed administrator, driving ahead from day to day on the tasks of the state. He reserved his deepest resentment for the Vermonters who had as he thought stolen New York's fairest jewel from her crown. That was unforgivable. He protested against the transfer of a regiment to Poughkeepsie, on the ground that the village was already overcrowded; but he yielded, and the young soldiers behaved most creditably, cutting their logs and building their huts with speed.

From Clinton's mail-bag a letter has been borrowed, written by the same Justice Rosewell Hopkins of Crum Elbow that put British Sergeant Cassidy in jail. For all his irritation Clinton must have enjoyed a hearty laugh.

"Amenia, July 20, 1780.

May it please your Excellency. I beg leave to acquaint your Excellency with a Remonstrance Concerning a certain Pressmaster, one George Tremble, who is a transient person that lives in Connecticut, who came to me on the 8th Instant and told me he wanted my team to carry forage to the Fishkills. I told him my circumstances was such that I could not let them go, for it would Ruin me for my wheat, about 130 bushels, all I had was in the field and it would spoil. My oats, 200 or 300 busshels all lay in the Swarth, and would be lost, for I had no help but one Son, and could not hire any man; my flax, a fine crop, was in the field and some hay in the meadow, and my grass lodg'd and rotting, but he said he cared not for that, but I should myself go with my team the next day. I told him if I could secure my wheat grain I would send my son and team the next week, but he said I should go the next day. I told I would not; he showed me a Coppy of a press warrent from your Excellency to Col. Hay with a line from him on the back authorizing said Tremble to impress teams & drivers in this state.

I told him that was no legal title to him; he rode off saying he would get a warrent for me & then told all about, he had got a warrent for me; but on the 14th he came again with a Sergeant & 8 men & entered my field, Seized my son & confined him under guard, drove out my fatten oxen that I was fattening for the army, took my horses, & forced my son to drive them with a lode of my own oats to the Fishkills, altho I consented if they must go they might carry my oats, he told me I was a disaffected person, had done nothing to support the cause, held bad Principles, was a dam'd Lyer and a dam'd rascal.

I have fin'd him for cursing; sued him for trespass, & issued a warrent against him in order to bind him to his good behaviour, & recorded a riot against him.

I think its a pity that there is not a man in this Precinct County or state that can be trusted with a press warrent, but such an outlandish, Irish, malicious, abusive fellow must be sent into this Precinct to press all the whiggs teams, & none in Charlotte, which is near 3 times as big, and half tories, for I cant larn of one being pressed there; after all the malicious fellow wrote a letter to Col. Hay sent by the Soldiers that my team Capt. Shepherd's & Mr. Ingersoll's teams were disaffected teams, and requested they might be kept in Service a month; he abused others besides me. I am, Sir, your most obedient Hum'e Serv't

Rosewell Hopkins.

P. S. One Stack of my wheat is spoiled being wet through & grown & I shall loose about six tones of hay. R.H.
His Excellency Governour Clinton."

In April, 1778, the Governor received Daniel Hammill, a Dutchess soldier who had been captured at Fort Montgomery and had turned loyalist. He had been sent upriver by Sir Henry Clinton to spy what he could, while ostensibly making advances to George Clinton and his brother James. His companion, Samuel Geake, got himself sent to Fort Schuyler, to recruit the disaffected Irish. He was soon detected, and Hammill with him, through a letter from an American prisoner in New York telling of Hammill's visits to Sir Henry. Though under sentence of hanging, Geake was reprieved and Hammill kept in jail in order to protect the informant. He escaped in August, and left the country.

Perhaps the busiest man in Dutchess County during the war was Colonel Udny Hay, Deputy Quarter-Master General 1776-1780, Purchasing Agent for New York State 1780-1783. A Scottish lumberman, he had left Canada and two thousand pounds' worth of tools and lumber when he threw in with the Americans. He had helped the men who fortified Ticonderoga, and came to Fishkill in 1778. His large correspondence with Washington and Governor Clinton bespeaks the man of affairs and the trained financier, who never allowed details to divert his judgment. Over his desk at headquarters went the orders for flour for the troops, forage for the horses and cattle, lumber for the huts and boats, lead, iron, and all the rest. He undertook the unpleasant business of impressing wagons and hay from the Dutchess farmers, and maintained a long struggle with his superior, Col. Timothy Pickering, insisting that the Congress should pay for these requisitions. Perhaps his defence of New York was the cause of his transfer to the office of Purchasing Agent for the State of New York in 1780. He left Fishkill and moved to Poughkeepsie, where he could be in daily touch with the governor and other officers. There in October he purchased the house on Main Street known as the "Clinton House", rebuilding it after a fire in 1783, at which time he lived for a few months in the Glebe House further up the street. In 1786, he got into debt, and removed to Vermont, where he lived on the slope of Mt. Mansfield near Burlington, the friend of Ethan Allen and other leaders. Allen appointed him executor of his will. On his own death in 1806, his influence there was described as "predominant without parallel."

Hay's letters are worth reading. He always looked for the

reason of things. He was the analyst in business, the philosopher of accountancy.

Hay became Ira Allen's agent for the sale of his vast holdings in Vermont. In his younger days he had been an ardent Son of Liberty, and his remove to Vermont may have been due to his disapproval of the growing Federalism of Dutchess. In Vermont he became a principal collaborator with Citizen Genet in the French Revolutionary propaganda. He was active in the promotion of a Revolutionary movement in Canada in which Genet took part in 1794. Lord Dorchester the Governor called upon the Canadian Indians to prepare for attack. Genet had married a daughter of George Clinton, and must often have visited Dutchess. No doubt Hay thought of him as approved by his admired leader.

Clinton managed to attend the higher courts when they met at Poughkeepsie, for Gen. de Chastellux on his brief passage in 1780 could not meet him, as he was in legal conference. During the twelve months of 1777-8 he was brigadier-general of New York Militia, brigadier-general of the Continental Line, governor and lieutenant-governor at the same time by election under the new constitution. His ordeal by fire began with his inauguration in July, 1777. His Poughkeepsie years wrought the tempered steel of character that brought him the governor's post from 1777 to 1795, and from 1801 to 1804. The vice-presidency of the United States would have been his honor much earlier, had the Constitution which he opposed been rightly drawn in its terms. When it was amended in 1804 he was elected, and reelected in 1808. He died in 1812 during the last year of his second term. In those years his home was in Dutchess, at Clinton Point. No other American served thirty years as governor and vice-president. Only the Virginia party kept him from the highest office.

Among our many men of the higher gifts he was the one most typically American. A fighter from boyhood, he had fought against Fort Frontenac in 1758 at 19. He led troops at White Plains in 1776, commanded in the Highlands in

1777, and took the field against Sir John Johnson in 1780. Yet his letters show no trace of the routine officer, of the bureau chief, or of the crafty politician. He was rather the straightforward man of action, but open to his friends' advice. In an age of patronage and flattery, he never flattered anyone nor broke a code to help a friend. No wonder that for his first ten years in office he had no opponent at the polls. The Governor's Poughkeepsie days brought forth several hundred of his letters. They make Poughkeepsie the wartime capital of the State, in no uncertain terms. Indeed, the real civic birth of Poughkeepsie dates from George Clinton, for he not only lived and ruled here, but he made its port the place of embarkation of supplies to the army north and south.

Here came Tadeusz Kosciuszko to call upon him in March, 1778, before assuming his duties in planning West Point fortifications. Kosciuszko was warmly recommended by the Governor to General Parsons, as one "disposed to do everything he can in the most agreeable manner." His opinion was borne out by other records. General John Armstrong of Barrytown, Aide-de-camp of General Gates at Saratoga was so charmed by his agreeable manner that he gave his son the terrific name of Kosciuszko Armstrong. The Polish hero planned to buy a Dutchess farm and settle here. Armstrong conducted inquiries about real estate for him. Unfortunately, Congress voted land in Ohio to his friend, and he, unable to wait to realize upon it, left it with Jefferson to use to set Negroes free, thus blotting out a part of America's tragic flaw. The money, however, at long last went to a distant Polish relative.

But the Indian menace filled the Governor's mail in '78 almost to the exclusion of other matters. It was filled with accounts from officers of the massacres at Wyoming and Minisink, Cherry Valley and Unadilla. The Catskills were invaded, and Col. John Morin Scott of Rombout wrote gloomily from Ulster that Clinton would do well to evacuate that rich county and concentrate on the eastern shore. Governor George was of sterner stuff, and plugged the gaps with one company or another whenever he could. Refugees were cared for, though in no very organized manner.

Mary Vanderburgh Geer arrived in the village with her seven children. Her husband was killed at Wyoming, and the young widow fled to the woods, coming finally to the Delaware and to safety. The Count de Chastellux found two forlorn refugee girls at Andrew Morehouse's tavern in Dover, in the summer of 1780. Evidently they helped to meet the employment shortage. They were sturdy enough, having walked over a hundred miles barefoot.

A whole company were sheltered at Pawling. From the accounts of Wyoming in John Holt's N. Y. Gazette, then published in Poughkeepsie, Thomas Campbell thirty years later got some helpful hints for his most famous poem, "Gertrude of Wyoming", published in 1809. Written at a time when America was anathema in English books, it was gratefully received in America. Campbell's father and uncle had settled in America, his cousin being a district attorney in Virginia. His southern connection may have led him to locate a "pastoral savanna" upon the Susquehanna, although the rhyme may also have wrought its charm.

But Campbell's thought was of sympathy and especially of regret for the war.

"Sad was the year, by proud oppression driven
  When Transatlantic Liberty arose,
Not in the sunshine and the smile of Heaven,
  But wrought in whirlwinds, and begirt with woes,
  Amidst the strife of Fratricidal foes.
Her birth-star was the light of burning plains;
  Her baptism is the weight of blood that flows
From kindred hearts—the blood of British veins,
  And famine tracks her steps, and pestilential pains."

Campbell may have learned of the "Fratricidal foes" from his relatives the Archibald Campbells of Dutchess and Albany

Counties, for they were on opposite sides in the war. Thomas' grandfather was an Archibald Campbell. Like the scholar he was, the poet read all he could find—Colden's "History of the Five Nations", "Jefferson's Notes on Virginia", and many English books of travel. At least he did not put hyenas lapping the brook as Milbert did, or tell of crocodiles sporting beneath Niagara Falls, as Thomas Moore wrote somewhat later.

Clinton's day was cheered, though "begirt with woes", by a lively account of two Hudson River boys who knew the backwoods. The account came from Colonel John Cantine at his out-post near Lackawack in Ulster. There are Cantines, Osterhouts, and Andries, in Dutchess, galore, but these three heroes were more likely of Ulster, perhaps of Saugerties. The narrative is almost as good as a Gary Cooper "Western".

"Aug 11 1778

George Andries and Jacob Oosterhout the two men that where lately tacken prisoners at Lackawack have made their Escape. Thay where on there way to Niagara and within twenty miles of that place under the Care of a Mohawk Chief (who Commanded the party that where at Lackawack) and two other Indians. Oosterhout a Weakly man, was not able to march as fast as the Indians. They where Resolved the next Day to kill him and take his Scalp. Andries Informing Oosterhout of their Danger and askt him if he could do Something for himself. Oosterhout Said he Could Not. Andries then advised him to Lye Still. When they Went to Sleep Andries as usual was put between the two young Indians, the Capt or Chief with two squaws on the other side of the fire. Once Andries found that they were asleep he got the ax on which he had prepared for that purpose and with it Laid his two Bedfellows much sounder asleep than they were before, When getting across the fire in order to Let the Capt. Shear the same fate, he started awake but Andries Handling his Ax so well that the third Blow Laid him asleep also. The Squaws made their Escape. Andries came in with Osterhout at his place, the

Nineteenth Day after he had performed this Exploit, with near the Vallue of One Hundred Pounds Worth of plunder on his back. Had when they set out on their jorney 2 quarts sinnemon and 5 young Ducks. He can give but little Information of the Enemy.

John Cantine."

# 28. The Watch on the Hudson. 1777

DURING THE THREE crucial years when the Hudson line was under attack the American headquarters were kept on the east shore, in Dutchess County. From 1780 to the end, Washington moved the bulk of his power to the West shore, and his headquarters to Orangeburg (Tappan) and Newburgh. Command of the Highlands locally remained in the east, under Arnold, MacDougall, and Heath.

Through the entire war the watch at the Highlands continued. From the hill fortress the Continental Grand Army faced both north and south; north against Indian raids and Canadian invasion; south against coastal raids and the breaching of the Hudson watergate. Burgoyne's great design was to drive Washington out of his fastness from the north, and capture him in north Jersey between his army and that of Howe issuing from New York City. The only trouble with this strategy was that Washington had all Jersey to retreat into. Accordingly Howe seems to have thought he would sail further south and march up through Jersey to Washington's rear. No escape would then be possible.

The trouble with this brilliant plan was the ghastly extent of it, and the unsought experiments by the way. Gates captured Burgoyne, and Philadelphia captured Howe. Weak as it proved in 1777, the Fishkill passage was held, and the Highlands with it. Not until Newport was reached could the British make a permanent dent in the line. With forts and troops on both sides of the River at West Point Washington could move his main army to Tappan, and remain closer in touch with the war in the South.

Although neither Putnam nor Heath perfected a good defense of the New England coast, it was kept as a force in being, and even raided Long Island at times, while the Spy Lane along the Taconics was used by the Congress as well as by the British, for learning what was going on in New York.

Thus, though no battles took place on the soil of Old Dutchess, its southern hills remained the essential Redoubt of the Revolution, while its wheat fields, stock, and iron fed the army. Burgoyne's army marched across it from Bull's Bridge to Fishkill, though not as victors. Clinton's fleet raided its shore. Tryon's raid skirted its eastern edge. But for the most part it is the story of a garrison, of supplies, hospitals, quarters, and engineering; of espionage and betrayal, of refugees, deserters to and from the enemy; of jails and sequestrations. All the while civil government goes on, both of state and county, precinct and town, and visitors find its outward look most flourishing. All this, we must remind ourselves, is also Revolution.

The chief contribution to this watch on the Hudson were the Regiments of the Line, the Militia, and the Levies, who stood watch.

There are two reasons for giving in some detail the figures of enlistment of the soldiers. The nation did not possess the experience or the resources for fighting a war. Mismanagement dogged every step of the way. Moreover, Dutchess, and New York in general, were "notoriously Tory." The actual achievement under these conditions is therefore interesting.

The Dutchess Continental Line, the Fourth New York Regiment, mustered 1880 soldiers. Of these 197 were mustered also in other regiments, of the Militia. To these may be added 300 Dutchess men mustered in the Second and Third Regiments of the Line. To this total of 1983 Continentals must be added the Militia muster rolls, of 4417 names. All of these but the Fourth Regiment are found in the Archives; the Fourth has been estimated at the lowest muster figure, 300.

| | | |
|---|---|---|
| First Regiment, Col. Swartwout | officers and men | 488 |
| Second Regiment, Col. Brinckerhoff | " " | 805 |
| Third Regiment, Col. Field | " " | 303 |
| Fourth Regiment, Col. Frear, | " "est | 300 |
| Fifth Regiment, Col. Humfrey, | " " | 506 |
| Sixth Regiment, Col. Graham | " " | 1309 |
| Seventh Regiment, Col. Luddington | " " | 637 |
| Coopers Rangers | | 69 |
| | TOTAL | 4417 |

No account has been taken of the two companies of Associated Exempts, men over age or otherwise disqualified, who were mustered as a Home Guard and Tory Watch; or of the Five Regiments of Militia Levies mustered from the Militia toward the end of the war for service outside their state.

An examination of the rolls gives 3% as a fair estimate of duplicates among the militia companies. This gives 4287 as the total militia muster, and 6270 as the County total. Of course no such number served at any one time. Most enrollments were for very limited periods.

An estimate of 1,500 as the average number under arms would seem reasonable. In crises this number would be enlarged: after Brooklyn, Burgoyne's invasion, Brant, the Sullivan march, Arnold's treason, the mutinies of 1780, and Yorktown.

With a population which did not exceed 30,000, this gives 5% as the average enrollment, a figure approximately that of 1944.

We may look at it another way. With thirty thousand souls, one-half women, and one-third Tories, we have ten thousand left. Of these, considering the then span of life, six thousand may be under sixteen, leaving four thousand. Then we subtract one thousand available men for Exempts (aged, or infirm, or civilian war workers). This calculation leaves three thousand men for enlistment in the Muster Rolls. Actually, with over six thousand names on them, we must supply the rest either from the refugees who fled to the county and took arms, from the invaded counties to the south, or the natural increase of sixteen-year-olds, coming of muster age each year. With these supplies, the muster roll of Dutchess is entirely acceptable.

No mutiny, and no undue desertions, mar the war record of Dutchess men. The Fourth New York Line was one of the trusted regiments selected to march to West Point in January, 1781, when the Great Mutiny spread among the Pennsylvania, New Jersey, and Connecticut line regiments. Its officers demanded improvement of condition in the same year, and resigned with the rest. Its soldiers sent a delegation to the State Legislature at Poughkeepsie. But this was not mutiny; and the remedies did not include the loss of whole regiments, with British agents among them.

Under Colonel Henry Beekman Livingston, the Fourth New York Line fought well at Brooklyn in 1776, and in every major engagement of the northern Line Regiments until its derangement in 1780, when it was brigaded with the Second Regiment. Lt. Col. Weissenfels commanded it in the later years. The Orderly Books later described tell its story more intimately.

When the British occupied New York in the summer of '76, the refugees streamed up to Fishkill by water and way, while loyalists slipped south to the redcoats' lines. The exchange provided some relief in housing the newcomers, but there was great overcrowding.

When Washington, after the battle of White Plains, retreated to the Jerseys, some of the regiments, with the wounded, found their way to Fishkill. The Wiccopee Pass was fortified, and a headquarters established at the VanWyck house north of it. An eye-witness report, well vouched-for, and recorded more than a hundred years, tells that the informant when a girl "went with her father through the streets of Fishkill, after the battle of White Plains, and in places between the Dutch and Episcopal churches the dead were piled up by the side of the road as high as cord wood."

Not only the wounded, but the hospitalized soldiers were

buried in the base of the mountain east of the highroad, Route 9. Conditions in Fishkill grew so serious that the surgeon-general in Fishkill, Dr. John Morgan, was dismissed from the service, and Dr. Shippen appointed in his place. Morgan was, however, restored to the service after investigation, and Shippen, who had been incompetent, was succeeded by Dr. Brown, and later by Dr. John Cochran as surgeon-general of the army.

The medical history of the Revolution is tragic. Nine times as many men died of disease as of wounds. The sufferings at Valley Forge were far surpassed by conditions in the hospitals. Incompetence in the staff was the chief cause.

Where, as in Albany, there were good beds in an adequate hospital, a competent head surgeon like Dr. Jonathan Potts, and a sufficient number of good surgeons, losses were small, less than two hundred out of several thousand.

One of the surgeons at Fishkill was Dr. James Thacher, whose "Military Journal" is a chief source-book of the war. He served at Boston and Saratoga, and left Albany in June, 1778. In that pleasant city, after the first crowded days, he had leisure to join his colleagues in dancing lessons taught by a Mr. Trotter. Thus equipped, he sailed with baggage and hospital supplies to Fishkill and with a pilot from New Windsor managed to land at Garrison's and take charge of the military hospital which had been set up at Beverly, the homestead of the Loyalist Colonel Robinson. Here with frequent visits at Fishkill and West Point, he managed to vary his professional duties with his favorite recreation. On July 8, 1778, he dined at the Fishkill hospital with his friends Drs. Adams and Eustis, and found them "pleasantly situated in a secure retreat for the accommodation of our sick and wounded soldiers." He reported next month, however, an excess of dysentery and putrid fever at his own base.

On August 28 he called on the Marquis De La Fayette, then convalescing from a severe attack of fever. The young general was "affable" in his broken English. He seemed not very elegant, "his shoulders being broad and high, nor is there a remarkable symmetry in his features; his forehead is high, his nose large and long, eyebrows prominent, and projecting over a fine animated hazel eye." The description seems worth recording of this reception in the county which later honored the Marquis by naming a village for him, and a town for his chateau.

On August 8 General Putnam visited the hospital. The old warrior was corpulent and clumsy, "but carries a bold, undaunted front. He exhibits little of the refinements of the well-educated gentleman, but much of the character of the veteran soldier." Learning that the young surgeon had never heard of curing the "ground itch" with tar and brimstone, he told him good-humoredly that he was not fit for a doctor.

Another Dutchess hospital was started in the meeting-house on Quaker Hill that autumn. The story there is not so pleasant. Most of the Friends were opposed to this use of their edifice. The army physician, Dr. James Fallon, wrote indignantly of his hardships to the Governor, on January 3, 1779.

"I want as a military officer to give the government my testimony (as the Quakers call it) and suspicions against certain persons on Quaker Hill; my verdict of applause in favor of the four Whig Quakers, and my account of the difficulties this met with." Dr. Fallon resented the hard-heartedness of the Quaker "Pharaohs" who would not let his poor sick and wounded soldiers go in their wagons to Danbury, when his own food and medical supplies had given out. He wanted his opponents punished. "I would not kill, but I would closely shear the wool."

In spite of ostracism and boycott on the Hill, Dr. Fallon managed to bring his men through with a mortality of only three, in a severe winter. The four saving Whigs were "old Ferris the pulpiteer (Benjamin Ferris) and his son, and Thomas Worth and his family."

It was during this season that Washington's Headquarters were on Quaker Hill, at the Kane and Reed houses. Here was celebrated the great barbecue and parade in honor of the first anniversary of the surrender of Burgoyne. Here, too, at his own request for a court-martial, General Philip Schuyler was acquitted of all charges against him for the conduct of the war in the north preceding his removal by Congress in favor of Gates. The Yankees not only caused his removal, but actually removed the Battle of Bennington from New York to Vermont. It occurred at Walloomsac. Dutchess did her best for Schuyler at Saratoga, for its regiments fought well there, and eight commissioned officers of the name of Livingston were present, some of them making Gates's life very uncomfortable.

In spite of Dr. Fallon's experiences, General Washington seems to have fared well at Quaker Hill. He generously rewarded a messenger who brought him a great cheese made by Mrs. Taber, who believed in the laws of hospitality.

The temporary encampment on Quaker Hill soon gave place to the more central position at Fishkill. Our friend Dr. Thacher left the inactivity at the base hospital for the life of a regimental surgeon, but he describes a visit at Fishkill in March and April, 1781, when 187 of the soldiers in his regiment were taken with the smallpox, and the entire encampment of Fishkill and Newburgh were inoculated. He especially mentions the event at Cold Spring, where Continental troops, mostly Connecticut line, were encamped on the plateau between Cragside and Undercliff. Drs. Cochrane, Thacher, Munson, and others performed it. Only four soldiers died in this early instance of mass inoculation.

It is difficult to realize now, that at this time inoculation was as much dreaded as the disease itself. In 1778 the New York Legislature had passed a law forbidding inoculation by anyone.—The first use of true vaccine was in 1796.

The small-pox epidemic followed by only a few weeks the great Mutiny of the Line in January, 1781, among these very troops, and also the Pennsylvania and Jersey camps in Jersey. There were desertions in York regiments, but no mutinies. The Fourth Dutchess was one of the regiments that could be trusted to put down the mutineers. Six months later they were all marching off to Yorktown most amicably.

Transferred to his light infantry Dr. Thacher took part in the feint against New York that preceded the Yorktown march. His regiment at first was sent forward against Kingsbridge, but soon "made the right about" and returned to the Highland Ferry (King's) and crossed the River. He well records the suspense of the soldiers as their guesses gave way to certainty that they were off for Virginia. "Bets have run high." With suspense ended, his regiment marched through the "splendid city of Philadelphia," blinded by the smothering dust-storm raised by the parading soldiers. "This was not a little mortifying, as the ladies were viewing us from the open windows of every house."

Lafayette had other memories than his illness to carry away from Fishkill. In one of his hero-worshipping letters he reminds General Washington of the night at Fishkill, and an interview with the devil, which an old friend experienced at his house, and which made the generals laugh so heartily. It is pleasant to read that Washington laughed at times, if only at "mesmerism" which had recoiled upon the contriver.

It was at Fishkill that this twenty-one year-old warrior gave his commander-in-chief his views on how to win the war. The general seems to have really loved the young gamecock. He recognized his real abilities but kept him in leash, as he did at Yorktown when Lafayette asked to command the American forces in order to give him prestige before the French troops. Washington preferred General Lincoln, but kept Lafayette's loyalty.

It was at "the Fishkills", too, that the French adventurer took his leave "most tenderly" from his general, when he went on his furlough to France. Lafayette writing from France used the plural form, showing that he knew the local name of the town as well as the official singular.

On December 15, 1778, Gen. McDougall wrote Clinton from Fishkill, "The abuses would shock you." There was a total scarcity of vegetables and want of covering for the troops. "The cattle have been eating their mangers for three days; others are dying". In a second letter he wrote:

"Connecticut won't have us but in the hour of Danger.
New York is reluctant we should have any Repose.
New Jersey complains they have had too much of us.
Where, my dear Sir, are we to go?
Can I defend the Highlands and the Rear Frontiers at the same time?"

The Congress forces spent much time in 1780 and 1781 fortifying West Point, on both sides of the river. The Connecticut line camped at Cold Spring during this period, while Fishkill remained the main depot of provisions and munitions for the works. An armory was built, where guns were repaired. In one of the shops James Bailey, a sergeant, made a sword which was presented to General Washington. Now at the Smithsonian, it bears the name of its maker. The Baileys were a well-known family in Rombout. Sgt. Bailey afterwards lived near Cold Spring.

At Fishkill gunpowder was made from supplies of saltpetre. John R. Livingston's powdermill supplied munitions. After 1778, on appeals from New England, where crops were poor, wheat was permitted to be sent east. The early sufferings were now mostly past, although Chastellux in 1780 noted that the soldiers at Fishkill wore their rags with dignity.

Dr. John Bard was grateful to the governor for his kind protection. He was suspected of trading with the enemy while in seclusion here.

"My Farm and Profession have wholly employed me, and I hope not altogether uselessly."

In defense of the Hudson in 1777 Clinton set Dutchess carpenters to work making fire-rafts for General Washington. He gathered wornout sloops and sank them in the channel. He built a chevaux-de-frise at Polipel Island. Perhaps his most ambitious task was the enlargment of the old Champlain chain, which had been made to keep the British out of the lake and was now sent down to the Poughkeepsie forges for enlargement. Unfortunately this sort of naval engineering was unknown to the Americans in 1776. The British artificers who dismantled it when they passed in 1777 thought it an admirable device. But it was never able to stand its own weight or to resist the tides. The Americans had miscalculated the lifting capacity of the spar-buoys, and the size of the clevis needed to swing the links against the strong tides. After several attempts, a new chain was set up at Constitution Island under West Point in 1779. This proved adequate, though the British never gave its engineers the satisfaction of proving it. It was removed in winter and rehung when the ice had gone down the river.

In 1778 occurred the massacres in the Minnisink and Wyoming Valleys. They were a diversion intended to protect the Canadian frontier, weakened by the loss of Burgoyne. General Sullivan's invasion of the Iroquois lands carried Dutchess regiments far to the westward in retaliation, but revealed our weakness in supply and in discipline and hygiene. The lessons were learned and applied.

In 1780 the line still held, from Middlebrook in Jersey up to Danbury. Then Major John André tried his hand at its overthrow. Benedict Arnold was now the weakest link in our chain.

Behind the screen of siege in 1781 Washington was able to maneuvre. Making a feint at Staten Island he could move his west wing at Connecticut to his extreme right in Jersey, and press the siege at Yorktown long enough to take Cornwallis, while slow Sir Henry Clinton fumed and flustered in New York. For the last time Washington's army crossed the Hudson at Kings Ferry, Dutchess' southern passway. The Dutchess regiments joined with the rest to the classical siege game in the Virginia trenches. From '81 to '83 the line still held, with diversions up the Mohawk to protect the frontier settlements—too late, of course, in many cases—and Washington could wait for the capitulation. Time was his best friend. His northern rival, Horatio Gates, after getting the mitten from a wealthy young Dutchess widow, Mrs. Richard Montgomery, met a worse fate in defeat at Camden in Carolina and was out of the picture for good. Greene of Rhode Island, his own man, trained in the Washington school, could retreat and win victory out of defeats by the mere pressure of the countryside.

The British retreat to Charleston, and the capture of the invading army at Yorktown, paralleled much too closely the adventure of New York and Saratoga. The war had become too expensive. German princes were raising their price for mercenaries. Many of the Burgoyne prisoners had defected to the Continentals. It was all rather annoying, and Parliament stopped their grants of money and closed the business down, not too graciously or decently. Cornwallis sulked in his tent at his capitulation, and an agent named Oswald was left to sign the fatal treaty of Paris, on which John Adams and Benjamin Franklin wrote their immortal names. Man for man, Britain was fairly outmatched for once in the power of mentality abroad and at home. British statesmen and generals were alike inadequate for the hour.

Two of the thirteen vessels of war authorized Dec. 14, 1775, by the Congress Committee were built at Poughkeepsie. Shipyard Point, where the *Congress* and *Montgomery* were constructed, was the guardian of a small cove now filled in, like so much of the old shore line. The ships were christened June 6, 1776. The continental shipyard was owned by Sheriff James Livingston, uncle of young Major Henry. There is no record to show that he gained any money from this use of his land. Against great odds the vessels were launched in November. The carpenters who made the ships were mostly New York refugees, ill-paid and worse housed in the crowded little town, "Contemporary records teem with references to plank, timber, iron, cordage, rigging, anchors, cables, tar, lead, glass, gun-carriages, muskets, cutlasses &c." But at last they were finished and secured in Rondout Creek, the best anchorage on the river.

Stephen Hendrickson, the genial taverner of Poughkeepsie, was left in charge of the ships' stores. The shipyard supplied fire rafts for defence of Fort Montgomery in 76 and cordage for Schuyler's galleys on Champlain. In June 77, the ships were brought back for final refitting, and in July went down river to their stations defending the chain at Fort Montgomery in the lower Highlands. They were burned on the night of October 6, 1777, when the British found no resistance.

General (Governor) George Clinton reported to General Washington that General Putnam had ordered the ships into the fighting zone, though they had neither sufficient anchors nor cables to maneuvre in the narrow river. The men on board were too few and too untrained for such a task, also, and could not handle them. Clinton had ordered the *Congress* up to Constitution Island to avoid disaster, but the order was not obeyed. Evidently the best watermen were upriver with Schuyler at the time. It was a sad blow to the little town that had made the two ships, and small comfort that the ships were not to blame for the incompetence that attended their first and only voyage.

The enemy against whom they were intended had an all too easy task all the way. Thanks to the interest of President Franklin D. Roosevelt in our local history, we have a completely documented account of the raid up Hudson River, which threw the only shot ever fired by enemies into Dutchess County. The documents were obtained by him by the courtesy of the British Admiralty. They contain a full log of British ship movements at New York during 1777-81, two ships' logs up the river, and naval correspondence in the raid.

Eleven hundred troops first occupied the heights of Tarrytown. General Tryon, the Tory Governor, led troops to Continental Village in Dutchess County, where he found barracks for 1,500 troops and "considerable" stores, all destroyed. Verplanck's Point was next taken, and 2,500 men landed at Stony Point, from which they marched twelve miles to Fort Montgomery, which they assaulted at night. George Clinton, at Fort Clinton further north on the same western side of the river, lost his own fort, and escaped under fire. Colonel James Clinton and 250 men were captured and one hundred were killed. The British lost 50 killed and 150 wounded, by their own report. A Lieut. Col. Campbell, Majors Lull and Grant, and Captain Stewart were among the killed, from which we may deduce that Highlanders led the assault. For three hundred and fifty to account for two hundred of the enemy argues a fierce fight while it lasted. These were Dutchess men, in great part.

Fort Constitution further up was assaulted after it had fired on a flag of truce. The British found 67 cannon and extensive stores. The guns were, evidently, among those taken at New York by Col. Willett, and were now restored to their original owners.

Commodore Hotham found the remains of the broken chain and boom, and kept what he could. "The construction of both gives strong proof of labour, industry, and skill."

From Fort Constitution the little force sailed upriver, 1,600 soldiers in all, while half as many were left to guard the forts. At Esopus Creek they found two little batteries of five guns in all and an "armed galley", all of which gallantly bombarded the big British ships. On this account General Vaughan determined to destroy them and the town as well, so that Kingston paid bitterly for her gallantry. Captain Wallace ends his letter announcing the burning of Kingston October 17, with two significant sentences:

"The officers and men upon this occasion behaved with the greatest spirit.

By all our information I am afraid General Burgoyne is retreated—if not worse."

The ship's logs bear witness to the bombarding from the forts before their capture. The artificers cut the chain, at "the rondout" according to the *Dependence* log. On October 18 Slipsteen Island was attacked and stores destroyed. The Livingston house at Clermont was burned for stores. On the 23d, after returning from Kingston, the *Dependence* saw "at 11 A M the Rebel Army posting themselves Advantageously behind the Heights at Pokeepsy". They brought to, in order to "scour the narrow pass (now the R R bridge pass), to fire "14 fourlbers. With round and Grape (shot) at them while the Transports were passing."

The troops engaged were "two battalions of Anspach" or Hessians, which destroyed Continental Village; the 17th Dragoons; the 7th, 26th, and 63d Regiments of the Line. The ships were the *Cerberus, Tartarus, Thomas, Preston* (Com. Hotham); brigs, *Mercury, Diligent;* Galleys *Dependence, Crane, Spitfire;* Sloop *Raven;* transport, tenders, horse ships, etc.

Lt. Genl. Sir Henry Clinton's narrative of the attack makes it read like a grand assault on the forts. He attributes to Col. Beverly Robinson, the Dutchess Loyalist, who commanded the Loyal American Regiment, great aid from his knowledge of the country, "to whose spirited Conduct in the Execution of it I impute in a great measure the Success of the Enterprise."

The 67 cannon were a serious loss to the Americans, as were the stores. But the most serious defection was the withdrawal from Verplanck's Point without a shot. Except for Oswald's little company of artillery the army of General Putnam, supposedly at least ten thousand, was conspicuous by its absence. Putnam was court-martialed, acquitted, and restored, to leap down Horseneck Rock next year into immortality.

Some appealing dispatches from Burgoyne were received by Sir Henry, who had gaily sent one of his own to Gentleman Johnny.

"Nous y voilà, and nothing now between us but Gates; I sincerely hope this little Success may facilitate your Operations."

Just how, Sir Henry did not elaborate. To General Burgoyne's desperate appeals for aid, he coolly sent word that "not having received any instructions from the Commander in Chief (Lord Howe) relative to the Northern Army, and unacquainted even of his intentions concerning that army, except his wishes that they should get to Albany, Sir H. Clinton cannot presume to give any Orders to Gen. Burgoyne," etc.

General Burgoyne certainly could not expect Clinton to go all the way to Albany with his small force!

A letter from General Vaughan expressed his own personal gratification at being the instrument of the destruction of

Kingston, "a Town notorious for harboring the most rebellious People in that part of the Country." But, as Putnam had 5,000 on the east shore, and Clinton 1,500 on the left, he found discretion the better part of valour, and retired in good order with his captured cannon.

Sir Henry's reward was succession to command when Lord Howe resigned after doing all he could for us. The Dutchess regiment fought well at Monmouth the next year, and retired with General Washington to White Plains in August. But this was too close to New York for comfort, and after losing his Indian scouts under Nimham he withdrew to Fishkill and Quaker Hill. Bedford had been raided and badly hit, and there was no food to be had in pillaged Westchester. The fortress of the Highlands lay behind him. He therefore sat within it.

# 29. The Flight from Beverly. 1780

THE UNFORTUNATE appointment of Arnold in command of the entire Highland region on both sides of the River was originally recommended by Chancellor Livingston, who urged it upon Washington. The General, who had fallen for the plausible self-advertisement of the traitor, and who was not averse to promote a foe of Gates, thought Arnold would do better in a more active post, but yielded to expediency. According to Arnold's sister, the Chancellor had been impressed by Peggy Arnold's charm no less than by the soldier's courage in battle. The Chancellor's brother Col. Henry liked Shippen girls, too, for he married Nancy Shippen, Peggy Arnold's cousin.

The black tale of John André's capture and Benedict Arnold's treason in September, 1780, needs no rehearsal here, although some of its incidents occurred in old Dutchess. Washington breakfasted at Fishkill before setting out for Beverly Robinson's house, where the famous luncheon was served. Arnold received there the letter telling him of his confederate's arrest. The flight to the river down the ravine saved his own skin, and convicted his comrade.

Ensign Tallmadge of the Fourth N.Y. thus recorded the army bulletin of the event, Sept. 26, 1780. It was probably written by Gen. Greene.

"Treason of the Blackest Dye, was yesterday Discovered. Gen'l Arnold who commanded at West Point Lost to Every sentiment of honour, of private, and public, obligation, brought

About to Deliver up that Important post into the hands of the Enemy. such an Event must have given the American cause a deadly wound, if not a fatal Stab, happily the Treason has been timely Discovered, to prevent the fatal misfortune, the providential Traine of Circumstances which led to it Affords the most convincing proof that the Liberties of America is the Object of Divine protection. At the same time that Treason is to be regreted the Genl Cannot help Congratulating the army on the happy Discovery. Our Enemy Dispairing of Carrying their point by force are practiseing Every base act to Affect by bribery and Corruption what they Cannot Accomplish in a manly way. Greate honour is due to the American army that this is the first Instance of Treason of the kind Where many were to be Exspected from the Nature of the Dispute, and nothing is so bright an Ornament In the Character of the American Soldiers, as there having been proof Against all the arts and Seductions of an Insiduous Enemy. Arnold has made his Escape to the Enemy but Mr Andre the Adjutant Genl to the british army who came out as a spy to negotiate the business is our prisoner. his Excelency the Commander in Chief has arrived at West point from hartford and is no doubt taking the proper measures to unravel fully so hellish a Plot."

The countersign for the next day, according to Samuel, was "Fortune favors America." Three Pennsylvania soldiers were that day tried and sentenced to death for robbery. No doubt Tallmadge took more interest in their fate than in André's, which took place four days later, October 1, and resulted in the sentence of death, "in the usual way." On the same day, by order of Colonel Weissenfels of Dutchess, John Tenney, who had left camp without leave, was ordered to appear at roll call with his "clog" still fastened to his leg, for the whole day. Other sentences occupied Tallmadge's Book on October 2, but John Barr, who was also at Orangetown that day, noted:

"Major Andre was executed at 12 O'clock this day concluding his Life with repeating his words—that he was reconciled to his death, but was disappointed as to the mode of it, & that the Spectators would bear witness that he met his fate like a Brave Man."

Tallmadge's bulletin announcing the trial summarized the evidence perfectly: André had landed from the sloop Vulture the night of September 21, "on an interview of Gen'l Arnold, in a private and secret manner. He had changed his dress within our lines, and "in a disguised habit passed our works at Stony and Verplanck Points, the evening of September 22". He had been taken next day at Tarrytown, being then on his way to New York, and when taken he had in his possession several papers which contained Intelligence for the Enemy."

The rank and file must have been vastly pleased to have been told the whole truth at once. They were also told, though the bulletin does not disclose it, that André had been captured by some private soldiers, which fact must have given them further pleasure. John Barr discloses this, and calls their leader "Mr. Polding", being more respectful than André's latest biographer, who calls him "a huge yokel." The honorific "Mr." was not loosely used in colonial times, and in this respect we may prefer the contemporary description. As for "huge", he was six feet tall.

Conditions in the Jerseys, and everywhere else that two armies faced each other at some distance, were exactly the same as in southern Dutchess and northern Westchester Counties. Soldiers off-duty did just what the armed forces did on a larger scale. They devastated their enemies' land, and sometimes their friends' too. Yet, such is the way of farmers, the farms kept on.

In the neighborhood of New York City, this lasted seven years. Rodgers' Rangers and other British forces swept the countryside to fill the empty bins in the city. General Heath in force raided Westchester for the same purpose, complaining as he did so that too many volunteers accompanied him.

The name "Cow Boys" is frequent in the letters of the day.

I have not found the name "Skinners." It seems to be the invention of the novelists fifty years later. So is "No Man's Land" used to denote the Highland region. By an act of New York volunteer militiamen might claim as their prize any property found on captured enemies.

Thus the soldiers John Paulding, David Williams, and Isaac Van Wart went over and above the call of duty in carrying out their own mission in close proximity to the enemies' lines.

The Spy Lane of the Hudson East Shore led down the Oblong to Salem where the Continental encampment lay. It would be natural for spies to turn down toward the River at this point to avoid it, and for Americans on private service to lie in ambush there. Paulding had just escaped from his imprisonment in New York City, and might have some scores to settle. But in any case he and his companions were engaged in an authorized activity. John Barr spent much of his time looking for American deserters in the Taconics.

John Paulding is enrolled in both the Sixth and Seventh Dutchess Militia. David Williams is enrolled in both the Fourth Dutchess Continental and the Sixth Militia. Isaac VanWart is not enrolled, though a number of the name are in several of the Dutchess regiments. He and Paulding lived in Westchester whose regiments were deranged and mixed with Dutchess forces.

The conventions of military romance, which have never done much for the common infantryman, have exalted André into the hero of this adventure, and have contrasted him with the sordid details of his capture by "banditti," "yokels," "bushmen," "Skinners," and the like. Colonel Benjamin Tallmadge, then a major, and in charge of the American spy route into New York via Long Island, late in life claimed a good deal more of the credit for the capture than he deserved, and in particular attacked the reputation of the three musketeers who actually made it. As a congressman he succeeded in defeating a move to increase their pension.

This was too much for Egbert Benson of Rhinebeck, President of the New York Historical Society, and in the Revolution

Attorney-General of New York State. He wrote a brochure in their defence. But though recent writers have respected these men who were honored by General Washington, and by Congress given each a fame and pensions of two hundred dollars, they still tend to contrast them with the romantic gentleman. Their keeping of the souvenirs is called robbery, though André had carried off a portrait of Franklin from his host's house in Philadelphia. If they talked with him about a ransom, it is imputed for banditry, though they brought André at once to their commander.

This history is therefore justified in making clear their true status, and in honoring them in their private service, approved by the custom of soldiers, and by law of the state, in doing exactly what they did; incidentally, saving West Point, and General Washington himself (for the thoughtful Arnold had told Sir Henry that Washington would be at that very time on the Hudson shore). Thus the "straying"—to use Washington's word for it—was to some purpose. No wonder he immediately sent for Paulding.

# 30. Yankees on Their Way. 1775

*For Yankees they are on their way*
*And the British? they're retreating.*

THE MARCH TO QUEBEC,
*Revolutionary Ballad,*
*Collected in Dutchess County.*

AT THE 79th milestone on the River Road from New York stood "the Locusts." The pleasant Dutch gabled farmhouse was the home of Major Henry Livingston, Jr., a father's gift to him upon his marriage to Sally Welles of Stamford in 1772.

Major Henry, poet, artist, musician, surveyor, justice and all-round good fellow, portrays himself in every line of his pen as a gay and debonair young soldier with a gift for description. Perhaps he wrote the song on "The March to Quebec" which gives us the title of this chapter. He was fond of writing for the postboys on their New Year tour of customers, and other occasional verse. At all events, his journal of the march is the liveliest one left by a Dutchess soldier. And like the song, it gives no hint of the fatal outcome of that march, for Major Henry was invalided home after the capture of St. Johns.

At twenty-seven Henry had been commissioned major by Colonel James Clinton. He embarked at Poughkeepsie on board Captain Jackson's sloop, August 25, 1775. Two days later he went ashore at Albany with the Ulster contingent which had joined them at Kingston. There he witnessed a war council of the Iroquois Indians, probably Oneidas and Tuscaroras only. War belts were given with the speeches in time-honored custom; one of them, Henry observed respectfully, was worth sixty dollars. In all, the gifts amounted to nearly two thousand pounds.

On September 6, while the troops were assembling, Major Henry went to see the Mohawk Falls at Cohoes, "Nistiquine," and Schenectady. On a five-day furlough he revisited Poughkeepsie and his Sally. With the delayed arrival of Captain Rosecrans' company from Fishkill, he set off to the northward. Five days of leisurely march brought him to the settlement of his fellow-countian, Abraham Wing of Quaker Hill, at the now Glens Falls. Henry was no soldier; he never mentioned his company. His eyes were all for the soil and the water, the abundance of pitch pines. Lake George seemed to him a continuation of the Highlands. He crossed it in a "petteaugre."

At Ticonderoga he had a chance to study the fortifications, and thus trained he reached Crown Point October 4. At Grand Isle "I catched five pike 2 feet long and a clever Bass with which kind of fish & yellow perch and sunfish the Lake abounds." He found the stones on the shore of Cumberland Point "as square as if made by art." Not a word yet of drill or musketry. Perhaps there were none, the farmers' sons strolling along on their picnic. It was interrupted on the ninth of October, when they joined forces with General Montgomery's troops, and saw the first shells fall. Next day the commander held a council of war, where he accepted the majority decision upon the site of a proposed battery. Major Henry with two hundred men set up the redoubt and with two 12-lb. guns fired away at the British lines for a week. Then Chambly surrendered, and the Major was sent forward with a hundred men under Capts. Morison and DuBois and Lieutenant Matthew Van Bunschoten.

On October 19, as the chilly fall came on, the soldiers had their first sight of Montreal and the St. Lawrence, at La Prairie. "The Inhabitants are strangers to many of the necessary & all the elegancies of a civilized life." The village he described in detail, noting the excellent vegetable gardens with onions and cabbages, the pease, potatoes, and turnips, and finding the bread coarse but palatable. "I never saw such a fine grass country in my life." The milk was the "best he ever tasted", but the cattle seemed small.

He liked "the urbanity of the peasants". "But altho their hearts are good, their Oeconomy is by no means so. After a peasant's house is built and the rain shut out, no more water ever touches their floors save a little holy water every morning which follows a partial sweeping."

On the other hand, "I never saw a Bad bed in Canada. It seems as if they were resolv'd to lie well if they liv'd poor—many of them have 2 feather beds on each other. Not a woman in twenty understood the art of knitting." He thought the men and women "alike idle, much more than the people among us." "A land of slaves will ever be a land of poverty, Ignorance and Idleness."

Only the women could read, not one in twenty of the men. But he found "a jolly fat Curate", "a thorough Whig." The people in general were extremely ignorant as to politics, but they seemed to prefer the Americans to the British. "The Regulars" abused them, he was told, and he found evidence of this in the attitude of captured British officers.

On October 21 at LaPrairie he entertained six chiefs from Caughnawaga at a tavern. Nimham may have been among them, for he was reported to have met the expedition. "They answered me with all that deliberation, firmness, and seriousness peculiar to the Indians." They seemed somewhat less articulate after eighteen bottles of claret. Major Henry kept the chiefs' plates full of turkey and beans. They were greatly pleased with the hospitality; British Guy Carleton had never deigned to dine with them. Major Henry went with them to their "castle", ascertaining that they could muster three hundred warriors.

On October 26 he sent three companies, only ninety-two privates, under Capts. DuBois and McCracken, to the relief of Colonel Warner of the "Green Mountain Boys." With this reinforcement Warner repelled Carleton's assault on him at Longeuil. St. Johns surrendered November 2. On the day before, when Montgomery's forces had effected a crossing to Isle St. Paul, Carleton fled down the river. Major Livingston entered Montreal on the 14th of November.

He counted there "twelve hundred houses of rough-coat stone, lime and sand; the streets unpaved."

And there his war ended in sickness. In storm and wind four days later he set out on his homeward way with other invalids. He nearly foundered on the rocks in Champlain in a storm. On December 3, taken very ill on his way from Lake George, he spent a week at kindly Parson Graham's at Stillwater, two years later the scene of Burgoyne's battle. He had been General Schuyler's guest the night before. On December 21 he had recovered sufficiently to reach "Bards", and next day he was greeted at Poughkeepsie: "The God of all mercy be adored for His goodness to an unworthy sinner."

His war service was over, but he served on commissions against the Loyalists. His life and works were ahead of him.

Colonel Henry Ludington of the Dutchess Seventh Militia had seen service. As a boy he had served in a Connecticut force against Canada, ending his four years of war after the victory at Quebec by conducting a company of wounded men to Boston, in the winter frosts. At twenty he married his cousin Abigail of Rombout and set up at Fredericksburgh. His wife at fifteen bore her eldest, Sybil. Eleven other children followed.

With a mill and a large farm Henry soon rose to good fame. In 1773 he served as captain in Col. Beverly Robinson's regiment, but resigned over the Intolerable Acts. He signed the Association pledge in 1775, and in June, 1776, was commissioned colonel of the Seventh Militia. The regiment was recruited from the whole of the South Precinct, and was soon divided, as it enrolled more than double its quota. Colonel Ludington received the command of the Philipse Patent recruits. He was immediately ordered by the County Committee to rid his precinct of "equivocal" persons. His performance earned him the price of three hundred guineas, offered by

Lord Howe for his capture dead or alive. Once Ichabod Prosser of Pawling attempted it, once some visitors tried while staying overnight, but the well-armed daughters and sons mightily discouraged them.

Fredericksburgh with its loyalism lay on the direct route of the British espionage, and Ludington led a charmed life to have escaped. After his courageous conduct at the battle of White Plains, General Washington appointed him in charge of counter-espionage. He worked in direct cooperation with Nathaniel Sackett, and the famous Enoch Crosby was one of his soldiers and worked under him.

Captain John Holmes, one of the most dangerous of the Tory recruiters, was captured by Ludington in a scrub oak kripplebush near Fishkill Plains, with his whole company. Nickerson, another enroller, was captured through the device of planting a young spy in his company. Ludington proved Nickerson's guilt by unscrewing the head of Nickerson's cane, which contained the roll of his recruits.

It was Ludington who drummed old John Kane out of town. When one of his companies was transferred to another commander the company deserted, to a man. But though he won such loyalty, he was deeply discouraged at times, and once wrote to Clinton that "it seems as if every power of Earth and Hell were enlisted against me." This was not, however, till toward the end of the struggle, when Ludington should have been furloughed for rest.

He had been for six years on the firing line. In April, 1777, General Tryon landed on the Connecticut shore and raided the stores at Danbury. At nine in the evening of Saturday, April 26, an alert notified Ludington at his home on the mountain. He could not leave, for his farm was the drill-ground. Sybil, now sixteen, roused the militia by a ride which took the whole night. This is, at least, the tradition in the family; the exact route has been outlined by trusting historians. To Carmel down the HorsePond Road, to Lake Mahopac, to Captain John Crane's house and through Red Mills to Peekskill Hollow, and back up the pike to Hortontown and Pecksville, a lot of territory for sixteen years in the No Man's Land. Forty miles or so in spring mud! No wonder Bert Braley jingled:

> Listen, my children, and you shall hear
> Of a lovely feminine Paul Revere.

On Sunday Ludington's regiment marched to Redding, and reached Ridgefield in time to take part in the bloody skirmish at that place. The British had no easy time of it on the return from this second Lexington. An American boy was captured and escaped, to tell of five hundred casualties among the enemy, as he saw them carried on board the fleet. "I congratulate you on the Danbury affair", wrote Alexander Hamilton to the Dutchess chairman, John Jay, and added his own estimate of the "pretty high price to the enemy." It must be added that Connecticut records at Ridgefield make no mention of Ludington's aid; but Hamilton's message to a Dutchess official strongly supports the tradition.

In June, that same year, Ludington's men garrisoned Tarrytown, and escaped Tryon who had sent them a command to surrender. With a force entirely inadequate to meet Tryon, the Dutchess men retired to Fishkill, while Tryon destroyed Continental Village. Putnam scurried up and down the Hudson shore like Halsey at the Philippine Sea, never firing a shot but always threatening, and scaring Vaughan from any thought of taking Albany.

Meanwhile Ludington was asked by Nathaniel Sackett to find a man in his regiment who was absolutely trustworthy, and who would be willing to go to New York as a spy. Ludington selected Benajah Tubbs, who duly took the oath, and no doubt served well. All this time, from 1777 to 1781, Ludington was a member of the Assembly, and again in 1786; a J P, supervisor, overseer of the poor (this included the New York City poor who had been evacuated to Dutchess under the care of Dirck Brinckerhoff, Jr.) He had also been sub-sheriff, church trustee, and so on.

Yet he survived it all, and lived thirty years, till 1812.

Enoch Crosby of Colonel Ludington's Seventh Militia attained greater fame than any other soldier of the county, as the original of Fenimore Cooper's "Spy". The story is now localized at the Wharton House on Route 9, which was the place of meeting of the State Committee of Safety after it had adjourned from the Stone Church at Fishkill because of its damp. The house, then known as the house of Isaac Van Wyck, was also the headquarters of the army when at Fishkill.

But Crosby had a real existence, and his own narrative is just as exciting as Cooper's. The latter always denied his original, but admitted that his story was inspired by a conversation with John Jay, who as chairman of the Dutchess Committee had every opportunity to meet Crosby.

On October 15, 1832, Crosby applied for a pension under the new act. He deposed before Judge Washburn in Carmel that in the spring of 1775 he enlisted in a Connecticut regiment and went to St. Johns with Montgomery when his term expired. The following August he enlisted in Col. Swartwout's regiment in Kent precinct and fought at Pines Bridge and White Plains, where he was captured but escaped. At this time he made his first capture of Tory recruits, leading Captain Townsend from Esy Young's, and giving Congress troops the chance to make the capture. At Fishkill he met Nathaniel Sackett and was bailed out by Jonathan Hopkins. He next engaged in secret service in Ulster at John Russel's. He lived with "Capt. Robinson" for a week in a cave, but managed to get away long enough to notify an American soldier named Purdy. At Bush Carrick's the whole company was captured by Capt. Melancthon Smith and Col. Duer in a barn. They were all confined in the Stone Church. Later he made shoes at Fishkill.

His next mission was to Vermont along the "Spyway" of the mountains. At Walloomsac he met a certain Wilcox (Stephen?), who gave to him a complete list of the Tories cooperating with the British all the way down.

Armed with this he was enabled to make his third and most

famous capture at Prosser's cave near Dover. In February, 1777, three miles from the tavern of old Judge Morehouse, he joined up with a company about to march to New York. His absence to notify the soldiers at Morehouse's had been noticed, however. Just as the Tories raised cries of "Betrayal", the echo resounded with the "Stand!" of the Congress men, and the whole company tied, two by two, were marched off to Fishkill. Enoch, however, was "considered such a dangerous man that he rode tied to Judge Morehouse himself." Naturally, he escaped at the proper time, and made his way to Colonel Ludington, who brought him to the Van Wyck house, where he met John Jay and told him the story.

As a marked man in Dutchess he was used next in the north with Col. Van Ness, where he picked up the helpful information that the vigorous work of the committees was discouraging to the Tories. He served in Swartwout's, and was at Stony Point. In 1780 he enlisted with Capt. Ludington in the Van Bunschoten regiment at West Point, where he was discharged in 1781.

The Tory cave in Pawling was raided by Captain Pierce in April 1781. He captured four men there, among whom were Samuel Tid, the friend of Woltimyer, and Solomon Baker of Beekman Precinct. The latter was tried as a spy, convicted, and sentenced to be hanged by a court presided over by Col. Zephaniah Platt. Among the witnesses examined was Ichabod Prosser, the Indian doctor, who admitted that he knew the cave well, since it was but a half-mile from his house.

The unfortunate Baker had gone to North Castle three years before, along the well-known underground line, and there enlisted in Col. Robinson's "disaffected" regiment. Captured at Crompond, he pretended to be a deserter and was permitted to return home. Later he went with Arnold to Virginia, and was captured there, at Westover.

Dutchess County may well be proud of the record of its highest ranking militia officer, Brigadier General Jacobus Swartwout. He had had military experience in the Canadian war, as a militia captain, and was elected Colonel of the Second Regiment of Minute Men. In 1775 he had been placed in charge of securing the signatures to the Pledge of Association. As senior officer of the Dutchess brigade of Militia, he fought at Kingsbridge in 1776, and served at West Point, and on the western frontier of Ulster and Orange. In 1777 working with Egbert Benson and Melancton Smith of the County Committee and the Exempts he labored to restore discipline in the discouraged Dutchess regiments. He fed his soldiers from his own farm. At interims he served on the County Committee against Conspiracies. On April 12, 1779 he received his promotion, to command "in defense of frontiers." In March 1781 he presided at the court-martial which acquitted General Robert Van Rensselaer. At the end of the war he was elected to Assembly in 1783 and later to the Senate, serving until 1795. In 1788 he stood on Clinton's side at the Constitutional Convention.

Only by the support of such men could New York have survived. No Continental army, however strong, could or would have protected the thousand-mile western frontier, in the absence of strong central authority. Militia service was not only highly honorable; it was indispensable. From its ranks came the replacement for the Continental Line. Its regiments kept the frontier, external against the Indians, internal against the Loyalists.

Major Elias Van Benschoten began the war as a lieutenant, obtaining his captaincy at Quebec, in November, 1775. With General Gansevoort he served in the defense of Fort Stanwix, in 1737. We find him later a captain of Exempts, protecting his county from internal troubles. With a major's commission after a term on the Ulster frontier, he followed Colonel Lewis DuBois to the Mohawk in 1780, and the defeat of Sir John Johnson. Back again in Dutchess, he carried out Governor Clinton's drastic conscription of reserves preparatory to the march to Yorktown. When Cornwallis fell he led our levies under Marinus Willett to the clean-up fight with the Mohawks.

Willett, one of New York's best officers, commended him for "his violent efforts."

The old veteran militiaman kept his uniform and as Lt. Colonel drilled a Dutchess regiment from 1786 to 1797.

The service of Colonel Frederick H. Weissenfels of Dutchess reads like a history of the whole war in the North. Born in 1738 in Saxony, he had served under Frederick the Great, and on coming to America entered British service as an officer of Braddock. From 1763 his name appears in our records. He must have been prompt to enlist, for he was first captain in Alexander McDougall's First Regiment. General Montgomery made him a Major, and he became Lieutenant Colonel of the Third Regiment in March, 1776. In May he left Canada to assume his new post. He brought word to General Schuyler that the American troops in Canada were starving.

On October 28 he commanded the regiment at White Plains. Colonel Ritzema's Tory proclivity had led him to absent himself from the field. The next month Colonel Weissenfels was transferred to the Second Regiment, which held more Dutchess men. In this command he fought the Hessians at Trenton.

His regiment was one of those sent by Washington to aid Gates at Saratoga, and was very active. Weissenfels is said to have employed his knowledge of German in persuading Burgoyne's Hessians to desert. On the way through Pennsylvania many of them dropped out of the prisoners' column to join the German settlers.

Back with Washington again, Weissenfels wintered at Valley Forge, and fought bravely at Monmouth. He was promoted to command the famous Fourth, but without change of rank, though recommended by both Willett and McDougall. He led the Fourth through the long march of Sullivan in '79, always active, especially at Newtown. In November 1780, after the regrouping of regiments, he led a command to the relief of Fort Schuyler. Arriving in time, he helped the exhausted garrison to make repairs and get new supplies. He wrote Governor Clinton: "My men are very naked, which makes Duty very severe. I do not expect to remain in the Service, and only wish that I may not be left to take the trouble and anxiety for others, who will enjoy the honor of the service." On January 1, 1781, he was relieved at his request and returned to Dutchess. All he needed was a furlough, for though his services had been unrewarded he soon applied for a new command, and in August he took charge of levies from Orange and Weschester Counties, of whom he proudly wrote, that they were "the best Levies, with respect to Exterior appearance, I believe, that have been raised in this state."

He took them to Albany in service, and was still guarding the frontier in 1782, when he commanded from the Catskills to the Ramapos. Some of his force served in final drives further north. In tardy recognition he was named one of the committee of thirteen to plan the reception to Governor Clinton, when he came to New York City in November, 1783.

Frederick Von Weissenfels (several times so listed, though never so signed by the modest officer) deserves to be ranked with Steuben and de Kalb as among the Germans who drilled our army well.

Major Andrew Billings emulated his friend Van Benschoten. A silversmith of note, he raised his own company of Poughkeepsie boys, and joined General James Clinton's Third Regiment. After Quebec, he continued under Colonel Ritzema, but later raised a company of Exempts. He and his wife must have been favorites of Washington, for she obtained a lock of the general's hair. Robert R. Livingston somehow secured it, and enclosed it in a portrait of the General by Archibald Robertson, the Scots painter imported by the chancellor. It hangs in Edinburgh, one of the best likenesses of the oft-painted hero.

Major Billings, meanwhile, returned to his trade, and many excellent pieces are still preserved of his art in silver.

When General Putnam chased the British fleet up and down the Hudson, Colonel Zepha Platt held the fort at Poughkeepsie with his Exempts, while he reported to Governor

Clinton that he would do his best. The slow moving fleet of the British on their return bombarded the narrows of the Long Reach, giving time for Putnam's men to post themselves on the rocks, while Lt. Colonel Oswald peppered the ships to good advantage.

Our Dutchess Indians deserve a place of honor among our fighting men. Most of them were then dwelling at Stockbridge, after Colonel Beverly Robinson had driven them from the Highlands. Mahikans and Wappingers were then one tribe, the Stockbridge, and were so known to the New Englanders who enrolled them for war.

Some of them were at Boston, after Lexington, under Captain Solomon. When pressed for more regular enlistment, he replied, "Our ways of fighting are not your ways. We cannot train as your soldiers do. Only show us where your enemies are. That is all we want to know."

Others of the tribe under Nimham appear to have gone with Montgomery. They were reported on the route with them. They served in New Jersey and Pennsylvania.

On August 31, 1778, the Wappinger company under Nimham on scout duty at Kingsbridge in New York drove back a British force, but two days later was ambushed and half their force cut to pieces by Tarleton's cavalry. Nimham, though severely wounded, refused to leave the field. He said, "I am an ancient tree. Let me die here." They left him to a hero's fame. A large boulder at the Brinckerhoff triangle in Dutchess bears a tablet in Nimham's memory. The Wiccopee hill-slopes look kindly down on it.

On February 9, 1778, Col. Udny Hay reported this fight at Tibbetts Brook. "The day before yesterday a party of our Indians fell in with a party of the Enemys light horse, who after a little skirmishing retreated (probably on purpose) and by that means drawed the Indians after them into an open field, after passing a small part of which they found themselves attacked in the rear by a body of infantry, and in front by the retreating light horse, which had returned to the charge:—

nineteen of the Indians are missing, others are supposed to be taken prisoners; we have likewise lost a Capt. and six soldiers in that affair."

The remainder of the scouts stayed with the army. General Washington after Yorktown gave Stockbridge an ox to roast. He had asked Congress to reward them more substantially. But the Oneidas, fellow-warriors in the field, were more hospitable. They invited the Stockbridge tribe to make their home with them. The Wappingers accepted, and named their home "New Stockbridge". Most of those who preserve tribal life can be found at Fox Lake, Wisconsin. The only report, made of them by an official for the General Court of Massachusetts, describes them as "among the very highest in culture and respectability."

The best available source for a picture of the life of a Dutchess County soldier can be found in "Samuel Tallmadge's Orderly Books". Young Samuel, a refugee from Long Island in 1776, and already a militiaman in 1775, enlisted in the Dutchess regiment, the Fourth New York of the Continental Line, in November, 1776. The next year he became ensign, and served in that rank till 1780, when he was appointed adjutant in July. On January 1, 1781, when the Fourth was "reduced", and its members transferred to the Second New York, Tallmadge went with them, obtaining a lieutenancy in October. He was promoted first lieutenant in April, 1782, and was mustered out, June 1783, at Newburgh.

Samuel Tallmadge's duties included a sort of secretaryship with his colonel, Henry Beekman Livingston. Thus his entries reflect the acts and discipline for which this prominent Dutchess soldier was responsible. His service also reflects the story of his regiment. His "Orderly Books," of which about half are in his own hand, the remainder collected and preserved by him, have been published by the state. They reflect a vivid picture, chiefly of the discipline, but also of the movements, the daily tasks, and some of the escapades of the day to day life of the regiment.

Tallmadge's Orderly Books run to over 900 pages of a large

quarto. They are in no sense a journal of the war, but they comprise a great number of the details that kept the soldiers busy.

Tallmadge served in the Battles of Long Island and White Plains in '76, in Saratoga and at Valley Forge in '77, in the Sullivan campaign against the Indians in '79, and near Tappan in Feb. 1780, at the time of Arnold's West Point flight. He served in the Mohawk against the Butlers and Johnsons. In June, 1783, he joined the New York Society of the Cincinnati, as a lieutenant in the regular army. In 1786 he was captain in the Dutchess militia, but was replaced in 1793, having moved away.

He had married an Albany girl the month after his discharge and set up a store in Rhinebeck, where his colonel lived, and a cousin, James Tallmadge, became a United States Senator, and found fame in opposing the Missouri Compromise of 1820. Like many other soldiers Samuel moved north to farm in Montgomery County. Of his seven children three were born in Rhinebeck. Until three years before his death in 1825 he asked no pension.

At Easton, 1779, after the return of General Sullivan from his wilderness march, he reprimanded his men. "The troops make Incrussions into the Countrey and Rob the Inhabitants of their property." He threatened to establish a "picquet" around the whole army. For breach of this order a soldier was given one hundred lashes "on his bare back." Later at West Point the commanding general noted stealing "horses hogs Sheep and poeltry", even open robberies. For such the lashes were "well laid on," but the number never exceeded one hundred at one time. Very rarely, lashes were repeated on successive days. Robbers of the stores were paraded with canteens hung around their necks, and coats turned inside out.

Samuel Tallmadge on Aug. 7, 1781, reported attempt of the Tories "to take off" Gen. Schuyler at his Albany house. This was apparently the Hans Woltimyer raid.

In addition to his Orderly Books, Tallmadge kept a Journal, covering the period from December 1780 to July 1782. It starts at Fort Schuyler in the Mohawk, and includes a journey to New Haven and back, the journey to Yorktown and the siege. He noted two Indian raids in March and May, 1781, but made no comment. In July he went with his regiment in "Battows" down the Hudson. They embarked in boats stopping overnight at Claverack, Rhinebeck, Poughkeepsie, and West Point, and joined the Grand Army at Kings Ferry Aug. 24. For a month they marched south, arriving at Yorktown Sept. 28. Two of the four weeks were spent between Baltimore and York.

The Dutchess Regiment (now the 2d New York under Colonel Philip Van Cortlandt) mounted the Yorktown trenches on October 12, "Completing our second parallel." This was only two hundred yards from the enemy's guns. Relieved on the 13th, the regiment returned the 15th, and participated in the repulse of the English counterattack, which ended the active fighting. The next day brought the capitulation.

"At two o'clock the american and french armies was paraded for the reception of the enemy, they marched through our armies, with sloped Arms Colours Cased, and drums beating a british march and grounded their arms, after which they returned again and was permitted to Continue in Town this night the army being composed of English, Scotch and Hussians amounting to about Seven thousand, sailors included, two Regiments of our army took possession of the arms and Colours of the Enimy."

And that's it. Two days later the militia "marched them off about 12 o'clock to conduct them to the back part of Virginia." On October 22 Tallmadge went into Yorktown and found it "much Distroyed by our Cannon and Shells." On the 28th the Yorkers reduced the second parallel which they had been at such pains to throw up. From October 31 to December 14, when the snow was eight inches deep, the New York Brigade was on the return march.

When on February 1, 1780, the officers of the New York Continentals resigned because of their wants and sufferings, Samuel Tallmadge signed with them. Protests continued through the year. Samuel became an adjutant in September. He records the letters of a "soldiers committee" of three members who went to Poughkeepsie to present their case. They were courteously received. Their demand for "Cash or Nothing less than a Real Security or Transfer of Lands", "Conveyed . . . bonified", was referred to a special committee of both houses of the legislature, then in session.

Throughout the year the reports of thefts of food and clothing proved the utter lack of good organization in the country and the army. Again and again General Greene was obliged to issue at West Point his orders against "violence and depredation." Rolls were called three times a day at one period, to make sure that soldiers were not out in the field. New York, and especially Dutchess County, suffered much because the camps were in this vicinity in the later years when morale was low.

On January 1, 1781, New York's five regiments were reassembled or "deranged" into two of infantry and one of artillery. Tallmadge was transferred to the Second New York, with most of the Dutchess boys. New York with her Indian frontier protected by militia levies had fewer regiments in the line, which had fifty-six in all.

Captain Lewis DuBois of Dutchess, who led one of the companies of the old Third Regiment, had been promoted colonel of the Fifth New York for good service at Quebec. When dropped from seniority in the 1781 reorganization, he raised a regiment of levies, and fought well in the Mohawk campaigns of '80 and '81.

It was Lewis DuBois' "Dutchess companies" that fought so well at West Canada Creek, in the affray described by Walter D. Edmonds (himself a Livingston descendant) in his "Drums along the Mohawk," one of the best of the New York stories. The soldiers no doubt took a grim pleasure in the rescue of the sons and daughters of Palatines who had left the Hudson for its beautiful tributary.

It was in this campaign that what may be called the Clintons' first canal was invented. General James Clinton, a surveyor and engineer, dammed up Otsego Lake, prepared his boats, and chuted down the swollen stream in 238 boats three abreast. He issued minute instructions for his land-lubbers. He forgot to organize his grammar, however, in his exultation at reaching Owego, August 19, 1779. Only one boat had been lost.

"General Orders.
The Guards to Parade at the Beating of the General in the Rear of the Artillery Camp", etc.

Scarcely more grammatical was John Barr of Amenia, whose Diary fills a hundred pages of "Tallmadge Orderlies."

"200 sick of Gen'l Sullivans Army Sent back."

The desperate state of the Commissary on the Sullivan Campaign is indicated by the General's efforts to collect shirts to clothe his naked men, the failure of flour and other foods, and one grisly occasion when human bodies were skinned to make hides for shoes. It was a ragged mob that returned, to be comforted by fresh clothes and an inspection by "his Excellency Genl Washington."

On Friday, May 19, John Barr tells how the noted "dark day" terrified even soldiers. Barr was at home in convalescence in Amenia.

"Friday 19 (May 1780) Thundered and rained some this Morning, but when the sun arose it appeared to be Eclipsed, tho, contrary to Nature, as the Moon fulled this Morning at 6 o'clock of the Preceding Day, this Phenomenon continued until 10 or Eleven OClock A M making a wonderful appearance both in the Horrizon and on the Earth, terrible indeed to all the beholders."

John Barr's furlough was also spent on less serious engagements. He would spend fifteen dollars drinking cyder with Mr. Elias Shavelears or Mr. William Young in the Oblong (Thomas Young's son), or he would join a frolic. He reaped and plowed with his host, Joseph Pennoyer, or rode with officers in search of deserters. He reported the draft of 800 militia to march to Fishkills in July, 1780. On the 6th of August he noted the arrival of 6,000 "land Troops and Eleven Sail of the Line your brave allies," and the impressment of all the teams of the neighborhood to remove the Continental army to White Plains. He spent fourteen dollars at a dance following the "raising" of a barn at Robert Freeman's. He paid 36 dollars for a pair of boots. Three months board at Pennoyer's cost him $443. His ride back to Tappan cost him $180 en route and $191 for the horse. He crossed the Hudson on Sunday, September 24, at Kings Ferry. Had he been earlier he would have seen H. M. S. *Vulture* (superbly named) bearing off Gen. Benedict Arnold after his flight from the luncheon table with Washington. When he got to camp he attended a general view of the whole army. Next day the Pennsylvania brigades marched to protect the threatened Point. Next week the New York Brigade followed.

Barr's stay in camp was dull most of the time. He suffered from rheumatism after his western raid. Now and then small bands of Indians raided the Ramapoes and Catskills, carrying off men and horses. Barr chased them but never caught any. An Ensign like Tallmadge, but better educated, he worked hard on his orders and rolls, but would catch "5 dozen of Trouts", or make one at a supper.

"Running the Gantlope" (gauntlet) was a not uncommon punishment. At Hqrs. in Highlands July 16, 1780, two men guilty of forging passes and of desertion were ordered to run bareback, through 500 men furnished with "A sufficient number of Switches," and "with a bayonet at each of their Breast to regulate their step." A third soldier for some favorable circumstances was to receive "only 100 lashes on his bairback".

At the Highlands, too, Baron Steuben kept up his stern and helpful discipline. With twenty-five old soldiers in a company the recruits were given intensive physical drill twice a day, at first without arms "for posture and carriage". Complete inventories of arms were kept and storehouse practices established. "The baron", as the entries list him, brought a respectable force into being, which the British never cared to challenge after 1780.

"June 25, 1780.

"The Genl. (MacDougall, succeeding Arnold) from undoubted Intelligence hears that Spies from the Enemy are out, with Intention to Obtain information of the situation of this post, Officers in Genl and officers of the day in perticalar are therefore rejoined to Scrutinize Strictly all Caracters not belonging to the Army who are found in the Camp or its Environs, and to confine those who do not give a perticular Account of themselves."

On Feb. 13, 1780, at the camp at Morristown General Clinton severely censured his troops for not keeping the standards set by Gen. Steuben. According to his inspectors the Second Regiment was neither well kept nor disciplined. Although arms were in good order, the Third and Fourth Regiments showed a shocking loss of arms, and what remained were in "Middling" or "pirty" good order. Their clothing was clean, however. The losses "exceeded All reasonable bounds." Probably, as was elsewhere reported, the men were so hungry they bargained arms and clothes with the country folks for food.

The regiments had already gone through Valley Forge and Fishkill, and now in the really desperate cold of '78-'79, the army was at one of its lowest points. Yet in the spring the regiments marched via Albany to Otsego, and thence to the Genesee River in the Sullivan campaign, a tough assignment of some 800 miles, and acquitted themselves well.

On Tuesday April 25, 1780 Barr went to Great Nine Partners "being election at Mr. Simeon Cooks . . . for Governor and Lieut. Governor Senate and Assembly, Expenses 16½ Dollars". But on May 11 he went to "Ellection in Sharon Connecticut".

On June 22 he attended "a training of the Militia at Mrs. Wheelers when there was a Detachment of the Militia to go to

West Point for 8 Days". On the 26 "A Genl alarm throughout this State". Next a detachment set off for Fishkill. July 6 came an order for 800 militia to be ready to march to Fishkills on the 14.

On August 18 Barr "found in the Fishkill News Paper the names of some Deserters from the 4 New York Regt went after one of them Job Randle found him dined with Lieut Isaac Darrow." He spent the next day looking for two more. Time after time the militia fell in lines and marched away to the next fight. Now and then the beacons lighted the skies from the Fishkill mountains.

"Thursday 24th Eat Breakfast with old Mr. Robert Johnson.
Friday 25th went to Town Meeting at Mr. Simeon Cooks
August, 1780. where the Minds of the Precinct was taken in Respect of Supporting the Credit of this New Emission, & getting a Law made to prevent the illegal Trade with the Enemy unanimously agreed to sign the following Petition.

"To the Legislature of the State of N. York, The Petition of the Freeholders and Inhabitants of Dutchess County, humbly Sheweth that our Petitioners for the Defense and Security of their Just Rights and invaluable Privileges are engaged in a Bloody and expensive war, with a Powerful and cruel Enemy, that should they overcome us nothing will remain but the blackest Prospect of abject Slavery, under the most cruel and relentless Taskmasters, that without Money we cannot carry on the war to any considerable Effect, that through the Scarcity of Specie, there is a Necessity of Substituting a paper Currency, that in Order to make Paper supply the Place of Specie, it is Necessary to prevent its Depreciation and give it a free Circulation—and your Petitioners beg Leave to observe further, that though Sufficient Funds may be Established for the Redemption of our Paper Money yet as a Great Part of the Inhabitants of this State are opposed to Independance, there is Reason to expect that they will do all in their Power to ruin us through our Paper Currency, and by every Means in their Power endeavour to depreciate its Credit and Stagnate its Circulation,—and your Petitioners beg Leave further to observe that there is within this State a vile Set of Men whose God is their Gain, who are lost to every Principle of Virtue, and distitute of any Regard for the Public Good, are carrying on a trade with the Enemy in hard Money, and refuse to sell their Goods otherwise than for Specie, to the Great Discouragement of those who endeavour to keep up the Credit of the Paper Money—and your Petitioners beg Leave further to observe, that the Disaffected People are confederate together to avoid as much as Possible the taking of Paper Money, and with that View refuse to sell the Necessaries of Life to those who Stand in Need, except for hard Money to the insuperable Discouragement of those whose wish it is to Support our Paper Currency—and your Petitioners beg Leave further to observe, that though they have a high Sense of the Wisdom manifested in the Legislature, at that last Meeting, by the Laws that were then made for the Security of the Paper Currency, yet they beg Leave to express their fear that unless further Measures are taken in the Premises the New Bills emitted by the Act of Congress of the Eighteenth Day of March last, will be in great Danger of depreciating, in Consequence of which we fear that we shall be reduced to the most deplorable and Remediless Situation,—we therefore beg Leave to request the Legislature to make Laws Effectually to prevent the illicit Trade with the Enemy, and to compell all those who have the Necessaries of Life to Spare to sell reasonable Quantities of the same, to those who stand in Need, for the Said New Bills at the Price that those Articles are usually sold for in Silver and Gold—and your Petitioners as in Duty bound shall ever Pray.

a True Coppy.

| | |
|---|---|
| "Friday 25th | Expenses to Day 8 Dollars |
| Saturday 26th | wrote three of the above Petitions for to circul-(ate) in the Different Precincts. |
| Sunday 27th | went to the Red Meeting House, no Minister. |

went in the After Noon to Mr. Lewis De Lavergne's delivered the three copys as above Mentioned to Judge Ephraim Paine, heard the Revd Mr. Elkanah Holmes Preach from these words, He that Standeth Take Care least he falleth, dined at Mr. Selah Trowbridge's."

A Song from Samuel Tallmadges Orderly Book.

"Come on my hearts of tempered steale,
And leave your girls and farms,
Your sports and plays and holidays, and hark away to arms,
*And to conquest w'll all go . . .*
A soldier is a gentleman, his honour is his life,
And he that wont stand by his post will ne'er stand by his wife,
*And to conquest . . .*
For love and honour are the same, or els so near allied
That neither can exist alone, but flourish side by side,
The spring is up, the winter flies, the trees all green and gay,
And all inviting honours call, away! my boys away!
In shady tents and cooling streems, with hearts all firm and free,
We'll chase away the cares of life in Songs of Liberty,
So fare you well you sweethearts, you smileing girls, Adieu!
For when the war is over, we'll kiss it out with you.
No foreign slaves shall give us laws, no Brittish Tyrant reign,
'tis Independance made us Free, and Freedom we'll maintain,

We'll charge the foe from post to post, attack
their works and lines,
And by some well laid stratagem we'll make
them all Burgoins.
Each hearty Lad shall take his Lass, all beaming
like a star,
And in hur softer arms forget the dangers of the
war,
And when the war is over, we'll set them down
at ease,
We'll plow and sow, we'll reape and moe, and
live just as we please,
The riseing world shall sing of us a thousand
years to come,
And tell our Children's Children the wonders
we have done,
So honest fellows here's my hand and heart and
very soul,
With all the joys of Liberty, good fortune! and a
bowl!
And to conquest we will go.

Finis"

Fort Schuyler Jan 10 1781

Orangetown Aug 17 1780

"it is Expected that the men for Daily Guards will appear in the Grand and other parades shaved, Combed, and powdered, and their clothes as clean as Circumstances will admit."

# 31. War Guests

IN DECEMBER, 1778, after a most unhappy year in Cambridge, the British prisoners of Saratoga were marched to Virginia. Gates's promised parole had been repudiated by Congress, although a few of the higher officers were exchanged. Among these was Lieutenant Thomas Anburey, whose letters along the way give a lively British picture uncolored by prejudice.

At Fishkill Anburey grasped the American design of defense as primarily one of keeping communication open between the states.

"The Americans, judging it was the plan of the campaign, 1777, to make ourselves masters of the North River, and thus to separate the Eastern from the Western States, after the taking of Forts Montgomery and Clinton, and our troops proceeding to Esopus and then returning to New York, they immediately began to fortify West Point, which is not at present compleated, but when it is will be impregnable and effectually prevent any fleets passing; it being a point of land that projects and makes a winding in the river and at the same time narrows it so as to have the whole command at that place.

"No doubt this was the reason for the choice of Fishkill as a place the best calculated for a depot of provisions and other stores, as being situated on the high road from Connecticut and near the North River. It is by this important post of West Point, that the Americans are enabled to keep possession of the North River, and a communication between the Northern and Southern Provinces, and I do once more assert, not only upon my own opinion, but of the Americans themselves that had we kept possession of the North River, the war would have been over by this time, early terminated in favor of Great Britain."

When Lieutenant Anburey and other officers passed through Dutchess they stopped at a house in Hopewell. "The people behaved extremely civil and attentive, would scarce permit us to pay for what we had from which circumstance we concluded they were friends of Government, and some officers opening their heart, spoke very freely about the Congress, Washington, etc. observing how great a shame it was that we should be put to such expense and that Congress ought to pay for us. The man went out of the room in a moment, and, just as we were mounting our horses, brought us an enormous bill, exhorbitant in every article, which he insisted upon being paid, and upon our urging that we had paid him what he demanded, he replied, 'Yes, gentlemen, so you have, but then I thought Congress was to defray all your expenses; now I know you are to pay me, I cant take a farthing less than this bill,' which we were obliged to discharge; however, it served as a lesson in future to be cautious before whom we railed against Congress."

In the long straggling line of British and German soldiers on their way from Massachusetts to Virginia in obedience to the orders of Congress there rolled along the wagon carrying the Baroness Riedesel and her children. She and her husband were enchanted with Dutchess though it was December, for the early winter was exceptionally mild. She overheard an American say "I believe God Almighty has turned Tory to give these Britainers such fine weather for their march." Some of the German soldiers were equally impressed with the country, and deserted on the promise of farms. But when Baron Riedesel tried to negotiate for a farm on the slopes of the Shongum, he was discouraged.

Lieutenant Anburey, meanwhile, was improving his knowledge of the fauna. It is to be feared that some Dutchess farmer's boy was spoofing him when he set down what he learned of the cuba (Yankee for catamount).

"There is an animal supposed to be peculiar to New England called the cuba. This animal, as if sensible that his family rely on him for protection, is extremely tender of them and never forsakes them until death dissolves the union." The lieutenant then moralizes on the failure of the human paterfamilias to profit by the cuba's example.

The Baroness, whose journal is one of the most entertaining of the period, described a veritable incident of the way, that was doubtless duplicated a hundred times.

One day we came to a pretty little place, but our supply wagon not having been able to follow us, we could not endure our hunger longer, I begged the hostess to let me have some food. "I have," answered she, "several different kinds. There is beef, veal, and mutton" My mouth already watered at the prospect. "Let me have some," I said; "I will pay you well for it." Snapping her fingers under my very nose she replied "You shall not have a morsel of it. Why have you come out of your land to kill us, and waste our goods and possessions? Now you are our prisoners, it is, therefore, our turn to torment you." "See," rejoined I, "these poor children, they are almost dead with hunger." She remained inflexible. But when finally my three-and-a-half-year-old daughter Caroline seized her by the hand and said to her in English, "Good woman, I am very hungry," she could no longer withstand her; she took her in a room and gave her an egg. "No," said the good little child, "I have still two sisters." At this the woman was touched, and gave her three eggs, saying, "I am just as angry as ever, but I cannot withstand the child". She then became more gentle and offered me bread and milk. I made tea for ourselves. The woman eyed it longingly, for the Americans love it very much; but they had resolved to drink it no longer, as the famous duty on the tea had occasioned the war. I offered her a cup, and poured out a saucer of tea. This mollified her completely.

In all the bitterness the little scene stands out. There was neither Whig nor Hessian when two real women met that day.

Best known of travelers in Revolutionary Dutchess was M. Le Marquis de Chastellux. His work, describing his journeys in 1780, 1781, and 1782, is widely known. Judge Hasbrouck gave an entire chapter to his notes on our county. Chastellux landed with the troops at Newport in July, 1780, and finding camp life a bore, set out upon his travels upon the continent. He took two friends, M. Linch and M. de Montesquieu, and five servants, not to mention two aides-de-camp, with an extra horse and a cart for the baggage.

He entered Dutchess at Bull's Ford, now Bull's Bridge, and reached Justice Andrew Morehouse's tavern in the Oblong. He found there a dozen farmers and 250 cattle, en route from New Hampshire to supply the army at Fishkill. He was interested to find the farmers requisitioned for 80 to 150 pounds each according to their means, for such supplies. The leader of the farmers gave up room and beds to the Frenchmen, and joined them during the evening. The room was filled with "huge men, the strongest and most robust I had yet seen in America".

Chastellux kept on next day to Fishkill through Hopewell, stopping at Colonel Griffin's tavern. He was out making fence-rails. Chastellux admired the long fine barracks, the stores, hospitals, and shops. He compared the American wooden log huts, which he described minutely, to the Roman winter quarters called "Hiemalia". The Marquis was amused to find army surgeons as well as physicians called "doctors" and treated on an equality with them. He noted that both groups were treated with the greatest consideration, "as with ancient Greeks". "Dr. Craig whom I knew at Newport, is the intimate friend of General Washington."

"In Fishkill, closely confined, were Tory soldiers in English uniforms, captured in the Mohawk fights." They had burned more than 200 houses, killed the horses and destroyed 10,000 bushels of wheat. The Americans guarded "these robbers in a close and narrow prison."

Chastellux soon pushed on to a convalescent camp where he found soldiers in nakedness, "not even rags," in November. On the way a little further, having met an escort sent by General Heath, he came out upon the Beacon plateau and "the most magnificent view I have seen in all my life."

By good luck he found 2,500 troops under General John Starke of Bennington fame, who gave him a dress parade, before he took his barge. Rounding Constitution Island, his party saw West Point, with its "formidable batteries", giving him a thirteen-gun salute with 24 lb. cannon.

"If one remembers that two years ago, West Point was a wilderness almost inaccessible, that this wilderness has been covered with fortresses and artillery by a people who six years before had never seen a cannon; if one reflects that the fate of the thirteen states has depended on this important post, and that a horse trader turned into a general, or rather became a hero, always intrepid, always victorious, but buying victory always at the price of his blood; that this extraordinary man, at the same time the honor and disgrace of his country, had sold and thought to deliver this Palladium of American liberty; if finally one groups together so many wonders, both of the physical and of the moral world, one may easily believe that my thoughts were indeed fully occupied and that I was not bored by my journey".

After a trip to Philadelphia and a night as guest of General Washington at Newburgh, he pursued his tourist way back to Fishkill Landing and Poughkeepsie. Finding the Court of Sessions at work, and the Governor engaged with them, he kept on to Pride's Tavern at Hyde Park. Next day, through hail and snow he plodded through "beautiful and well-cultivated country"; what he could see of it.

At "Strasbourg," which the inhabitants of the country called "Strattsborough," he learned from a polite French-speaking citizen, Mr. LeRoy, that his comrades Vicomte de Noailles, Comte de Damas and Chevalier de Mauduit had passed that way. Hurrying on he took shelter from the biting snow with Mr. Thomas at Rhinebeck, a big man of good mien, a hunter, a horse merchant and disposed to talk. With him at his good fireside, he learned of Thomas' dealings with Benedict Arnold, and of Thomas' starting him in the importation of horses from Canada. At one time Thomas had traveled to Montreal and back with horses in fifteen days, by riding Lake George on the ice.

Chastellux learned much: that one bushel of wheat sown brought from thirty to forty at Rhinebeck, (twice the average); that his fine dogs were foxhunters; that they killed bears and deer in winter(!); that New York people were eager for the conquest of Canada. And so the Marquis arrived at Claverack.

# 32. The Cincinnati. 1783

THE SOCIETY of the Cincinnati was formed on Thursday, May 13, 1783, at Major General Steuben's headquarters at Mt. Gulian, the estate of the Verplancks near Fishkill. Samuel Tallmadge as lieutenant in the Dutchess Regiment joined the Society and in his Orderly Books has left a complete record of its beginning. It is not without significance that his narrative follows pages denoted the settlement of pay for officers of the army.

By the terms of the founding, membership in the Society was open to all officers of the American army of three years service, or in service at the end of the war, or deranged by act of Congress, who were eligible on payment of one months pay. Thereafter, "as a testimony of affection to the memory and the offsprings of such officers as have died in the service, their eldest male branches shall have the same right of becoming members, as the children of the actual members of the society." Foreign officers were admitted, and honorary members provided for.

The insignia displayed Cincinnatus, who stood receiving honors from "three senators presenting him with a sword and other military ensigns—on a field in the back ground his wife standing at the door of her cottage—near it a plough and instruments of husbandry—round the whole: "Omnia reliquit servare Rempublicam": on the reverse "Sun riseing—a City with open gates and vessels entering the port—fame crowning Cincinnatus with a wreath inscribed Virtutis Proemium.

Hands joined supporting a heart, with the motto Esto Perpetua.

"Societas Cincinnatorum instituta A. D. 1783." Election was immediately made of the officers of the French command and the Ministers who had come to America.

The plan was the work of General Henry Knox, with some modifications. The Boston bookseller was elected secretary and his beloved chief accepted the presidency.

The society has not realized the fears of the more democratic leaders of the day. It gave birth to many other orders with more or less rank and title as their terms of admission, but in the great hurly-burly of American life these have done little harm, and have operated as useful pastimes for those with a taste for such. By far the most famous product was the city of Cincinnati, christened by General St.Clair seven years later.

The society also created, by a natural antipathy, its rival, the Tammany Order. St. Tammany, a worthy chieftain of the Lenape nation on the Delaware, had been friendly to the white man, and led a blameless and completely unknown life. Popular among the soldiers in their hours of play, he was set up in New York as the rival of Cincinnatus. The limitation of membership to the eldest branch was the chief point criticized, as was, of course, the rank of officer. But Tammany after a short time remained local, though an old house in Rhinebeck still goes by the name of Old Tammany Hall, and is supposed to have been Aaron Burr's headquarters. Certainly, in later years, from Rhinebeck and her sister Hudson villages to the north, came Grand Sachem Schell of Tammany, and such famous Democrats as Van Buren and Tilden.

In reflecting on this event, which has given lustre to the county, comes the memory of Washington's refusal to make himself king by right of the army, which took place across the river at Newburgh. The two events supplement each other, the one providing a certain place for privilege in a private capacity, the other setting the example of the legal basis of rule over all, privileged or unprivileged. Dutchess County has been through the years the outstanding example in electing men of means to office, and thus starting them on political careers, while at the same time preserving a democratic attitude of equality towards such aspirants. A president, vice-president, governors, generals and admirals have lived in the countyside, our neighbors and friends.

The Cincinnati, whatever its later history, started with the loftiest ideals, a chivalry of the republic. The "exalted rights of human nature," . . . "that union and national honor," and "the cordial affection subsisting between the officers," were the three ideals to which the members pledged their faith.

The cordial affection was not always maintained. Aaron Burr, frequently a Dutchess visitor, sat in the back of the room in New York while Alexander Hamilton, president of the Society after Washington's death, stood on the table and sang "How Stands the Glass Around?" Next morning Burr killed his fellow-member, and became a haunted man.

Twenty-three of the original members, at least, were Dutchess men, and certainly more.

When the Cincinnati were founded times were hard. The rewards of officers were small. The government had no prestige, and the name "continental" sank to become synonymous with "worthless". Some banner, some ideal, was needed to give the tired men new courage for the day. The Cincinnati met that need. Democracy as we conceive it was not yet a common faith. Many laws were still to be enacted to end inequality before the law—Gentlemen still came before yeomen. By swearing the higher ranks to defend the national honor, the Cincinnati aided in creating an atmosphere in which democracy might thrive without exciting retaliation on the part of the wealthier group. Washington's one fear was that some one would use the army to effect a military coup d'état, as in other American states too often was to be the custom. For this reason he rejoiced in the new society at the Verplanck house.

# VII. WE, THE PEOPLE

## 33. The Constitution, State of New York! 1777

THE FIRST CONSTITUTION of New York State deserves to be called the Franchise of Youth. Of the three men, who not only wrote the original draft but guided it through the many changes at the convention, Robert R. Livingston was twenty-nine, Gouverneur Morris was twenty-four, and the aged John Jay was thirty-one.

Gouverneur Morris, to whose skilled hand was later entrusted the polishing of our Federal Constitution before its final adoption, must have smiled as he noted that even a Representative must be at least twenty-five. The Yorkers had not been so particular. The only reference to the subject merely required voters to be "of full age."

John Jay, the eldest, was apparently chief author. Certainly he led the debates in which the articles were finally hammered out. But the others had their share. Livingston proposed the most original of the amendments that were adopted. His interest in the state constitution had caused him to miss signing the Declaration of Independence. The Third Provincial Congress, of which Livingston had been a member, adjourned on June 30, 1776, and its successor, the Fourth, met on July 9 at the same place, White Plains. Livingston was there, with the rest of the Dutchess representatives: Judge Zephaniah Platt, John and Henry Schenck, Jonathan Landon, James and Gilbert Livingston, Anthony Hoffman, Cornelius Humphreys, Joseph Crane, Thomas Hopkins, and Nathaniel Sackett. All but Hopkins had been members of the Third Congress. The whole county was represented from Crane and Hopkins of the Highlands to Hoffman of Red Hook.

The convention next moved to Harlem, then to Kingsbridge, to Odell's in Philipse Manor, and settled down in Fishkill. But accommodations there were limited, and the refugees crowded them out, so that after finding Poughkeepsie equally crowded the convention moved in March to Kingston, where the Constitution was adopted. It was printed, however, in Fishkill by Samuel Loudon. According to the biographer of Morris, the original draft was composed in that village. John Jay was at the time in a double capacity, serving also as chairman of the Committee of Safety. He was, of course, a refugee in Dutchess for most of the war.

Actually, he served in a triple capacity, for such was the exigency, with the British fleet threatening New York, that a secret committee was appointed to block off the Hudson. Livingston and Jay were both members of this committee. Under this pressure no progress on the Constitution was made till December, when the convention met in Fishkill. The committee then announced its work ready, and asked for a secretary to copy it. Thus Dutchess County may fairly claim to have been the place of composition of New York's first constitution. No doubt it would have been adopted there, if Abraham Yates, chairman of the committee, had not been taken ill, causing a postponement.

Not till the following March 12 did the committee's report reach the floor of the Convention at Kingston.

The long legal preamble of the new instrument recited the several steps taken by the Provincial Congresses, the Declaration of Independence, and closed by affirming that "all power whatever therein (in the conventions) reverted to the people." Having thus established the legality of their procedure, the convention proceeded to its articles.

The impetuous Gouverneur Morris was a young man in a hurry. He had made the original motion that the Third Provincial Congress appoint a committee to recommend to the people "to frame a government." John Morin Scott opposed this as too hasty, and unauthorized, and a committee was appointed merely to consider the suggestion of the Continental Congress on the subject. This committee reported that the New York Congress had as yet no legal warrant for such action, and proposed that a Fourth Congress be elected, on terms giving it precisely this power of framing a constitution. Thus for the fourth time in thirteen months the good people of this state had to choose a Provincial Congress; but the demands of the lawyers were at last satisfied. The Fourth Congress merely voted itself the Constitutional Convention; and when it adopted the state constitution, no further ratification by the people was necessary, nor did anyone ask for it. They had had their fill of voting; and the war was on.

But law takes time, and New York, the legal State, was one of the last to frame a state constitution, as it was the eleventh to adopt the national one. Connecticut and Rhode Island had merely scratched out the King's name and put in "the people," and lo! their constitution was ready. Others were almost as simple. But New York had to debate, and ten months must pass.

The Fishkill instrument was thoroughly examined and many amendments passed, before it was satisfactory to the men at Kingston. As adopted, it consisted of forty-two articles, each a single paragraph. The first declared (in the negative form of a Bill of Rights which forbids the wrong), that "no authority shall, in any pretense whatever, be exercised over the people or members of this state, but such as shall be derived from and granted by them."

The next sixteen articles dealt with the assembly and the senate, and the legislative function. Thirteen articles were devoted to the governor and executive branch. Article XXX deals cleverly with the election of delegates to the general Congress of the United States. The senate and assembly were each to prepare a full list. Names on both lists would be delegates;

the two houses would then vote jointly to elect one half of the remainder. Five articles then disposed of the judicial branch. The remaining seven confirmed royal land grants up to October 14, 1775, required Indian lands to be granted by consent of the legislature; gave complete religious toleration; forbade clergymen to hold civil or military office; provided for militia; continued trial by jury; and gave the legislature the power to naturalize whom they might think proper, requiring the oath only of those who entered from outside of the United States.

This constitution, with but five brief clarifying amendments, remained the law of the state for forty-five years. The experience gained with it changed New York from the legal to the Political State, in this respect overtaking Massachusetts and Virginia, and bringing to power the progressive energies of the nation. The Clintons, Van Buren and Edward Livingston, Wm. H. Seward, Samuel Tilden, Cleveland, the Roosevelts, Alfred E. Smith, and the rest make a group which alike in victory or defeat added much to American law and politics. Equally gifted were those of New York who differed from them in their conservatism; Jay, Kent, Robert Livingston, Charles Evans Hughes. The strength of all these has been their primary interest in justice as expressed in law, and in their ability to carry legislation through, often experimentally found wanting, but usually leading to some new advance in the popular thought.

This direction clearly showed itself at the Constitutional Convention. Gouverneur Morris and John Jay brought in amendments that would have abolished slavery. The Convention refused them, and contested eventual freedom. The event was the outcome of a legal tangle that was never resolved. Actually the Convention put itself on record in favor of adopting both the preamble and the enactment of freedom for slaves, but no final vote was ever taken combining the two. Livingston, from obscure motives, moved the previous question, and debate ceased therewith, thus leaving the matter till the Second Constitution in 1821.

Robert Harpur moved that all money qualifications be removed from voters, but this was defeated. Morris succeeded in reducing the property qualification for electors of assemblymen from £40 to £20, and Livingston managed to insert a clause giving suffrage to tenants with an annual rent of 40s., but there it ended. These really limited the voters to owners or renters of land; the original draft required only the payment of taxes and six months residence. At Jay's desire freemen of Albany and New York were exempt, but the landlords had their way upstate.

One of the most interesting debates dealt with naturalization. The Federal concept was new; other states, though leagued with New York, were still foreign territory in a legal sense. After long debate it was decided, under Jay's leadership, that the citizens of other states needed no measures of naturalization in New York.

Equally debatable was the article on religious freedom. Legally the metropolitan counties round New York had an Established Church, that of England. This was disestablished by the article, which forbade any preference or discrimination, and was better phrased than that in the Federal Constitution. The whole paragraph reads:

"And whereas, we are required, by the benevolent principles of rational liberty, not only to expel civil tyranny, but also to guard against the spiritual oppression and intolerance wherewith the bigotry and ambition of weak and wicked priests and princes have scourged mankind, this convention doth further, in the name and by the authority of the good people of this state, *Ordain and declare* that the full exercise and enjoyment of religious profession and worship, without discrimination or preference, shall forever be allowed within this state to all mankind: *Provided,* that the liberty of conscience so far granted, shall not be so construed as to excuse acts of licentiousness, or justify practices inconsistent with the peace or safety of this state."

In view of the history of this state, which has given birth to more sects than would have been expected, this declaration in the year after the Virginia statute is worth recording. The conditional provision, suggested by our Robert R. Livingston, was offered as a substitute for stronger conditions opposing authoritarian religions whose members might owe prior allegiance to a foreign potentate.

The article (XIII) guaranteeing civil rights of the Constitution through due process of law and the judgment of one's peers, we owe to a Dutchess Livingston, this time to Gilbert, a county official and a devoted follower of George Clinton. This is, in effect, the heart of Magna Charta. Its omission almost lost us our Federal Constitution.

Article XIII. No member of this state shall be disfranchised, or deprived of any rights secured to him by this Constitution, unless by the law of the land, or the judgment of his peers.

The two articles completely original with this Constitution, and not continued in its successors, provided for the Council of Appointment and the Council of Revision. Both sprang from the heads of lawyers versed in jurisprudence, and accustomed to see judges the chief governing officers in every village and town.

The Council of Appointment took away the power of the governor, and gave it to a council consisting of one senator from each of the "great districts" (Metropolitan, River, Albany, and Western) chosen by vote of the assembly; these with the governor merely as a voting member, to appoint all officers not elected. Thus the legislative branch took over an executive function.

It might work when the governor's party had a clear majority, but not otherwise. We may understand the unwillingness to repeat the history of British governors, but after all a governor must govern. Jay, with the cooperation of Livingston and Morris, devised this plan; it threw him on the rocks when he was governor twenty years later. He claimed the exclusive right of *nomination* of officers, but was defeated by a special article in 1801. The article was abolished in 1821.

The Council of Revision seems to have been mainly the idea of Robert R. Livingston. A plan for an executive council had been given up, by the substitution of the elected senate; but it was desired to curb the governor's power of veto, and the new chancellor or chief justice and the judges of the supreme court or any two of them were constituted a council to revise all bills. If the council deemed the bill improper it must send the bill back within 60 days. A two-thirds majority was then needed to pass it.

As a result of this article XI, one of the last adopted in point of time, the many questions of constitutionality and the vexatious delays incident to our present practice were avoided. Laws were drawn more carefully on revision, and almost no constitutional law or interpretations resulted during the next half-century.

But the trouble was, that it embroiled the judges in politics. In practice less than two per cent were vetoed in the twenty-four years under Chancellor Livingston. But disappointed partisans became bitter when pet bills were vetoed, and the bitterness engendered brought the judges into a poor repute, it was claimed.

The Fourth Provincial Congress, now the Convention, was dissolved on May 17, 1777. It had appointed on the 8th of May a Council of Safety of fifteen members, to act until a Legislature and Governor should be chosen. The Council of Safety met May 14, and required all sheriffs to give notice of the elections. The Legislature was convened on August 1, and sat till October 5, adjourning at Kingston on news of the loss of Fort Montgomery. A second Council of Safety followed, convening the legislature at Poughkeepsie on January 5, 1778.

We may well be proud of our first essay in lawmaking. The first Constitution was conservative, like the people. It was brief, simple, and clear. It did not put in the constitution what belonged in legislation or try to regulate everything. Modern state constitutions are lawbooks nobody reads. Its authors were not afraid to trust legislatures or to try experiments. Most of them were successful. The Bill of Rights was there in essence, but not in detailed form.

Under it a great governor, George Clinton, was able to make

his influence felt without being constantly at loggerheads with opponents. The state doubled in population and in prosperity. The legislature's terms at Poughkeepsie were fruitful. Its fame as the state capital brought it into being as a town of real character. In a sense it may be said that the Poughkeepsie of later days was the child of the First Constitution.

# 34. Our Federal Constitution! 1788

THE ADOPTION of the Federal Constitution must have confirmed General Washington's belief that a special Providence guided the faltering steps of this infant Republic. How, otherwise, could John Paulding's patrol have stumbled upon André? How, after years wandering in a wilderness, murmuring and mutinous, could America suddenly put on the whole armor of confidence and discipline, and produce a great instrument of order?

Throw a dozen votes the other way, divide them among the conventions of Virginia, Massachusetts and New York, and you would have no constitution. Our own state won by three votes, the narrowest margin of all. They were Dutchess votes, for it was the desertion of the three Dutchess spokesmen from Clinton's side that broke the deadlock and led the parade to the Federal victory.

The Old County was true to her role as mediator between north and south in York State. Dutchess shared the reasonable concern of her stout governor for the preservation of every state privilege, every foot of the new empire she had won in the eight years of war, every right her citizens had claimed.

But we also looked out from Hudson shore upon a maritime future, a great inflow of new people and an outlet for new industry. Dutchess had outgrown Orange and Ulster Counties in population, and had built stronger ties with Manhattan.

The years in which New York Legislature had met in Poughkeepsie had left their mark on the townspeople. James Kent, who had come here to live, and had married General Bailey's daughter Catherine, had not felt isolated in the pretty country village during the years when Washington, Kosciuszko, Lafayette, Jay, Robert and Edward Livingston, and the great governor had visited its courts and offices of government. Alexander Hamilton had pleaded here, and Judge Egbert Benson, most distinguished of local citizens, had built up a great reputation for learning, wit, and judgment. Judge Zephaniah Platt stood high in esteem, and had embarked on a great land venture of 30,000 acres on Lake Champlain, with a town bearing his name. Melancton Smith, Platt's close associate in the doubtful days of Whig and Tory, had joined in backing the new state by putting his savings into land also.

Gilbert Livingston, brother of the Rev. John and Major Henry the mapmaker and poet, was perhaps the busiest lawyer in the county, and had invited Kent to join him. There was a stir and a promise in the air of this lucky little town. A band of young lawyers would soon make the village known throughout the country.

For five years Dutchess had been Clintonian. Its people had looked north and west to the new counties which the governor had created by the County Act of 1788. Some of them would settle in them. Vermont attracted the patriot Colonel Udny Hay. The new lands were an outlet also for the discontented Tories who had returned with peace, but found little rest in meeting the stony faces of their Whiggish neighbors. So they packed up and took the covered wagons over the Fishkill and Rhinebeck ferries to the great western roads, or floated upriver to Essex and the other new counties beyond Saratoga.

Even so prominent a "neutral" as Dr. John Bard found life in Dutchess wearing, and advertised his Hyde Park farms for sale. Fortunately his children would not desert Old Dutchess. But Theophilus Anthony sold his estate, the mill and dock at Union Street. Cornelius Luyster of Fishkill, the obstreperous militia captain who tried to take his company over to the British, advertised his Verplanck leasehold. Nathan Birdsall, first on Quaker Hill, was sold out by the sheriff. So it went.

Dutchess showed little regret, their leaving did not lower farm prices materially. New faces were everywhere. In spite of the loyalists who had gone to Canada and Nova Scotia, and their friends who were migrating to more tolerant life in New York, Dutchess grew rapidly.

There were all the confiscated estates to be split up and resettled. Much of South Precinct was now divided up and sold in substantial acreage to speculators and farmers. The Township Act, which followed the county act, split up the old estates still further, by running new administrative lines through them. Dutchess took a slice from Rhinebeck and added it to Charlotte, renaming its largest town after her beloved Governor Clinton. Alongside his name none but Washington was fitting, and half of Amenia was split off to do honor to Clinton's friend.

Not till after 1793, when General Washington led the Federals, did Dutchess take Stanford away from him. These were the heart of the county, the land of the levellers, where the father, Colonel Charles Clinton, had surveyed the old lines, and radicalism was in the very air.

Except for leaseholds in the Old Beekman tracts, there were few acres in Dutchess that complained of their landlords. Most of the land was in fee simple. Dutchess Clintonianism had nothing to do with tenancy, though radical campaigners made political capital out of attacks on landlords in general.

Actually, the county stood on the threshold of a real land boom. Every acre was being cultivated. A new agrarian interest, the breeding of horses, had suddenly sprung up. It took capital and skill to develop, but by 1788 Dutchess newspapers were filled with advertisements of numerous imported and American stallions at stud ready to cover the mare for five to twenty dollars the stint.

The fine horse "Cincinnatus" was far more interesting than the Society of the Cincinnati, though the latter had been founded at Mt. Gulian in Dutchess. "Bold American," son of "Bold Briton," challenged the farmers. There was "Fearnought" of "Wildair;" "Hyder Ali" and "Bajazet" boasting Arab lineage; "Old Rainbow" and "Young Lath;" "Pilgrim" and "Pastime," "Fox" and "Jolly Sportsman," "Phoenix" and "Golden Farmer," "Molton and Hermit." All these in the two years before the Poughkeepsie Convention. Notices of them jostle the Convention bulletins.

That august body had scarcely adjourned before the "Country Journal" advertised "a Purse of Twenty Pounds Current Lawful Money of the State of New York, to be run for on the 9th of October next, at Mr. John B. Shears, Inn-keeper, in Fishkill township on the farm late in possession of George Bloom, about one mile and a half above Philip Verplanck's Mills—one mile heats, the Two best out of three; free for any horse, gelding, or mare, belonging in Dutchess County at this date, and not elsewhere, carrying weight for blood and age, viz.

"Full blood and full age, to carry 10 stone, and so in proportion for blood and age. Entrance money to be run for, the day after running for the purse, as a Scrub race. Sept 1, 1788."

What has all this to do with the Constitution? A great deal. Horses were a most valuable product, sloops carrying thirty horses at a voyage were sailing regularly to New York. County farms were furnishing stock for the western trek. All this meant, that the Dutchess did not live to herself, and that her people, especially on the river shore, were in active trade. Her prosperity was tied to Federalist New York City.

The Country Journal put forth articles on the improvement of agriculture. In great detail the culture of flax was taught. A "French gentleman" who had bought an estate near Poughkeepsie was delighted with the soil, and already experimenting with new plants. Even opium was suggested as a valuable crop, though "Strim Stram" in a burlesque of this and other proposals urged the increased planting of Skunk Cabbage, for its known medicinal value. Skunk root was of course a known specific.

There were other ties with the south. Dutchess had sheltered many refugees from southern New York, who now returned, taking with them pleasant memories. Melancton Smith was among the Dutchess men who went with them, to try their luck in the city, though they still kept lands and friends in old Dutchess. There was also the opposite movement, as when Captain Jesse Ames and his friend James Williams, who had escorted Burgoyne's men to Virginia, and had liked Dutchess landscape, returned to buy farms and marry.

In all this stir and striving, the depreciation of the currency, the issues of paper money, the loss of foreign trade, and the unemployment in the seaports made no great impression up-state. A serious depression struck in 1786, but it soon passed, though it left city residents resentful at the failure of Congress to aid them.

The North-West Territory Act of 1787 was perhaps the only work of the Congress to attract Dutchess folks. The text of it was printed at once in Poughkeepsie, though no comment was made on New York's leadership in surrendering western territory to the nation. This had made the Ordinance possible. It called for a strong government to manage the new lands.

New York, indeed, had been among the first states to call for such a change. As early as July, 1782, the legislature had instructed Governor Clinton to propose a convention to the other states, for the purpose of revising the Articles of Confederation. It had no success in the years of war. Now, in 1787, Clinton was still of a mind to revise the Articles, but not to surrender any part of New York's hard-won privilege. To the neighbor states that had coveted the great harbor for so many years of boundary disputes, it was exasperating to see the great upstate expansion of the Empire State financed by taxes on the use of the harbor which was theirs by right of charter and Puritan determinism. Both Connecticut and Massachusetts still claimed extensive lands in western New York. The Hamiltonian threat uttered in the Poughkeepsie debates, that the lower counties might secede and form a great maritime state along the coast, was no chimaera. State boundaries were being adjusted everywhere, in Maine, Vermont, Massachusetts, Pennsylvania, and further west. Anything might happen.

The merchants of the city grumbled when their port dues paid the costs of upstate development. The phenomenal growth of the city and its commerce was suddenly threatened in this convention by the closing of West India ports to American ships, another reminder that Britain did not relish the role of almsgiving to impoverished loyalists whom the Congress had pledged its faith to reimburse.

Clinton was much more disturbed by the blunt refusal of Britain to comply with the treaty terms of evacuation of the outposts in the Northwest, on the ground that the States had not fulfilled their promise to aid loyalists. The Governor knew well enough that the real reason was the profitable fur trade, now covering Michigan territory; but he thought he should defend New York's frontiers, and New York militia could gain the five posts in York State from the old enemy. He refused Congress' aid, and repelled the suggestion of Massachusetts troops as a garrison. No foreigners on York soil!

George Clinton was still smarting from the loss of Vermont. He had no intention of letting New England get a toehold anywhere along the Genesee. In this resolve Dutchess stood with him to a man.

Yet the more conciliatory policies of Robert R. Livingston had their supporters also. He and his friends had slowly but steadily sapped the antiloyalist laws, until by 1786 they were repealed. The Chancellor, as he was then known, had even adopted the daughters of a Tory Livingston relative, and introduced them to New York, on the ground that you could not fight a beautiful Tory.

When he talked about "a nerveless Congress", no one really feared that he would advocate one which would be so strong as to endanger New York State. Moreover, under Attorney General Egbert Benson a whole new code of state laws had been devised and adopted during a three year period preceding the Convention, which had touched every aspect of jurisprudence. The publication of the laws filled many pages of the Country Journal. Yorkers were gratified. The reforms abolished primogeniture and entail, and ended quitrents by commutation on a fourteen-year basis. But they did far more. Judge Benson could now go further, and make New York law precedent throughout the country. James Kent of the American Commentaries, who studied with Benson at Poughkeepsie, thought he had done more for the amelioration of legal practice while on the bench than had come about in a whole previous century.

But Benson was a Federalist. His work for the State laws had brought him election to Congress, and when in 1786 the states of the Potomac-Chesapeake region felt the need of interstate cooperation, Benson was elected with Hamilton and others on the New York delegation. No other state outside the region was represented. The Annapolis Convention requested the Congress to call a convention for revision of the Articles of Confederation.

Egbert Benson of Red Hook is a delightful figure. A man of many parts, he was interested in local history, and became the first president of the New York Historical Society. He wrote a comprehensive memoir on Indian and Dutch names and their meaning. In his later years, indignant at the attack on the captors of André, he wrote an excellent defence.

As Attorney-General of the State in 1781, and member of the Assembly for Dutchess in 1788, Egbert Benson was clearly a friend of the Governor, and not marked out as a real antagonist. He was in Congress for the same reasons, and not as a party man. The fact is that Federalism was a mushroom of very sudden growth, and all attempts to ascribe its rise to party divisions before the Constitutional Convention are quite futile.

Benson was also a good friend of John Jay, his next-door neighbor in Poughkeepsie who had been elected Chief Justice of New York. In 1781 he had removed from Fishkill to Poughkeepsie. With Jay, Benson, young Kent, and the rest, the village could challenge any town in America for Constitutional law.

Thus when Benson joined Jay and Hamilton in championing the Constitution, he was never accused of deserting the Governor. It cannot be too clearly stated, that the issue was not between a new Constitution or none. Nor did anyone defend the old Confederation. That was a dead horse. The issue was upon the necessity of amendments, and primarily upon the necessity of their adoption prior to New York's ratification. In the heat of the debate many taunts were flung to and fro which clouded this issue; but the leaders such as Hamilton, Jay, and Benson on one side, and Clinton, Melancton Smith and John Lansing of Albany on the other, never descended to the level of the mudslingers. The issue was primarily legal and procedural, and though it involved other questions, social and economic, it is impossible to line up the antagonists on such broad issues as aristocracy, land tenure, or capitalism. There were too many exceptions.

Certainly the "Country Journal" and its readers up to the very month of the Convention, were treated with an exposition of the merits and faults of the new Constitution on the highest grounds, unencumbered by political bitterness. Hamilton, it is true, wrote of Clinton's indifference toward the old Congress, and his early lack of hospitality to it, but the terms were guarded, and Clinton, though he answered, made no issue of it.

The pamphleteers all felt the greatness of the hour, and remembering the days of the early Roman republic signed themselves Cato (Clinton), Publius (the Federalist leaders). Richard Henry Lee, whose essays the Journal reprinted, wrote as a "Federal Farmer".

The most distinguished pamphleteer of Dutchess was Melancton Smith, who in December, 1787, under the name of "a Plebeian" penned "An Address to the People of the State of New York." The pseudonym is significant. Smith was not even a tribune of the people, he was one of "the democratical mob", that bugbear of colonial aristocracy. "Cato" and "Publius" were not for him.

He argued in terms addressed to the simplest artisan. What was wrong with New York, that people should want a super-government? New York had no need of a new Constitution. Every man in New York sat under his own vine and figtree, with none to make him afraid. If New York had any debts, they were from the continental war, and would soon be paid off. Nobody wanted to fight us. The French were gone, the savages had had their lesson. No civil war between the states could be imagined. If improvement must come, let it grow naturally out of the Articles of Confederation.

Smith defended New York's hold upon the impost as the easiest means of meeting New York's debt to the Congress. He saw with prophetic eye the extension of powers by interpretation of vague and general phrases like public welfare. He deprecated the increase of executive and legislative power which would surely be exerted in fields not prescribed in the Constitution, but which were not expressly prohibited there.

He would reserve to the States the power of direct taxation and the conduct of elections. He thought that the provision of one representative for each 30,000 inhabitants gave much too small a House, and wanted it doubled. What he would have said to the present ratio can be imagined.

Smith's address was sober, modest, and well written. Clinton's party has often been represented as the party of the small farmer, rural storekeeper, and poor tenant. If this be so, it is strange that in the "Address" of his chief spokesman no appeal to these groups is made. This Dutchess address is made to the respectable citizen, whether rich or poor. Its appeal is only to practical good sense, conservative dislike of change, and a real loyalty to the State which had struggled so long to make its citizens free men. The quarrel, if it could be called such, was with minor points rather than with the ideal of a strong central government. Let the government be strong, but let it not get out of hand and overpass the bounds of discretion.

"Friends, countrymen, and fellow-citizens:
The present is the most important crisis at which you have ever arrived. You have before you a question big with consequences, unutterably important to yourselves, to your children, to generations yet unborn, to the cause of liberty and of mankind; every motive of religion and virtue, of private happiness and public good, of honour and dignity, should urge you to consider coolly and determine wisely.

"Almost all the governments that have arisen among mankind have sprung from force and violence. The records of history inform us of none that have been the result of full and dispassionate reason and reflection. It is reserved for this favored country to exhibit to mankind the first example.

"This opportunity is now given us, and we are to exercise our rights in the choice of persons to represent us in execution, to deliberate and determine upon the constitution proposals: it will be to our everlasting disgrace to be indifferent on such a subject: for it is impossible, we can contemplate anything that relates to this life of half the importance.

"The only question between us is simply this, Shall we accede to a bad constitution, under the uncertain prospect of getting it amended after we have received it, or shall we amend it before we adopt it? Commonsense will point out which is more rational. . . .

A Plebeian."

Melancton Smith and his Dutchess fellow-delegates Zephaniah Platt and Gilbert Livingston were able attorneys, men of some means and of high standing among their neighbors. All three had land in the county, and had practised law for years. Smith and Platt had served on the County Committee during the Revolution, and had helped to sell the loyalist lands. They certainly represented no poor or underprivileged group. Gilbert Livingston was not, as has often been stated, Clinton's brother-in-law, nor was he specially honored among the thirty-six Livingstons listed in the Governor's correspondence. He came from the more humble Poughkeepsie family of Henry Livingston, a younger son of Gilbert, husband of Cornelia Beekman, who owned one third of the Great Beekman Patent. Little of this had descended to the younger Gilbert.

After the Convention Smith returned to his lucrative law practice in New York. Platt, who had acquired extensive grants in Lake Champlain, went on to found Plattsburg, a pioneer at 60. Gilbert Livingston served the county as Surrogate, and at his death in 1806 was Clerk of the County.

It seems strange, if Clinton were so ardent for defeat of ratification as he has been represented, that he did not bestir himself to select a more subservient team in this pivotal county. But Clinton's letters, signed Cato, though skillfully and correctly pointing out the dangers inherent in the Constitution, did not depart from the most formal and dignified style. Here were no Sons of Liberty from the water-front, no Levelers from the Back Country like John Kane and Samuel Munroe.

Clinton bestirred himself to see to it that Dutchess County did not choose Robert R. Livingston, John Jay, or Egbert Benson as delegates. Alexander Hamilton had suggested them, but in vain. New York City sent all but Benson. It seems clear that in the Dutchess' choice the prejudice against the landlords' party had no influence. Indeed, the very election of a grandson of Gilbert and a nephew of Robert Gilbert Livingston, the two landlords most unpopular in Dutchess after the Philipses, proves that memories of old tenancies no longer dictated voters' choices.

As for Alexander Hamilton, the young statesman fully realized he was leader of a minority. The odds seemed hopeless, if his opponent was seriously bent on full rejection of the Constitution. But there was evidence that this was not the case. When the Federalist Senate of New York had proposed its slate of delegates to the Federal Constitutional Convention, Clinton's Assembly had compromised with a combination of three, of which Hamilton was to be one. The others, Robert Yates of Albany and John Lansing of Lansingburgh, were good sober men enough. Evidently Clinton was not sufficiently alarmed to pick a delegation that should really fight Federal organization.

As it turned out, Hamilton was the best choice Clinton could have made. He was so far over on the side of authority, aristocracy, life tenure, and centralization, that after a speech or two he found himself in a minority of one, and contributed little to the formation of the Constitution. Meanwhile Yates and Lansing took a walk, and returned to New York, telling their Governor that their longer stay was futile. Thus the Constitution, it could be said, was none of New York's making.

But when Clinton's temperate papers of "Cato" began to appear, Hamilton saw light. Here was not an intransigent opponent of any constitution, but a keen and logical critic. Such a man might listen to reason. In any case, it would eternally damage the defenders of authority if such a critic went unanswered.

This was the origin of "The Federalist", with its two New York authors and James Madison of Virginia. "Publius", their common pseudonym, began to appear in New York, and to be read on all sides. Others responded, and no legal document ever got so full and extended a treatment before enactment as did our Constitution in New York. In a sense, every point raised in Poughkeepsie had already been discussed, and its merits judged, before the debate began in the Dutchess Courthouse.

In Dutchess, at any rate, the people seemed familiar enough with the arguments. The Country Journal reprinted the Antifederalist paper of "The Federal Farmer" of Richard Henry Lee, but its columns were chiefly filled with the acts revising state laws which poured out of Albany. One ardent Federalist alone poured out his eloquence in defence of the Constitution. On December 19, 1787 it appeared.

"Shall we, and shall the fates of future generations, be submitted to a government which has been deliberately planned and recommended by our best and wisest men, or shall we, as all other nations have been obliged to do, leave these matters to be dictated by the sword? The alternative is awfully serious. It touches every consideration in life."

This was, indeed, the real crux: action, not argument over details. The makers of the Constitution were no despots but Washington, Franklin, and their friends. They made no extravagant claims for their production, except that it would work.

The true Bill of Rights was the Constitutional provision for the short terms of office of the President and the legislature, who could not keep themselves in office if the people willed otherwise. Connecticut had no Bill of Rights, but was freer than most. Rhode Island had a Bill, but was in a tyrant's hands.

Check upon check had been provided, that could work against this branch or that securing a monopoly of power. As the author looked upon the many safeguards provided in the foundations, firmly riveting the parts together, he became "pretty indifferent as to the ornaments or superstructure because he knew they could at any time be modified for the public good."

"The patronage of genuine liberty is worthy of the noblest minds."

With this not oversubtle compliment to the noble Dutchess people the writer concluded. He urged his readers to peruse the "Publius" letters, of Madison, Hamilton, and Jay. He admitted they were too numerous to be printed in the "Journal," but proposed to print an abridgment of them.

"They treat on the necessity of Union, from every point of view, and in all its consequences, in such an able manner, and with such strong and able painting, as to denote the hand of a master."

The last paragraph points directly to a disclosure of the author's name. James Kent, afterwards Chancellor of New York, was a young student of law in Judge Egbert Benson's office. In a letter to Mrs. Alexander Hamilton, written many years after the event, he told her that he reprinted the first 36 letters of "The Federalist", and that Judge Benson and he took them to the caucus at which the delegates to the Poughkeepsie Convention were to be chosen, and distributed the copies to the voters personally. This was in May, 1788.

Thus James Kent made his first appeal to Dutchess voters, and fulfilled the proposals which he had advanced as the "Country Federalist." Perhaps the voters read "the Federalist;" perhaps not, as Josh Billings remarked. In any case they had been informed. Their choice of middle-of-the-road delegates may have been modified by Kent's action. Certainly they chose the most popular men in the county, Benson excepted.

Judge Benson had been at Annapolis with Hamilton to discuss joint state action on navigation and trade with the states of the Potomac Chesapeake area. They had recommended to Congress a revision of the Articles of Confederation, instead. Benson was a committed Federalist. Doubtless he worked tirelessly among the delegates from his Poughkeepsie home.

Modern times have witnessed so many fruitless conferences that the story of the Poughkeepsie Conference seems an illusion. Do conferences ever convince anyone? As the opening day convoked opposing parties, the atmosphere was strangely free from political rancor and personal friction.

This continued throughout the six weeks' debate. The Clintonians possessed Poole's Inn, on the corner of Market and Cannon Sts., the Hamiltonians filled Hendrickson's Inn, the present Nelson House. Yet cordial personal relations persisted through the session.

The debate was dignified, and free from trivial quibbling and jeering, except in one person, the last that could possibly have been suspected. Chancellor Robert R. Livingston, who led off for the Federalists with an able overclassical keynote address, was thereafter of little use to his party. His jibes were calculated to bring retaliation rather than conviction to his opponents. He was particularly cutting upon his own relative, Gilbert Livingston. The occasion of the latter's offense was a mixed metaphor.

Gilbert had been attacking the terms of the United States Senators. Since they could be continuously reelected, they might become a wall.

"What wall?" he was asked.

"A wall of gold," he replied, "flowing into the Senate from all parts of the country."

A hearty laugh filled the courthouse, and the abashed Gilbert continued his argument. But thereafter he could not rise to his place without a stinging reference by the Chancellor to his opponent's "fluid wall." Perhaps the proprietor of Claremont could not forgive a village relative's defiance of the law of the Livingston. It was not a gracious exhibition.

Hamilton and Jay, the real Federal leaders, had no time for such bickering. While Hamilton hammered away in the style of the Federalist upon the merits of the Constitution, and showed how its failings were either illusory or susceptible of amendment, John Jay, Chief Justice of New York, and Chief Justice of the United States to be, worked upon the feelings of the Clintonians. He assured them that he recognized the imperfections, and pledged himself to work for their amendments, in the manner provided in the Constitution.

He urged that the Constitution had anticipated criticism and itself provided the readiest way to amendment by those who accepted it in good faith.

While Hamilton's exposition filled the minutes of the early days as reported in the Country Journal, the later crucial days were not fully reported in the Poughkeepsie press, and the only detailed account I have read are the notes of Gilbert Livingston, who faithfully followed most of the speeches. In these notes Jay's name appears more frequently than Hamilton's.

Chancellor Livingston had been given the honor of moving that the Constitution should be considered article by article, before a vote was taken upon any section. This was unanimously adopted. The extended coverage of this action was useful. Both sides were sufficiently confident to feel that time was on their side. The Clintonians were 46 to the Hamiltonians 19, and feared no defection because of Hamilton's eloquence.

They hoped that Virginia then in session would enter into an agreement with New York to stay out until their joint amendments had been adopted at a second conference. They hoped also to convince the downriver men that, a fair field having failed to change their vote, they would yield to upriver, which was the New York State of the future, and from which alone their wealth could come.

Hamiltonians had nothing to lose, and all to gain by delay. The Constitution had been completed in September, 1787. George Washington had publicly announced it, with a letter prefacing its introduction. His enormous prestige had launched the great debate with favor. Delaware, Pennsylvania, and New Jersey had declared for it in December; Georgia and Connnecticut followed in January; Massachusetts joined in February, Maryland in April, and South Carolina in May. Thus seven states for, none against, was the record when dilatory New York came to elect delegates. New Hampshire, the ninth state, clinched the union by ratification the week before New York's delegates gathered at Poughkeepsie.

Clinton in January, 1788, had sent his message to the legislature without any inclusion of his wishes as to a Convention to consider it. It was Egbert Benson of Dutchess who moved in the Assembly to hold a convention; the vote showed a majority of two in favor. This was in February.

The New York legislature, hoping perhaps to increase the Clinton vote among the disfranchised, opened the voting, for the first time in New York's history, to all citizens without any property qualifications. On such occasion it sometimes happens that over-confidence reduces the number voting. Whatever the cause, only 6% of New York's men voted for delegates to this all-important convention. At least the New Yorkers were not over-impressed with the value of franchise at this time.

The people of Poughkeepsie showed a greater interest in their big show. The standing room behind the members benches were always filled. Young James Kent's eager face could be seen every day, and near it that of the Governor's nephew, young DeWitt Clinton, already a promising student of law. Ladies were in attendance, also, Mrs. Hamilton, daughter of Gen. Philip Schuyler, leader of the New York Senate, being one. The Chancellor referred gallantly to the ladies as deserving of some gayety in the debate.

He did not get it; the people wanted the real thing and they got it. "A gentleman in Poughkeepsie" wrote to his friend in Connecticut (favoring the *Journal* with a copy, of course): "The Chancellor pours forth a stream of eloquence deep as the Ganges, irresistible as the Cadaraqui. Jay's reasoning was weighty as gold, polished as silver, and strong as steel. Smith, the 'anti' champion, adds the stability of Locke to the candour of Sydney. If his elocution is hesitating, it is still eloquent, and the exertions of his mind exhibit a man formed for investigation and debate.

"Upon the whole I believe that in no place in America has the new constitution been fairer convassed, abler defended, more powerfully opposed. What will be the result I dare not divine . . ." (he believed) "peace with all her delightful appendages will probably erect a stone to be shaken only with the dissolution of the globe".

Yet it may be questioned whether nine-tenths of the debate accomplished anything not already decided. On not one of the chief points of attack: the term of office of presidents and legislators, scope of legislation, function of the courts, taxation, slavery, bill of rights, and the rest, was there any change of opinion. Nor did Hamilton persuade anyone to vote to ratify the Constitution. Everyone had come prepared to vote for it. The only question really before the conference was one of timing: whether to ratify before or after amendments had been adopted. On this vital point honors must be shared between Hamilton and Jay: the former persuaded the Dutchess members that there were legal difficulties in the way of expecting help on amendments either from the then existing Congress or a second convention to be extra-constitutionally convened. The latter may fairly be said to have carried the day with the rest of the Clintonians from lower York State, by giving his pledged word to cooperate in securing the desired changes, and by his tactful address.

The popular story that Hamilton by sheer superiority in

eloquence wore down the opposition, and changed a thumping majority into a vanishing minority, is a pure myth. Certainly Hamilton's skill in argument aroused the highest praise from Chancellor Kent in his later years—in a letter addressed to Hamilton's widow,—but it is exploiting Melancton Smith's generous acknowledgement of a conviction on a single point of expediency, to use it as a confession of surrender along the whole Clintonian line of offence.

On the contrary any thoughtful perusal of the first fortnight of debates will convince the reader that the Dutchess lawyer more than held his own in argument on the Constitution and its defects. One example may suffice: the debate on the reservation to the states of powers not delegated to the United States by the Constitution, nor prohibited by it to the states—the 10th Amendment, in short. Hamilton argued that Constitutions should consist of general propositions. "The reason is that they must necessarily be permanent, and that they cannot calculate for the possible change of things. I know that the states must have their resources, but I contend that it would be improper to point them out in the constitution."

This was all very well, as an opinion of Mr. Hamilton, but why not state it in the instrument? Smith rejoined. The reservation to the states must be clearly set forth. Smith knew that Hamilton's thought was imperialist in scope, and that he had little sympathy with state rights. His assurance that all powers not conclusively given the United States were "of course" retained by the states carried little weight with those who knew the arguments Hamilton had advanced in his few speeches at the Federal Convention.

Smith stated with conviction that a great Constitutional question was at stake. Good men might differ upon it. The question must be clearly set forth in the Constitution.

He was right, and the tenth amendment proved it. But a clearer and fuller definition of state rights might have anticipated the civil war, and rendered needless such obsolete provisions as that the United States could not pass bills of attainder, or ex post facto laws, or confer titles of nobility. These were essentially part of a Bill of Rights, which had been left incomplete. If the United States had not been given the power by the Constitution, why not deny the power, unless the United States *did* lay claim to powers not expressly given it? It was a nice point, and Smith's reasoning was quite as good as Hamilton's.

In forensic and rhetorical display Hamilton's talents were recognized, though that they played any great part in the outcome must be doubted. Certainly during the fortnight which ended July 2, 1788, the anti-federalist arguments for amendments were as strong as ever, and the reports showed no sign of weakening.

The situation changed suddenly with the next stage of debates. Up to this time the Constitution had been discussed as a whole, members having the right to bring up anything they pleased to say about it, for or against. Now they began to discuss it article by article, in accordance with their early decision. Only a week was necessary, most of the sections meeting approval with little comment. It became immediately clear that the delegates had no intention of scrapping the great instrument.

On the same day that the Convention took up the serious business of reading the articles of the Constitution, their task was rendered almost an academic exercise. The most dramatic moment in the Convention thrilled sportsmen quite as much as the politicians.

"On Wednesday last (July 2) at half after 12 Col. William Smith Livingston arrived at this place with the news of the ratification of the new Constitution by the State of Virginia.

"It arrived at New York at 37 minutes after two on the same day. The difference between New York and this place is 82 miles, and from the stoppings in the road the journey was performed in 7 hours and one quarter. The ruffness of the road and the change of horses being but twice rendered the expedition an act of contemplation, and it appears from information to have been performed with more expedition than has hitherto been known on this road."

The Country Journal, which scooped the press at the time, carried on July 15 also the full text of the Virginia ratifications with its objections and its proposed amendments. Its form probably suggested to Melancton Smith his own proposals two days later.

Col. Livingston was received with great joy by the Federal Party, and in the evening 10 guns were fired in honor of the 10 states which had ratified the Constitution.

Although the delegates attended to their knitting on July 4, they celebrated Independence Day in entire harmony. Poughkeepsie had wakened them to cannon fire, and adjourned them at noon with thirteen rounds. The Governor's party dined at Hendrickson's, the Federalists at Poole's across Market Street. John Jay, ever solicitous about accord, wrote his wife with satisfaction that though "Two tables but in different houses, were spread for the convention, the two parties mingled at each table and the toasts (of which each had copies) were communicated by the sound of drum and accompanied by the discharge of artillery."

This good example, though followed by the county so far as we know, was neglected by New York and Albany where dangerous riots took place. Elsewhere in Dutchess good feeling ing prevailed. At Matthew Patterson's in Fredericksburgh (Patterson) toasts were tactfully tendered to the "Federal Farmer" (Lee) and the "Plebeian" (Mr. Smith). Nothing matched, however, the victory barbecue on August 5 at Henry G. Livingston's in Dover, the week after ratification, where five hundred persons disposed of a great roasted ox, and drank 11 toasts in honor of the 11 ratifying states. In the evening there was a grand bonfire, and the whole village lighted every candle and shouted for victory.

A second fortnight must pass after July 4 before it was, indeed, all over but the shouting.

Specific amendments continued to appear, Smith's proposal that the president should enjoy one term of seven years being offered on the very morning of Independence Day. The convention later expressed its preference for a limitation of two terms, and this was duly forwarded to Congress. Smith's amendment thus reached its fulfillment 163 years later.

By July 11 men's ideas had begun to flag, and John Jay moved adoption of the Constitution as a whole. Smith on the 15th moved amendments, which were later incorporated as resolves in the final action. The discussion became general again, and the rural delegates were restless. Harvest was coming on. They came out for flat rejection. Clintonians seemed likely to split. To avoid this, the committee to which the amendments had been referred brought in a complete plan for ratification on condition of the adoption of a bill of rights and other amendments. Extended speeches by both Jay and Hamilton kept the convention in session for a week. Here Hamilton achieved his moment of triumph in his argument that no future congress would possess power to receive New York on terms and conditions. Congress could not suspend any part of the constitution, yet conditional acceptance amounted to so much. Even if Congress passed a law to effectuate Amendments, it could be repealed at any time. An unconstitutional approach to a constitutional alteration was self-defeating.

Clinton knew he was licked, and his wrath rose. "I see the advocates of the constitution are determined to force us to a rejection," he said. "We have gone great lengths, and have conceded enough; but nothing will satisfy them. If convulsion and civil war are the consequence, I will go with my party."

This defiance frightened the Federalists, who moved an adjournment. Their speeches kept the motion before the convention for several days, during which passions had time to cool. Smith had been doing some very serious thinking. Clinton's threat might easily lead to secession of the northern counties. He now lived in New York, and his interests still lay in his loved Dutchess. He could not face such a tragedy.

On July 17 Melancton Smith achieved his great compromise. He admitted the justice of Hamilton's argument that acceptance of conditions by Congress was impossible. The Constitution had been ratified and was now in effect. Congress of itself could not alter it or any part of it.

The one thing now to strive for was a plan which would bring the union about. He reviewed his course of opposition listing seven main points:

1 Vagueness of terms expressing the most important powers of Congress.
2 Lack of precision in definition of federal and state relations.
3 Revenue powers indefinite.
4 Congress too few in number.
5 Congressional regulation of elections.
6 Senate enhanced by executive and judicial powers.
7 Judicial powers so vague as to threaten state justice.

The convention nevertheless desired to remain with New York's neighbors for the common good of the union.

"They have therefore agreed to assent and ratify the Constitution in the firmest confidence that an opportunity will be speedily given to revise and amend the constitution, in the move pointed out in the fifth article, expressly reserving to this state a right to secede and withdraw from the constitution in case such opportunity be not given in—years."

He called on Congress to convene a second convention, and proposed that a circulatory letter be sent to the states, inviting them to join in so requesting Congress.

Next day the convention sat in silence. Federalists awaited the next move, Clintonians were at a loss to proceed. Finally they adjourned, agreeing to meet on July 19, and to discuss the Smith plan in detail before all other business.

Melancton Smith had drawn to his breast the lances of the opposition. For a week he defended his course, the Federalists exercising forbearance with respect to the preparation of the amendments, the Clintonians passing the amendments but breaking out against Smith's acceptance of Hamilton's point.

As the discussion kept on, Smith and his friend Samuel Jones, antifederalist of Suffolk, now and then voted against an amendment. The defection had begun. The good feeling engendered by Jay's frequent assurances, that his friends would loyally support the amendments, had borne fruit; and the amendments and resolves had been rapidly approved, many without discussion. Meanwhile Hamilton, to strengthen his case, had appealed by letter to Madison for confirmation of his contention that the state could not reserve a right to secede. Madison of course agreed. His letter was read to the convention.

It was pointed out that threats would not sway the other states, and that the only way to win good will was to exhibit it. In this amiable frame of mind Samuel Jones, whose votes on amendments had already classed him as no mere Clintonian, came to Smith's aid by moving to insert Smith's "in fullest confidence" in place of the conditional acceptance with the right of secession. "In full confidence" was then suddenly voted, 31 to 29, in committee of the whole.

Next day John Lansing, Clinton's closest man, tried to repair the loss by moving that New York reserved the right to withdraw if a second convention were not called after a specified time. Hamilton opposed it, an adjournment was voted, and Clinton had to face the fact that he no longer led enough of his party to defeat unconditional ratification. His downriver men had deserted him, perhaps fearing secession from New York which would be a worse fate than the Constitution. Staten Island would go to the Jerseys, Long Island to its logical geographical owner, Connecticut; Manhattan might follow Westchester into Yankee arms. At the time, it is recalled, New York and Connecticut were about equal in population. The threat was real, though upriver men might not think so.

On July 25 the Lansing amendment was defeated by 31 to 28. On July 26 the final affirmative vote to ratify "in full confidence" passed 30 to 27. The seven upriver counties stayed with Clinton, (1 vote excepted). Dutchess County's four delegates voted with Hamilton and Jay (one delegate had gone home ill). Woodhull of Orange; all of Queens; and all but one of Suffolk voted for them. Thus no county north of Dutchess and Orange gave the Constitution a vote; no county south of them refused it (with one exception, a Suffolk vote). The seaboard had won over the back country.

Gilbert Livingston and Zephaniah Platt stuck manfully with Melancton, but felt it necessary to explain their shift, before the final vote was taken. They did so modestly and without bitterness.

What George Clinton thought of his departed friends can be surmised. Melancton Smith pleaded with his colleagues: "What security can anyone have respecting any right, but the confidence you put in the government which exercises the power?"

Clinton tartly inquired: "If the confidence we have in government is to be our only safety, why have we sot here so long? Let us have these rights clearly expressed."

On the final "question" after the committee rose, the vote was 30-25 for an unconditional approval.

The legislature sulked in its defeat. No presidential electors were appointed and no New York Senators or representatives attended the opening session at New York. Ironically, the inauguration took place in Wall Street, and Governor Clinton banqueted Washington on his arrival. Dutchess shared in the ceremonies, for Chancellor Livingston administered the oath of office.

Clinton got his ten rights three years later, but New York had joined the Union. Had the Federalists been less eager to protect the interests of property, the prerogatives of office, and the authority of the law, many long years of struggle in interpreting the vague clauses of the Constitution might have been saved. But time was very important in 1788; a few more months and we might have had three nations for one, perhaps four, if the West be considered. These men did their best.

So bring on the roasted ox! Up the Constitutions! To the President! The Congress! These United States! The Sovereign State of New York!

# 35. The New Look. 1790

SUDDENLY DUTCHESS turned modern. The Age of Transit, of Communication, of Machinery, of Organization, came all at once upon the quiet county. Expansion and improvement struck the keynotes of the new age. Just as a new and untried Constitution became the frame of reference in the first days of suspicious cooperation, the nation plunged into some of its greatest problems: British fulfillment of the peace terms; wider access on sea; Louisiana; the Barbary pirates; the French and British wars; the revolutionary ideas; the beginnings of a truly continental system; all these whirlwinds of feeling and action engulfed the country and the county.

Internal politics were no less disturbing. New York had to fight for her newly won frontiers. The disfavor of the people endangered the Constitution. The Bill of Rights of 1791 only half satisfied them. The teeth of the great instrument had not been drawn. The nation might still submerge the state. Alexander Hamilton, whose brother-in-law Philip J. Schuyler represented Dutchess in Congress, and whose able assistant, Nathaniel Pendleton, was a Dutchess judge, held the country true to the Federalist cause for fifteen years, but only by a slim majority. Fishkill and the Highland towns were anti-Federalist most of the time. After Hamilton's death—Nathaniel Pendleton was his second at the fatal encounter in 1804—Dutchess went "Constitutional Republican," a new name for Federalist. As war clouds gathered toward the close of the period, Dutchess voted for De Witt Clinton against Madison. Twice, in 1804 and 1808, pro-British sentiment grew so strong as to give thoughtful minds concern lest New York with New England should seek Britain's aid in secession. Early politics excelled later days in vituperation.

In the midst of all this hurly-burly, the individual emerged. People began to realize they lived in history, and to keep records of other things than the sale of land and the bounties on bears' heads. We begin to see the county through the unguarded eyes of people like ourselves.

Maps were made. Henry Livingston, Jr. made a set of maps of Dutchess towns, unexcelled today in clearness of detail, and in style of topography. Hills are gently shaded in. Roads are named by destination. In the corners, lightly sketched, you find shepherds and shepherdesses out of French paintings, for Major Henry was an artist and musician, too, who would be quite at home with us today.

Newspapers flourished. Holt left his New York Journal behind him as the Country Journal, to which the Poughkeepsie Journal under Nicholas Power succeeded. Toward the end of our period Paraclete Potter took it over, and with his comfortable bookshop made his rooms, with their circulating library, the center of village culture.

It is no wonder that the Reverend Timothy Dwight thought well of the village and its county. In his famous book of travel he wrote: "Poughkeepsie is the shire town of Dutchess County, one of the best tracts of land in this State, and indeed in the United States. It is filled up with inhabitants, and remarkably well cultivated. Poughkeepsie is excellent land. In 1790 its inhabitants were 2,529; in 1800, 3,242; and in 1810, 4,670.

"Many of the houses are pretty buildings, surrounded by neat appanages. The situation is elevated, and sufficently level to be handsome. The soil in which it stands, is rich. The streets, which are of a good breadth, are handsomely set with trees. Gardens neat and productive, and lots covered with verdure are often beautiful ornaments to the houses. This town contains a considerable proportion of intelligent and polished society, a small circle of which made our little stay very agreeable."

Among the small society that so pleased the stately clergyman was a very small replica of himself, Master Timothy Dwight, II, to whom Henry Livingston addressed a little gem of verse that would be hard to parallel in New Haven of that day, where poets did not run to pleasure little boys on their birthdays.

Letter sent to Master Timmy Dwight, 7 yrs old,

Dec. 7, 1785.

Master Timmy, brisk and airy
Blythe as Oberon the fairy,
On thy head thy couzin wishes
Thousand and ten thousand blisses.
Never may thy wicket ball
In a well or puddle fall;
Or thy wild ambitious kite
Oe'r the elm's thick foliage light.
When on bended knee thou sittest
And the mark in fancy hittest,
May thy marble truly trace
Where thy fancies mark'd the place.
If at hide and seek you play
All involved in the hay
Tittering, hear the joyful sound:
"Timmy never can be found."
If you hop or if you run
Or whatever is the fun,
Vict'ry, with her sounding pinion,
Hover o'er her little minion.
But when hunger calls the boys
From their helter-skelter joys,
Bread and cheese in order standing
For their most rapacious handling,
Timmy, may thy luncheon be
More than Ben's as five to three.
But if hasty pudding's dish
Meet thy vast capacious wish,

Or lob-lolly's charming jelly
Court thy cormorantal belly,
Mortal foe to meager fast,
Be thy spoonful first and last!

The poem was printed in the Country Journal in 1787, and suggests that others by the same hand may be sought there.

Dr. Dwight was not so happy when he crossed the Oblong near Sharon. The lonely defile he thought "remarkably disagreeable, and the "dismal swamp" at the bottom was no better. Near the "weekwams at the Indian camp at Schaqticoke the inhabitants are poor, and look as if they were forsaken of mankind."

But the good doctor soon recovered his comfort in quiet Amenia. "I know not where absolute retirement could be found in more inviting circumstances."

Rhinebeck, "everywhere filled up with plantations," and "the inhabitants appear to be in easy circumstances," pleased him no less. He thought the "Kaatskill" mountains varied and fine, and greatly enjoyed "the ever-varying view of that magnificent stream, with the mountains rising majestically."

Dr. Dwight noted that the town of Fishkill, then including practically the whole Rombout patent, had more inhabitants than Poughkeepsie town and village. "The soil of the Fishkill valley is excellent. The stream which flows through it is a large and very sprightly mill-stream, bordered by a chain of rich and elegant intervals, the more delightful to us, as we had seen nothing of this nature since we left Kinderhook. It is not often that beauty and grandeur are so happily combined as in this spot, nor is the sense of stillness and retirement often excited in a higher degree."

But Philipstown pleased our sentimental traveler also. He had feared the mountain road; instead he found a fine pike through the hills, the work of Isaac Van Wyck and Isaac Haight of Fishkill. He liked the Highland people, "many settlements which appeared to be sprightly and promising.

The houses appeared to be neat, and the owners were plainly in very comfortable circumstances."

Other travelers of the period sang their praises of the Dutchess. Thomas Fowler, a few years later, paid it the last compliment: it resembled his native Gloucestershire. But two young carpenters, like him from England, outdid him in their appreciation; not in word, but deed.

They walked from New York to Poughkeepsie; to Albany, Buffalo, and Western Reserve, to the Beaverkill and the Ohio. They rafted down the river to New Orleans, then walked back overland to Washington, thence to Boston. Then, in order to see charming Poughkeepsie once more, they returned to New York by way of Dutchess, and so to the sea, and home. The two young men, twenty and twenty-four years old, thought nothing more attractive anywhere as a village than Poughkeepsie and its shady lanes. One of them, along the way, stopped to paint a hundred and fifty waterfalls, thus evidencing a certain aesthetic taste, at least.

Substantiation of Dwight's estimate of Dutchess' fertility appears in the choice of two other young Englishmen, Thomas and James Vassar, who sailed in 1795 from England in search of good farmland. Though they went from New York to Buffalo they found nothing "to fill their idea of farmland or culture", and were about to turn back for England when they met two good Dutchess salesmen, "Young and Newhouse," and were persuaded to try Wappingers Creek. Here they found their haven. Sunrise Hill gave them pasture, and their herd drank the clear kill water, standing deep in good English fashion. The little English herdboy who drove them was Matthew Vassar.

Years afterwards he recalled "tending the cows with sister Maria in the Wappingers Creek, being no fences to prevent them crossing over to our neighbours—how we amused ourselves, Cutting Willows, making whistles of the rind & fishing with pinhooks in the limpid flowing stream—how we waided need deep on its sloping banks how a huge water-snake chased us—how in fishing we caught *not* a tartar but an immense snapping Turtle, how we cut off his head to get the hook out of his mouth, and ten days after saw the creature crawling about headless at the bottom of the cristal waters."

Matthew always had an eye for the thrill. On the voyage over he remembered "Sea sickness, the waves breaking over the vessel, sweeping me from the companion-way to the Lard-board side of the Ship, loosing my new London bought hat, and just escaping a watery grave."

Recuperating from a second attack of "typhus" the little boy "walked out with rude made crutches to a Hickory Tree near the house to gather nutts, under which was strewed black, broken, and crooked limbs, & one appearing to my dim vision more smooth & tapering I reached to pick it up, when, lo, on touching it flew from me, It was a monstrous Black Snake. Unlike the Brazen Serpent, It frightened but did not Kill, I lingered many days.

"Following this incident I remember ascending the summit of a Hill lying west of the Hudson with my sister Jemima and child—like chinning up on the top of a tree to look at the Po! Church Steeples (in the intervening space lies the now College grounds this plot of level land was well known as the Dutchess County Club Horse-Race-Course, associated by a Charter with the Long Island Club Horse-Race Society for the Promotion of the Breed of Horses. I remember attending one of these former races with a Gentleman acquaintance by the name of "Brush" who came with his Lady to my house, but as the amusement brot together many Gamblers and Black-Legs it was not regarded verry Respectible, so I hired a close Carrage, and went out with them to avoid being seen by as few as possible.

"It was during this period of my boyhood I had many wandering thoughts—Had a fancy for shows, comical exhibitions, fitted up in the Garret of the house a rude Theatre had quite a Corps of Children actors. This fancy took my mind by seeing a performance in the Village.

"I was also found of painting, Bot me a small Box of water

colours painted rude Christmas pieces filled them up with doggery Rhimes and went in the Country to sell them, Remember selling one to old Richard Davis Lower Landing who gave me a Crown Spanish Piece for it."

The boy's town thus described was just like every other village in America, a wonderful place to grow up in. Its lanes were the only school Matthew ever attended, though for a short time he went to night school under "old Gabriel Ellison, had a fracas with him, because he struck me over the head with a round heavy Ruler, flooring me, how I got up and sent an Ink Stand at his Yellow Breeches, besmeering his White Cotton Stockings to a pepper and Salt colour. Left school under L. B. Van Kleeks Great Coat when School was dismissed at noon. Quite a Rumpus was made by this event, how Father insisted my returning to School, how Mother interceeded for me and finaly sent me to John Harbottle's Night School in Union St. So sum it all up between my own temper and fathers severity & indifference to giving me an Education I got none—Scarcely to read & write."

Matthew Vassar's "temper" turned out to be his fortune. Two or three years after the inkbottle he ran away from home because he would not be apprenticed to a tanner. "Started privately on my journey and on Monday May 8th, set off to seek my fortune with 6/ in my pockett, two corse East India Muslin Shirts, a pair of Wollen Socks, Sow Skin Shoes, all tied up in a Cotton Bandana handkerchief."

His mother knowing his determination furthered it, and walked with him to the ferry at New Hamburg. An old gentleman befriended him on the other shore of the River, and thus the first citizen of Poughkeepsie began his upward march to affluence.

President of the Farmers and Manufacturers Bank, a director of the Savings Bank, heading the subscription list to build the Hudson River Railroad, leader of the Improvement, stockholder in two whaling companies, with sloops sailing from his landing to the West Indies for supplies to the brewery, Matthew Vassar's complete independence and originality of thought led him at fifty to commit the unprecedented act of retiring from business and consuming ten years in deciding how to spend his money, and ten years more in launching his great idea—Vassar College. That story belongs to a later era. But nowhere else outside the all too few pages of reminiscence can the picture of old Poughkeepsie be found.

On the Dutchess countryside, with its ample farms averaging over a hundred acres, there was no need of greater population. Farming was not intensive, nor were the soils too rapidly exhausted. Sheep and cattle abounded. Banks were founded to handle the business, one from New York, a branch of the Bank of Manhattan, one by charter from the State, the Middle District Bank.

Machinery began to enroll its workers. Invention lured the ingenious. But even more, the importation of new plants, new breeds, new products suggested an endless possibility of improvement. In fact this word became the refrain of the age, taking in every meaning. Mrs. Maturin Livingston lamented that one of her daughters had "practically no improvements," by which she meant the arts of the new drawingrooms.

These conditions prevailed everywhere in New York, rapidly taking its place as "the seat of Empire," in Washington's phrase.

People were beginning to think that, upon the whole, city life was more agreeable, though less bountiful, than life on the most prosperous farm. Already the city began to lure folks bent on a holiday. The Bartows of Brinckerhoff would make it in a day, taking a week to see the sights and get dresses; then back over the hills in another day's ride of sixty miles behind a sprightly team. This was years later, but typical of an old-established custom.

Among the pioneers who found fortune in the city was Cornelius DuBois of Fishkill, son of Peter and Mary (Van Voorhees) DuBois and stepson of Dr. 'Dorus Van Wyck. The proud and self-reliant boy resented the doctor's strict ways. He had read Benjamin Franklin's autobiography, and caught the likeness to his own case. So at fifteen, and with his mother's encouragement, he said goodby to his half-dozen brothers and half-brothers, and landed in the great city of fifty thousand in 1786 with nothing but a letter to Dr. VanBeuren of Flatbush.

In five years he was a partner with Isaac Kip in wholesale supplies, in ten years he bought out his partner, and for over forty years on Water and Front Streets handled the produce of Dutchess County for his farmer friends. A successful man, he was a trustee of a dozen charitable institutions. His wife's gifts alone, according to his calculation, were over a hundred thousand dollars. In later years a Dutchess man, Isaac A. Storm, was his partner. He died in 1846.

His letters to his brother Coert DuBois, a farmer in Dutchess, give a good impression of the busy merchant, not too busy to help other boys get a good start in the city. He advises his nephew Thomas not to go into business without more experience, but when his advice is not taken he helps the lad over his tight places. He goes shares with his brother in raising merino sheep, the current craze.

In 1812 he writes his brother: "I have a Negro Boy for sale, and think he may suit you—about 17 years. Strong healthy, and of the best disposition, but wants a master to keep him at his work. He is bred in thc country, and accustomed to Labor —but unsuitable as a house servant (except washing and scrubbing)—I gave 200 Dols and will take the same—he says he wants to live in the country—he has no idea of freedom."

On July 4, 1812, he noted with satisfaction that his uncle "the Squire" is as great a Demo as ever", but his brother has nearly given up the party.

"How any intelligent man, or good Christian man, can longer adhere to this abhominable and destructive war, is not very easy for me to imagine.—By the by, if peace is not soon made, we shall all be in danger in this City, for Britten has it now in her power to lay our Cities on the sea coasts in ashes, this City certainly lays at this moment at the mercy of the Enmy, and my family perhaps before Winter may have to seek an assylum elsewere.

If our Government in their madness are determined not to give up the principal of allowing our Vessels searched for British subjects (naturalized) this war will be waged on the part of Gt Britten with greater vigor than heretofore—and this fall, I think will determine, a peace on honorable terms (which I never doubted the British were willing to give) or a renewed War which may bring us to the last hopes of the nation."

# 36. Shire Town. 1799

IT WILL BE RECALLED that during eighteen years, from June 24th, 1719, to December 16th, 1737, Dutchess County had three Wards; the South, including the High Lands and up to Wappingers Kill; the Middle, from the Kill to Kline Sopus Island, a mile below Staatsburg; and the North to the present boundary. At the division of Beekman and Nine Partners, in 1737 a new plan was adopted of seven precincts:

South, the High Lands; Rombout, the Rombout Patent south of Wappingers Kill; Beekman, the Beekman Patent; Poughkeepsie, the patents north of Wappingers Kill and south of Nine Partners; Crum Elbow, Nine Partners, Fauconniers (Hyde Park) patents, to Kline Sopus; Rynbeck, Pawlings Purchase, Kipsbergen (Roosa and Co.) Beekman's Upper Patent, Schuyler Upper Patent (Red Hook); North East, the Upper Nine Partners.

The original precincts were thus run strictly along the old Patent lines.

On December 17th, 1743, the newly organized Oblong was annexed to the precincts bordering on its western line.

The influx of settlers from New England led to the division of Crum Elbow, on March 20, 1762, into Charlotte, the western, and Amenia, the eastern part. Seven years later, after Colonel Beekman's death, Beekman followed suit, on May 20th, 1769. Pawling was then named for his sister, the remainder kept under his own name.

On March 13th, 1786, special honor was done to the popular Governor in Clinton Town including the whole of Crum

Elbow Precinct. Two years later, included in the comprehensive Township Act of March 7th, 1788, "towns" were substituted for precincts, and Rhinebeck, Northeast, Clinton, Amenia, Washington (set off from Amenia), Poughkeepsie, Fishkill (the Rumbout), Pawling, and Amenia. The South precinct included Philipstown, the great western area, Fredrickstown, in the East, Southeast, and the Oblong. In 1795 Carmel, Frederick (later Kent), and Franklin (now Patterson) were set off from Frederickstown and Southeast. Putnam Valley later was set off from Philipstown.

Pressure continued, however, for further division. A general standard had been adopted for central and western New York, (and later through the North-East Territory) of six miles square for a town. Dutchess, with twenty towns and a city and an incorporated village, now approximates this average, with about forty miles to the town.

To bring this about, Stanford was first set off from Clinton, March 12th, 1793. Hyde Park followed January 20th, 1821, Pleasant Valley January 26th, and Freedom on February 29th of the same year. Union Vale followed, March 1st, 1827, the rest of Freedom becoming LaGrange, 1828.

Little Nine Partners set off Milan, March 10th, 1818, and Pine Plains, March 26th, 1823.

East Fishkill finally got free on November 29th, 1849, and Wappingers, May 20th, 1875.

Of the lower area on the River, Fishkill had become the natural center. As migration westward increased, the road from Bulls Bridge to Fishkill Landing became a chief avenue of approach. The ferry to Newburgh, already active in war days, now became perhaps the busiest on the River. Rapidly increasing settlement of the former Philipse Patent, now sold in fee, brought in a thrifty and independent addition in the valleys, who liked the shops in Fishkill, and thought Poughkeepsie too far away. Fishkill Town, including almost all of the old Rombout Patent, was considerably larger in population than Poughkeepsie Town, and more productive.

It was time, indeed, for the little village to bestir itself. When Governor Clinton's School Act was passed in 1795, the allotment of public school moneys to the three chief towns of the county were:

| | £ | s. | d |
|---|---|---|---|
| Fishkill | 267 | 12 | 3 |
| Rhinebeck | 216 | 5 | 3 |
| Poughkeepsie | 152 | 1 | 6 |

The village could boast only one drygoods store, one grocery store, a hardware, a lumber, and a "general" store at the Landing. There was also a small hat factory. There seems to have been no regular ferry before 1798.

The slow growth of the town may partly be accounted for by the large farms that hemmed the little neighborhood on the town roads. A map of 1770 shows the whole area north of the Fallkill to have been held in one man's name, the Scot Leonard Lewis. Practically the whole north side of Main Street was in the ownership of six men.

The passage, by the state legislature at a Poughkeepsie session, of the County and Town Acts in 1788 was the first real danger signal. The State meant business, it appeared, and was prepared to divide any slothful county or town that was not measuring up to its responsibilities. With the act went many changes in the towns of Dutchess. The village Road Commissioners straightened out some of the roads approaching the village, though there was never any thoroughfare north and south,—nor is there now. But the village remained till the turn of the century in the hands of a few proprietors, for the most part.

Henry Livingston, the county clerk, and his brother James, the county sheriff, got possession of most of the south tract, from the Killetje Cove. Bartholomew Crannell, the village's leading attorney for the quarter-century before the Revolution, and son-in-law of Peter Van Kleeck, got most of Main

Street on both sides from Crannell Street and Catherine Street, named for him and his daughter. His sons-in-law, Dr. Peter Tappen, Gilbert Livingston, and Rev. John Beardsley, were given, or obtained, a great area along Main Street to the east, as far as the village extended. Beardsley alone had a hundred acres or so, and Crannell much more. Both the reverend gentleman and his medical brother-in-law went also into politics. Crannell kept Poughkeepsie in the Tory way until the very last minute, while Tappen held several offices in the opposite party, including one as alternate on the Committee to Detect Conspiracies. Yet he and his brother-in-law Livingston joined amicably to buy in their father-in-law's property, and aided the old Tory to recover some of it.

Further south, another county officer, Henry Vanderburgh, acquired a great property. Smaller parcels were retained by the heirs of the first settlers, Van de Bogart, Van Kleeck, and Sanders. The large landowners farmed their properties, for the land was rich (Winnikee, rich land) along the Fall Kill. There Crannell owned his big mill, which he claimed had the greatest promise in the state.

To these facts may perhaps be attributed the slow growth of the village, and the still slower planning of the lesser streets. As late as 1770 there was scarcely more than a cross-roads at the courthouse. The village officers did not even trouble to straighten the King's Highway, which turned left and right at the Court-house, (and continued to do so until the time of the late honored James Sague). It may be noted in passing, that the earliest club in Poughkeepsie was called "The Deliberating Society."

The real impetus to expansion of the village came with Governor Clinton in 1776, and the legislature in 1777. When the courthouse burned in 1785, the legislature did not return till 1788, when Peter Tappen's fine building, remembered in the design of the present Post Office, had been completed. This building burned in turn in 1806.

The County and Township Acts were adopted at Poughkeepsie. So, too, Poughkeepsie may claim to have fostered the first act for education, for it was at the village in January, 1795, that Governor Clinton recommended an act for the encouragement of schools by state aid. The legislature passed the bill at an adjourned session in New York City. Under this act £2,100 were voted for use in Dutchess County, and not long after a "school lot" is printed on the map, at the southeast corner of Church and Market Streets.

The Dutchess County Academy, incorporated by the Regents of the University of the State, gave its dignified name to Ragged Lane in 1791 or shortly after. It made no difference to the boys, who no doubt still went barefoot. The Academy, later transferred to Hamilton Street, served the boys until 1866, when it reopened as a public High School with the transfer of the Free School from Church Street.

A few small schools for girls were started, and advertised in the press. But for many years girls' education remained a family matter. Those that had any education were sometimes well trained, and would have laughed at Mary Ball's or Catheryna Brett's spelling. For the greater number the harsh criticism of William Smith was still true, that the ignorance of women must remain the greatest deterrent to the fair fame of New York.

Incorporated on March 27th, 1799, the village adopted its rules, only to be reincorporated, through some technical oversight of its untried officers, on April 18th, 1801. Minutes were kept from 1803, when a market, a pound, and a fire house were listed. The County jail was sufficient. In 1807 the market, on the southeast corner, was moved to the west side of Market Street (the center of the present street) and continued there in some form for many years.

Slow progress wrought out the village gridiron on time's anvil. In 1800 Main Street, which up to that time had ended at the Court House, was extended to the Hudson. Mill Street was extended to the winding road to the Upper Landing and Livingston's mill. Union Street and Pine Street took travelers to the lower landings at the Killetje. Clover Street connected with all these. All of them, according to the travelers' accounts, were well shaded, and boasted lovely gardens, the best being those by the Fallkill from Mill Street. Here the Dutch love of gardens outdid itself.

By 1806 there were at least thirty named thoroughfares, and the pattern of the early city was fully laid. Most of the growth was at first on the new streets running parallel with the river and west of Market Street. The river view, unobstructed by warehouses, enhanced the charm of the lanes with their young trees, while pleasant strolls ran by the mill-ponds and their splashing overfalls. Toiling wagon-teams plodding up from the sloops did not diminish their charm, nor the white sails scudding down the busy stream.

The Dutchess Turnpike was opened in 1804, the Highland Turnpike about 1806, the Beekman and Pawling Turnpike about 1812 (Manchester Road). A pike also went Northeast to Salt Point. Five mills were using Fallkill water power by the close of the period; a saw mill, two grist mills, a nail factory and a plaster works. George Booth's woolen mill stood near a pond, where pins were later made. A cotton mill was a little farther up. First at Vassar Street, then on the river dock, was James Vassar's, later his son Matthew's Brewery. It was burned in 1811 and the father, shaken by his elder son's loss, turned the business over to the energetic second son.

Teunis Van Kleeck's advertisements of his hat factory begin in 1808. A score of shops and small factories filled Main Street, making good the chosen seal of the village, a beehive.

Platt quotes Spofford's 1812 Gazetteer as listing seven public buildings, five churches, 471 houses and stores in a village of 3,000. The Dutch Reformed church was oldest by fifty years. Then came an Episcopal church, revived after the Revolution, (though never wholly closed in the war), a Methodist in 1805, the work of Freeborn Garrettson, and a Baptist in 1807. Vassars were active in the last.

Of the newspapers, the old Country Journal became the Poughkeepsie Journal, later adding "and Constitutional Republican." From 1801 a second paper, the Guardian, next year the Political Barometer, the Barometer in 1805, in 1811 the Republican Herald. All these were Republican, but only in 1806 was the County of that color, owing to a division of Federalist sentiment caused by Hamilton's death and Burr's defection. From 1808 to 1812 Federalists carried the county, becoming more outspoken against the French and for the English.

The Journal was purchased by Bowman, Parsons, and Paraclete Potter, the latter purchasing sole control in 1815. This interesting man, and his still more brilliant family lent color to the local scene. Of Episcopal faith, they came of old Quaker stock, which furnished the town with its postmaster McKeen, the shipbuilder Southwick, the trader Valentine Baker, and many others of its leading men. Quaker thought greatly affected the sentiments of the town.

The cultural change in the quarter-century between the adoption of the Constitution and 1812 was probably the most rapid of the century. The people of the earlier periods had been content with survival; now, all of a sudden, they sought a complete life; in society, in art and science, in outlook upon the world. What happened in Dutchess was only a microcosm of the greater world.

France under Napoleon made her great bid for world empire, until England's alliances drew the noose tight upon her. In the United States the Federalists sided in sentiment with Great Britain, belittling the discomforts of Orders in Council and the impressment of seamen. The Virginians and Clintonians kept their sympathies for France. George Clinton's daughter married Citizen Genet, and fashions went French in society.

Twice during the period, in 1804 and 1808, the Federalist denunciation of the Government took on almost the note of secession unless hostility toward Britain were tempered. John Jay's treaty with Britain in 1795 excited the greatest antagonism, on the other hand, and marked the first step leading to the Federalist downfall. All this was fought out in our little country paper, and influenced local sentiment. Gradually, out of the welter of opinion, there emerged a Northern and Central Dutchess Federalism that stuck through thick and thin, while the townships of the South were equally Clintonian. Fishkill and Poughkeepsie wavered between the two, though more often Federalist in sentiment. Both towns thought of trade and intercourse first, but were also moved by the more radical sentiments of town workers.

Yet most of this conflict came home to the County only when it affected a local issue. The people of Dutchess were deeply engaged in the full flowering of their region. Starting late, handicapped by delay in the division of patents, molested by aggression in the east, and threatened with war to the north, the Dutchess's County had been pinched back, the last of the old Provincial areas, until suddenly with power released it had outdistanced its competitors. In 1800 Dutchess stood first in the state, in the success of her agriculture and the promise of her manufacture and trade.

One-third of all the flour shipped to New York came from Dutchess, and her mills ground more than any other. Throughout the period the breeding of horses spread rapidly. In the years 1806 and 1807 sloops carried large cargoes of horses to New York for export. In 1807 a high pedigreed bull was advertised. In 1807 Robert R. Livingston, Jr., in a contribution to the Country Journal, announced the success of his breeding merino with other sheep, and claimed that three to four times the profit could be obtained from fleeces of the half-merino stock. His wool had all been sold to George Booth, an English arrival who had married Matthew Vassar's sister, and had set up the first carding machines, it was claimed, in the country.

A whole fleet of sloops was employed in the river trade of the Dutchess landings. The Davis landing mentioned by Dr. Dwight was only one of a half dozen at Poughkeepsie. There were five at Hyde Park alone. Landings in Fishkill, Wappingers, and Rhinebeck were equally active. The building of sloops and schooners increased at Low Point (Chelsea), Poughkeepsie, and Rhinebeck.

Many of the sloops bore the names of admired leaders of Dutchess. Samuel W. Hopkins of Litchfield came in 1791 to Poughkeepsie, finding it easier to reach New York in this way. "I embarked at Poughkeepsie in the good sloop 'John Jay' and soon saw the wonderful city, the compact parts of which extended up to St. Paul's Church and then up Chatam Street to the Tex Water Pump, or nearby."

The Hudson River sloop was about 100 tons' capacity, and less than 75 feet in length. It had a high quarter-deck, and the mast was well forward, allowing a large sail. The jib was small. The packet sloops sailed fast, often reaching Dutchess in seven or eight hours. Their broad deck was good for parties and dances, and the voyage was a favorite diversion for everyone.

In the flyleaf of W. E. Verplanck's "Sloops of the Hudson", at the New York Public Library, is pasted a letter from John Bigelow of Malden, once Ambassador to Russia, who stated that in his youth he could count from his house, at one time, more than a hundred sail on the river. The old fashioned paintings of the river dotted with the little ships were no artist's fancies, but purely realistic.

Mr. Verplanck's co-author was Captain Moses W. Collyer of the famous river family of Low Point, who was a river captain for half a century. By 1806 sloops sailed on regular schedules for New York and Albany. The "horse ferry" was started at New Hamburg in 1803. Earlier ferries were rowed.

In the early days before the river channel was kept clear, or buoys posted, sailing in the river required pilots of skill and experience, as tides were treacherous and storm-gusts sudden. The annals of the sloops are full of losses, especially in the Worragut above Constitution Island, and the reaches above Crum Elbow.

Along the river grew up a seafaring population, for the larger sloops and schooners did not hesitate to sail the Coast, or even to the West Indies. Fishing, too, employed many; shad by the barrel were advertised in the Journal, and Albany beef (sturgeon) was a brisk article.

Booth's Mill, like the Vassar brewery, was built on the shore near the Upper Landing. Other factories joined them there; an iron foundry, a nail mill, as well as Gilbert Livingston's flour mills.

In 1807 the voyage of the "Clermont" was a Dutchess picnic. Not only did the little steamboat skirt fifty miles of county shore, but at Staatsburg the Maturin Livingstons boarded the craft, adding greatly to the gaiety and beauty of the passengers. Eight lovely Livingstons were the chief attraction. Harriet Livingston, daughter of Walter of Teviotdale, and sister of Robert, who married the Chancellor's daughter, was introduced at Clermont as the betrothed of the young inventor, Robert Fulton, Chancellor Livingston himself making the dramatic disclosure. The famous lawyer was never in happier vein. His long series of experiments and failures, first with John Fitch, then with the young Scotch inventor, was now crowned with success.

But for a dozen years steam was to remain supplementary on the river. Two hundred sloops plied its waters, bringing cargoes from fifty to two hundred tons swiftly and cheaply to every little landing in the river. The great river trade was soon to be increased four-fold by the canal system. To Christopher Colles must go the credit for the first suggestion. His maps of county roads are useful and accurate. The Napoleonic wars abroad and repressive measures at home, aroused widespread discontent in England after 1795, and promoted emigration. Of the list of naturalized citizens in Dutchess about this time, the great majority were English weavers. George Booth, and his friends Thomas and James Vassar, were typical imports of the day. Thomas Fenner, with his handsome place Richmond Park (College Hill), did his best to show countians what an English country estate looked like. The name Richmond Hill clings to another drumlin today.

The English immigrants brought new machinery and new farming methods, and added to the favor in which public opinion held the British cause against the French excesses. John Jay's treaty of 1795, heavily favoring Britain, was praised, while Jefferson was denounced.

French influences were also at work. Refugees from the Terror came to Dutchess, joining the many descendants of Huguenot days to make an agreeable seasoning of the Dutchess pudding. Richard De Cantillon's landing was one of the most active on the River. Half a dozen families settled in Red Hook.

The Dutchess did not reach her heyday in this period, but certainly the dawn appeared. Another quarter century, and Dutchess production would astonish her oldest inhabitant, with a thousand hogs in a single barge, and as many as 20,000 cattle passing down the Harlem Valley to market in a single day. This would last till 1840, when mass production in the West would overtake the local farms, while fertility here would decrease. But for the time being New York with Vermont would furnish nearly half the sheep in the country, and Dutchess would top the list.

Only in the light of this production would her sudden leap into pivotal importance as the political center of the nation explain New York, and rationalize the extraordinary output of political figures of the day in what were called at the time "the Poughkeepsie Schools of Law."

In 1799 the growth of the village led to its incorporation. The charter, printed in the state laws, was adopted on March 27. The essential feature of the incorporation was the board of village trustees, elected annually by the freeholders. Five assessors, a collector, a treasurer, and five wardens were also elected.

To the trustees were given powers of regulation and supervision. Town constables remained the only police, however.

The boundaries of 1799 remained for a hundred years and more. The maps of Poughkeepsie, village and town, and the other maps of the Dutchess towns all by Henry Livingston, Jr., are beautiful pieces of surveying, and a joy to use in the volumes of the Historical Society.

Oddly, as it seems now, Main Street did not go down to the

river dock at first. The Kaal Rock Landing was reached by a road branching off from what is now Mill Street. The lower landing was reached by Pine Street and Union Street. Main Street ended at Washington Street, North Road, while Market Street (South Road) fed Union and Pine and Montgomery Street. Scarcely a home stood upon what is now Hooker Avenue, or the Creek Road (Crom Elbow Creek). From its beginning as a "rest place" for runners along the river trail, Poughkeepsie had been chiefly a station on the King's Highway between New York and Albany. Stores, inns, and offices lined Market Street along this road, while dwellings extended up Main Street, a name which did not exist before this period.

But as agriculture and the river traffic increased, the east-west avenue won its way, and the village expanded to northeast and southeast with Main Street as its division line. Law still monopolized the vicinity of the courthouse. Kent, Bailey, Emott, Oakley, Livingston and others resided within a hundred yards of it. The market stalls and pavilions filled the center of the street, and farmers' wagons piled their loads here. But stores moved up Main Street, in a traditional Dutchess fashion still practised. first as a front addition, then as the ground floor of a house, and finally taking over the whole dwelling.

Edmund Platt tells how Levi McKeen, postmaster on Main St. east of Liberty, stopped a run on the private bank he maintained by unloading a wagon filled with small kegs at his door. "Two men struggled into the building through the crowd of anxious depositors and noteholders, carrying one of the kegs, which at the proper moment slipped from their fingers and burst, scattering coins in every direction." All the other kegs were later said to contain nails, but the burst keg stopped the run."

A circulating library was started about this time, the proprietors holding one of their annual meetings on July 17th, 1806.

While the Poughkeepsie Journal flourished under Paraclete Potter, the Democratic-Republican press did not do so well.

The county was conservative, too, in its response to the great migration from New England. Not until 1802 were the first steps taken, and for long after this date the highways connecting with the east were in bad condition.

Not until after 1800, when Poughkeepsie finally decided to name its streets officially, did its main thoroughfares meet the turnpikes. The Dutchess Turnpike, chartered in 1802, was initiated by men with larger connections: Dr. Thomas Tillotson of Rhinebeck, a surgeon of the Revolution who had married Margaret Livingston was the chairman. Peter J. Schuyler, Daniel C. Verplanck, Edward Livingston and Jacob Radcliffe, made up the imposing company. It did not meet plain sailing, however, and several supplementary acts were required to get it in motion. Three years later it was open, at least in part. Indignant farmers had held riotous massmeetings about it, a Shunpike had been started in the cantankerous Nine Partners, and protests were filed against its invasion of valuable orchards. But it got through at last, with branches to Dover and Sharon, though it never became a favored route of the pioneers. The Highland Pike was in operation about the same time, and by 1806 actually controlled Market Street, according to the street commissioners.

The Great North Pike to Montreal was begun in 1806, a most ambitious project. The Beekmans and Pawling Turnpike was completed by 1811, too late to save the county from division. The Sepasco road on the old trail to Salisbury, and the road from Dover to Fishkill had been longer travelled, but were difficult going over the Ridge. Stages followed the tollpikes almost as soon as they were open. A few plank-roads were tried, one of them the road to New Hackensack, a shortcut to Wappingers Falls and Beekmans, but its planks soon rotted out. Colles' map, however, in 1799, showed it as the road to New Haven.

The Pikes were great boons to the farmers, and Poughkeepsie's growth as a river town was chiefly due to them. But although the state gave them its sanction, the capital was in almost every case derived from private sources. They were the first great ventures in which the right of eminent domain was asserted by the state; they opened the path for the railroads. Timothy Dwight and Thomas Fowler expressed appreciation of them, from which one may infer that they were superior in maintenance to their connections in neighboring counties.

# 37. The Great Split. 1812

THE TOWNS of the Dutchess Highlands followed rather closely the lines of the Philipse Patent's division arranged by William Livingston, as attorney for the heirs of Frederick Philipse. Philipstown and Putnam Valley shared the western lots. The central lots included Kent and Carmel, while Franklin (later Patterson) and Southeast took most of the eastern tier and the Oblong.

From a rough count of the 1800 census it appears that not more than 2% of the Highlanders were of Dutch origin. Except for the Scots names in the Patterson neighborhood, they seemed wholly of New England stock. From 5,900 in 1790 to over 10,000 in 1910, the ratio of growth was much faster than in northern Dutchess.

So long as Matthew Patterson's influence prevailed, the sentiment in the upper towns was loyal to Dutchess. This worthy Scot, a merchant of some means, had purchased a substantial property in Fredericksburgh, and immediately became a leader. His son John married Sarah Livingston, and his daughter married Harry Livingston. John was a supervisor and in 1804 a member of Assembly. In 1797 and again in 1798 the town of Kent had voted unanimously "that Dutchess remain in its present situation without any division," and had so instructed its Assemblyman to report.

This reply may have been made to an enquiry from Albany rather than from any discontent within the county at the time. It was an era of change, and all over the state counties and towns were undergoing realignment to meet the needs of the waves of migration. If the turnpikes had been built ten years earlier there might have been no division. But the leaders of the growing towns began to be restive under the dominance of the powerful group of attorneys at the shire town.

A sharp division in political opinions had begun to assert itself between the Highlands and central Dutchess. Federalism still held sway in the north and center, while the south, borrowing perhaps from the radicalism of western Connecticut, supported George Clinton and his Democratic Republicanism against the landlords. A certain isolationist sentiment kept its people from mingling with the older stocks. Their trade was mainly with Danbury, and their river traffic with Cold Spring and Peekskill. On the other hand, the old Dutch stock recalled the Tory troubles of the Oblong and its Spy Lane.

Thus there was more than met the eye in a letter printed in the Journal on May 10, 1803.

"To the enquiry made at the Poll of the late election in Pawling by—Inspector and others, "Who the D - l is this Henry Van der Burgh?"—This Henry Vanderburgh, Sir, is a respectable freeholder in the Town of Clinton, and is a descendant of an ancient and respectable family in Dutchess, his father was Col. James Vanderburgh, late of the Town of Beekman in Dutchess, whose commissions civil and military, bore equal date with "the times that tried men's souls" it is, Sir, the same Henry Vanderburgh that served as an officer in Col. Du Bois' regiment in the American Revolutionary Army, it is the same Henry Vanderburgh, Sir, that was wounded in a battle with the Tories and Indians at the Northward, when Capt. Brown and some others with whom I suppose you was not acquainted, fell fighting for American Independence. I have now informed you who Henry Vanderburgh is—now, pray, Sir, who the D - l are you?

Spectator

May 10 1803"

Some of the dissatisfaction seems to have been attributed to the persistence of the old patent lines in Dutchess, which had neither the justification of geography or economics. A writer in September, 1804, asked a complete revision in the town bounds of the Beekman and Rombout lands. He urged the adoption of a standard of six miles square, such as Vermont then enjoyed. On this plan five new towns would replace Beekman, Fishkill, and Pawling. Two years later as if in response, Dover was taken off from Pawling, while in later years East Fishkill, Lagrange, and Union Vale would complete this early plan.

The road problem was well urged in a letter dated November, 1805. Signed "A Beekman-Town Farmer," the writer very reasonably put his case for better roads to east and west. "If a road was sufficiently worked from Poughkeepsie in the most suitable direction to the intersection of the new road from Pawlings through the Mountains to Beekman and the improvement continued to Bull's Bridge it would become the shortest and best market road for the people generally of those extended and populous country places, where as the rough hilly course and zigzag direction of the present road prevents the people from going to market unless an extraspecial need renders it compatible with their views. The more business can be brought to this centre the more a good market will be accelerated. There is now a good road from Hartford to Bull's Bridge. Many now bend their course to Peekskill or SingSing, choosing a circuitous route in preference to the rough road through Pawlings and Beekmans."

But the Board of Supervisors were more concerned with keeping the home market away from Hartford than with all the profit accruing from the Great Migration from New England, now in full swing. The shire town was content to hold the trump cards of the new pikes leading to Poughkeepsie, the courthouse, and the County Clerk's office. Then, suddenly, a reasonable accommodation in geography was interpreted as an act of historical aggression, and two misfortunes brought Dutchess pride in the dust.

On March 14th, 1806, the Legislature allocated to Fishkill the northwest corner of the town of Philipstown. North of

Breakneck Mountain the river shore was practically inaccessible except by water, and in winter over the ice, if thick enough. On the other hand all the farmers in the triangle did their business in Fishkill, and some of them were very substantial producers. But Philipstown of course objected to the loss in taxes, and deplored this destruction of old bounds; forgetting that this very land had been won in a most unjust lawsuit by the Philipse heirs. But what was to prevent Pawling from laying its hand on the Prendergast farm?

So, at Franklin (Patterson) on November 6, 1806, it was voted unanimously that the County of Dutchess ought to be divided into two counties. On November 14 Samuel Towner of Franklin, Stephen Hayt, and Stephen Barnum prepared a letter for circulation throughout the county. This was signed also by John Hayt of Philipstown and John Patterson of Franklin. The younger generation was in action.

The Fishkill grab was not the only provocation for this radical step. On September 14th, 1806, died Gilbert Livingston, Clerk of the County of Dutchess, a man widely respected, and, if we may believe his eulogium, even loved. For some reason Morgan Lewis, Governor of New York and a resident of Red Hook, failed to appoint his successor.

Then on September 25th of the same year the Dutchess Courthouse, famous as the scene of the ratification of the Federal Constitution, burned to the ground. Optimistic examiners of the ruins thought it might be rebuilt upon the same foundations, with its cellar-jail. Others who had perhaps shared its accommodations thought otherwise.

At a meeting in Poughkeepsie not long after the fire, a subscription list was proposed, to start the movement for Poughkeepsie's fourth courthouse. At this juncture Levi McKeen, a well-to-do merchant and the postmaster, offered a lot for the new building, eight times as large and on high ground, as a better site than the market-place of the village. Unfortunately his lot lay to the north of the village. It started people talking.

The trouble with legal business was that it was too far already, without moving it any further north. The writers of the Franklin petition referred to "an almost unanimous petition" to the legislature that had been ignored. It had asked the magistrates might acknowledge, and town clerks record, the transfer of real estate through deeds without reference to Poughkeepsie.

Still the county seat just sat tight. It was a fatal attitude in the new America. It had a case, but it did not present it. No one of all its brilliant lawyers sprang to its defence, or undertook pacification by promises of new roads or a better traveling service to be afforded by the office of the County Clerk, or by any other concession. The defence was simply, that Poughkeepsie knew best.

Within two months after the first signed letter every town in Dutchess had acted. At first it looked as though the movement would sweep the whole county. Rhinebeck and Fishkill were particularly enthusiastic, anticipating a transfer to their villages of the two courthouses. Some wit took the wind out of their sails by proposing that the neighborhood of Shanadore (Shenandoah) be chosen for the lower courthouse, as the exact center of the south county; and that "the Pine Plains be the site of the north courthouse. Both were on flat lands, accessible by good roads to all."

Rhinebeck soon changed its mind, but Fishkill, Clintonian by temperament, kept longer with the malcontents. Washington and Amenia, with their good pike, stood fast for Poughkeepsie.

Meantime, after the spate of massmeetings, the legislature took up the petition. The senate voted in March, 1807, by 16 to 13 for the division. In the House the measure was considered in committee of the whole, and approved by 48 to 47. Next day, March 4th, the vote in the assembly to pass the bill was 49 to 49, when the Speaker cast the deciding ballot against it, and Dutchess' life was reprieved. A bill authorizing the county in 1809 to build a new courthouse was defeated by a large majority. The Journal reported that all who voted to reject it were "Tompkinsonians."

From this time on the contest was political. Clinton's men were for the division, others against. The gubernatorial campaign waned. Lewis lost stature by declaring himself completely neutral in the matter. Meantime Pawling was divided into two towns, thus keeping the matter of division before the people.

In the election Tompkins carried Southeast, Philipstown, Carmel, Franklin, and Fishkill, but lost Frederick by ten votes. Division votes in all his towns were carried. In the state Tompkins won handsomely, and division seemed inevitable.

To please Fishkill the 1808 bill carried the division line from the mouth of the Wappingers straight east to Connecticut. Fishkill was made the county seat, while the northern fragment was given Stanford for the courthouse. This was plain retaliation. Actually, the Croton Valley people would not be too content with Fishkill, while Stanford was absurd.

At this crisis a group of the more serious-minded started a non-partisan move to save Dutchess. In the ensuing election, the delegation, which had been solidly Lewisite, became divided with two each for Dewitt Clinton, Lewis, and Tompkins. Clinton, who was state senator and party leader, was now removed from his New York mayoralty by the Council in Appointments, to make room for the Poughkeepsian, Smith Thompson.

Dewitt Clinton was in position to wreak any vengeance he pleased on the defenceless county. But his eye was already fixed on greater things, in his own governorship. In four years he was to run for the presidency, and to miss his goal by no more than a fraction of the vote of Pennsylvania.

In committee of the whole assembly the new bill was passed on March 2, 1808 by a vote of 59 to 34, a strictly Clintonian majority. In the senate Clinton moved to postpone, and an order was set for March 22. On that day Clinton's man Barlow moved to discharge the committee, and this was passed. Thus for the second time division had been defeated.

The split election that followed, the non-partisan line-up in the county, and the re-election of George Clinton as vice-president may provide the answer to this puzzle. George Clinton had made his home on the river at Clinton Point, a few miles below Poughkeepsie. His wife's brother was deep in county politics. It is not unlikely that he spoke a word to his nephew that he should not too grievously vex his own future neighbors. Perhaps, too, he remembered the war days, when he had lived so pleasantly in the village.

There is another possible motive. Clinton had made up his mind to try for the nomination to the presidency in 1808. It would be unfortunate for him to have his home neighborhood hostile because of his nephew's retaliations. Madison defeated him, as it turned out, and he continued as vice-president, dying in April, 1912.

The only admission by any Clintonian that the Dutchess deal was politically inspired came from Clinton's man Cheetham, who remarked, "Dutchess' Federal majority is too large and therefore requires the anatomical knife." To this the Journal questioned: "Why should the legislature whose duty it is to provide for the general welfare, be anxious to divide us against our wishes and to the destruction of the best interests of the County?"

Whatever it was, the discussion suddenly ended for four years, except when the legislature refused to go ahead with the erection of a new courthouse. Yet the 1810 elections were very bitter, and the Journal printed a famous attack on Clintonian nepotism with a catechism detailing its extent. Clinton did not invent the spoils system, but he certainly had practised it to a far greater extent than the Chancellor had ever done. Such abuse of nepotism had its reward and deprived both families of the highest posts, as well as of the posthumous fame they had earned. It must be remembered that family succession was much stronger then than now, and no one objected to it in moderation. Meanwhile, as James Kent wrote his brother Moss in 1811, "Democracy is raging in all its fury at the capitol."

From 1810 to 1812 nothing more was heard of the Dutchess' division. Then, in the most troubled times since the Revolution, the legislature took up the matter again. On March 12th, a few days before George Clinton died, a bill was introduced. Poughkeepsie was in the midst of a serious epidemic, probably of cholera, and the Medical Academy had appointed a committee to make researches to find out what it was. The country was on the brink of war with Britain. A Federal victory had just won at the polls. De Witt Clinton had been nominated for President, and Governor Tompkins had just prorogued the legislature, to get them quiet after their battle over the State Bank.

Meeting in May at the end of the prorogued session, the old legislature, with a majority of twenty for the Clintonians, determined to act on Dutchess before the Federalists came in. By a majority of 18, all Clintonians, the division passed the senate, the committee of the whole house, and the assembly, and became a law June 12, 1812.

"We trust our friends in the south will not ask again for a division of Dutchess."

So spoke the young Republican Herald, a Clintonian paper, which had pledged "the conciliatory hand of Concord" in the county, in the hope of shortening her period as "the sport of dissension and for some time the seat of federal triumph."

The Poughkeepsie Journal had nothing to say. The act had been passed over the protest of Jacob Radcliff, who had asked that the affidavits of a number of persons, whose names had been falsely signed to petitions, should be examined.

Dr. Robert Weeks, member of the Assembly from the south towns, was appointed one of the committee to report out the measure to the Assembly. A resident of Carmel, he was credited with having been the active agent in securing the majority of 18. He was not without personal interest, for he immediately sold (or gave) to the new county a halfacre site in the center of Carmel village, on condition that if the lot were at any time sold for another purpose, the property must return to his heirs. In later days, when Putnam tired of Carmel and sought a transfer, this clause blocked the way, and was a high consideration in keeping the courthouse where it stands today.

Thus, in entire peace and good will at last, so far as the

evidence takes us, Putnam County took its place on the River. The newcomer has retained its close relations with Peekskill in Westchester, with Beacon in Dutchess, and with Danbury over the line, but it has also a sprightly tradition of its own, and a thriving interest in things historical, which has been an inspiration to neighboring regions along the Hudson shore.

evidence takes us, Putnam County took its place on the River. The newcomer has retained its close relations with Peekskill in Westchester, with Beacon in Dutchess, and with Danbury over the line, but it has also a sprightly tradition of its own, and a thriving interest in things historical, which has been an inspiration to neighboring regions along the Hudson shore.

# Acknowledgements

THIS book, the product of five years of study, has been written in part payment of obligations incurred during forty years of residence among friends and neighbors in the County of Dutchess. Their enthusiastic participation in my studies has been inspiring. To all who have so indulgently listened to my brief talks about our county —considerably more than a hundred now and still in progress, over Station WEOK—I am most grateful. Those who have attended my courses in county history at Arlington High School's adult programs under Mr. Walter R. Neidhardt, and my hearers in the many addresses given at schools, churches, and clubs, have rewarded me with encouragement and often with materials of historical value.

Outstanding among my students and colleagues at the High School is Mr. Frederick A. Smith, Clerk of Dutchess County, who suggested to me the task of cataloguing fifteen thousand documents of the eighteenth century filed in his offices. With the skilled help of his staff, and particularly Mrs. Lyberta Paquet, this collection has been made available to students. The catalogue, listing over thirty thousand names, is now in use. Reference in this book to many documents quoted by name and date is to this catalogue of ancient documents (A D). I hope at some future time to extend this service among the nineteenth century documents, with Mr. Smith's generous encouragement.

I am deeply indebted to the Dutchess County Historical Society (D C H S), of which I have been a member many years, and am now serving as trustee. Lasting gratitude is due their members, and especially to past members, the late Helen Wilkinson Reynolds and Dr. J. Wilson Poucher, my friends, whose many articles among others I have quoted.

The Franklin Delano Library has kindly permitted me to use the Montresor map in President Roosevelt's collection as the jacket design. Its many courtesies to this reader, and Mrs. Aimée Buchanan's assistance, as curator of the collection of the county historical society, have been warmly appreciated.

I acknowledge with sincere thanks the permission to quote from documents in their collections, or admission to their manuscript rooms, of our great public libraries; the Library of Congress; the New York State Library, Miss Edna Jacobsen of the manuscript room, and the State Historian, my friend Dr. Albert B. Corey; the New York (city) Library, and permission to quote the Gilbert Livingston MSS.; the New York Historical Society, and permission to quote from MSS. relating to the Prendergast uprising; the New York State Historical Association, for permission to quote its publications, and my thanks to Dr. Louis C. Jones and Miss Dorothy Barck, Director and Librarian; the Henry A. Huntington Library of San Marino, California, for photostats from the Chandos letter-books; the New York State Museum, Director Dr. William H. Ritchie; and the Frederick Barnard Memorial Law Library, Poughkeepsie, Mr. G. N. Mahar, Librarian.

Permission to quote has been kindly granted by the University of North Carolina Press, from Carl Bridenbaugh, Gentleman's Progress; the Muhlenberg Press, Philadelphia, The Muhlenberg Journals; Mrs. Martha C. Bayne, County at Large; Mrs. Shirley H. Strong, the Rhinebeck Gazette; Mr. Charles Weygant, The Sacketts of America; The Poughkeepsie New Yorker, Mr. Clifford H. Nuhn, Editor; Barnes and Noble Co., Narratives of New Netherland, Danckaert's Journal; Mrs. Mary Butler Lewis, articles on archeology; Mrs. Emerson D. Fite, the study, still in manuscript, of the Constitutional Convention at Poughkeepsie; Miss Hattie and Miss Ellen Ballard, for permission to quote the deed of Nimham; and my old friend Harry T. Briggs, for the use of his unpublished and published materials on Dutchess sports.

My best thanks are due, for friendly counsel, for loan books and maps and other materials, to my neighbor, the Honorable John A. Mack; Mr. Peter H. Troy; the late Edward E. Perkins; Mr. and Mrs. Orville R. Wright; Mr. and Mrs. J. A. Wallberg; Mrs. John Gilchrist; Miss Mary Taber; Miss Cornelia K. Allen; the Akin Library of Quaker Hill; Mrs. Christie L. Nash, of the Ridgefield, Conn. Library and Historical Association; Rev. Horace E. Hillery, County Historian, for his valued labors in leading history seminars fruitful in scholarship; Miss Ida Bartow; Mrs. W. J. Reagan; Mr. James DeLancey

Verplanck; Mr. Chester Winslow; Mrs. DeWitt Davis; Mr. H. K. Staley for the lost book on Sepasco Lake, (when it shall be found); Mr. Thomas M. Murphy; Miss Genieve Lamson; Mrs. Araminta N. Mahoney; Dr. John Rogers; Mrs. Harry G. Hill; the late Lewis Stoutenburgh Ring, Mr. David Stoutenburgh Ring; Mr. P. E. Bahret; Miss Catherine M. Bacon; Mr. Charles Nutter; Mrs. Catherine Snell Crary; Mr. William Millar; Mr. James H. Shafer; Mr. Almon Beneway: Mrs. W. F. Linder; Mr. Robert L. Hall, curator, State Historical Museum, Madison, Wis.; Mr. John DuBois Freer; Mr. Lewis Ludington Young; Mr. Chester Eisenhuth.

I am greatly indebted to friends of the Vassar Faculty and of much experience in the ways of history and other matters: Miss Violet Barbour; Mrs. Mary Landon Sague; Miss Vera B. Thomson; Miss Florence McCaleb; Mrs. Keene Richards; Mrs. Evangeline Darrow; Mrs. Julia C. VanDeWater; Mr. Richard A. E. Brooks; Miss Jane T. Swenarton; Miss Marion Bacon; Miss Eileen Thornton; Miss Luella R. Pollock; Miss Mary Lee McDonald; Mr. Carl H. Degler; Miss Helen Garrett; Miss Helen Pendleton Wheeler, Mrs. Clarice H. L. Pennock.

Mrs. Mary Doyle has skillfully deciphered my painful scrawl. Mrs. Marie M. Tompkins (Mrs. Elijah Tompkins) has worked throughout the period of composition as documentary analyst, bringing order out of chaos. Miss Mabel V. Lawson has been of real assistance.

My very special thanks for help as fellow-workers in the field are due to Mrs. Amy Pearce VerNooy, librarian, scholar, and editor; Mrs. Clara Steeholm, once curator of D C H S collections, who has cooperated in research; Miss Helen Myers, journalist and historian, with innumerable studies and articles in Dutchess County lore. And to my dear friend and representative of all that is best in Dutchess, for loans and unceasing assistance, Mrs. Margaret L. Chanler Aldrich.

# Bibliographical Notes

## COUNTY HISTORIES

PHILIP H. SMITH. *General History of Duchess County from 1609 to 1876,* inclusive, illustrated, etc, Pawling, New York. Published by the author, 1877.

JAMES H. SMITH, assisted by H. H. Cole and W. E. Roscoe. *History of Duchess County, New York,* Syracuse, 1882.

*The County of Dutchess,* FRANK HASBROUCK, editor. Poughkeepsie, New York. 1909. Valuable, especially for early years.

*Commemorative Biographical Record of Dutchess County.* Chicago, 1897.

HENRY DUBOIS BAILEY. *Local Tales and Historical Sketches,* Fishkill Landing, New York. 1874.

*Tales of the Shongum.* By the same.

Norrie Fellowship Reports on Dutchess County, especially *The Dutchess County Farmer,* and *County at Large,* MARTHA COLLINS BAYNE, 1936.

*Books of the Supervisors, D.C.* 3 vols. Vassar Bros. Institute, 1907-1911.

## TOWN AND LOCAL MATERIALS

JOHN N. LEWIS. *Annandale, Reminiscences of,* Pamphlet.

NEWTON REED. *Amenia, History of Early,* Amenia. 1875.

THOMAS HUNT. *Clermont, Historical Sketch of the Town of,* Hudson, 1928.

RICHARD F. MAHER. *Dover, Historic,* Dover Plains. 1908.

*Fishkill, Historical Sketch and Directory of the Town of,* etc. Fishkill Landing. 1866.

FRANCIS M. KIP. *First Reformed Church, 150th Anniversary Discourse,* 1866.

F. D. SPAIGHT. *Looking Backward,* Fishkill-on-Hudson, 1896.

ALICE CRARY SUTCLIFFE. *Homestead of a Colonial Dame,* Poughkeepsie, Haight, 1901.

VAN VOORHIS. *First Reformed Dutch Church, Tombstone Inscriptions,* Putnam.

HENRY S. HACKETT. *Hyde Park,* DCHS XXIV, 75.

ISAAC HUNTTING. *Little Nine Partners, History of, -of North East Precinct, and Pine Plains,* Amenia, 1897.

*Pleasant Valley, Original Settlement in the Town of*. DCHS V, 23. Mills in, III, 26. *Presbyterian Church* XXVIII, 36.

*New Hackensack, Records of the Ref. Dutch Church of*, Carpenter.

EDMUND PLATT. *Poughkeepsie, The Eagle's History of, from the Earliest Settlements,* 1683 to 1905. Poughkeepsie, 1905. Very valuable.

JOHN HAVILAND and WM. M. BIRDSALL. *Nine Partners Quarterly Meeting, and Creek or Clinton Corners Meeting of Friends.*

WARREN H. WILSON. *Quaker Hill, A Sociological Study,* New York, 1907.

Quaker Hill Local History Series, Pawling, New York, 1902-.

EDWARD M. SMITH. *Rhinebeck, Documentary History of, in Dutchess County, New York,* Rhinebeck, 1881.

HOWARD H. MORSE. *Rhinebeck, Historic Old,* 1908.

*Hyde Park, Records of the Town of, Dutchess County,* edited by FRANKLIN D. ROOSEVELT. Hyde Park, 1928. DCHS.

REYNOLDS, HELEN WILKINSON, principal writings. *Poughkeepsie, The Origin and Meaning of the Word.* Poughkeepsie, 1924. *Dutch Houses in the Hudson Valley before 1776.* Poughkeepsie, 1920. *Dutchess County Doorways and Other Examples of Period Work in Wood,* 1730 to 1830. New York. William F. Payson, 1931.

*Notices of Marriages and Deaths . . . at Poughkeepsie, New York,* 1930.

*Records of Crum Elbow Precinct,* Dutchess County, edited by FRANKLIN DELANO ROOSEVELT, DCHS Collections, 1940.

### CHAPTER 1

BUTLER, MARY. *Notes on Archeology in Dutchess County,* American Anthropologist, Jan.-Mar., 1951.

*Table of Cultures,* New York State Museum, Publications, Educ. Series, No. 6, Leaflets 1, 7.

*Archeological History of New York,* Bulletins 235, 236.

RUTTENBER, E. M. *History of the Tribes of Hudson's River,* J. Munsell, 1872.

SMITH, CARLYLE S. *Archeology of Coastal New York,* N. Y., 1950.

*Bulletin 10,* Eastern States Archeological Federation, 1951.

SHAFER, JAMES H. *Report on Bannerman Site in Southern Dutchess County,* E. States Arch. Fed., Bulletin 13, 7, 1954.

JAMESON, J. FRANKLIN. *Narratives of New Netherland,* Scribner's, 1909.

### CHAPTER 2

RAESLY, ELLIS LAWRENCE. *Portrait of New Netherland,* Columbia University Press, 1945.

JAMES, BARTLETT BURLEIGH and JAMESON, J. FRANKLIN. *Journal of Jasper Danckaerts,* Scribner's 1913, p. 167.

O'CALLAGHAN, E. B. *The Documentary History of the State of New York,* (DHNY) Albany, 1819, Vol. 1, Dongan Report p. 145, Dutch p. 160, Census p. 368, 693.

O'CALLAGHAN, E. B. *History of New Netherland or New York Under the Dutch* (HNN) Appelton, 1846.

O'CALLAGHAN, E. B. *Laws and Ordinances of New Netherland,* (LAWS), Albany, 1868.

BRODHEAD, JOHN ROMEYN (collected by). *Documents Relative to the Colonial History of the State of New York,* edited by E. B. O'Callaghan. (DCH), Albany, 1856.

BRODHEAD, JOHN ROMEYN. *History of the State of New York,* (HNY), 2 vols., Harper, 1871.

BRODHEAD, J. R. Ibid., Vol. 2 p. 409. Two Wappinger chiefs attended the Peace of 1660 at Esopus: Isseschahya and Wisachganio.

BERESFORD, JOHN. *The Godfather of Downing Street,* Houghton Mifflin, 1925, pp. 134-139.

## CHAPTER 3

*Narratives of New Netherland.*

DANCKAERTS, J. *Journal.*

*Hist. New York,* 2, p. 385; for the Charter of Privileges, 2, p. 383.

*Hist. New Netherland, Doc. Hist. N. Y.,* for county boundaries.

WADSWORTH, BENJAMIN. *Journal,* Mass. Hist. Society Collections, Boston, 1852. Quoted by permission.

## CHAPTER 4

MILLBERT, J. G. *Itinéraire Pittoresque du Fleuve Hudson,* Paris, 1828. On Goethe, information received from Professor Ada Klett Bister, Vassar College.

JESPERSON, OTTO. *A Modern English Grammar on Historical Principles,* Heidelberg, 1922, Vol. 1 Section 2 p. 744, "After the time of Caxton *tch* became the usual spelling at the end of a native as well as of some French words." (Also in the middle, of course: *hatchet,* etc.).

SMITH, P. H. (PHS) *General History of Dutchess County,* Pawling, 1877, Introduction.

## CHAPTER 5

*Queen Mary of Modena,* Dictionary of National Biography.

HAILE, MARTIN. *Queen Mary of Modena,* London, 1908.

## CHAPTER 6

*Colonial Laws of New York,* etc., 5 vols. Vol. 2.

*New York Colonial Manuscripts,* 1638-1800.

N. Y. Col. Mss, *Land Papers,* 1642-1803.

*Books of Letters Patent,* Secy of State, Albany.

*Doc. History of N. Y.* vol 2.

*Ancient Documents,* Office of the County Clerk, Poughkeepsie; Beekman deed. (quoted as Anc. Doc.)

*Dutchess County Historical Society, Yearbooks,* 1914-. Vols. 1-40. quoted as DCHS. *Collections,* 1916-1940, vols. 1-7.

Beekman letters, DCHS, 6; 26. 12; 34.

New Hampshire Grants, New Hampshire Historical Society, vol. 26.

HANSCOM, ELIZABETH D. *The Heart of the Puritan,* Macmillan, 1917; Belcher to Chandos, p. 159.

COOPER, WILLIAM. *A Guide in the Wilderness,* New York State Historical Society, reprint.
RIFE, C. W. *Land Tenure in New Netherland,* Essays in honor of C. M. Andrews.
Poughkeepsie's first lease to VanKleeck and Oostrum, DCHS, 15;32.

## CHAPTER 7

ANDREWS, CHARLES M. *The Colonial Period of American History, The Settlements* III, Yale University Press, 1937.
For the patents see: *Land Papers,* New York Colonial Manuscripts, New York State Library, Albany.
*Books of Letters Patent,* Secretary of State, Albany.
REYNOLDS, HELEN WILKINSON. *Poughkeepsie, the Origin and Meaning of the Word,* (HWR) Dutchess County Historical Society *Collections* Vol. 1., 1924, for patents No. 1, 2, 3, 5, p. 80, for possible clue to Rombout's Purchase p. 75.
MORSE, HOWARD H. *Historic Old Rhinebeck,* Rhinebeck, 1908, for patents No. 4, 6, 7, 10, 11.
SMITH, JAMES H. *History of Dutchess County,* N. Y. 1863-1882, Mason, 1882, for patents No. 1, 3, 13.
HASBROUCK, F. The County of Dutchess, Poughkeepsie, 1909, for patents No. 3 p. 38, No. 11 and other patents. DCHS, for patents No. 1 Vol. 3 p. 10, No. 8 Vol. 2 p. 28 (VAN VLIET), No. 9 Vol. 24 p. 75 (HACKETT, H. T.,), No. 11 Vol. 3 front (map), No. 12 Vol. 8 p. 29, Vol. 16 p. 27 (record book), Vol. 20 p. 26, No. 13 Vol. 22 p. 71 (HUNTTING).
PELLETREAU, WILLIAM S. *History of Putnam County, New York,* Philadelphia, 1886, for patent No. 14. DCHS Vol. 5 p. 180, 255 for Hunter, Bellomont, Viele. DCHS Vol. 25 p. 43 first settlers. DCHS, Vol. 3 for Staats.

## CHAPTER 8

Wards and Precincts, DCHS, 1;21.
Sackett, DCHS, 25;51.
SCHOONMAKER, MARIUS. *The History of Kingston,* N. Y. 1888.
*Packet of Old Letters,* DCHS, 6;26.
*Rats' Nest, Letters found in a,* DCHS, 12;41.
*Brett Letter,* DCHS, 6;39.
SUTCLIFFE, ALICE CRARY. *The Homestead of a Colonial Dame,* Poughkeepsie, 1909.
REYNOLDS, H. W. *Dutch Houses.*
*Farmers' Landings,* DCHS, 21;74.
*Mrs. Brett's Will,* NYHS. Colls. 1897. DCHS 12;32, for discarded will.
Musiar *Document,* Anc. Doc.
On Staats and Schyler; DCHS, 3;228. Morse, H. H. n., *Historic Old Rhinebeck.*
On Hyde Park, DCHS, 24;75.
On Lower (Great) Nine Partners, DCHS, 24;52.

Freeholders, Doc. Hist. NY., 4;134.
Verplanck Map of 1728, DCHS, 19;23. In Adriance Library (copy).
Fox, Dixon Ryan. *Caleb Heathcote, Gentleman Colonist,* etc., N. Y., 1926.

CHAPTER 9

Materials gathered in many rambles on dusty byways. Numerous maps in DCHS, especially early volumes. Good collection of maps in County Clerk's Office.

CHAPTER 10

Schoonmaker. *History of Kingston.*
VanBuren, Augustus H. *A History of Ulster County under the Dominion of the Dutch,* Kingston, 1923.
Goodwin, M. W. *Dutch and English on the Hudson,* New Haven, 1919.
*New Paltz,* Address on, Hon. Frank Hasbrouck, DCHS, 9;17.
Dutch in English, *Dictionary of American English.* Study of dialect of Hudson River Region, by Vassar College students. Ms. in library.
Elting, Irving. *Dutch Village Communities on the Hudson River,* Baltimore, 1886.
*Lure of the Living Past,* Mrs. T. De LaPorte, DCHS, 12;75.
Kilpatrick, W. H. *The Dutch Schools of New Netherland and Colonial New York,* U.S. Bureau of Education Bulletin No. 12, 1912.
Reynolds, H. W. *Poughkeepsie,* Dutch Glossary.
Reynolds, H. W. *Dutch Houses.*
Kittredge, G. L. *The Old Farmer and his Almanac,* Boston, 1904.

CHAPTER 11

Knittle, Walter Allen. *The Early Eighteenth Century Palatine Emigration,* Philadelphia, 1936.
Helen Reed DeLaPorte. DCHS, 21; 29. Dr. J. Wilson Poucher, DCHS, 22; 87. Helen W. Reynolds, DCHS, 22; 94.
Wallace, Paul A. *Conrad Weiser,* etc. Phila. 1945.
Beauchamp, W. R. *Life of Conrad Weiser,* etc. 1925.

CHAPTER 12

Scots names and all documents from A. D. For Cottam, see G. S. Van Vliet. DCHS 26; 42.
Crèvecoeur, St. Jean de. *Sketches of 18th Century America,* Yale U. Press, 1925. (Quoted by permission.) *Negroes in DC in 18th Century,* HWR, DCHS, 26; 89.

CHAPTER 13

*Boundaries of New York State, Report of the Regents of the University of the State of N. Y. on,* 2 vols., Albany, 1874. Especially vol. 2.

CHAPTER 14

*Muster Rolls,* NYHS, Colls. 1891. In 1758 out of 80 men in Capt. Joseph Crane's Dutchess company for the French war, 52 were born in

New England (Boston 20, Conn. 24), 11 in Dutchess, 9 in Westchester, the rest scattering.

DeVries, David. *Short History,* Narr. New Neth.

Reynolds and Poucher. *Old Gravestones of Dutchess County,* DCHS, Collections, 1924.

Gottesman, R. S. *Arts and Crafts of N. Y.,* NYHS, 1938.

Reynolds. *Dutch Houses.*

Rev. Benjamin Shove. *Thomas Taber and Edward Shove,* Quaker Hill, 1903.

Higgins, Ruth C. *Expansion in New York,* Columbus, 1931.

Briggs, Harry Tallmadge and J. G. *The Colonial Ancestry of J. G. Briggs and Isabell Gibbs DeGroff.* Typical of Dutchess intermarriage.

Miller, Perry. *The New England Mind, from Colony to Province.* Permission of W. Sloane Associates, copyright.

Documents, Anc. Doc.

## CHAPTER 15

Heckewelder, John. *Narrative of the Mission of the United Brethren,* Phila., 1820.

Loskiel, S. H. *History of the Missions of the United Brethren,* tr. C. J. Latrobe, 1849.

Wallace, *Conrad Weiser.*

DHNY, 3;1013-1027.

Anc. Docs., for Ross, Treat, and Sackett.

Bridenbaugh, Carl, *Gentleman's Progress,* Univ. N. Carolina Press, 1945.

Dyer, Edward O. *Gnadensee, the Lake of Grace,* Sharon, 1903.

Hamilton, J. T. *History of Moravian Missions of Dutchess County,* P. Schaff, Amer. Church History Series, 8;451ff.

## CHAPTER 16

[Note: Earlier histories give detailed accounts of early churches. This chapter is limited to sketches of a few outstanding leaders. With our limited records, the story is one of pioneers.]

Muhlenberg, H. M. *Journals,* Vol. 1. 1942. Muhlenberg Press, Philadelphia. Other Lutheran material from Anc. Doc.

Nathan Bangs. *Garrettson, Life of the Rev. Freeborn,* J. Emery and B. Waugh. N. Y. 1830.

Hamilton, J. T. *History of the Reformed Church (Dutch),* Schaff, Church Mission Series, vol. 8. Coetus Documents in John Tabor Kempe Papers, NYHS. *Records* of Reformed Churches in Poughkeepsie, New Hackensack, and Fishkill.

Morse, H. H. *Historic Old Rhinebeck,* p. 173, for Robert Scott.

Wilson, Warren H. *Quaker Hill in the 18th Century,* Q. H. Series, 1902; *Quaker Hill, A Sociological Study,* 1900.

Allen, Mary C. and Caroline K. *North Quaker Hill and its Traditions,* Q. H. Series, 1950. Map.

Swartz, W. C. *Colonial Presbyterian Churches in Dutchess County,* DCHS, 28; 34.

Hoefgoed at Poughquag, DCHS, 9;48. Also DHNY, 3;975.
KIP, REV. FRANCIS M. *First Reformed Church of Fishkill,* Address on the 150th Anniversary, of.
*Glebe House, The,* at Poughkeepsie, DCHS, 28;58.

### CHAPTER 17

Doc. Hist. N. Y., 7;795, for Bellomont's remarks, among others.
REYNOLDS, H. W. *Dutch Houses;* DCHS, 20;60, *Country Seats on Hudson's River.*
LIVINGSTON, EDWIN BROCKHOLST. *The Livingstons of Livingston Manor, New York, 1910.*
*R. R. Livingston, Family of,* DCHS, 4;12-21.
MRS, MONTGOMERY. *Reminiscences of,* DCHS, 15;25.
CROSBY, M. S. *Grasmere,* DCHS, 14;24.
DELAFIELD, BRIG. GEN. JOHN ROSS. *Montgomery Place,* DCHS, 14;26. *The Hermitage,* DCHS, 24;30. *Teviotdale,* DCHS, 24;40.
*The Hill,* DCHS, 26;23.
*Francis Filkin's Book,* H. W. REYNOLDS, DCHS, 23;52.
*Account Book of a Country Store Keeper,* Vassar Bros. Institute, 1911.
*Abstracts of Wills,* NYHS, vol. 32.
GRANT, MRS. ANNE, of Laggan. *Memoirs of an American Lady,* London, 1808.
SMITH, WILLIAM. *History of New York,* Albany, 1814.
CRÈVECOEUR, ST. JEAN DE. *Sketches of 18th Century America,* H. W. REYNOLDS, DCHS, 18;41.
FOX, DIXON RYAN. *The Decline of Aristocracy in the Politics of New York,* Columbia University, 1919.
CAMPBELL, MILDRED. *The English Yeoman,* Yale Univ. 1942.
*Ancient Documents,* Clerk's Office, Dutchess County.
*Physicians and Medicine in the Eighteenth Century,* DCHS, 26;78.

### CHAPTER 18

*New York Council, Minutes of,* 1668-1783, New York State Library.
HANDLIN, OSCAR. *The Eastern Frontier of New York,* New York History, 18;50.
MARK, IRVING. *Agrarian Conflicts in Colonial New York,* 1711-1775, Columbia Univ. 1940.
PARGETTIS, S. M. *The Four Independent Companies of New York, Essays presented to C. M. Andrews,* 1931.
GEORGE BANCROFT. *Interview* with Mrs. Garrettson, N. Y. Public Library. Livingston Mss.
CHEYNEY, E. P. *Anti-Rent Agitation in the State of N. Y.,* 1839-1846, Phila. 1887.
*Docs. Col. Hist.,* 7;765. Sir William Johnson attributed lawyers' opposition to British rule to the taxes imposed on law business.
ATTY.-GENL BRADLEY. *Docs. Col. Hist.* 6; 901. "While assemblies dare act thus and seem to have it in their power to obtain what laws they please, how can his Majesty's interest be secured in so remote a country where people multiply so fast?"

*Memoir on Thomas Young,* Mass. Colonial Society Transactions 21;138. Young was an intimate of Samuel Adams.

## CHAPTER 19

County records and court-minutes on micro-film. *Ancient Documents* in County Clerk's office.

DEXTER, F. B., *History of Yale Alumni,* 1885-1912.

HANDLIN, OSCAR. *The Eastern Frontier of New York,* NYH, 18;50.

RYCAUT, CAPT. PAUL. *Report on Riots, Poughkeepsie, 1761,* Doc. Hist. N. Y., 3;984.

*Clinton, George, Public Papers of,* New York, 1899-1914. Counterfeit money, 7;217.

*Civil Administration in Dutchess County,* DCHS, 24;58, 25;41.

BECKER, CARL L. *The Eve of the American Revolution,* Yale Press, 1918.

THOMPSON, HAROLD. *Body, Boots, and Britches,* Phila., 1940.

SCOTT, KENNETH. *Counterfeiting in Colonial New York,* New York History, 35;73.

## CHAPTER 20

MILLER, PERRY. *Jonathan Edwards.* Copyright, Wm. Sloane Associates, 1949.

SMITH, CHARD. *The Housatonic,* Rinehart, 1946.

ALEXANDER, JAMES. Papers, boxes on Dutchess County, in NYHS.

HANDLIN, OSCAR. *Eastern Frontier of New York,* NYH, 18;50.

LIVINGSTON, EDWIN B. *The Livingstons of Livingston Manor.*

## CHAPTER 21

HANDLIN, OSCAR. *Eastern Frontier of New York,* NYH, 18;50.

MARK, IRVING. *Agrarian Conflicts in Colonial New York.*

*Boundaries of the State of New York,* Report of the Regents of the University on the, Albany, 1872.

BARCK, DOROTHY C. *LetterBook of John Watts, Merchant and Councillor,* 1762-1765, NYHS, 1928, p. 401.

*Hist. New Neth.* 2;402.

*Express* from Pittsfield, London Chronicle, in NY Pub. Library.

DELAFIELD, GEN. J. R. on Lady Mary Allen, DCHS, 26;30.

MARK, IRVING, and HANDLIN, OSCAR. *Land Cases in Colonial New York,* New York Univ. Law Review, 1942, 19;165-194. Print of *Notes on July Assizes,* in part.

## CHAPTER 22

MARK, IRVING. *Agrarian Conflicts in Colonial New York,* 1940.

*Nine Partners Patent,* DCHS 8;29.

KEMPE, JOHN TABOR. *Papers,* Box 6, New York Historical Society.

*New York Council Minutes,* New York State Library.

COLDEN, CADWALLADER. *Letters and Papers of, 1711-1755; 9 vols.,* N. Y. 1918-1937; For Cane, Richard, Anc. Doc.

*A Geographical, Historical Narrative or Summary of the Present Con-*

*troversy between Daniel Nimham . . . and Messrs. Roger Morris, Beverly Robinson, and Philip Philipse, Legal Representatives of Colonel Frederick Philipse, deceased,* etc., Library of Congress, transcript of MS. Lansdowne Ms. 707, British Museum, pp. 1-55. The *Brief Case* is the first part of this text. Other papers in the Shelburne collection of the Library are quoted.

RUTTENBER, E. M. *History of the Indian Tribes,* etc., p. 51, for Nimham's testimony, Oct. 13, 1730.

SULLIVAN, JAMES. *Papers of Sir William Johnson,* Univ. of the State of New York.

POUCHER, J. W. DCHS, 23;24, on the Nimham Monument at Brinckerhoff.

SUTCLIFFE, A. C. *Homestead of a Colonial Dame.* See also REYNOLDS, H. W. *Poughkeepsie,* for Mrs. Brett's troubles with Indians.

New York Colonial Manuscripts, *Land Papers,* 18;128, for Indian claim.

PELL, JOHN. *Ethan Allen,* Boston, 1929.

*American Archives,* vol. 4, section 2, p. 713. 1837.

HUNTTING, ISAAC. *History of Little Nine Partners,* etc., Amenia, 1897.

Docs. Col. Hist., 7;825,868,879, for principal Nimham papers.

[NOTE: A tradition survives that the last Indian did not leave Wiccopee till the close of the nineteenth century. They dwelt at Barrett's Pond, below Wiccopee Pass, west of Route 9. This report was furnished by Mrs. Sara, a local resident. Other survivors have been reported at Chelsea, New Hackensack, Hyde Park; aged couples making a livelihood by the art of basket-weaving.]

### CHAPTER 23

HANDLIN and MARK. *Land Cases,* loc. cit.

HANDLIN, *Eastern Frontier,* loc. cit.

MARK. *Agrarian Conflicts,* loc. cit.

KEMPE, JOHN TABOR. *Papers,* NYHS, for testimony of Peter Pratt and of defendants in July Assizes.

PELLETREAU, W. S. *History of Putnam County,* Phila. 1886. Robinson's letter.

Prendergast, sale of property, manuscripts in Akin Hall Library, Quaker Hill.

SABINE, WILLIAM H. W. *Historical Memoirs of William Smith,* Hollis, N. Y. 1956.

COLDEN, CADWALLADER. *Letters and Papers.*

CARMER, CARL. *The Hudson,* chapter 9. Farrar and Rinehart, N. Y., 1939.

The New York Gazette or Weekly Post Boy, account sympathetic to Prendergast.

WING, CONWAY P. *John Wing and his Descendants,* 1888. Full account of Mehitabel Wing.

MONTRESSOR, JAMES AND JOHN. *The Montressor Journals,* NYHS, Collections, 1881, p. 384.

### CHAPTER 24

*History of Manchester, Vermont.*

HOWSON, PROFESSOR HOWARD. *Notes on the Marsh Family,* Ms.

MARK, IRVING. *Agrarian Conflicts,* for the Pawling Petition, p. 170.
*Young, Thomas, Memoir on, Mass.* Colonial Society, Collections, loc. cit. Ancient Documents.
JONES, MATT B. *Vermont in the Making,* 1750-1777 Harvard Press, 1939.
DE LAPORTE, MRS. T. *Danby, Vt.,* DCHS, 20;55.
New Hampshire Historical Society, 21, for town purchases.
REYNOLDS, H. W. *Berlin, Vt.,* DCHS, 26;65.
Doc. Col. Hist. N. Y., 4;529-1034.
THOMPSON, CHARLES M. *Independent Vermont,* Boston, 1942.
BENTON, R. C. *The Vermont Settlers and the New York Land Speculators,* Minneapolis, 1894, p. 21.
PELL, JOHN. *Ethan Allen.*
Doc. Col. Hist. 7;917.

CHAPTER 25

VAN TYNE, CLAUDE H. *The Causes of the War of Independence,* Boston, 1922.
VAN DOREN, CARL. *Benjamin Franklin,* Viking Press, 1938.
POUCHER, J. WILSON. *Richard Sackett,* DCHS, 25;51.
SABINE, WILLIAM H. W. *Historical Memoirs of Wm. Smith,* 221.

CHAPTER 26

American Archives, vol. 4, Amenia Document; also Benson's report.
*Committee to Detect Conspiracy, Minutes of,* Albany, for Hallenbeck, Woltimyer, Taylor, Haft.
*Clinton Papers,* for Taylor.
HASBROUCK, FRANK. *The County of Dutchess,* Poughkeepsie, 1909, 212-213, letter of Abraham Swartwout to Col. Peter Gansevoort, 29 August, 1777, asking for "8 yards broadcloth to replace blue cloak, which was used for colors at Ft. Schuyler."
Ancient Documents.
REYNOLDS, H. W. *Peter Mesier,* DCHS 5;7.
The same, *Bartholomew Crannell,* DCHS, 7;39; also 37;58.
POUCHER, J. WILSON. *Events on Hudson's River in October, 1777.* DCHS 23;34. Documents procured by Franklin D. Roosevelt.
BARD, JOHN, DCHS 21;68.
JONES, THOMAS. *History of New York* etc., NYHS 1879.
FLICK, ALEXANDER CLARENCE. *Loyalism in New York,* Columbia Press, 1901.
FRENEAU, PHILIP. *Poems,* 1903, III, 238.
*Rombout Committee of Observation, Minutes of,* 1775, NYHS, 29;295.
YOSHPE, HARRY B. *The DeLancey Estates,* New York History, 1936, 7;167.
*Laws of New York,* 1783. Dutchess Tories' estates were given immediate sale.

CHAPTER 27

REYNOLDS, H. W. *Col. Udny Hay,* DCHS, 10;49.

*Clinton, Gov. George. Public Papers of,* Publications of the Univ. of the State of New York, Albany, 1899.

POUCHER, J. W. *George Clinton,* DCHS, 24;48. Also DCHS, 11;31.

CHAPTER 28

HASBROUCK, FRANK. *The County of Dutchess* for Muster Rolls.

THACHER, DR. JAMES. *Military Journal of the American Revolution,* Hurlbut, 1862.

PATRICK, LEWIS S. *Washington's Headquarters at Fredericksburgh,* Quaker Hill Series XVI.

CLINTON, GOV. GEORGE. *Public Papers.*

REYNOLDS, H. W. *The Congress and the Montgomery,* DCHS, 21;95.

Roosevelt, Franklin D., Papers obtained by, DCHS, 20, 86,88.

LOSSING, BENSON J. *Pictorial Field-Book of the American Revolution,* Harper, 1860.

PLATT, EDMUND. *History of Poughkeepsie,* chapter 3.

NYHS, Proceedings, 1881, *Trial of Gen. Philip Schuyler* at Quaker Hill.

CHAPTER 29

VAN DOREN, CARL. *Secret History of the American Revolution,* Viking, New York. 1941.

THACHER, DR. JAMES. *Military Journal,* Chapter 28.

FLEXNER, JAMES THOMAS. *The Traitor and the Spy,* Harcourt, Brace. 1953.

BENSON, EGBERT. *A Vindication of the Captors of Major Andre.* 1817.

SARGENT, WINTHROP, *André.*

Such was the concern in Dutchess over spies that the N. Y. Legislature on Nov. 2, 1778, created a night-watch in the county, drafting every able-bodied man that might be needed.

CHAPTER 30

LIVINGSTON, MAJOR HENRY, JR. *Journal* to Canada, Ms. copy in DCHS, Collections. See also DCHS, 27;85, 21;81, 23;39.

LUDINGTON, COL. HENRY, DCHS, 30;75. JOHNSON, WILLIS F., COL. *Henry Ludington,* a Memoir, privately printed by Lavinia E. and Charles Henry Ludington. Contains material also on Enoch Crosby. See Riker Ms. NYPL, for Benjamin Montanye, Fishkill refugee, who was employed by Gen. Washington in his famous ruse. The papers Montanye carried, in his boot like André, were found by his captors, and deceived Sir Henry Clinton by disclosing Washington's pretended plan for seizing New York. Instead, Yorktown was the objective. See also Clinton Papers, for Montanye, whose descendants are of Dutchess.

Dr. J. Wilson Poucher wrote many particular notices of Revolutionary soldiers, which appear in the Year-Books of the Dutchess County Historical Society. I mention some of them: *Gen. Benjamin Swartwout,* DCHS 13;67. *Col. Frederick Weissenfels,* 27;74; *Col. Lewis DuBois,* 20;71. *Capt. Zephaniah Platt,* 29;51. *Major Andrew Billings,* 25;30. *Sheriff James Livingston and his Children,* 28;67. *Judge*

*Robert R. Livingston, his sons and sons-in-law,* 30;54. *Dr. Peter Tappen,* 19;38. 37;58 (by Amy Pearce VerNooy. *Elizabeth Tappen,* letter 13;46. *Major Elias Van Benschoten,* 21;90. (He was very active with levies at Ft. Stanwix, and with Col. Willett on the Mohawk.) *Col. James VanderBurgh,* 15;36. *Gov. Morgan Lewis,* 13;35. *Dr. Cornelius Osborn,* 4;39. *Orderly Books of the Fourth New York Regiment,* etc., Univ. of State of New York, 1932. Chiefly written by S. TALLMADGE and J. BARR. When Tallmadge represented the soldiers' complaints at the Poughkeepsie legislature, Nathaniel Sackett moved the Assembly's vote of sympathy.

BARR. ibid. p. 831, for Amenia Resolutions.

CHAPTER 31

ANBUREY, LT. THOMAS. *Travels through the Interior Parts of America,* Riverside Press, Cambridge, 1923. Vol. 2;83.

REIDESEL, BARONESS FREDERICKE E. L., *Letters and Journals,* etc., translated by Wm. M. Stone, Albany, 1867. Page 147.

DE CHASTELLUX, GENERAL LE MARQUIS. *Travels,* in HASBROUCK, FRANK, *The County of Dutchess.*

CHAPTER 32

STEVENS, F. R. *Cincinnati, Founding of the,* DCHS, 28;23.

TALLMADGE. *Orderly Books,* p. 780.

Verplanck House, Scene of the Founding, picture, DCHS, 31;36.

POUCHER, J. W. *Baron Von Steuben,* DCHS, 31;36.

CHAPTER 33

LINCOLN, CHARLES Z. *The Constitutional History of New York,* 5 vols., Rochester 1906. vol. 1, texts.

ABBOTT, WILBUR C. *New York in the American Revolution,* Scribner's, 1929.

SWIGGETT, HOWARD. *The Extraordinary Mr. Morris,* New York, 1952.

CHAPTER 34

I have followed the course of the debates on the proposed Constitution in the Country Journal at Poughkeepsie. Pamphlets in the NYPL have been valuable, especially that of Melancton Smith. Ms. notes of Gilbert Livingston at the Poughkeepsie Convention are important, and are quoted by permission of the Librarian.

A Ms. book by the late EMERSON D. FITE. *The Struggle in New York over the Federal Constitution,* has been studied (kindness of Mrs. Alice Fite and Miss Katherine B. Fite, State Department.)

SPAULDING, E. WILDER. *New York in the Critical Period,* 1785-1789, New York State Historical Series, 1932.

KENT, JAMES. *Sometime of Dutchess County,* H. W. Reynolds, DCHS, 8;21. Contains his map of his home region in Doanesborough.

HORTON, J. T. *James Kent, a Study in Conservatism,* Appleton, New York, 1939.

CHAPTER 35

*Poughkeepsie Journal,* for the period. The chief source in my study.

FOWLER, JOHN. *Journal of a Tour in the State of New York.* Whittaker, 1831.

SUTCLIFFE, ALICE CRARY. *Robert Fulton and the Clermont,* Century Co. 1907.

STRONG, G. S. *Early Landmarks of Syracuse,* Times Co. 1894, for Forman.

REYNOLDS, H. W. *Sheep-Raising in Dutchess County,* DCHS, 26;71.

HEDRICK, U. P. *History of Agriculture,* New York, 1933.

ROGERS, DR. JOHN F. *History of Dutchess County Medicine,* 1806-1956. Pamphlet, Poughkeepsie, 1956.

REYNOLDS, H. W. *Physicians and Medicine in Dutchess County in the Eighteenth Century,* DCHS, 26;78. Also see DCHS 13;29, 18;22, 30.

HAIGHT, ELIZABETH H. *Autobiography and Letters of Matthew Vassar,* Oxford Univ. Press 1916.

CUTTEN, G. B. and VERNOOY, AMY PEARCE. Silversmiths of Poughkeepsie, DCHS, 30;23.

REYNOLDS, H. W. The Poughkeepsie Courthouse, DCHS, 24;69. See also folder of papers on Courthouse in NYHS, Misc. Mss.

COLLYER, MOSES M. and VERPLANCK, WM. E. *Sloops of the Hudson.* Putnam, 1908.

REYNOLDS, H. W. *DeLaBigarre,* DCHS, 21;23, 14;45.

DUBOIS, CORNELIUS. *Letters,* loaned by the kindness of a descendant, who owns them, Mr. John DuBois Freer, of Hyde Park.

CHAPTER 36

PLATT, EDMUND. *History of Poughkeepsie, from the earliest Settlements, 1683-1905,* published by Platt and Platt, Poughkeepsie, 1905.

REYNOLDS, HELEN WILKINSON. *Poughkeepsie, the Origin and Meaning of the Word,* Collections of the Dutchess County Historical Society.

Chapters on Poughkeepsie in the histories of Philip Smith, James H. Smith and Frank Hasbrouck are valuable.

CHAPTER 37

PELLETREAU, W. S. History of Putnam County, 1886, Chapters 1-4.

*New York State Laws, 1806-1812.* On the Fishkill slice of 1806.

*Poughkeepsie Journal,* files, Adriance Library.

*Republican Herald,* files for the later years of the debate.

*Clinton, George, Public Papers,* for his life in Poughkeepsie.

# Index

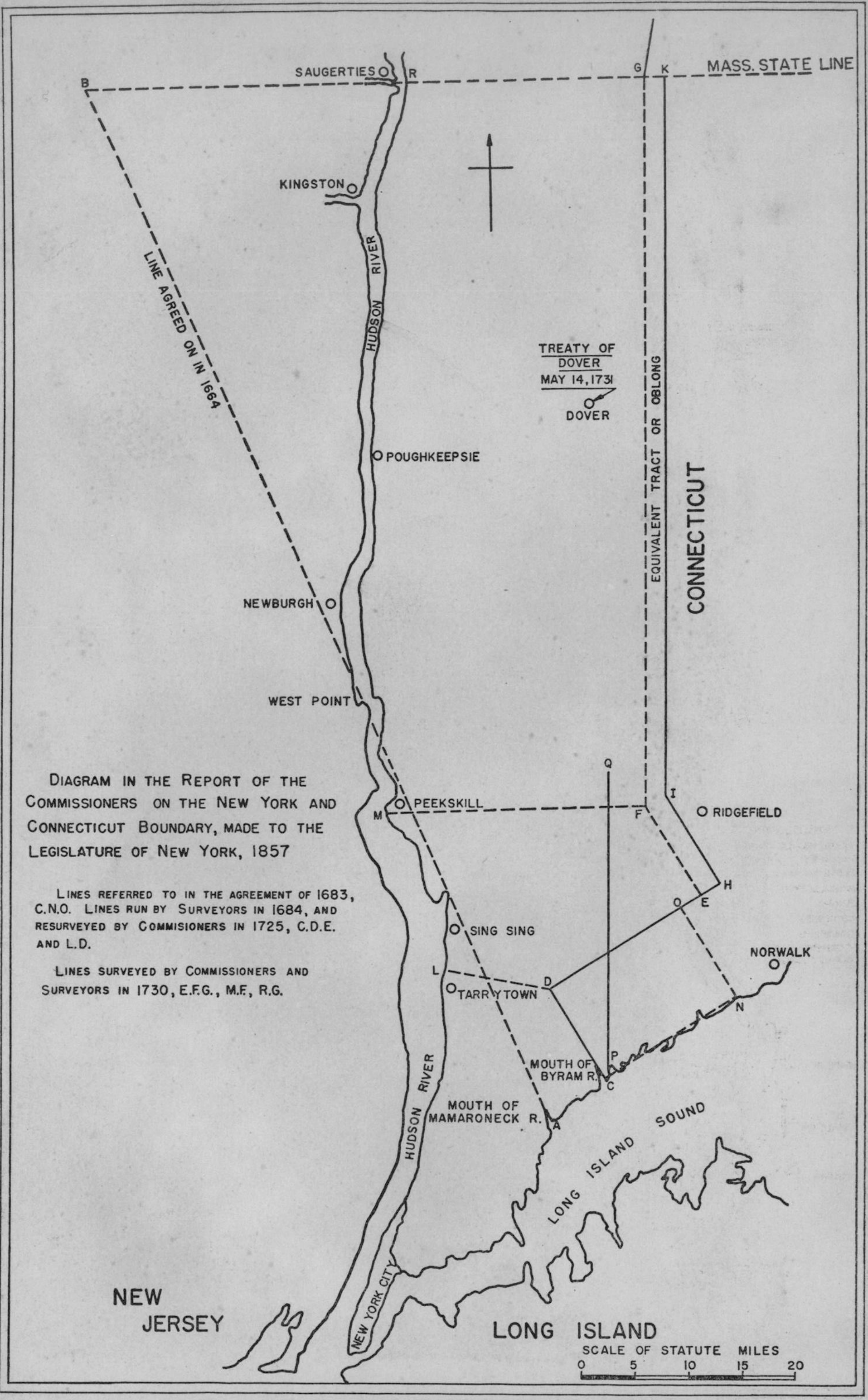
MASS. STATE LINE
SAUGERTIES
KINGSTON
HUDSON RIVER
LINE AGREED ON IN 1664
TREATY OF DOVER MAY 14, 1731
DOVER
POUGHKEEPSIE
EQUIVALENT TRACT OR OBLONG
CONNECTICUT
NEWBURGH
WEST POINT
PEEKSKILL
RIDGEFIELD
SING SING
NORWALK
TARRYTOWN
MOUTH OF BYRAM R.
MOUTH OF MAMARONECK R.
LONG ISLAND SOUND
NEW YORK CITY
NEW JERSEY
LONG ISLAND
SCALE OF STATUTE MILES
0 5 10 15 20
Diagram in the Report of the Commissioners on the New York and Connecticut Boundary, made to the Legislature of New York, 1857
Lines referred to in the agreement of 1683, C.N.O. Lines run by Surveyors in 1684, and resurveyed by Commisioners in 1725, C.D.E. and L.D.
Lines surveyed by Commissioners and Surveyors in 1730, E.F.G., M.F., R.G.